# GRAND
# ALLUSIONS

# GRAND
# ALLUSIONS

## A LIVELY GUIDE TO THOSE EXPRESSIONS, TERMS AND REFERENCES YOU OUGHT TO KNOW BUT MIGHT NOT

*by*

## Elizabeth Webber

*and*

## Mike Feinsilber

Farragut
Publishing
Company

*Washington, D.C.*

PRINTED IN THE UNITED STATES OF AMERICA

Second printing 1990

Library of Congress Cataloging-in-Publication Data

Webber, Elizabeth, 1946–
    Grand allusions : a lively guide to those expressions, terms & references you ought to
know but might not / Elizabeth Webber and Mike Feinsilber.
        p.   cm.
    Includes bibliographical references.
    ISBN 0-918535-09-3 : $21.95—ISBN 0-918535-03-4 (pbk.) : $12.95
    1. English language—Etymology—Dictionaries.    2. English language—Terms and
phrases.    3. Allusions—Dictionaries.
I. Title.
PE1580.W33    1980
422'.03—dc20                                                        90-34023
                                                                       CIP

*To*
*Betty Webber*
*E.W.*

*Doris Feinsilber*
*M.F.*

# ACKNOWLEDGEMENTS

We want to express our thanks to the many people who helped bring this book to completion.

Word mavens Paul Dickson and Robert Greenman, for lending materials and invaluable research suggestions; Garry DeLoss, public interest lawyer and walking reference library, for generous research assistance, editing and advice; and for special assistance with hard-to-find terms, Merriam Webster, Inc. and Randy Roberts of the Peter G. Tamony Collection, University of Missouri, Columbia, Missouri. Thanks also to Bill Adler, Jr. for his generosity and patience in assisting us with NEXIS searches.

For assistance with pronunciation of foreign language words and phrases: Ursula McManus, Anne Kessler and Mark Kessler, Lynn Flexner, Washington writer Ellen Hoffman and Stanley Meisler, graduate of the Workmen's Circle Yiddish School on Vyse Avenue, The Bronx, New York.

For help in reviewing and correcting the manuscript: Barry Schweid, the Associated Press's diplomatic writer at the State Department; James Bigger, Washington classicist; Frank Jackman, erudite Washington journalist and world-class trivia buff; Irwin Manning.

Special gratitude with oak leaf cluster to Merideth Menken, whose computer wizardry and editorial eye produced a coherent manuscript out of masses of scrawled corrections.

And finally, special thanks to publisher Daniel Rapoport for the idea, as well as for continuous support and creative meddling. In retrospect we realize that he was often right.

*E. W.*
*M. F.*

# PREFACE

The legendary editor Harold Ross, founder of *The New Yorker*, is said to have once expressed plaintive bewilderment to his magazine's star writer, James Thurber: "Is Moby Dick the man or the whale?" This book is for people like Ross.

Like him, we're not so dumb, we readers, but we don't know everything about everything. We might know what's flotsam and jetsam, but not what manner of mammal was Moby Dick. This book will help.

Writers blithely write about Mickey Finns, or Parkinson's law, or sea changes, or apparatchiks, or drinking hemlock or the witching hour or the Fabulous Invalid, never explaining, never looking back to see if we're still with them.

All of us run into (and sometimes use) these sideways references that are intended to add color and vigor to language. But they are lost on us if we have forgotten or never knew what they meant. We could stop reading and try to search out their meaning in a reference work—but that can be frustratingly difficult—or take an educated guess, or read on in a fog.

This book is an eclectic collection of those allusions, figures of speech, terms of art, terms of the trade, foreign language phrases and jargon that appear in our daily reading without accompanying explanation. (We chose our title to suggest the zest and punch these expressions add to the way we communicate ideas. *Grand Allusions* is a play on the title of the memorable 1937 French film *Grand Illusion*, about French prisoners of war during World War I.)

Now when a phrase brings your reading to a halt or when someone tosses off a puzzling reference, turn to these pages. This book explains terms the dictionaries don't, like the Dreyfus case, silent spring, beggar-thy-neighbor, lounge lizard, the artful dodger and what someone does when he vets. The terms come from literature, sports, mythology, Wall Street, history, headlines, Shakespeare, politics, standup comics and the Sunday comics, the locker room, the board room—and chiefly from the authors' everyday reading.

We show how these terms are used, with examples from magazines, newspapers, books—and the odd bit from radio or *Doonesbury*. You'll notice that many of our examples are drawn from *The New York Times* or

*The Washington Post*, the papers that we read regularly but whose dispatches, these days, are likely to turn up in newspapers everywhere, thanks to supplemental wire services and syndicated punditry.

We've tried to convey solid information without being stuffy about it. Sometimes we've run off on a tangent if an anecdote or a quotation struck us as intriguing or enlightening.

We've also tried to make the book convenient to use or browse through. Each term is defined and illustrated by an example from contemporary media. Where useful, there is a guide to pronunciation. Everything's arranged alphabetically. Terms defined elsewhere are shown in boldface type.

You'll be bemused by some of our choices. Some will seem too obvious and some too obscure. A generational factor sometimes may account for that; anyone over 50 would know what Dunkirk means but someone under 30 might not. A computer buff will be familiar with terms that might bewilder a musician. Everyone knows some of the terms here, but we doubt anyone would know them all. We didn't. We had to look them up in a variety of sources, from medical to medieval guides. And there may be some surprises even if you are acquainted with a term here; see Gothic, for example.

English, especially in written form, is so full of figures of speech that depend on a shared association that no book could capture them all. Your nominees for additions to Volume 2 are welcome. Send them to Farragut Publishing Company, 2033 M Street N.W., Washington, D.C. 20036. And if you find an error, or can contribute an additional meaning for a term we have used, please let us know.

A word about style, the rules writers follow to achieve consistency. We've adhered to our chosen rules, but did not alter the style used by the authors of the examples we cite. So you'll notice some style inconsistencies between our comments and the examples.

We've had fun putting this book together and learned a lot. We hope you have fun reading this book—and learn a lot.

*Elizabeth Webber*
*Mike Feinsilber*
Washington, D.C.
July, 1990

# A WORD ABOUT PRONUNCIATION

The pronunciation assistance we have provided is phonetic; we tried to avoid all those peculiar little symbols that turn up in dictionaries. Accented syllables are printed in upper-case letters. We admit they look odd, but if the parts are spoken in a natural way, they work.

To foreign language experts, we apologize: there are some sounds that American tongues and sinuses cannot easily duplicate, so we went for simplified sounds that come close. Our goal was the best approximation that would avoid public embarrassment. And in some cases, we provide Anglicized pronunciations, especially in Latin, since these are more commonly used.

The following examples illustrate how the sounds are set forth:

| | | | |
|---|---|---|---|
| hat | (hat) | phone | (fohn) |
| art | (ahrt) | boot | (boot) |
| bear | (bair) | boil | (boyl) |
| fall | (fawl) | hour | (OW-er) |
| date | (dayt) | show | (shoh) |
| end | (end) | above | (uh-BUHV) |
| heat | (heet) | face | (fays) |
| server | (SER-ver) | faze | (fayz) |
| wit | (wiht) | good | (good) |
| try | (trigh) | gem | (jem) |

# List of Terms

Achilles' Heel
Acton, Lord
Ad Hominem
Agitprop
Al Fresco
Alarums and Excursions
Alger, Horatio (see Horatio Alger)
Alphonse and Gaston
American Century
A Modest Proposal
Amour-propre
Ancien Régime
Angst
Anschluss
Antebellum
Antichrist
Antihero
Aperçu
Apparatchik
Aquarius, Age of; Aquarian
Ark of the Covenant
Armageddon
Arriviste
Art Deco
Art Nouveau
Artful Dodger
Au Courant
Augean stables
Ausländer
Auto-da-fé
Avatar
Axis
Babel
Babbitt
Bacchanal
Bad Seed
Balkanize, Balkanization

Banquo's Ghost
Barbie and Ken
Bardic
Baroque
Bauhaus
Beau Geste
Beggar-thy-neighbor
Bell, Book and Candle
Belle Époque
Belles-lettres
Belling the Cat
Bellwether
Below the Salt
Beltway, the; Beltway Bandits
Bertie Wooster
Best and Brightest
Bête Noire
Beyond the Pale
Big Bang
Billingsgate
Bimbo
Bitch Goddess
Black Hole
Bligh
Blimp, Colonel
Bloody Shirt (see Waving the Bloody Shirt)
Bloomingdale's
Bloomsbury
Boilerplate
Bon Mot
Borscht Belt
Boswell
Bowdlerize
Brahmin
Brave New World
Bread and Circuses

Brobdingnagian
Bully Pulpit
Bunker Mentality
Burkean
Byronic
Byzantine
Cain, Mark of (see Mark of Cain)
Canute
Captain Queeg (see Queeg, Captain)
Cartesian
Cassandra
Casus Belli
Catch-22
Caveat Emptor
Center Cannot Hold, the
Cerberus (see Sop to Cerberus)
Checkers Speech
Chernobyl
Cheshire Cat
Chiaroscuro
Children's Crusade
Chimera or Chimaera
Chinese wall
Chutzpah
Cinéma Vérité
City on a Hill
Cloud-Cuckoo-Land
Cloud Like a Man's Hand, a
Cognoscenti
Colonel Blimp (see Blimp, Colonel)
Colossus of the North
Comédie Humaine
Comstockery
Consent Decree
Conspicuous Consumption
Cordon Sanitaire
Cotton Mather (see Mather, Cotton)
Coxey's Army
Cri de Coeur
Critical Mass
Crypto-
Cult of Personality

-Cum-
Dada
Damascus, Road to (see Road to
    Damascus)
Damon and Pythias
Damon Runyon (see Runyon,
    Damon)
Dantesque
De Facto
Defarge, Madame
Defenestration
Déjà Vu
De Jure
Delphic
Dernier Cri
Deus Ex Machina
Deutschland über Alles
Diaspora
Dickensian
Die is Cast, the
Dienbienphu
Dionysian (Bacchic)
Disinformation
Disraeli, Benjamin
DNA
Doctors' Plot
Dog in the Manger
Dooley, Mr. (see Mr. Dooley)
Don Quixote (see Quixote)
Doppelgänger
Dorian Gray
Double Helix
Doublespeak
Doyen, Doyenne
Draconian
Dreyfus, Dreyfus Affair
Droit du Seigneur
Dunkirk
Dybbuk
East Lynne
Echt
Eddie Haskell

Edwardian
Élan
Elmer Gantry
Éminence Grise
Emperor's New Clothes, the
Enfant Terrible
Enlightenment, the
Epicenter
Epiphany
Eton, Playing Fields of (see Playing
    Fields of Eton)
Et Tu, Brute?
Everyman
Ex Cathedra
Fabulous Invalid
Fall on One's Sword
Falstaff, Falstaffian
Faulknerian
Faustian Bargain
Fawkes, Guy (see Guy Fawkes)
Feet of Clay
Felliniesque
Fifth Column
Film Noir
Fin de Siècle
Final Solution
Fire and Brimstone
Fire When Ready, Gridley
Fleet Street
Flotsam and Jetsam
Foggy Bottom
For Whom the Bell Tolls
Force Majeure
Four Horsemen of the Apocalypse
Fragging
Full Court Press
Future Shock
Gang of Four
Gantry, Elmer (see Elmer Gantry)
Gatsby
Gemütlichkeit
Genius Loci

Genre
Gestalt
Gilded Age, the
Gladstonian
Glick, Sammy (see Sammy Glick)
Global Village
Goldberg, Rube (see Rube Goldberg)
Golden Parachute
Gonzo
Gordian Knot
Gothic
Götterdämmerung
Grand Guignol
Gray, Dorian (see Dorian Gray)
Great Leap Forward
Great White Fleet
Great White Hope
Greek Chorus
Greenhouse Effect
Gresham's Law
Gridley (see Fire When Ready,
    Gridley)
Grub Streeter
Gulag
Guy Fawkes
Habeas Corpus
Haiku
Half-life
Hamlet
Hardball
Harpy
Haskell, Eddie (see Eddie Haskell)
Hastings, Battle of
Hat Trick
Heart of Darkness
Hearts and Minds
Hegemony
Hegira
Heisenberg Uncertainty Principle
Hemlock, to Drink
Herodotus
Hindenburg

Hit the Wall
Hobson's Choice
Hoi Polloi
Hoist with One's Own Petard
Holy Grail
Homeric
Horatio Alger
Horatius at the Bridge
Hors de Combat
Hot Stove League
Hubris
Iago
Icon
Id
Idée Fixe
Idiot Savant
Immaculate Conception
In Flagrante Delicto
Invisible Hand
Iron Lady
Iron Triangle
J'accuse
Jacobean
Jacobins
Jihad
Jingoism
Kafkaesque
Karma
Kitsch
Know-Nothings
Kristallnacht
Kulturkampf
Last Hurrah
Lazarus
Lebensraum
Leitmotiv
Lèse-majesté
Let a Hundred Flowers Bloom
L'État, C'Est Moi
Level Playing Field
Leveraged Buyout
Leviathan

Libido
Lilliputian
Lingua Franca
Literati
Loaves and Fishes
Lochinvar
Loman, Willy (see Willy
   Loman)
Long March
Loose Cannon
Lord Acton (see Acton, Lord)
Lounge Lizard
Loyal Opposition
Luddites
Lumpenproletariat
Machiavellian
Madame Defarge (see Defarge,
   Madame)
Magic Bullet
Maginot Line
Main Street
Major-domo
Malthusian
Mandarin
Man For All Seasons
Manichean or Manichaean
Manifest Destiny
Man On Horseback
Mano a Mano
Manqué
Mantra
Mark of Cain
Mather, Cotton
Mau-mau
Maven
Mc-
Mea Culpa
Medium Is the Message, the
Meltdown
Ménage à Trois
Mensh
Mephistophelean

Mess of Pottage, to Sell One's
  Birthright for a
Micawberesque
Mickey Finn
Mirabile Dictu
Miranda, Mirandize
Mise en Scène
Mitty, Walter (see Walter Mitty)
Möbius Strip
Moby Dick
Modus Operandi
Modus Vivendi
Mr. Dooley
Mullah
Munchkin
Munich
Nabob
Neo-
Ne Plus Ultra
Night of the Long Knives
NIMBY
Ninety-five Theses
Noblesse Oblige
Nom de Guerre
Normalcy
Nostalgie de la Boue
Nouveau Riche
Number-crunching
Nuremburg Defense
October Surprise
Oedipal
Offending Adam (see Whip the
  Offending Adam)
Old Guard
Orwellian
Outré
Ozymandias, Ozymandian
Pale, Beyond the (see Beyond the
  Pale)
Panglossian
Papal Bull
Parkinson's Law

Parvenu
Pas de Deux
Patois
Pavlovian
Pax Americana
Peck's Bad Boy
Pecksniff, Pecksniffian
Persona Non Grata
Peter Principle
Peyton Place
Pharisees
Philistine
Phillipics
Phoenix Rising From the ashes
Photo Opportunity
Pickett's Charge
Pilgrim's Progress
Plato's Cave
Play in Peoria
Playing Fields of Eton
Plus ça Change, Plus C'Est la
  Même Chose
Pogrom
Poison Pill
Polonius
Pooh-Bah
Portmanteau Word
Potemkin Village
Pour Encourager les Autres
Praetorian Guard
Preux Chevalier
Pro Bono
Procrustean
Promethean
Protean
Proust, Proustian
Ptolemaic Universe
Pumpkin Papers
Putsch
Pygmalion
Pyrrhic Victory
Quantum Leap or Quantum Jump

Queeg, Captain
Queen of Hearts
Quisling
Quixote, Quixotic
Rabbi
Radical Chic
Raison d'Être
Rara Avis
Rashomon
Realpolitik
Red Queen
Reductio ad Absurdum
Redux
Regency
Road to Damascus
Robber Barons
Robespierre
Rogers, Will (see Will Rogers)
Roman à Clef
Rosetta Stone
Round Up the Usual Suspects
Rube Goldberg
Rubicon, To Cross the
Runyon, Damon; also Runyonesque, Runyonese
Salad Days
Samizdat
Sammy Glick
Sang-froid
Sans-culottes
Sarajevo
Savile Row
Savonarola
Scarlet Pimpernel
Schadenfreude
Sclerosis, Sclerotic
Scorched Earth Policy
Scylla and Charybdis
Sea Change
Second Coming
Secular Humanism
Segue

Shanghai
Shangri-la
Shermanesque
Sherpa
Shot Heard Round the World
Shtik or Shtick
Sick Man of Europe
Silent Spring
Sine Qua Non
Sinister Force
Sisyphean
Situation Ethics
Skunkworks
Slam Dunk
Slouching Toward Bethlehem
Slough of Despond
Sobriquet
Social Darwinism
Sodom and Gomorrah
Solon
Sop to Cerberus
Sotto Voce
South Sea Bubble
-Speak
Spear Carrier
Spin Control
Star Chamber
Stockholm Syndrome
Sturm und Drang
Sui Generis
Sulk Like Achilles in His Tent
Svengali
Sword of Damocles
Take to the Woodshed (see Woodshed, Take to the)
Talmudic, Talmudistic
Tammany, Tammany Hall
Tar Baby
Teapot Dome
Tectonic Plates
Tet, Tet Offensive
Theater of the Absurd

xviii

Thermopylae
Thin Red Line
Through a Glass, Darkly
Tilting at Windmills
Titanic
Torquemada, Tomas de
Troglodyte
Trojan Horse
Trompe l'Oeil
Trouble in River City
Tumbrel or Tumbril
Tweedledum and Tweedledee
Twist Slowly in the Wind
Type A
Über
Ugly American
Ur-
Valhalla
Vast Wasteland
Vet
Volte-face
Wagnerian
Walter Mitty
Waterloo

Waving the Bloody Shirt
Weltanschauung
Whip the Offending Adam
White-Bread
White Man's Burden
White Noise
Whitehall
Will Rogers
Willy Loman
Witches' Sabbath
Witching Hour
Woodshed, Take to the
Wooster, Bertie (see Bertie Wooster)
Wunderkind
Xanadu
Yalta
Yellow Journalism
Yin and Yang
Young Turks
Zaftig
Zeitgeist
Zen
Zero-sum Game
Zut Alors!

# GRAND
# ALLUSIONS

**Achilles' Heel.** (uh-KIL-eez) A point of maximum vulnerability.

In Greek mythology, the hero Achilles was invulnerable to mortal wounds because his mother, Thetis, had dipped him as an infant into the magical waters of the River Styx, which flows around Hades, the underworld. But she held baby Achilles by the heel. And inevitably, in the war against Troy, Achilles was killed by an arrow which struck him in that one vulnerable spot.

Achilles also gave us his tendon, which joins the calf muscle to the heelbone, and the Achilles reflex, also known to medicine as the ankle jerk, caused by a sharp tap on the Achilles tendon.

The term in use, by Philip K. Verleger, an energy specialist quoted by *The New York Times*, November 12, 1987:

> "Oil is the Achilles' heel of the trade picture now."

Another example, from Peter H. Lewis, *The New York Times*, March 21, 1989:

> "The key to a fax machine's power, and also its Achilles' heel, is that it works over regular telephone lines. Any boor with a fax machine and your phone number can deluge you with unwanted documents."

And from Rick Wartzman, *The Wall Street Journal*, July 24, 1989:

> "Some think it's the DC-10's Achilles' heel: a cluster of hydraulic lines that, if cut, can send the plane plummeting."

**Lord Acton.** He gave us the maxim, "Power tends to corrupt, and absolute power corrupts absolutely."* He was a brilliant and obviously

---

* George Bernard Shaw's view, as reported in *Days With Bernard Shaw* by Stephen Winsten, was: "Power does not corrupt men; fools, however, if they get into a position of power, corrupt power."

quotable Victorian. His name was John Emerich Edward Dalberg and he lived in the last two-thirds of the 19th century. As a Roman Catholic, he couldn't attend Cambridge University, but later he was appointed to a professorship in modern history there.

A friend of de Tocqueville and other prominent intellectuals of his day, celebrated as one of the most learned men of his age, Acton was an ardent Liberal and a close friend of **Gladstone.**

In addition to his observation on the corrupting nature of power, this comment on secrecy is attributed to him: "Everything secret degenerates; nothing is safe that does not bear discussion and publicity."

His lordship invoked, by Elizabeth Janeway in her review of Jonathan Yardley's *Our Kind of People, The New York Times Book Review,* March 19, 1989:

> "The WASP group (and I speak from experience since my own kind of people are much like Mr. Yardley's) has combined the comfort of belonging with long dominance of American power and culture. This assumed entitlement naturally infuriates many people. It also complicates its members' lives and visions: reality itself, not mere wishful thinking, has seemed to confirm the rightness of their beliefs and behavior. Here, I suspect, lies the root of that corruption by established power which Lord Acton, a White Anglo-Saxon Catholic, told us humans to fear."

Another example, from Charles Paul Freund in his column "Rhetorical Questions" in *The Washington Post,* April 11, 1989:

> "Never mind Lord Acton; in Washington, power homogenizes. Look at Newt Gingrich."

**Ad Hominem.** (ahd HAW-mih-nem) An appeal to someone's prejudices, emotions or special interests rather than intellect or reason. In politics, an ad hominem attack is an attack on an opponent's character rather than an answer to his or her arguments on matters of substance. The phrase is Latin, meaning "against the man."

Discussing negative campaign advertising in a *New York Times* column, August 19, 1987, William Safire offers a play on the expression, declaring that "politics is a nicer place without the ads hominem of negative campaigning."

Another example, from Michael Newman in *The New Republic*, February 6, 1989, on freshman Congressman Ben Jones of Georgia (and formerly of television's "The Dukes of Hazzard"):

> "That's not to say Jones hasn't been around the block a time or two. He prevailed in one of the most ad hominem congressional campaigns of 1988."

**Agitprop.** Propaganda, pure and simple, and, more sinister, alien propaganda. It's a marriage of agitation and propaganda, a tactic to arouse the people, and its method is selective and manipulative use of facts and falsehoods.

As you might guess, the term comes from the communists: Lenin used it, and the *agitatsia propaganda* section of the Central Committee secretariat was set up by the Communist Party of the Soviet Union in 1920. Its function was to control the ideological conditioning of the populace.

In western usage, it is usually a pejorative term for arguments used by someone on the other side of an issue (and therefore wrong).

The term in use, by columnist George Will in *The Washington Post*, December 27, 1987:

> "The director, Oliver Stone, who also directed *Salvador* and *Platoon*, makes political films that frequently become agitprop."

And from John Buckley, spokesman for the Republican Congressional Campaign Committee, in praise of Congressman Newt Gingrich, quoted in *Time*, June 12, 1989:

> "Gingrich is classic agitprop—great with devising the arguments to forward our revolution. I see him as one-third Thomas Paine, one-third Winston Churchill and one-third Genghis Khan."

**Al Fresco.** (al FRES-koh) Sounds like the name of your waiter, but actually it is where you eat when you dine at a sidewalk cafe or

5

somewhere else in the open air. It's Italian, and literally means "in the cool." As an adjective or an adverb, it puts you and your activities outdoors.

The term in use, by Tony Kornheiser in *The Washington Post*, September 20, 1988, describing the pratfalls of the U.S. Olympic boxing team and its coaches:

> ". . . Coulter [a coach] kept having public relations problems. A story surfaced alleging that he had gotten off a bus to urinate, as we say, *al fresco*, during a U.S. boxing team visit to Moscow."

**Alarums and Excursions.** Stage directions occurring in slightly varying form in Shakespeare's *Henry VI* and *Richard III*, for the noises offstage that simulate the sound of battle, such as trumpets and the clash of arms.

"Alarum" is an obsolete form of "alarm," which was originally a call to arms. "Excursion" is also of military origin, meaning sallies against an enemy.

Today the phrase is used playfully to describe skirmishing, confused fighting, sudden rushings to and fro.

The term in use, by James Brady in a column in *Advertising Age*, August 31, 1987:

> "Be still, my heart. All these alarums and excursions about Gary Hart have me in a high state of excitement."

Another example, from Bob Weimer, *Newsday*, March 5, 1989:

> "The medium [television] has always been dedicated to the hard sell, and that most certainly has not changed. If anything, the coming of cable has only introduced a more frenetic quality to the pitches, which, like Shakespearean stage directions, are keyed to action. Instead of 'alarums and excursions,' cable television has 1-800 numbers. From the herky-jerky glitz of MTV to the unrelenting pedagogy of the Discovery Channel, they are the punctuation marks of salesmanship."

**Alger, Horatio.** See Horatio Alger.

**Alphonse and Gaston Act.** Two people engaging in an excessive and sometimes self-defeating or silly deference to one another.

The term originates from two comic strip characters, Frenchmen who did everything with exaggerated and self-defeating politeness. They were created by Frederick Burr Opper in 1905 (he also originated "Happy Hooligan"). According to Coulton Waugh, *The Comics*, they were national figures, and their elaborate courtesies became catch phrases: "After you, my dear Alphonse!" and "No, after you, my dear Gaston!"

The damage arises when deference turns into destructive delay, as with two baseball fielders deferring to each other with the result that the ball falls between them.

The term in use, by television critic Tom Shales in *The Washington Post*, September 16, 1987, reviewing the opening of Senate Judiciary Committee hearings on the Supreme Court nomination of Robert H. Bork:

> "Perhaps the real contest of the day was, who could be slipperier, Biden or Bork? And who could be more unctuous to the other? . . . So instead of Ali and Frazier, one gets Alphonse and Gaston."

Another example, from Alex Heard, *The American Spectator*, May 1989, writing on the Senate debate on the nomination of John Tower to be secretary of defense:

> "It was Senator Symms, not I, who compared this Alfonse [sic] and Gaston Nerf-Mitt boxing match to the truly rancorous old days, so it's fair to look at Then versus Now."

**American Century.** A term introduced by Henry Luce, creator of the Time-Life publishing empire, in *Life* magazine, February 17, 1941: "to accept wholeheartedly our duty and our opportunity as the most powerful and vital nation in the world, and in consequence to exert upon the world the full impact of our influence, for such

7

purposes as we see fit and by such means as we see fit. . . . [T]he world of the 20th century, if it is to come to life in any nobility of health and vigor, must be to a significant degree an American century."

Luce's statement was a powerful call to a country that had not yet entered World War II and still had strong isolationist impulses.

At the end of the war, when the United States' supremacy in military and economic strength was clear, it did seem that the American Century—the **Pax Americana**—had arrived. From the perspective of the post-Vietnam and post-industrial 1990s, things look different. Has the Century shrunk to Andy Warhol's 15 minutes of fame? Nevertheless, George Bush revived the phrase in his 1988 presidential campaign: "The American Century has not drawn to a close," he asserted in a speech in Chicago. "We are not in decline."

Another view, from George Scialabba, in the *Village Voice Literary Supplement*, December 1988:

> "The Golden Age, the American Century, ended with a sudden and sustained surge of international economic competition in the 1970s. Between 1969 and 1979, the value of our imports nearly doubled."

And from John Judis, *The New Republic*, April 10, 1989, reviewing *The Price of Empire* by J. William Fulbright:

> "When Fulbright became a senator during World War II, he was a champion of the American Century. When he left 30 years later, after years as the chairman of the Senate Foreign Relations Committee, he was its foremost critic."

**A Modest Proposal.** A proposal that's anything but modest—one that's outrageous, in fact.

The expression is the shortened title of A *Modest Proposal for Preventing the Children of the Poor People in Ireland from being a Burden to their Parents or Country; and for making them beneficial to their Publick*, a pamphlet written by Jonathan Swift in 1729. He suggested that the answer to the grinding poverty of Irish peasants was for them to raise their children as livestock and sell them for food. Just to make sure you got the idea, Swift helpfully included recipes.

The proposal was a classic example of Swift's bitter satire. He wrote it as an attack on the wrongheadedness of British government policy toward the Irish. And ever since, "a modest proposal" has been one which carries an idea to ridiculous extremes to make a point.

The term in use, by columnist Ron Shaffer, who writes on traffic woes under the **sobriquet** "Dr. Gridlock," *The Washington Post*, September 9, 1988:

> Under the heading "A Modest Proposal," Shaffer printed a letter from a pothole-weary reader proposing that the armed forces be called out to complete a long-delayed freeway segment through the District of Columbia, and that highway construction firms be sent overseas to defend the country against a Soviet invasion: "All they'd have to do is work on their roads."

**Amour-propre.** (ah-MOOR PROH-PR) A French term for self-love or self-esteem; one's wish to be admired.

The term in use, by Gore Vidal in *Matters of Fact and Fiction*, speaking of the Adams family of American statesmen and men of letters:

> "Yet it is true that their overwhelming amour-propre was such that they were hopeless when it came to the greasy art of survival in American politics. Although they were sly enough to rise to the top, they were never sufficiently adhesive to stay there."

**Ancien Régime.** (AHN-see-en RAY-JEEM) French, meaning the old order, the government or power structure that has been displaced.

Capitalized, it refers to the aristocratic order existing under the Bourbon monarchy which was overthrown by the French Revolution of 1789. The phrase came into use during the Revolution to sum up the obsolescence of the previous system.

The term in use, by Paul Valentine in *The Washington Post*, September 18, 1988, discussing politics in Baltimore, Maryland:

> "Rawlings said the incident may be a temporary sting to [Mayor Kurt] Schmoke, who entered City Hall here last

January as a rising young black political star promising to replace the ancien regime of William Donald Schaefer, now Maryland governor."

Another example, from Fouad Ajami, *U.S. News and World Report*, June 19, 1989, commenting on the death of Ayatollah Khomeini:

"Above all, Khomeini was a state builder. The real legacy he leaves is the clerical state he built on the ruins of the *ancien regime.*"

**Angst.** (ahngst) A German word meaning a feeling of dread, anxiety or guilt.

The term in use, by Mark Stevens, art critic, in *The New Republic* May 18, 1987:

"It's been said that Andy Warhol took an interest in the homeless. This seems apt, not just because he was kind-hearted or interested in the most celebrated of current causes, but because he and his art seem no less homeless. Warhol appeared to live at parties, and the images with which he worked have a drifting nomadic presence . . . The world is a **Bloomingdale's** of images, among which one poses and shops. A little angst is added for flavor."

Another example, from Tony Kornheiser, *The Washington Post*, October 3, 1989:

"My friend Larry, a Chicago native and man of independent spirit—a White Sox fan!—says: 'I don't hate the Cubs so much as I hate Cubs fans. They're so precious and self-pitying.'

"Cubs fans, spare us your angst.

"Spare us your phony-baloney conceits about baseball as a metaphor for life. (If it is, then when you lose, how come you don't die?)"

**Anschluss.** (AHN-shloos) The forcible annexation, by Adolf Hitler's Germany, of Austria in 1938. It was Hitler's first external conquest, the fulfillment of a vow made in the first paragraph of *Mein Kampf,* to seize his native land "by any means." Literally, the German word means "joining together."

The Austrian government attempted feebly to hold off the Germans; Chancellor Schuschnigg announced a plebiscite on the question of Austrian independence in which only pro-independence ballots would be distributed. Those wishing to support annexation would have to produce their own ballots. This effort had significant popular support, which led Hitler to demand a postponement of the election and Schuschnigg's resignation. Unable to control events, the chancellor resigned on March 11, 1938, and was replaced by a Nazi sympathizer. On March 12 the German army invaded. Ruthless revenge was taken on their opponents.

A plebiscite conducted by the Nazis after the fact gave a favorable 99.75 per cent vote in favor of union.

The term in use, by Paul Gigot in *The Wall Street Journal,* June 9, 1989, on the implications of Chinese repression for the scheduled British turnover of Hong Kong to China in 1997:

> "So is an Asian Anschluss inevitable? Perhaps not yet.
>
> "Even after last Saturday's massacre [of Chinese student demonstrators in Beijing], the British have found excuses. The stiff-upper-lip foreign secretary, Sir Geoffrey Howe, first said only that Hong Kong's future remains 'inextricably bound . . . with mainland China.' Some may recall that many in Britain used similar arguments, in 1938, to justify the Anschluss. Austrians spoke German, after all, and what could the British do anyway?"

**Antebellum.** (AN-teh-BEL-uhm) "Before the war" in Latin, but in the United States it always means before the Civil War. "A beautiful antebellum mansion" is one built before 1860. In the United Kingdom, antebellum refers to the period before the Boer War (1899-1902) or either of the world wars.

The term in use, by Florence King, in *Reflections In A Jaundiced Eye* (1989), as quoted by Jonathan Yardley in *The Washington Post,* March 29, 1989:

"I graduated from college qualified to do nothing except crossword puzzles in ink. Though a scholarship student, I received an aristocrat's education, designed for people like the antebellum Ashley Wilkes who have the money and leisure to enjoy it for its own sake."

And another example, from Michael J. McCarthy in *The Wall Street Journal*, March 28, 1989, writing on Marietta, Georgia:

"The town square, the bleached-white gazebos and the antebellum mansions give Marietta a misty feel of the Old South. But Old Dixie never had anything like Marietta's 'Big Chicken.' Perched atop a Kentucky Fried Chicken outlet, the 56-foot metal fowl is so visible that Mariettans use it as a guide when giving directions. Pilots even use it to navigate."

**Antichrist.** In Christian belief, the Antichrist is an adversary of Christ who will appear before the **Second Coming** as the last oppressor of the Christians, to be defeated by Christ on his return to earth.

However, the concept of a demonic "man of sin," a devilish figure who will engage God in the final battle at the end of time, is older than Christianity. It is found in the prophecies of Daniel in the Old Testament. Some scholars trace the idea back to the myths of Babylon.

As the Christian church evolved, so did its enemies, and the label of Antichrist was applied to such figures as the Roman emperors Caligula and Nero. In the Middle Ages, the term was used against opponents in religious, or even political, quarrels. During the Reformation's battles over the power of clergy, reformers Luther and Calvin charged that the papacy was the Antichrist. The church responded with similar claims against its critics.

In more recent times, the term has been applied to contemporary figures such as Kaiser Wilhelm and Hitler. What it comes down to, of course, is that the Antichrist is sure to be someone on the other side of a bitter dispute.

The term in use, by the Rev. Ian Paisley, who obviously believes in old-fashioned insults. The militant Protestant clergyman loudly interrupted an address by Pope John Paul II before the European Parliament in Strasbourg, France on October 11, 1988: "I denounce you as the antichrist."

Another example, cited by Henry Allen in *The Washington Post*, November 22, 1988, on the Kennedy assassination and aftermath:

> "We seem to resent not only success where Kennedy failed, but the idea of anybody else having those ideas at all. Jack Newfield of *The Village Voice* attacked [Lyndon] Johnson as the 'Antichrist.' "

Also, from Randy Sue Coburn, writing in *Premiere*, October 1989, on the making of the movie *Fat Man and Little Boy*, about the building of the atomic bombs dropped on Japan:

> "Around the movie set, [Dr. Edward] Teller is something of an Antichrist, the man who resisted Oppenheimer's guilt and caution to push ahead with ever more powerful nuclear bombs. Now, of course, Teller is one of the fathers of America's 'Star Wars' program."

**Antihero.** The central character of a work of fiction who lacks what traditionally are the attributes of heroes—brains, courage or other admirable characteristics. Antiheroes may be foolish, cowardly, dishonest or wicked, but still manage to stir the sympathies of the reader. Famous antiheroes are Yossarian in Joseph Heller's **Catch-22**, Cervantes' **Don Quixote** and George MacDonald Fraser's Flashman.

The term in use, by Eugen Weber in a review in *The Washington Post*, March 19, 1989, of *Citizens*, by Simon Schama, a history of the French Revolution:

> "Speaking from the ruthless precinct of the Committee of Public Safety, Saint-Just, who is one of Mr. Schama's favorite antiheroes, insisted that the Republic stood for the extermination of everything that opposed it."

**Aperçu.** (a-pehr-SYOO) French; quick impression, glimpse or insight.

13

The term in use, by Janet Malcolm, in *The New Yorker*, March 13, 1989:

> "In [Daniel] Berrigan, [author Joe] McGinniss finds the expansive interlocutor he has been seeking, but the morning after their boozy late-night conversation, McGinniss opens the notebook in which he inscribed Berrigan's aperçus, and instead of 'the disciplined, accurate notes of a trained professional' he finds only illegible scrawls and the punch line of a coarse joke."

**Apparatchik.** In Russian, it's a member of the Communist Party organization. The word has a Latin root—apparatus—meaning instrument. The Russian word for the Party organization is "apparat." Thus an apparatchik is a member of the apparat, a functionary, agent or spy. In contemporary use, the term has broadened to refer to bureaucrats, government officials—functionaries who carry out policy. It's not a friendly word. The western connotation is someone who mindlessly carries out orders from above.

The term in use: During Senate confirmation hearings on his nomination by President Ronald Reagan to a Supreme Court seat, Judge Robert Bork had to defend his actions as solicitor general in the "Saturday night massacre." On October 20, 1973, President Richard Nixon ordered Attorney General Elliot Richardson to fire Watergate Special Prosecutor Archibald Cox for refusing to withdraw a subpoena for Nixon's tapes. Richardson resigned rather than carry out the order. Deputy Attorney General William Ruckelshaus also refused to fire Cox and resigned. That left Bork in charge of the Justice Department, and he did the deed. In his Senate testimony 13 years later, he said it was his intention to fire Cox and then resign—to demonstrate that he was "not just an apparatchik"—but Richardson talked him out of resigning on the grounds that it was necessary for someone to stay on and provide continuity of leadership.

Another example, from Arch Puddington in *The American Spectator*, March 1989:

> "Ironically, in view of the New Left's intellectual pretensions, the movement produced many more apparatchiks than great thinkers."

**Aquarius, Age of; Aquarian.** A term from astrology. The age takes its name from the astrological sign of Aquarius, the water bearer. The Aquarian Age is the next great age after the Piscean Age, which was considered to be the Christian era in Western culture. Astrologers disagree on just when we are supposed to enter this new, post-Christian era—or whether we are in it now. Characteristics of the period are great changes in society and culture, especially in the role of women; increased violence and the threat of global disaster—nuclear, ecological or both.

The term was popularized in the 1960s, with the hit musical "Hair" and other popular and commercial celebrations of the hippie counterculture. These suggested a more benign view of the changes anticipated in the new era—harmony, peace and understanding were to be the order of the day. The term today is used to invoke this romantic, naive spirit—or used ironically to sneer at the misjudgments of the period. The idea retains some life in the so-called "New Age," an amorphous successor to the counterculture.

The term in use, by William Safire in *The New York Times*, May 9, 1988, on the flap over First Lady Nancy Reagan's reliance on an astrologer:

> "As a result of the score-settling by former White House chief of staff Don Regan in his million-dollar memoir, the inclination of the First Lady to consider star signs in the scheduling of her Age-of-Aquarius husband will be endlessly spoofed."

Another example, from Robert R. Harris, reviewing *Woodstock: The Oral History*, by Joel Makower, *The New York Times Book Review*, July 23, 1989:

> "Woodstock, of course, has attained legendary status as a symbol of the youth revolt of the 1960's. This intriguing book—for all its faults, by far the best of those on the subject published this year—will do little to dispel that image, despite its eye-opening reminders of some of the distinctly non-Aquarian behavior at the concert: intense battles between producers and greedy food concessionaires,

rock groups demanding cash before they would go on-stage."

**Ark of the Covenant.** A wooden chest, possibly a model of a temple overlaid with gold, in which the presence of God was supposed to dwell when he communicated with biblical Israel. The ark is thought to have contained the stone tablets of the law, as given to Moses, and was carried into battle. For example, it was carried around the walls of Jericho. Kept in the Holy of Holies of Solomon's temple in Jerusalem, it disappeared after the fall of Jerusalem in 586 B.C. Its fate is unknown.

The term is now used figuratively to mean something sacred or reverenced, a revealed truth.

The term in use, by British Prime Minister James Callaghan, quoted in *Time*, April 19, 1976, warning the members of his Labour Party that he intended to maintain party unity at all costs:

> "I want no cliques. None of you hold the Ark of the Covenant."

Another example, quoted by *The Washington Times*, October 9, 1989, on issues in the Virginia gubernatorial race:

> " 'They used to call [right to work] the ark of the political covenant,' said James Sweeny, a historian at Old Dominion University in Norfolk. 'It's a holy of holies. You just don't trifle with the right-to-work-law.' "

And from Murray Kempton, *Newsday*, March 4, 1988, on the struggle between the midwestern and eastern factions of the Republican Party:

> "That struggle reached its highest pitch in 1952 when Senator Robert Taft lost the Republican nomination to Dwight D. Eisenhower in what was not so much a political contest as a civil war between Ohio and New York.
>
> "Taft was, in those days, the ark of the conservative Republican covenant and the troops that overthrew him were commanded by Gov. Thomas E. Dewey, who was

especially hated by the orthodox as little better than a liberal Democrat."

**Armageddon.** (AHR-muh-GED-uhn) From the book of Revelations in the New Testament. Armageddon is the site of the climactic battle between the forces of good and evil at the end of the world. Today it is used to describe a battle between irreconcilable forces, a confrontation resulting in terrible destruction.

In fundamentalist Christian belief, "Armageddon theology" prescribes the sequence of events in the forthcoming destruction and recreation of the world. One step in the sequence is the Rapture, the moment when the select are whisked off the earth by God—out of bed, out of cars, etc.—leaving everyone else to die in the destruction of the world. (Apparently out of clothes, too: T-shirt observed in downtown Washington on buxom female reads, "In case of rapture, this shirt will be EMPTY!")

"Armageddon" has become a cliche to describe nuclear war. In a *New York Times Book Review* article by Michael Dorris and Louise Erdrich, March 13, 1988: "In the years since Aug. 6, 1945, writers of fiction have repeatedly and variously attempted to conceive a future beyond an Armageddon which, if and when it comes, is guaranteed to exact casualties on a scale beyond precedent, beyond comprehension."

The term in use, by Dan Balz in *The Washington Post*, March 5, 1989, describing the political battle over the nomination of John Tower to be secretary of defense:

> "The fact that the Senate appears on the brink of rejecting not only a new president's Cabinet nominee but a former colleague as well has produced an extraordinary spectacle. There is a sense that the rules have been changed but not yet fully redefined. Is this the breakdown of the Club? Is it the transfer of sharp partisan lines from the House to the Senate? Is it a power grab on the part of Democrats still licking their wounds after a bruising presidential campaign? Will it produce lasting damage?
>
> "Senate Republican Whip Alan K. Simpson (Wyo.) curtly dismissed the Armageddon analogies last week."

Also from the *Post*, film critic Rita Kempley's review of *The War of the Roses*, December 8, 1989:

> " 'The War of the Roses' is yuppie Armageddon, an explosion of empty values and curdled peevishness that blows a marriage and blasts a decade."

**Arriviste.** (ahr-ee-VEEST) One who has just acquired wealth, and who lacks the gentility of "old money." Sometimes it is used as a derogatory word for a self-important newcomer.

Literally, in French, it is the newly arrived, but it is most frequently used to mean those who have newly arrived into big bucks. See their first cousins, **nouveau riche** and **parvenu.** Count on the French to have such a variety of ways to convey scorn for this particular group. English can't come close.

The term in use, columnist Jonathan Yardley, writing in *The Washington Post*, December 15, 1986, about fashion designer Ralph Lauren:

> "Lauren may sell his products across a wide range of social and even economic classes, but his primary market is among the *arrivistes*: those who have come lately to wealth, or an approximation of the same, and are now attempting to fashion the appropriate 'life style' for themselves. If you've just leveraged your way into a duplex on the Upper East Side and know how neither it nor you should be furnished, Lauren is the man for you; from him you can purchase instant image."

Another example, from William M. Bulkeley in *The Wall Street Journal*, April 28, 1989, on celebrations of a pre-Plymouth Rock Thanksgiving in El Paso, Texas:

> "This may strike some Yankees as ludicrous, but they, after all, have embroidered a pot-luck supper by English *arrivistes* into a national extravaganza. As for Texans, the discovery that Spanish pioneers feasted here a generation before the Mayflower has become something of a coup."

And also in the *Journal*, Alexandra Peers, writing about the boom in portraits of pets, November 20, 1989:

> "One of the leading animaliers of this century is Count Bernard de Claviere d'hust. He earns as much as $250,000 per work for his paintings—commissioned by arrivistes who seek instant aristocracy, and by members of the old guard who cling to their love-affair with beasts."

**Art Deco.** A design style that emerged in the 1920s, remained popular throughout the 1930s, died out and then experienced something of a comeback in the 1980s.

Art Deco grew out of many influences, including **art nouveau**, modernist painting and efforts to have the arts represented in the products of a new era of mass production. It took varying forms between classical design and the "International Style" which was the embodiment of the anti-ornamentation sentiment of radical modern. Generally it is characterized by streamlined, flowing lines, black and white, flat color, geometric lines and a lack of symmetry.

In architecture, art deco reworked traditional types of ornamentation into new themes, combining modern materials and motifs—illustrations of modern travel and industry, for instance—with traditional decorative tools. For example, the great aluminum doors of the Federal Trade Commission in Washington have panels showing ocean liners and airplanes.

Art deco made use of new materials such as glass block, neon and aluminum. And old materials were used in new ways—circular mirrors, highly polished dark stone. New themes appeared: Egyptian or Aztec motifs were worked into streamlined modernity.

Other examples of art deco style include New York's Chrysler Building, Radio City Music Hall and Rockefeller Center and those gleaming black-and-white nightclubs with polished floors where Fred Astaire and Ginger Rogers danced in all those 1930s movies.

Preservationists have saved an entire neighborhood of such buildings in Miami Beach, where the Art Deco District has become a tourist attraction.

The term in use, by James Wolcott in *Vanity Fair*, May 1989, discussing the movie *Batman:*

> "Conceptually, Burton has left behind the candy-mint camp of the TV series to scale the Deco spires of *Metropolis* monumentalism. Gotham City is not a cardboard playhouse, as it was on TV, but a nocturnal beast of black metal."

Another example, from P.J. O'Rourke, *Holidays in Hell*, visiting South Africa:

> "I did see one homeland that worked, beautiful and severe bushveldt taken back from Boer farms and restored to its natural state with blesbok and gemsbok and springbok boking around all antlered and everything and herds of zebra—art deco on the hoof—and packs or gaggles or whatever-they're-called of giraffes (an NBA of giraffes would be the right term)."

**Art Nouveau.** (AHR noo-voh) An art movement that developed in the late 19th and early 20th centuries, characterized by flowing lines and ornamentation that uses floral motifs, twining plant tendrils and other natural forms. It developed most successfully in the decorative arts, furniture, book design and illustration, jewelry and architecture, and represented a break from the traditional conventions in art and decoration.

It owed much to a revived interest in medieval art and the intricate patterns of Celtic art. Literally, in French, it means "new art." Tiffany in the United States and Lalique in France (glass and jewelry) were well-known practitioners.

Since the 1960s, art nouveau has enjoyed a revival in the United States and Europe, especially in advertising, interior decoration and fabric design.

The term in use, by David Richards, reviewing *A Midsummer Night's Dream*, *The Washington Post*, September 29, 1989:

> "When Arena Stage produced 'A Midsummer Night's Dream' in 1981, the set consisted of a huge *art nouveau*

tree of twisted metal branches, a forest floor that resembled Gruyere cheese and an onstage swimming pool, into which the cast members were forever plunging headfirst, like so many smiling extras in an Esther Williams movie."

**Artful Dodger.** A street thief, especially a young one; more broadly, a trickster or con artist.

The term derives from a character in Charles Dickens' novel *Oliver Twist.* He was the star of Fagin's gang of child thieves, the most accomplished pickpocket of them all. His name was Jack Dawkins, but in tribute to his skills he was called the Artful Dodger.

The term in use, by Kevin Thomas in *The Los Angeles Times,* March 17, 1989, reviewing the movie *Rooftops:*

". . . Alexis Cruz is the 'Artful Dodger' of the plot, a gifted, diminutive graffiti muralist whose own long coat sports some of his best work."

Another example, from Walter A. Hackett, *The Christian Science Monitor,* March 16, 1989:

"My baggage handler slid up, handed me my stubs. I gave him a $2 tip. 'You must be a rich Japanese,' he said grinning. He took off like the Artful Dodger."

Finally, the term applied to former British prime minister Harold Wilson, by *The Economist,* February 25, 1989, reviewing *Breach of Promise: Labour in Power 1964-1970,* by Clive Ponting:

"Alternatively he might have offered a rollicking narrative of what was, after all, a bizarre administration filled with bizarre people: the dipsomaniac-genius George Brown, the crafty but shallow Richard Crossman, the Artful Dodger himself, Mr. Wilson."

**Au Courant.** (oh koo-RAHN) Up-to-date, well-informed, in with the in crowd, hip. It's French, a chic way of saying someone knows what's what, what's in, what's up to the minute.

The term in use, by Maureen Dowd in *The New Republic,* August

1, 1988. Dowd reviews the NBC series "Tanner '88," about a Gary Hartish presidential candidate, which features a mix of real and fictional characters:

> "A Nashville fundraiser during Super Tuesday featuring Waylon Jennings was filmed at a real fund-raiser for Al Gore, and stars the real local television reporters (**Ken** and **Barbies** or Twinkies, in the film's au courant argot) and real local officials who switch their allegiance from Gore to Tanner for [director Robert] Altman's camera."

And from Richard Stengel, *Spy*, December 1989:

> "No matter how society shifts—hairdos evolving from flips to shags, male movie stars metamorphosing from small and dark to tall and blond, economic theory changing from demand to supply, buttoned top shirt buttons going from geeky to cool—Jack Nicholson, Tom Wolfe, Mike Nichols, Phillip Johnson, Mick Jagger, Felix Rohatyn and the rest always manage to seem of the moment, to be au courant, to become the very exemplars of their age. Chameleons are news that stays news."

**Augean Stables.** (aw-JEE-uhn) Where Augean stables are involved, look for an awesome cleanup job, often of massive corruption.

According to Greek myth, cleaning the stables of King Augeas was one of the 10 heroic labors of Hercules. Just how heroic can be judged from the statistics: the stables housed 3,000 oxen and hadn't been shoveled out in 30 years. Hercules accomplished the task by diverting two rivers through the stables.

A crusading district attorney elected in a pledge to reform an entrenched political machine is said to face a Herculean task in cleaning out the city's Augean stables.

The term in use, by Celestine Bohlen in *The Washington Post*, November 18, 1987, in a report from Moscow on the excitement caused by the ousting of the Moscow Communist Party leader:

> "As spectators later recounted the remarkable outburst, the leading actress in 'The Seventh Feat of Hercules,' a new

and topical play about the cleaning of the Augean stables, departed from her script last Saturday and accused the audience of standing by while a new 'Hercules' who had come to clean up the city was ridden out of town on a rail."

And by James Traub, *The New York Times Magazine*, May 9, 1989, referring to HUD secretary Jack Kemp's plan to evict from public housing those suspected of illegal drug activity:

"It was a new-breeze, clean-the-Augean-stables kind of idea, but civil libertarians have complained that you can't deprive someone of shelter based on an allegation of drug peddling or use."

**Ausländer.** (OWS-len-der) Foreigner, or alien, in German. The word is often used pejoratively, with a connotation of boorishness.

The term in use, by Richard Cohen, in *The Washington Post Magazine*, September 6, 1987:

"I recognize that weirdness in me when it comes to rock music. Loathing it made me an outsider as a teen-ager and yet again an *auslander* in college. Now I hear people say rock defined my generation, and I haven't the vaguest idea how listening to rock would make the values of my peers significantly different from mine."

**Auto-da-fé.** (AW-toh dah FEH) Unjust or arbitrary proceedings that are literally or figuratively fatal to the victim.

The term is Portuguese and means act of faith. (The Spanish form is auto-de-fé.) It's the name of the ceremony in the Spanish Inquisition during which sentences were pronounced. Although victims were not usually executed at these ceremonies, the term has come to apply to both sentencing and execution. In fact, during the Inquisition, the prisoners—unrepentant or relapsed heretics—were handed over by the church to the government, which carried out the death sentences, usually by fire. [See **Torquemada**.]

The term in use, by Michael Kinsley in *The New Republic*, April 28, 1988:

> "It is the liberal nightmare come true. In the twilight of the Reagan era, conservatives finally get a secure lock on the Supreme Court and begin methodically overturning all the liberal decisions of the postwar era. It certainly looked like the beginning of a judicial *auto-da-fé* April 25. Lawyers for both sides in *Patterson v. McLean Credit Union* thought they were arguing about a minor point of interpretation of a 12-year-old civil rights ruling. Out of the blue, by a 5-4 vote, the court asked them to discuss whether the whole ruling shouldn't simply be reversed."

Another example, from Maria Margaronis, *The Village Voice*, January 30, 1990:

> "For those who need reminding, Charles Stuart killed his pregnant wife in Boston's Mission Hill on October 23, 1989, shot himself in the gut for an alibi, and conjured up the generic white nightmare of a black criminal to take the rap. Within hours, he'd triggered a racist auto-da-fé that almost culminated in the indictment of William Bennett, a 39-year-old African American from Roxbury. . . ."

**Avatar.** (AV-uh-tahr) The embodiment of a principle, attitude or view of life.

It's from a Sanskrit word meaning "descent." In Hindu belief, it means the descent of a deity to the earth in a visible form.

The term in use, by Henry Allen in *The Washington Post*, October 27, 1988, in a piece about Zsa Zsa Gabor:

> "She is still what she has always been—the epitome of the triumph of shamelessness over hypocrisy, of the feminine ethic of doing what you can with what you've got, a sort of avatar of that Vaseline-lensed heaven you see on the covers of a billion paperback books, and a combination of three personas, the 'adventuress,' the 'glamour girl,' and the 'woman with a past.' "

**Axis.** A term of anatomy, botany, analytic geometry, aeronautics, fine arts and politics, in all of which it means a real or imaginary straight line on which an object rotates, or a central line around which the parts of a thing or a system are symmetrically arranged. Thus the earth's axis is an imaginary line through the center of the earth that links the North and South Poles. The earth turns on its axis.

In politics, it is an alliance between nations, groups or individuals. In World War II the Axis Powers were Germany, Italy and Japan, with junior partners Bulgaria, Hungary and Rumania.

The term in use, by Erik v. Kuehnelt-Leddihn in the *National Review*, October 24, 1986:

"Is there such a thing as a Washington-Moscow axis?"

# B

**Babel.** (BAY-buhl) A scene of noisy confusion and misunderstanding, a tumult of voices or sounds.

The story comes from the Bible's Book of Genesis, explaining the origin of the variety of languages found on earth. After the Flood, Noah's descendants planned to build a great tower in the land of Babylon that would reach to heaven. Such presumption offended God, and he prevented the completion of the project by causing the people to speak in different languages. Unable to understand each other, they couldn't complete the tower.

The term in use, in *The New York Times*, as quoted by Robert Greenman in *Words That Make A Difference*:

> "Urumqi seems more like a Central Asian bazaar than a city of the People's Republic. The resemblance is especially close at the animated 'free market,' a babel of Turkic tongues at the intersection in front of the Red Hill Department store."

Another example, by George J. Church in *Time*, December 1, 1986, describing the confusion of explanations and recriminations in the Reagan White House in the wake of exposure of the Iran-contra affair:

> "In their efforts to explain and justify the secret U.S. sales of weapons and spare parts to Iran—which shattered the entire foundation of the Administration's fervent public efforts to take a strong stand against terrorism—Reagan and his aides last week seemed only to be erecting a Tower of Babel abuzz with conflicting voices."

**Babbitt.** The chief character in the scathing 1922 novel of the same name by Sinclair Lewis—and the synonym for a smug, middle class, unimaginative, insular and conformist American.

Reread the novel and you'll discover that George Follansbee Babbitt was a little more complicated than that. He was dimly dissatisfied with his life, had a tentative fling with bohemianism, took up a flirtation with an attractive widow, even uttered a few unconventional opinions. Alas, social pressure and fear led him to abandon his small rebellion and return to conformity and boosterism.

H. L. Mencken, the acerbic critic, pounced on this character with joy:

> "As an old professor of babbittry I welcome him as an almost perfect specimen—a genuine museum piece. Every American city swarms with his brothers. . . . He is no worse than most, and no better; he is the average American of the ruling minority in this hundred and forty-sixth year of the Republic. He is American incarnate, exuberant and exquisite. Study him well and you will know better what is the matter with the land we live in than you would know after plowing through a thousand such volumes as Walter Lippmann's *Public Opinion*. . . ."

The term in use, by William McGurn, writing in *The American Spectator*, March 1989:

> "In the half-decade since I forsook the secure environs of Reagan's America for shores unknown, journalism has taken me (and kindly paid my way) across a healthy swath of the globe. Mostly it has been smooth sailing, for even the most wide-tied Babbitt soon learns that it is possible to recreate the comforts of **Main Street** USA in the most incongruous of places."

**Bacchanal.** (BAK-uh-NAL) Riotous, drunken orgies. The adjective to describe such events is bacchanalian.

The term comes from the name of Bacchus, the Greek and Roman god of wine (and vegetation and fertility, too). [See also **Dionysian.**] Bacchus was worshiped in an annual festival called the Baccanalia, an orgiastic rite.

The term in use by *The Economist*, June 10, 1989, in a description of the Indianapolis 500:

> "While out-of-town guests of sponsoring companies watch the race from comfortable penthouse boxes lining the track, thousands of Hoosiers, as people from the state of Indiana are known, invade the area inside the oval track. There, nestled in trailer trucks and cordoned off from civilization by metal fences, the natives enjoy what has been called a 'blue-collar bacchanal.' Sitting on or beside their cars, they drink beer, grill meats and implore women to remove their shirts. Some comply."

**Bad Seed.** An evil child, whose evilness is innate, a seemingly genetic trait.

The term comes from the 1955 play *The Bad Seed* by Maxwell Anderson (based on a novel by William March), about a little girl who is a calculating murderess.

The term in use, by Myra McPherson, in her examination of the life of serial killer Ted Bundy in *Vanity Fair,* May 1989:

> "The major missing link to Bundy, of course, is his unknown father. Who he was might explain Bundy's monstrous nature, a possible genetic 'bad seed' misfire."

In use again, by Courtland Milloy in *The Washington Post,* January 31, 1989:

> "Are we talking about a 'criminal personality' or 'bad seed' as some might say? No way, the authors say, what we have here is the making of a delinquent—with poor parenting skills as a main ingredient."

**Balkanize, Balkanization.** The process of dividing (or the disintegration of) an entity into small, quarrelsome and ineffectual pieces, leading to turmoil, fragmentation and disorder.

The term comes from what happened on the Balkan Peninsula in the 19th and 20th centuries as the Ottoman Empire broke apart. The European powers muscled in, creating new states and spheres of influence for themselves, while powerful nationalist feelings and antagonisms among the former Turkish subjects grew explosively.

Failure to resolve these problems helped set the stage for World War I, which was touched off in the Balkans by the assassination of Archduke Francis Ferdinand of Austria in **Sarajevo.** Problems continued after the war, with quarrels among the states and ethnic clashes within their borders. These tensions were aggravated by economic difficulties.

The term in use, from a *Washington Post* editorial of April 1, 1988, on proposals that the Postal Service be removed from the budget so as to protect it from congressional spending cuts:

> "The Postal Service is not the only agency with its own source of revenue. They all want to escape the budget— the highway and the air traffic people, the Social Security recipients. Balkanize the government and let someone else pick up the tab. That's what they say, and who's to blame them?"

**Banquo's Ghost.** Someone who appears, seeming to materialize out of thin air, welcome or not.

Banquo and his ghost show up in Shakespeare's *Macbeth.* A nobleman and general who is a good and loyal man, Banquo is murdered at Macbeth's direction because the witches foretold that when Macbeth became king, Banquo's descendants would rule Scotland.

After the murder, the bloody ghost appears at a feast, visible only to the horrified Macbeth, who cries: "Thou canst not say I did it; never shake thy gory locks at me." The ghost disappears and reappears, and Macbeth's agitated reactions startle his guests.

The term in use, by Stephen Birmingham, describing Andy Warhol, *The Washington Post Book World*, October 15, 1989:

> "All at once I noticed that the Master himself had materialized in our midst. He had not stepped off the elevator, and he had not entered through any door. He had simply appeared, like Banquo's ghost, with his prison pallor, his acne-scarred face, his potato nose, wearing one of his silver fright wigs."

In use again, by *The Economist*, May 6, 1989, discussing the New Zealand political scene:

> "The bad slide began in December, when the leftish Mr. Lange sacked the architect of the economic reforms, his free-market finance minister, Mr. Roger Douglas. Like Banquo's ghost, Mr. Douglas refuses to go away."

**Barbie** and **Ken.** Two good-looking airheads.

The Barbie doll is the most commercially successful doll in history. She was introduced to the market in 1959 by the Mattel Corporation and has been a bestseller (500 million) ever since. She has a boy-friend, Ken, and friends, and most important, a gigantic and ever-changing wardrobe. Barbie represented a dramatic departure in the dolly world. She was grown up or, at least, out, with a fashionable and extensive (and expensive, some parents might think) wardrobe, in-cluding shoes to fit her preformed high-heeled feet.

Although millions of little girls love Barbie, she may have trau-matized generations of females who lack the bosom and impossibly long legs (and preformed high-heeled feet).

So while sales climb ever upward and imitators come and go, Barbie's name has become something of an epithet. For a woman to be characterized as a "Barbie" suggests she is empty-headed and plastic—too perfect to be real, with superficial good looks and dumb to boot. A "Ken" would be a male with the same attributes.

The epithet in use, by Maureen Dowd, in *The New Republic*, August 1, 1988, writing about the Home Box Office series "Tan-ner '88":

> "A Nashville fund-raiser during Super Tuesday featuring Waylon Jennings was filmed at a real fund-raiser for Al Gore, and stars the real local television reporters (Ken and Barbies or Twinkies, in the film's **au courant** argot) and real local officials who switch their allegiance from Gore to Tanner for Altman's camera."

Another example, from Andrew Ferguson, *The American Specta-tor*, October 1988:

"The speaker was a fellow named William Paxon, introduced as the candidate for Jack Kemp's seat from Upstate
New York. Young Bill stood at the podium with the splendid posture (and haircut) of a Ken doll. As I walked along
the upper rows, searching for my assigned seat, I listened to
him in mounting disbelief."

**Bardic.** An adjective describing the style or substance of heroic
storytelling—the recounting of epic stories about or great deeds by
kings, warriors and gods. These were celebrated by bards, minstrels or
poet-singers.

Such oral traditions served (and still serve) to preserve and convey to
succeeding generations the common history, myths and religious
beliefs in societies where the written word is little known. The term
comes from ancient Gaelic.

(The Bard, with a capital B, incidentally, refers to Shakespeare.)

The term in use, by Paul Gray in *Time*, September 26, 1988, on A.
Bartlett Giamatti, commissioner of baseball:

"He is convinced that major league baseball plays a bardic,
mythic role in American society: the long, recurring seasons are an ongoing epic, **Homeric** or Vergilian or **Dantesque,** a vital locus of rapt assembly where enduring
values are enacted and passed on."

**Baroque.** (buh-ROHK) A French word meaning a rough or imperfect pearl; something irregularly shaped, odd or whimsical. The word
was applied to a florid style of European art, primarily architecture,
that dated from about 1550 to 1750. Today it is applied to any
creation that's heavily ornate. Saying a politician delivered a baroque
testament to the oil depletion allowance wouldn't necessarily be a
compliment.

Lots of curving, swirling lines, flocking cupids and cherubim, gilt
and gold characterize the Baroque. Its most extreme form is called
rococo, an architectural style that developed in France in the early
1800s.

The term in use, in *The Washington Post*, July 19, 1988, in a description of a feature in *Elle* magazine:

> "In one fashion spread, called 'Beatnik Goes Baroque,' the piling-on of different patterns, beads, batik sashes and fringes is dizzying. The photographs are rich and textural, the styling is imaginative, but it's like listening to 10 voices talking at once."

And a twofer, in Eugen Weber's review of *Citizens*, Simon Schama's book on the French Revolution, *The New York Times Book Review*, March 19, 1989:

> "Baroque eloquence and rococo sparkle make the book long but never long-winded. All in all, it is an intelligent book for intelligent readers that is also a delight to read."

**Bauhaus.** (BOW-hows —say "ow" as in "cow") An influential school of modern design founded in Germany in 1919, an attempt to bring together modern methods of mass production and the design arts. The artists rejected traditional forms and conventions and struck out in new directions, creating much of what we know today as modern design in architecture, furniture and other areas.

Artists and designers associated with the school include Breuer (as in the chair), Gropius (architecture), Mies van der Rohe (architecture and the Barcelona chair), Kandinsky and Klee (abstract art).

The school was closed by the Nazis, as part of their suppression of modern art (which they regarded as degenerate), but members of the group dispersed to other countries, particularly the United States, where they became influential.

The Bauhaus influence (and its spawn, the International Style) became especially strong in the U.S., and indeed is the subject of much controversy. In recent years there has been a reaction against Bauhaus style—the monotonous boxes, the flat roofs and strip windows flush with the facade, the monolithic and overpowering starkness of it all. Le Corbusier called a house a "machine for living", and journalist Tom Wolfe spoke for much of the opposition when he said such structures resembled insecticide refineries (*From Bauhaus to Our House*, 1981).

The term in use, by Alessandra Stanley in *The New Republic*, December 12, 1988, "Presidency by Ralph Lauren":

"Snobbery has always sold well. But no one has ever mass-marketed the mystique or so widely popularized the yearning as Bronx-born Ralph Lauren, né Ralph Lipschitz. . . . The Laurenification of America reaches far beyond clothing. Surveying the **neo**-classical opulence of Philip Johnson's AT&T building in New York and Robert Stern's neo-Georgian mansions, *New York Times* architecture critic Paul Goldberger recently concluded that Ralph Lauren is the 'real design symbol' of our age. He calls the clothes designer a 'one-man Bauhaus.' "

**Beau Geste.** (boh jhest) A French phrase, meaning a grand gesture, a display of magnanimity, a gracious or self-sacrificing act or statement, usually costly to the person making it.

*Beau Geste* was the title of a 1924 novel by P.C. Wren in which three English brothers (named Geste, actually) heroically join the French Foreign Legion to save the family honor. Two of them, including the hero, Michael (nicknamed "Beau," of course), die gallantly in the desert. Hollywood loved the story, and made and remade it; both Ronald Colman and Gary Cooper played the title role.

The term in use, in *The New York Times*, June 28, 1988, describing French efforts to raise and preserve the wreck of the Confederate privateer *Alabama*, sunk off the Normandy coast on June 19, 1864 by the federal warship *Kearsarge*:

"Although the weaker Southern ship might have been able to sneak out of Cherbourg at night, its commander agreed to fight. Captain [Raphael] Semmes knew John Winslow, the commander of the Kearsarge, named after a New Hampshire mountain, because they both went to Annapolis.

" 'For Captain Semmes, it was a matter of honor to fight,' said Paul Ingouf, a Cherbourg native who has written a book on the Alabama. 'It was a beau geste.' "

**Beggar-thy-neighbor.** A policy or activity that seeks to gain at the expense of others—and results in hurting everyone, including the originator. "Beggar" is used here as a verb, meaning to reduce to beggary or to impoverish. In international relations, the term could be applied to protectionist trade policies.

The term in use, by Paul M. Kennedy in *The Rise and Fall of the Great Powers:*

> "If the democracies of the West weathered these storms better, their statesmen were forced to concentrate upon domestic economic management, increasingly tinged with a beggar-thy-neighbor attitude."

**Bell, Book and Candle.** A reference to the elements of the ritual of excommunication.

In excommunication from the Roman Catholic Church, a bell is rung, the book (the Bible) is closed and a candle is extinguished to symbolize the darkness to which the excommunicant is consigned. He is denied the sacraments of the church and the company of its adherents.

*Bell, Book and Candle* is also the title of a 1950 play by John Van Druten about a beautiful modern-day witch who falls in love and loses her supernatural powers.

The term in use, by Fleur deVilliers, asserting the ineffectiveness of economic sanctions against South Africa, in *The American Spectator*, March 1988:

> "Those who wielded bell, book and candle blithely ignored the fact that sanctions without the threat of military intervention have had a dismal record in the conduct of international affairs."

**Belle Époque.** (BEL ay-POCK) Literally, in French, it means beautiful era, but specifically it refers to the years from about 1890 to 1914—a time nostalgically considered to be one of great glamour and elegance. In general use today, the name evokes the gorgeous sunset of European peace before the horrors of World War I.

However, not for everyone was it so belle. As historian Barbara Tuchman notes in the foreword to *The Proud Tower*: "The period was not a Golden Age or Belle Époque except to a thin crust of privileged class. It was not a time exclusively of confidence, innocence, comfort, stability, security and peace. All these qualities were certainly present . . . Our misconception lies in assuming that doubt and fear, ferment, protest, violence and hate were not equally present. . . . "

The term in use, by Paul Chutkow, *The New York Times*, January 3, 1988, in "Belle Epoque Visions in Paris," describing the city's nightlife:

> "But the good news for visitors to Paris is that the dance [the cancan] does survive. The Lido, the Moulin Rouge, the Folies Bergère and a handful of smaller halls bravely play on, trying to keep alive a gay Paris still echoing with legendary names . . . a Paris still dancing to the timeless visions of Degas, Renoir and Toulouse-Lautrec.
>
> "This may not be the Belle Epoque, but Paris is still good for a night on the town."

**Belles-lettres.** (Bel LET-ruh) Serious literature, such as essays, criticism, aesthetics, quality fiction, drama and poetry. Literally, in French, beautiful writing.

The term in use, by Nick Ravo in *The New York Times*, November 25, 1988, reporting on the impact of a poem about the decline of a small-town family grocery on the real-life store owner:

> "Mr. Albamonti, who admits he wouldn't know belles-lettres from Belgian endive, found the poem so insulting, so embarrassing, that he has packed up the produce and sold Roland's, and now plans to leave the town that has been his home for all of his 40 years."

**Belling the Cat.** Sticking one's neck out in a very special way. The fable illustrates: A mouse suggested to the other mice that they should hang a bell on the cat's neck to warn all mice of approaching danger. "Excellent," quoth a clever young mouse, "but who is to undertake the job?" In other words, who's going to take the risk to save his neighbors?

The expression is an old one. The fable appears in "The Vision of Piers Plowman," written in the 14th century. A hundred years or so later, Archibald Douglas, 5th Earl of Angus, won the nickname "Bell the Cat" when nobles met to determine how to put down upstart favorites of the weakling King James III of Scotland. Lord Gray asked, "Who will bell the cat?" (In other words, who would act to eliminate these undesirables?) Responded Douglas, "That will I," and he killed them in the very presence of the king.

The term in use, by *The Economist*, July 16, 1988, discussing political developments in Kampuchea [Cambodia] and the problem of the Khmer Rouge guerrillas:

"Even China, their arms supplier, seems prepared to qualify its patronage. . . . It has supported the Khmers Rouges
to get at Vietnam. Now that Vietnam seems to be withdrawing at least some of its soldiers from Kampuchea, the
Khmers Rouges are perhaps becoming less helpful to Chinese interests.

"Intentions are one thing. Controlling the Khmers
Rouges is another. Who, in the words of the fable, is to bell
the cat?"

**Bellwether.** A forecaster, guide, leader or leading indicator.

In shepherding, from whence the term comes, the bellwether is the castrated sheep that leads the flock and wears a bell around its neck. In politics, it's those precincts which historically have voted for the ultimate winner: find out how they're voting and you'll know, pre-sumably, whether your candidate is going to win. Michael Barone and Grant Ujifusa's *The Almanac of American Politics* 1984 notes there are three bellwether counties in the United States with the distinction of having never voted for the loser of a presidential elec-tion: Coos County, New Hampshire, Palo Alto County, Iowa, and Crook County, Oregon.

In other uses, bellwethers are signs which give early evidence of trends, or are leading indicators, as in this usage in *The Wall Street*

*Journal*, December 16, 1987, describing the events of the October 1987 stock market crash:

> "But as the bellwether stocks such as IBM were delayed in trading, Mr. Friedman had second thoughts about owning any futures. 'All of a sudden, you realized some things were really different here,' he says. 'There was pandemonium.' "

**Below the Salt.** Among the common folks, the **hoi polloi.**

In medieval homes of the upper crust, the salt cellar (container) was placed in the middle of the long dinner table in the baronial hall. The family and its noble guests would sit on one side (above the salt), and dependents and those of less status would sit below the salt, with the lower orders.

The term in use, by William H. Gass in his review of *Arabesques* by Anton Shammas, *The New York Times Book Review*, April 17, 1988:

> "There are those, of course, for whom the question is never a question, who arrive in the world at a comfortable station and whose identity papers are made unnecessary by their wealth, their breeding, the games they play, their accents and their clothes; there are those, at the other extreme, who are told they are untouchable, that they are slaves, Jews, below the salt and **beyond the pale.**"

Another example, from E.L. Doctorow on Jack London, in *The New York Times Book Review*, December 11, 1988:

> "He was a workaday literary genius/hack who knew instinctively that Literature was a generous host, always having room for one more at her table. He sits now below the salt, while the cooler, more sophisticated voices of modernist irony take up the conversation."

**Beltway, the; Beltway Bandits.** Washington, D.C., is encircled by an interstate highway known as the Beltway. In addition to its notoriety for often creating, rather than eliminating, traffic gridlock, the Beltway serves as a geographical, rhetorical and psychological rampart. "Inside the Beltway" is used pejoratively to suggest an inward-turning, elitist, self-obsessed cabal of insiders who are ignorant of what's going on in the rest of the country. "Outside the Beltway" lies "the real world"—where theoretically "the people" live who agree with the individual brandishing the term. Of course, the users of the term are usually those who have lived and worked within the Beltway for years.

The Beltway is also the locus of the celebrated and occasionally investigated private consultants known as "beltway bandits." Their offices are located in the glossy and glassy new buildings which sprang up in the suburbs around the Beltway in the 1970s and 1980s. These consultants are often former government experts who have stepped through "the revolving door" (another term with a distinct Washington meaning) between government and private business operations which feed off government activities.

The term in use, by Sarah Booth Conroy, in *The Washington Post*, December 11, 1988:

> "The question came the other day at a Friends of Art and Preservation in the Embassies dinner for George Schultz. The guest who asked it came from Kansas City, the heartland of America, decidedly beyond the Beltway (which ill-informed locals interpret to mean **beyond the Pale.**)"

And again, by Walt Harrington, in *The Washington Post Magazine*, November 13, 1988:

> "But Washington's professional work force more and more includes consultants, Beltway Bandits, office managers, stockbrokers, real estate lawyers and others who prosper at the fringes of the government-driven prosperity."

**Bertie Wooster.** A fictional character created by British writer and humorist P.G. Wodehouse (1881-1975). Bertie is invoked today to suggest genial incompetence and silliness in the upper classes.

Wodehouse wrote numerous whimsical novels and stories featuring Bertie and his ilk; among the best known are *Leave It To Psmith* (1923), *Jeeves* (1925), and *The Code of the Woosters* (1938).

Bertie is the archetypical British upper-class twit: good-natured, idle and not too bright. He leads a life of ease, is a member of the Drones Club, and is saved from numerous scrapes by the imperturbable competence of his man Jeeves, who is equal to any crisis. The plots of Wodehouse's novels featuring the Honourable Bertie and similar characters are farcical tangles involving madcap young women, mistaken identities, dragon aunts, grumpy fathers and eccentric animals.

Bertie invoked, by David Nyhan in *The Boston Globe*, February 28, 1989, reporting on the political struggle to confirm President Bush's nomination of John Tower as secretary of defense:

> "Bush seems intent on trying to salvage Tower, without somehow alienating those conservative Democrats such as Sen. Sam Nunn of Georgia. The ever-affable Bush, our Bertie Wooster in the White House, trusts that John Sununu and Bob Dole will pull this one out."

**The Best and the Brightest.** A term sometimes used in an ironic or sarcastic tone, referring to leaders who are carried away by **hubris** into gross policy errors. The phrase was given currency in our own time as the title of David Halberstam's best-selling book on America's slide into the Vietnam war.

The title refers to the many men of recognized brilliance brought into government by President John Kennedy, who boasted of the number of Rhodes scholars in his administration. Halberstam explored how government decision-making could go awry through arrogant self-confidence, misinformation and unwillingness to examine fundamental policy assumptions.

The origin of the phrase is uncertain. Halberstam says that as far as he can remember he made it up. Mary McCarthy, in a savage review of the book in *The New York Review of Books*, January 25, 1973, suggested that the author even got the title wrong. "Bishop Heber had a better ear; shouldn't it be 'The Brightest and the Best?' " she asked, referring to an Episcopalian hymn written by Reginald Heber (1783-1826), bishop of the Anglican church.

Halberstam, however, can claim some impressive company for his version. Charles Dickens in *Little Dorrit* (1855-1857), referred to the youngest of a family of unspeakably arrogant and unhelpful bureaucrats in the "Circumlocution Office" as "the best and the brightest of the Barnacles." And Rudyard Kipling, in his poem *The Files* (1903), parodies obituaries of the famous-but-quickly-forgotten:

> Very great our loss and grievous,
> So the best and brightest leave us,
> And it ends the Age of Giants, say the files.

The term in use, by Henry Allen in *The Washington Post*, November 22, 1988:

> "And Washington is still full of Kennedy people waiting for the restoration or the resurrection with the ennobling fury of exiles who never feel the need to explain anything to anybody—aging Hamlets in pin-striped suits, best and bright at law firms and dinner parties and endless booksignings."

**Bête Noire.** (bet NWAHR) Something that provokes fear, trepidation or loathing.

In French, it literally means black beast.

Here's Chalmers Roberts using the term in a review of Eugene McCarthy's book, *Up 'Til Now*, in *The Washington Post Book World*, April 12, 1987:

> "Scattered through this rather slim memoir are such items as: Nixon offered McCarthy the UN ambassadorship and McCarthy wanted it. . . . Common Cause is too goody-goody; and the press, most especially *The Washington Post*, is a recurrent *bête noire*."

Another example, from *The Washington Post Book World*, January 15, 1989, in Dennis Drabelle's review of *AIDS and Its Metaphors*, by Susan Sontag:

> "By now, more than a decade later, cancer is no longer the national *bête noire* it once was."

**Beyond the Pale.** In today's usage, beyond the limits of propriety, courtesy, protection, safety; behavior that is beyond the boundaries of civilization. The term comes from the Latin word "palum" which means stake, thus a fence, a barrier or a territory with defined borders.

The sense in which anything beyond the borders was out of civilization's reach came from the English Pale, a name given to an area of Ireland in which there was English settlement and effective control of the territory. The settlement had been established by Norman aristocrats from England in the mid-12th century.

The most infamous pale was the Pale of Settlement, the only area in Russia where Jews were permitted to live, a region created from land gained in 1792 from a partition of Poland. During the 19th century, as successive czars alternated between policies of liberalism and repression, Jews were allowed outside the Pale and into industry and professions, and then reconsigned to the Pale and subjected to repression, including murderous pogroms.

The term in use, in *Spy*, February 1989:

> "Last November there was one senator whose stupidity went beyond the pale, and the voters of Nevada sent Chic Hecht packing. His defeat ended one of the most unimpressive Senate careers ever. 'He's really not playing with a full deck,' says one congressional staffer. 'You don't expect to meet guys like that in a gas station.' "

Another example, from a *New York Times* editorial, November 15, 1989:

> "But Israel's aid for South Africa's missile is clearly beyond the pale. Such aid flouts a U.S.-backed U.N. embargo on arms to South Africa. In any case, Pretoria could have no use for these weapons except to terrorize its neighbors."

**Big Bang.** A theory explaining the creation of the universe that has become generally accepted among astronomers: the universe was created by a single event, similar to an explosion. This is based on the observation that distant galaxies are moving away from the Earth—in other words, the universe is expanding. Scientists have worked their way backward from this observation and concluded there was a point about 15 billion years ago at which all the matter in the universe—

41

stars, galaxies—was packed into a small, dense space. This matter was then dispersed by the "event"—the Big Bang.

The term has since come into general use to describe a single, cataclysmic event that creates dramatic change.

The term in use, by Martin Peretz in *The New Republic*, September 4, 1989:

> "I don't mean to put [novelist E.L.] Doctorow exactly in the camp of those who find the United States less morally glamorous than societies governed by a big-bang revolutionary idea."

Another example, from *The Washington Post*, September 3, 1989:

> "Helmut Norpoth, of the State University of New York-Stony Brook, and Michael R. Kagay, director of news surveys for *The New York Times*, argued that the striking gains of the GOP among young voters 'point toward a party realignment in slow motion, not the big bang it may have been at earlier historic moments.' "

Another, from a Polish economist quoted in *The New York Times*, October 1, 1989:

> "Our big debate was whether to grow our economy step by step or to make it a Big Bang."

In the financial world, the term describes the changes in regulations which took effect overnight on the London Stock Exchange on October 27, 1986. Regulators chose to put their changes into effect all at once, rather than incrementally, and the date became known in anticipation as the Big Bang. An example, from *The Economist*, May 20, 1989:

> "For all its criticisms of British industrialists, the City [the British version of Wall Street] has not exactly come through Big Bang with flying managerial colours. Just when the end of old cartels and of fixed commissions was bound to increase competition and reduce profit margins, the financial industry acted as though its market and profits were about to expand exponentially, raising salaries, handing out

Porsches and increasing its cost base immensely. Stockbrokers used to small partnerships had little idea of how to
manage big integrated firms. Within a year, reality hit the
City with an even bigger bang. Firms' combined losses in
1988 totalled around £ 500m."

**Billingsgate.** Foul, abusive, vulgar language. A vocabulary of the
sort one would hear at Billingsgate, an ancient gate in the walls of the
City of London and site of the London fish market.

Therein a tale, irrelevant, but irresistible. According to Henry
Blyth's *The Rakes*, the sixth Earl of Barrymore was a noted 18th
century rake whose greatest accomplishment was that he produced an
entire family of incorrigibles even worse than he was. Their distinction lay in their colorful nicknames. Who got which when is unclear,
but all ended with the suffix "-gate." Richard, oldest and heir to the
title, was called "Hellgate" in recognition of his profligacy; he died at
age 24, having squandered a fortune of 300,000 pounds. Henry, the
second son, born with a club foot, was known as "Cripplegate."
Augustus, the third son, was "Newgate," after the city's famous
prison, which accommodated debtors as well as other prisoners. And
Caroline, the foul-mouthed daughter, was, inevitably, "Billingsgate."
(All the names, with the exception of Hellgate, were derived from the
names of gates in the walls of the city of London.)

Which shows, maybe, that gates got hung on scandalous behavior
a long time ago. Today "-gate" serves to describe American political
scandals—Koreagate and Irangate are two—but the derivation, of
course, is from Watergate, a Washington complex on the Potomac
River containing apartments, a hotel, and an office building, where
the celebrated burglary of the Democratic National Committee took
place in 1972.

The term in use, by Tom Wicker in *The New York Times*, November 8, 1988, commenting on the negative presidential campaign
waged by George Bush:

"That went beyond expectable campaign billingsgate into
the personal character of Michael Dukakis; it not only
vilified him, but in both cases it did so unfairly—with the
clear suggestion that Mr. Dukakis deliberately *chose* to bar

43

the Pledge of Allegiance from Massachusetts schools and
visit a murderer on a defenseless family."

**Bimbo.** A slang term for a woman of easy virtue and, often, of
scanty smarts.

Its origins are unclear. The *Oxford English Dictionary* says it
comes from a form of the Italian word for baby, bambino. But the
term, and variations of it, were often applied to men, usually those of
unsavory character. English comic novelist P.G. Wodehouse referred
to men who had discarded their wives and made passes at innocent
young women as bimbos. Bimbos also appeared as bank robbers and
other menacing characters in the tough-guy detective novels of
writers such as Raymond Chandler. *The Oxford English Dictionary's*
earliest citation of the term's application to women was in 1937, in
*Detective Fiction Weekly:* "We found Durken and Frenchy LeSeur,
seated at a table . . . with a pair of bimboes (sic) beside them."
Finally, there's Robert L. Chapman's *New Dictionary of American Slang*, which says bimbo is a word for the organ grinder's
monkey.

The term in use nowadays, by Joanne Lipman in *The Wall Street
Journal*, November 5, 1987, proclaiming 1987 (when disclosures
about their sex lives eliminated Gary Hart as a presidential candidate
and brought down evangelist Jim Bakker) as "the year of the bimbo."
She went in search of the species and wrote:

> "True to the advance billing, the average age of the men at
> the party seems to be close to 40; the women, by and large,
> appear a decade or two younger (among the youngest, we
> learn, are bimbettes, or bimbos in training.)"

And the August 1989 *Esquire* recalled Christine Keeler, a central
figure in the Profumo affair, a sex scandal of the 1960s which brought
down a British government, as "a pioneer bimbo."

Finally, from Chuck Conconi's "Personalities" column, *The Washington Post*, November 30, 1989:

> "It never stops for Vice President Dan Quayle. MTV's
> 'Rate the '80s' viewer poll to be announced next Wednesday
> presents the vice president with the 'Nobody's Home: The

Bimbo of the '80s Award.' For this honor, Quayle beat out such tough competition as Jessica Hahn, Rob Lowe, Brigitte Nielsen and Vanna White."

**Bitch Goddess** or **Bitch-Goddess.** A destructive obsession, an unworthy goal to which good is sacrificed.

In modern parlance, according to *The Oxford English Dictionary*, a bitch is a malicious, treacherous woman. The first use of the combination "bitch-goddess," according to the *Dictionary*, is from William James (1842-1910), American philosopher, physiologist, psychologist, teacher and brother of Henry. "A symptom of the moral flabbiness born of the exclusive worship of the bitch-goddess success."

D.H. Lawrence used the term in *Lady Chatterley's Lover* (1928):

"He realized now that the bitch-goddess of success had two main appetites: one for flattery, adulation, stroking and tickling such as writers and artists gave her; but the other a grimmer appetite for meat and bones."

In contemporary use, she has diversified, as in this example from Jerome Holtzman, *The New York Times*, July 31, 1988:

"Wrigley Field has succumbed to the Bitch Goddess of Progress."

Another example, from Playthell Benjamin, *The Village Voice*, November 8, 1988, describing a young drug dealer:

"Like most young men of his class and experience, he was tempted by, and in his case, temporarily succumbed to, the highly seductive life of the successful drug dealer. It is a fast-paced life of vulgar opulence populated by a new leisure class of wealthy adolescents who have struck a **Faustian bargain** with the bitch goddess of success."

**Black Hole.** A term from astronomy, applied to a region of space containing a collapsed star whose gravitational field has become so intense that radiated light can no longer escape to outer space, and

45

therefore can no longer be directly seen. The intense gravitational pull drags at surrounding bodies.

Outside its celestial context, the term has come to refer to a vast void into which things disappear, never to emerge. The term may have been influenced by "black hole," derived from the Black Hole of Calcutta, and referring to a cramped, dungeon-like room. This reference comes from an episode in 1756, in which the Nawab of Bengal confined 146 British prisoners in a cell eighteen feet by fourteen feet ten inches. All but 22 of the prisoners suffocated.

The term in use in a *Wall Street Journal* headline of September 1, 1988:

> "Why a Space Station That Costs $25 Billion May Never Leave Earth/NASA Wants It For Research, But Many Scientists Call It A Black Hole For Funds."

Another example, from Joe Queenan, writing in *The American Spectator*, March 1989, on Stephen W. Hawking's book *A Brief History of Time: From the Big Bang to Black Holes*:

> "Last year, Hawking unveiled what his publisher, Bantam, calls 'a classic introduction to today's most important scientific ideas about the cosmos.' Well, not quite. What he's actually written is a dreadful, boring, sloppy, incomprehensible book. His book isn't about black holes: It *is* a black hole."

**Bligh.** A British naval officer whose last name has become a byword for tyrannical and cruel discipline.

William Bligh (1754-1817) is known to the ages as the dictatorial captain of H.M.S. *Bounty*, scene of the most famous naval mutiny in history.

In 1787, Bligh and the *Bounty* were on an expedition to the Pacific to obtain specimens of the breadfruit tree. Although the causes of the mutiny remain mysterious, Bligh's extreme, unbending discipline is popularly supposed to have precipitated it. The mutineers set the captain adrift in a small boat with 18 crewmen who had remained loyal.

In a tremendous feat of seamanship, Bligh navigated the small open boat to safety across nearly 4,000 miles of open sea. He was later cleared of responsibility for the loss of the ship by a court-martial and continued his career.

Bligh was involved in two more mutinies. On May 19, 1797, a mutiny broke out throughout the British fleet, and Bligh, like other officers, was put ashore by rebellious crews. This one could hardly be blamed on him, however. The third mutiny against his authority took place on terra firma (Australia, actually) where Bligh was serving as governor of New South Wales. After another round of courts-martial, Bligh was promoted to rear admiral. But he never went to sea again.

The story of the *Bounty* gained fame through the 1932 novel *Mutiny on the Bounty* by Charles Nordhoff and James Norman Hall, and various movie versions, the most memorable of which (1935) includes a scenery-chewing portrayal of Bligh by Charles Laughton.

The captain invoked, by Steve Dale in the *Chicago Tribune*, February 17, 1989, on learning to sail:

> "Your best friend may seem to speak perfect English until he or she begins shouting instructions during a sailboat ride on Lake Michigan. You're eager to help until your friend turns into Captain Bligh, yelling at you in another language. 'Sheet the jib!' the captain screams. 'Come about!' "

Another example, by Eliot Asinof in *The New York Times Magazine*, March 26, 1989, writing on New York Yankees manager Dallas Green:

> "Green ran the Phillies the way Captain Bligh ran the *Bounty*. No more card playing in the clubhouse; no more ballplayers' children on the field before the game; everyone runs in practice, including the future Hall of Fame pitcher Steve Carlton, who had other ideas about conditioning."

**Blimp, Colonel.** A cartoon character created by British cartoonist David Low after World War I. His name came from the nickname for observation balloons used during the war. The Colonel was a caricature of the archetypical elderly British Tory, a paunchy, harrumphing John Bull opposed to all change, and rather dim mentally.

A play on the term, in *The Economist*, January 28, 1989, as the title of an item on Japanese production of miniaturized airships: "Corporal Blimp."

Another example, from Robert Brustein in *The New Republic*, March 6, 1989, reviewing a London production of Strindberg's play *The Father*:

> "John Osborne's adaptation occasionally suffered from Colonel Blimp Anglicisms ('You'll jolly well provide for the child, take it from me') but it's the strongest, most lyrical version of the play I know."

**Bloody Shirt.** See Waving the Bloody Shirt.

**Bloomingdale's.** A large New York department store whose name has become a metaphor for the consumer culture of America in the 1970s and 1980s.

Bloomingdale's went through a dramatic change in the 1950s and 60s, transforming itself from a sedate and dignified emporium selling necessities into a glitzy upscale store noted for its highly energized (some might say frenzied) atmosphere. (Affectionately known to its customers as "Bloomie's," the store applied this term of endearment to the seats of ladies' panties. The store dubbed some of its customers "Saturday's generation," which presumably means the folks who shop and perchance meet friends at Bloomingdale's on Saturday.) To some, Bloomie's stands for empty, status-seeking acquisitiveness.

Bloomingdale's also has made its appearance in movies: In the 1984 film *Moscow on the Hudson*, Robin Williams plays a Russian whose head is so turned that he defects in the store. This is perhaps the ultimate use of the store as a symbol of capitalist culture, the cathedral of consumerism in which the refugee from Soviet austerity can seek sanctuary.

The term in use, by Mark Stevens in *The New Republic*, May 18, 1987:

> "[Andy] Warhol appeared to live at parties, and the images with which . . . he worked have a drifting, nomadic presence. Such artists approach tradition as something to be widely quoted, not possessed or earned or challenged. The

world is a Bloomingdale's of images, among which one poses and shops."

**Bloomsbury.** A London neighborhood, near the British Museum and the University of London, traditionally an area where influential writers and intellectuals reside.

References today to "Bloomsbury intellectuals" are often barbed; the term is used to suggest an offbeat Bohemian or radical tinge. The neighborhood has a reputation akin to New York's Greenwich Village or Paris' Left Bank.

Bloomsbury is associated with some famous people who banded together to further their ideas and goals. One group was the Fabian Society, founded in 1884 and dedicated to improving social welfare through state intervention. George Bernard Shaw and Beatrice and Sidney Webb were members.

Another group that took its name from the neighborhood and in 1904 started meeting in each other's homes there included economist John Maynard Keynes and writers E. M. Forster, Virginia Woolf, Lytton Strachey and Vita Sackville-West.

The term in use, by Rachel M. Brownstein in her review of *Writing for Their Lives: The Modernist Women 1910-1940* in *The New York Times Book Review*, March 12, 1989:

> "As [authors] Gillian Hanscombe and Virginia L. Smyers see it, not only the wordlings of the Left Bank and Greenwich Village, but Amy Lowell cultivating her garden outside Boston and Marianne Moore in Brooklyn were members of what the authors call 'another Bloomsbury,' who lived and wrote 'anti-conventionally.'"

**Boilerplate.** Material that has been written in advance and used over and over again, such as the standard language that appears in contracts, wills or other legal forms.

In the world of heavy lifting, boilerplate is a plating of iron or steel for making the shells of boilers or covering the hulls of ships.

The journalistic use goes back to pre-computer days, when "boilerplate" referred to syndicated material (such as features, columns and editorials) that was widely distributed to newspapers, especially weeklies. It came in plate form for the presses, so that the type didn't have to be set. It offered a way to fill the paper with innocuous stuff.

The term in use, by Sidney Blumenthal in *The Washington Monthly*, October 1987, in a review of the writings of columnist George Will:

> "Much of this slight book is filled with commonplaces that can be gleaned from the daily newspaper. . . . Most annoying of all, Will puts forth this boilerplate as if it were derived from a close reading of Aristotle."

Another example, from George Will, *The Washington Post*, December 14, 1989:

> "Beneath all the measured diplomatic boilerplate about the inconvenience of a united Germany's economic power, and what reunification might do to the 'stability'—that golden calf, again—of the Tinker Toy project of European federalism, there is a plain prejudice against Germans."

**Bon Mot.** (bon moh) A witty comment or memorable remark. In French, it means good word.

The term in use, by James M. Markham in *The New York Times*, December 19, 1988 on the chaos caused by Christmas season strikes in Paris:

> "The snaking lines of weary citizens peering anxiously for a subway or a bus recall food queues in Warsaw or Bucharest, and the agglutinated, unmoving traffic jams make one think of the vehicular horrors of Lagos and Mexico City. Jean Cocteau's bon mot that the French are Italians in a bad mood seems timely."

**Borscht Belt.** (borsht) An area in the Catskill Mountains near New York City known for its Jewish resort hotels. Borscht is a beet soup (a Russian dish) frequently found on the menus of such establishments, reflecting the tastes and origin of many of the patrons. (Spellings vary: borsht, borsch.)

The Borscht Belt served as the training ground for many comedians, including the likes of Milton Berle and Henny Youngman, so the name came to be associated with standup comics delivering fast one-liners.

Other "belts" turn up here and there as a shorthand way of summing up cultural, ethnic, ideological or economic attributes of a region: H. L. Mencken is credited with coining the most commonly used of them, the "Bible Belt," in the 1920s to refer to areas where fundamentalist Protestantism flourishes. Later came the "Sun Belt" and the "Rust Belt."

The term in use, by Howard Kurtz in *The Washington Post*, December 15, 1988, discussing the reelection prospects of New York's mayor:

> "Mayor Edward I. Koch was on his turf, fielding questions from middle-class homeowners at a town meeting in Queens, when a woman dared to ask why the dozen commissioners and deputies at his side were all male.
>
> " 'Listen, I wanna tell you, you are so unfair, it's unbelievable!' Koch bellowed into the microphone. 'I have appointed more women to high positions than any mayor in history,' he said, rattling off a list of names.
>
> "With Borsch Belt timing, Koch paused a beat, turned to the woman and said: 'Apologize!' The junior high school auditorium filled with applause."

**Boswell.** James Boswell (1740-1795) was a Scot who gained fame as a diarist and as the biographer of Dr. Samuel Johnson, the English lexicographer, critic, poet and conversationalist, whose every witticism was faithfully recorded later by his friend.

Today, to be someone's "Boswell" is to serve in that same role as admiring friend and biographer.

The term in use, by Joanne Lipman in *The Wall Street Journal*, November 5, 1987:

> "Just who, or what, is this fabled creature, the **bimbo**? Given the word's currency—and many contexts—this year, it's hard to tell. So in an effort to discover more about

this wonder of the late '80s, we decided to turn to some experts on the subject—and who is more expert, we reasoned, than the bimbo's Boswell, the gossip columnist?"

**Bowdlerize.** To engage in prudish, arbitrary, foolish censorship that expunges from a book or play anything that could conceivably be considered obscene or off-color.

The term comes from the name of Dr. Thomas Bowdler (1754-1829), a retired doctor and self-appointed literary critic who applied his literary scalpel to the works of Shakespeare and Edward Gibbon's *The History of the Decline and Fall of the Roman Empire*, excising expressions "which cannot with propriety be read aloud in a family" and "whatever is unfit to be read by a gentleman in a company of ladies." He maintained that Shakespeare would have approved.

*The Family Shakespeare,* published in 1818, became a best-seller in which "God" as an expletive was replaced by "heavens"; famous speeches were severely cut; such major characters as Macbeth, Hamlet and Falstaff were seriously altered and some bawdy characters disappeared completely. Sometimes Bowdler had to admit defeat, as he did with *Othello:* The play was "unfortunately little suited to family reading."

Ten years after his death, his name made its appearance as a verb.

The term in use, and an example of bowdlerizing in action, by Robert Stone in his review of *A Bright Shining Lie: John Paul Vann and America in Vietnam,* by Neil Sheehan, in *The Washington Post Book World,* September 18, 1988:

"Speaking to the press and on the record, Vann called the ARVN [South Vietnamese army]'s conduct 'A miserable ———— performance just like it always is.' Headline writers in the United States grabbed the phrase and it appeared in bowdlerized form on front pages all over America."

**Brahmin.** An Americanism referring to a member of the cultural, social and political elite; the "Establishment."

It comes from Hinduism, where a Brahman is a member of the highest, or priestly, caste.

In 19th-century America, the term changed spelling and was applied to the close-knit intellectual, social and political aristocracy of Boston by Oliver Wendell Holmes, Sr., prolific author and father of famed U.S. Supreme Court Justice Oliver Wendell Holmes. And in the bare-knuckle politics of Boston, the term often was used as an epithet by ethnic politicians taking shots at the blue-blooded elite.

Today the linkage to Boston is diluted; what we are talking about is the Eastern Establishment. Members are linked by backgrounds of wealth, social standing, education at elite schools, and positions of influence in finance, law, foundations, think tanks, and the executive branch of the federal government, especially in intelligence and foreign policy.

The term in use, from *The New Republic*, November 2, 1987:

> "In the October *Atlantic*, investment-banking Brahmin
> Peter G. Peterson writes the standard **Cassandra** scenario."

And by David Margolick, *the New York Times*, December 1, 1989, on a dispute among lawyers in Boston's elite law firms:

> " 'It is not Ms. Ryan's intention to turn her defense into an
> attack on other lawyers,' said her own Brahmin lawyer,
> Paul B. Galvani of Ropes & Gray, in court papers."

**Brave New World.** Used ironically, as Aldous Huxley (1894-1963) did in his satirical 1932 novel by that title, the term stands for a world that is sterile, regimented, unbearable, without soul. The phrase is pejoratively applied to unnerving modern social and scientific developments.

The novel is set in the future, in the year 632 AF (for "After Ford," that is, Henry Ford, the inventor of the assembly line and thus of the modern mass production, mass consumption society).

Huxley stood values on their head to make his point. In the novel, the traditional family is abolished, monogamy and parenthood viewed with horror. Human beings are hatched in laboratories, predestined and programmed for various classes of society and work. People are anesthetized by promiscuous sex and drugs.

53

A "savage" who has educated himself reading Shakespeare is found on an Indian reservation. He is brought to "civilization" as an experiment. Thrilled at first, he quotes Miranda in Shakespeare's *The Tempest*. Like him, Miranda has been raised in isolation, and upon meeting the stranger her father has brought, she cries, "O brave new world/That has such people in't."

The term in use, by Robert Darnton, *The New York Review of Books*, January 19, 1989, on the bicentennial of the French Revolution:

> "Two hundred years of experimentation with brave new worlds have made us skeptical about social engineering."

Another example, from a *Wall Street Journal* editorial, August 28, 1989, berating activist Jeremy Rifkin for his opposition to genetic engineering:

> "Today, Mr. Rifkin argues that a cure for cystic fibrosis will lead inexorably to a totalitarian Brave New World."

And also, by Michael Specter, *The Washington Post*, December 14, 1989, writing on medical ethics and experimental therapies:

> "But many people who closely follow the brave new world of medical progress say that having obtained consent, doctors often feel they can do whatever they want, including risking the lives of a few with the hope of helping many."

**Bread and Circuses.** Public spectacles or entertainments that distract the public from important issues, or government policies that may alleviate discontent in the short run but provide no fundamental solutions.

The term comes from the work of the Roman satirist Juvenal (c. A.D. 60-140), who wrote:

> *Duas tantum res anxius optat,*
> *Panem et circenses.*
> The people long eagerly for two things—
> Bread and circuses.

Juvenal knew a thing or two about government. Another memorable saying of his comes up in contemporary discussions of government versus individual rights: *Quis custodiet ipsos custodes?* (Who will watch the watchers?)

The term in use, by Thomas Boswell in a commentary on Super Bowl XXIII in *The Washington Post*, January 22, 1989:

> "Nothing stops, or even deflects, the NFL—which did not cancel a single game the week President John F. Kennedy was shot—from fulfilling its self-appointed role as national purveyor of bread and circuses."

And from Jeremiah O'Leary, *The Washington Times*, November 8, 1989:

> "There are only two causes of military dictatorship in Latin America: either poverty and chaos become unbearable or the surging ambitions of armed men prevail. When the people become surfeited with chaos, they will welcome almost any power figure as a **'man on horseback'** if he seizes control with the promise of restored order or a modern version of Roman bread and circuses."

## Brobdingnagian. (BROB-ding-NAG-ee-uhn) Anything large, huge, gigantic.

It comes from Jonathan Swift's satire, *Gulliver's Travels*, (1726) in which Brobdingnag was a country of giants, 12 times larger than ordinary men.

The term in use by television critic Tom Shales in reviewing the 1988 Republican convention in *The Washington Post*, August 17, 1988:

> "Gipperless and glitterless, the Republicans slogged through the second night of their convention in New Orleans last night. . . . By the time Gerald Ford began a meandering, hackneyed speech, after 11 p.m., the boredom level was Brobdingnagian. Stupefaction set in. Ennui, anomie, delirium and depression. One began to wonder if,

55

once the speech ended, the network newscasters might have all just gone home."

And in *The Economist*, November 25, 1989, in a discussion of the U.S. defense budget:

"Brobdingnagian dreams of an ever-rising defence budget have been rudely dashed. Mr. Dick Cheney, the defence secretary, has asked the three services to suggest how they might change their spending plans if, instead of seeing their budgets rise after 1991 . . . they were given 5% cuts in each of the next five years."

**Bully Pulpit.** The use of the prestige of the presidency (or some other high office) to focus the public's attention on an idea or to bring the public around to the official's point of view.

The term comes from the irrepressible Theodore Roosevelt, first to call the presidency a bully pulpit. For TR, "bully" meant just grand, splendid. He understood the modern presidency's power of persuasion and the way it gives the incumbent the opportunity to exhort, instruct or inspire. So did other presidents of this century—Wilson, FDR, Kennedy and Reagan.

The term in use, by Edward B. Fiske in *The New York Times*, September 18, 1988:

"As successor to T.H. Bell, Education Secretary in Mr. Reagan's first term, Mr. Bennett viewed his role differently from any of his predecessors and quickly took advantage of its potential as a bully pulpit."

Another example, from *The Economist*, May 20, 1989, on the Bush administration's efforts against crime:

"He [Bush] sees an opportunity for virtuous use of the bully pulpit without the need for many dollars to back it up."

**Bunker Mentality.** A bunker is a military dugout, a reinforced shelter designed to withstand attack. This use became current during World War II, in addition to the earlier meanings of a golf hazard and the place where coal used as fuel is stored on board ship. The most famous bunker of all, of course, was Hitler's heavily-fortified shelter in Berlin, where he committed suicide on April 30, 1945, as Soviet forces took the city.

In American politics, a "bunker mentality" is an embattled outlook or frame of mind, often with an aggrieved sense of being unfairly under attack.

Picture a ragged remnant of a force, the remaining faithful adherents to the cause, withdrawn to a last-ditch defensive position (similar to "circling the wagons"). The term is most often applied to American presidents who suffer political reverses and assume a surly defensive posture—all critics are enemies, if you're not for us you're against us, etc.

The term in use, in *The Washington Post*, March 10, 1989, on the aftermath of the bitter fight over President Bush's nomination of John Tower to be secretary of defense:

> "[Democratic political consultant Richard] Moe warned the White House against adopting a bunker mentality because of the Tower defeat and urged instead that the president and his staff examine how the Tower fight went sour."

**Burkean.** An adjective meaning of or pertaining to Edmund Burke (1727–1797). Frequently quoted by today's politicians and pundits, he was a British parliamentarian, statesman and friend of the American colonies.

Burke was born in Dublin, the son of an attorney and the product of a mixed Catholic-Protestant marriage. He was elected to Parliament in 1766, where he opposed the Tories' uncompromising policy toward the American colonies, calling instead for cooperation and reconciliation. He wanted to give the colonies a parliament of their own under the British crown—essentially the dominion status later granted to Canada and Australia.

Burke wrote papers on the appalling poverty of his native Ireland and advocated Irish legislative independence, cautioning that: "If laws are their enemies, they will be enemies to law."

Fundamentally a moderate, he felt revulsion for the excesses he saw in the French Revolution and spoke in defense of traditional institutions and political restraint. Prudence, he said, is "in all things a Virtue, in Politicks the first of Virtues."

Contrary to what Barry Goldwater would say almost two centuries later about moderation (in defense of liberty, no virtue), Burke found it a commendable quality, "not only amiable but powerful . . . a disposing, arranging, conciliating, cementing Virtue."

Here's some typical Burkean advice: "Dare to be fearful when all about you are full of presumption and confidence." Finally, he was an ardent advocate of hands-on government:

> "I must see with my own eyes, I must, in a manner, touch with my own hands, not only the fixed but the momentary circumstances, before I could venture to suggest any political project whatsoever. I must know the power and disposition to accept, to execute, to persevere. I must see the means of correcting the plan, where correctives would be wanted. I must see the things; I must see the men."

In "The Lightweight Philosopher," *The Washington Monthly*, October 1987, writer Sidney Blumenthal critiques columnist George Will:

> "In *Statecraft as Soulcraft* he [Will] argued that American conservatism, if it were to endure, required a more Burkean deference to established custom and institutions. In particular, he suggested, the right-wing ought to take a more benign attitude toward the welfare state."

**Byronic.** An adjective meaning like or pertaining to the English Romantic poet, George Gordon, Lord Byron (1788-1824). Byron made a name for wickedness and debauchery and was described as "mad, bad and dangerous to know" (by one of his paramours, Lady Caroline Lamb, no slouch in that category herself).

Byronic heroes are usually handsome, melancholy and brooding, defiant of social convention and haunted by some mysterious sorrow, which of course makes them devilishly attractive. As the poet himself puts it in *Lara*:

There was in him a vital scorn of all:
As if the worst had fall'n which could befall,
He stood a stranger in this breathing world,
An erring spirit from another hurl'd.

Depending on whom you read, Byron was notable for his physical beauty, which was only enhanced by his club foot. (In other views, he was decidedly unhandsome: short, chubby, with a limp.) Much of his life was spent abroad, where he wrote, hobnobbed with the poet Shelley, had numerous affairs and championed the causes of Italian and Greek nationalism. Byron died in Greece, where he had gone to aid the struggle for independence.

His most famous works include *Childe Harold, The Corsair, The Prisoner of Chillon, The Destruction of Sennacherib* and *Don Juan.*

The term in use, by Tom Wolfe, in his 1987 novel, *The Bonfire of the Vanities,* in which hung-over reporter Peter Fallow contemplates his reflection:

> "Head on, he looked a young and handsome thirty-six rather than fortyish and gone to seed. Head on, his widow's peak and the longish wavy blond hair that flowed back from it still looked . . . well, Byronic . . . rather than a bit lonely at the dome of his skull. Yes, at this head-on angle . . . it was going to be all right!"

And from columnist George Will, *The Washington Post,* September 28, 1989, on rocker Mick Jagger:

> "Jagger, a Byronic figure for generations unschooled in poetry, excited young people 25 years ago as someone mad, bad and dangerous to know."

**Byzantine.** (BIH-zin-teen) Pertaining to or reminiscent of the politics and style of the Byzantine Empire; more broadly, an organization or situation or personality that is devious, intricate, and virtually unintelligible to outsiders.

The term, as it is used in describing human activity, derives its meaning from the bureaucracy and internal politics of the Byzantine Empire, rife with coups, plots, murders and intrigue. The Byzantine

Empire was the eastern segment of the Roman Empire, with its capital at Constantinople (now Istanbul), founded in A.D. 330 by the Roman Emperor Constantine on the site of the ancient city of Byzantium. Constantine hoped to strengthen the entire Roman Empire by creating an eastern capital. In A.D 395, the Empire was divided into East and West and never reunited.

The Byzantine Empire sustained itself long after the collapse of Rome in A.D. 476. It was Christian in belief and Greek in culture and, during the European Dark Ages, a beacon of civilization, culture and wealth that resisted barbaric invasion. Constantinople fell to the Turks in 1453 after enduring for a thousand years.

The term in use, by Paul M. Kennedy in *The Rise and Fall of the Great Powers*, describing the situation of czarist Russia at the start of the 20th century:

> "Czar Nicholas II was a **Potemkin Village** in person, simple-minded, reclusive, disliking difficult decisions, and blindly convinced of his sacred relationship with the Russian people (in whose real welfare, of course, he showed no interest). The methods of government decision-making at the higher levels were enough to give 'Byzantinism' a bad name: irresponsible grand dukes, the emotionally unbalanced empress, reactionary generals and corrupt speculations, outweighing by far the number of diligent and intelligent ministers whom the regime could recruit and who only occasionally could reach the czar's door."

In use again, by J. Hampton Sides in Washington, D.C.'s *City Paper*, April 29, 1988:

> "Founded in 1974 with a $500,000 grant from the Rockefeller Brothers Fund, the Worldwatch Institute has always been an anomaly in the Byzantine world of the Washington think tanks."

And in *The Wall Street Journal*, November 9, 1989, Leon Wynter comments on the election of David Dinkins as mayor of New York City:

"As Mr. Dinkins kissed, hugged and high-fived his way through the Palladium, a black lawyer who knows Mr. Dinkins well conceded that it would be a while before the new mayor tries to restructure the city's byzantine political order."

# C

**Cain, Mark of.** See Mark of Cain.

**Canute.** A king of Denmark and England who, legend has it, commanded the tide not to come in—a deed misinterpreted by those who use Canute's act as an example of arrogant pride.

Not so, according to the original 12th century story. Canute demonstrated to his subjects the limits of a king's power by ordering the tide to hold back. He knew it waited on no man. Modern recounting frequently stands the lesson on its head with its portrayal of Canute as a vain and foolish king who imagined he could command the tide, rather than the wise ruler who understood the limits of kingly power.

Canute the Great, as they called him, lived from 944 to 1034. He became the king of England after 1016 and of Norway in 1028. He ruled wisely and maintained peace, a significant achievement in those troubled times.

The term in use correctly by *The Washington Post* in an editorial on April 16, 1988, entitled "Canute and the Trade Deficit":

> "No sooner had the seven governments pledged to keep exchange rates stable than the American trade figures appeared—and the dollar lurched downward again. The stock market promptly followed it. King Canute would understand the position in which James Baker finds himself. Canute demonstrated that even a royal command won't stop the sea, and Mr. Baker is showing the world that the secretary of the Treasury, even when joined by a chorus of the finance ministers of the six other strongest trading countries, can't hold the market steady in the face of a bad trade report."

And from George Will, *The Washington Post*, May 18, 1989:

> "Bush seems outmaneuvered by the subtle Gorbachev and the brutal Noriega. Like King Canute commanding the

waves, Bush commands Noriega to obey and Noriega, like the waves, disobeys."

**Captain Queeg.** See Queeg, Captain.

**Cartesian.** (car-TEZ-ee-an) Pertaining to the philosophy of René Descartes, the 17th century French logician who formulated the famous "Je pense donc je suis"—"I think, therefore I am." It is most frequently quoted in Latin form: "Cogito ergo sum."

Descartes' philosophy can be summed up in two words: systematic doubt. He, along with Francis Bacon, brought modern techniques of analysis to studying the world about them.

Their methods challenged the Aristotelian method of the Middle Ages, which adopted a general proposition, then went about seeking to discover what further knowledge could be deduced from that accepted idea. Descartes and Bacon reversed the process. They believed the truth is not something to be stated at the beginning but emerges from a process of investigation and experimentation. This was the beginning of the scientific method.

To aid the search for truth, Descartes called for systematic doubt, to sweep away past ideas and consider things afresh.

The term in use, by Norman Sherman in "Pity the Poor Vice President," an op-ed piece in *The Washington Post*, January 20, 1988:

> "Vice presidents frequently are sent to funerals of heads of state to represent our country. Their visits with living heads of states are only marginally more productive. Yet, vice presidents all brag about what those visits mean. I can deal with a head of state, therefore, I myself can be a head of state. It is a kind of Cartesian proof of both existence and importance, but it is nonsense."

**Cassandra.** (kuh-SAN-druh) A person whose warnings of disaster are ignored; a prophet of doom.

And therein lies a myth, Greek of course. Cassandra, daughter of the king of Troy, spurned the romantic advances of the god Apollo. He cursed her in a particularly nasty way: he gave her the power of

63

prophecy, but assured that her forecasts, while invariably accurate, were inevitably ignored. In today's usage, the word is applied to those who foretell disaster, usually economic.

The term in use, by Kenneth R. Sheets, *U.S. News & World Report*, September 28, 1987:

> "The new Cassandras don't envision an angry God or a nuclear disaster that would bring the end of the world to a '**big bang**' ending, but they argue that society as we know it is ready to unravel into unprecedented economic and political chaos."

Another example, from *Barron's*, January 16, 1989, an article on financier Peter G. Peterson, known for his predictions of deficit disaster, is entitled:

> "The Cadillac Cassandra: Pete Peterson's Quest for Fame"

And *The Wall Street Journal* editorializes on economic forecasts, September 25, 1989:

> "But the Cassandras ought to recognize that America's corporations and workers are participating in, indeed are creating, a modern, dynamic economy characterized by increasingly global transactions."

**Casus Belli.** (KAH-sus BEL-ligh) An occurrence that is the cause or justification for war. It's Latin.

The term in use by Major-General F.C. Graham, C.B., D.S.O., Colonel, Argyll and Sutherland Highlanders (who should know whereof he speaks) in his foreword to **The Thin Red Line**, by John Millin Selby:

> "The Crimean War has exercised a strange fascination among historians, poets, artists and novelists.
>
> "How was this fascination inspired? The cause for which the British and their Allies fought was not particularly honourable or glamorous. The basic casus belli could be simply the desire to teach a salutary lesson to the Tsar and his looming legions."

**Catch-22.** A predicament in which the solution is the problem and vice versa. Result: no way out of the predicament.

The term comes from the title of a 1961 novel about World War II by Joseph Heller. Yossarian, the book's hero, is a captain in the Army Air Corps desperately trying to avoid the increasing odds that he will be killed. He seeks to get out of flight duty by claiming to be insane. An army doctor tells him he is following the correct approach, that the army will ground someone who is crazy. But he adds that there's a catch in the regulations. "Catch-22," he tells Yossarian. "Anyone who wants to get out of combat duty isn't really crazy." Consequently Yossarian is doomed to continue flying. If he becomes truly crazy, he will be eligible for grounding but he won't be sane enough to apply for it.

The term in use, by Myra McPherson in *The Washington Post*, September 2, 1988, writing about the revival of alligator hunting in Florida and the determination of state game officials that hunters be qualified:

> "There's an admitted Catch-22 in trying to find out just who is a gator expert. Since it has been illegal to hunt alligators for a quarter of a century, it is hard to find anyone who admits to having done it."

And from Chris Weller, University of Maryland women's basketball coach, quoted in *The New York Times*, March 31, 1989 on playing opportunities in the 60s:

> "The girls had 'honor teams,' she recalled, with just a trace of scorn. 'You could play six games a year. I asked why and they had no arguments. It was a Catch-22. You had no interest so you couldn't have a gym so you had no interest."

**Caveat Emptor.** (KAV-ee-AT EMP-tuhr) Latin for "let the buyer beware." In other words, the buyer is responsible for determining the quality of whatever he or she is purchasing. In some cases, as in the example below, the phrase is not just a warning that the product *might* be defective: it is meant to warn you off a definite bad choice.

65

The term in use, by music critic John von Rhein reviewing recent compact disc releases in the *Chicago Tribune*, March 19, 1989:

> "What the early symphonies need in particular are leaner textures and more rhythmic bite than Rostapovich and/or the recording engineers are willing to bring to them. Only the Fifth Symphony merits an unqualified recommendation. Otherwise, caveat emptor."

And from Jerome Groopman, *The New Republic*, February 13, 1989, on the debate over Food and Drug Administration regulation of new drugs:

> "Enter the gay activists, charlatans, and *Wall Street Journal* editorialists. The *Journal* is incensed by the denial of any American's right to have virtually anything he wants without government meddling. Caveat emptor! Let drugs rapidly enter the doctor's office, be given willy-nilly to patients, and eventually rise or fall on their merits."

**The Center Cannot Hold.** A cry of despair conveying the sense of the world spinning out of control—or the restraints of civilization breaking apart.

It is from *The Second Coming*, a poem by Irish poet William Butler Yeats (1856-1923) that perfectly expresses 20th century **angst:**

> Things fall apart, the center cannot hold;
> Mere anarchy is loosed upon the world,
> The blood-dimmed tide is loosed, and everywhere
> The ceremony of innocence is drowned;
> The best lack all conviction, while the worst
> Are full of passionate intensity.

[See also **Slouching Toward Bethlehem.**]

The term in use, by Leonard Silk in *The New York Times*, October 18, 1987:

> "Wall Street, plunging into a downturn that many analysts and investors feared was the end of the big bull market of

the last five years, behaved last week as though the center would not hold."

**Cerberus.** See Sop to Cerberus.

**Checkers Speech.** A **genre** of speeches given by embattled politicians in which they portray themselves as unjustly victimized and play on emotion to gain sympathy. Such speeches often are fraught with self-pitying personal detail embarrassing to the listener, if not the speaker.

The original was a nationwide television address given by Richard M. Nixon in 1952 when he was Dwight D. Eisenhower's vice presidential running mate. In the speech, Nixon dealt with charges that he was the beneficiary of a secret political fund. As news coverage of the issue mushroomed, Eisenhower first stood aloof, then reportedly said that Nixon would have to prove himself "clean as a hound's tooth" in order to avoid being dumped from the ticket.

Nixon's decision to respond to the situation on television was innovative at the time. In a 30-minute speech he described the fund and went into lugubrious detail about his modest personal finances. Mrs. Nixon did not have a mink coat, he said, but a "respectable Republican cloth coat." And his family had also been given a dog:

> "It was a little cocker spaniel dog . . . black and white, spotted, and our little girl Tricia, the six-year-old, named it Checkers. And you know, the kids, like all kids, loved the dog, and I just want to say this, right now, that regardless of what they say about it, we are going to keep it."

Response to the speech was overwhelmingly warm, Nixon stayed on the ticket, and a term was coined.

The term in use, by *The Washington Post*, July 9, 1987, commenting on the testimony of Oliver North during the Iran-contra congressional hearings:

> "A new classic in the annals of melodramatic political rhetoric, Lt. Col. North's appearance before the Iran-

contra committees yesterday ranks right up there with Richard Nixon's 'Checkers speech.' "

Another example, from Mark Lilla, *The American Spectator*, May 1989, on French president Mitterrand's reaction to stock-trading scandals involving his friends and government:

"He [Mitterrand] came right to the point. After a short, Checkers-like monologue about the humble virtues of his friend Pelat ('his mother was a washerwoman'), he turned to the real culprit: corporate capitalism."

**Chernobyl.** (chur-NOH-bil) The scene of the worst nuclear reactor disaster in history—and now used as a metaphor for any huge catastrophe, particularly an atomic one.

A nuclear power plant exploded in the Soviet town of Chernobyl, 60 miles north of Kiev, on April 26, 1986, causing a fire and the release of massive amounts of radiation which drifted across northern Europe. The area around the plant was evacuated permanently and the damaged reactor entombed in millions of tons of cement. The long-term scope of this disaster remains to reveal itself.

There's an ironic biblical twist to the name, as noted by *The Christian Science Monitor*, April 20, 1989:

"Chernobyl means 'wormwood,' the biblical name given to the great star in Revelation 8:10-11 that fell from heaven 'burning as if it were a lamp' when the third angel sounded his trumpet. According to Revelation, the star poisoned one-third of the Earth's waters 'and many men died of the waters, because they were made bitter.' "

The term in use, by Mary McGrory, *The Washington Post*, September 18, 1988:

"The functioning of the Strategic Defense Initiative would require sending 'as many as 100 nuclear power plants' into orbit, according to an American Physical Society panel. Lt. Gen. James Abramson, who is in charge of the program, says it would be crippled without nuclear power.

"Maybe [Democratic presidential candidate Michael]

Dukakis hasn't heard about the Chernobyl in the sky. Most people haven't. But it is an issue tailor-made for him."

Another example, from Robert Houston's review of *The Cloning of Joanna May* by Fay Weldon, *The New York Times Book Review*, March 25, 1990:

". . . they band together to readjust their lives and their men, share what children they have and begin at last to have a good time, while Carl goes down in his own private, ego-triggered Chernobyl."

**Cheshire Cat.** When someone grins like one, he or she wears a broad grin that's enigmatic, or at least ambiguous.

The expression was popularized by the mysterious and talkative cat in Lewis Carroll's *Alice in Wonderland* (1865) who grins from ear to ear. The cat is able to vanish and materialize at will, sometimes leaving behind only its grin.

The expression was used by British writer Peter Pindar (Dr. John Wolcot, 1738-1819) who gained fame for his satiric verse and caricatures of the great, including King George III. The origins of the phrase go back further than that, but no one is certain of the source. *The Oxford English Dictionary* says it is "of undetermined origin," but theories abound. One is that cheeses from the county of Cheshire were molded in the shape of a cat, or stamped with the emblem of a grinning cat. Another is that an inept pub sign painter in Cheshire made all of his lions look like cats, or that a forest warden of Cheshire named Caterling presented himself at the hangings of poachers, grinning "like a Cheshire caterling" which was then shortened to "cat."

The term in use, by Frances Fitzgerald in *Rolling Stone*, February 25, 1988, reviewing the Reagan years:

"Yet he has never chided any one of his appointees for betraying the public trust. His smiling face has hovered over them all like that of a Cheshire cat."

Another example, from George Will, in *The Washington Post*, May 18, 1989, on embattled House Speaker Jim Wright:

"Soon he will disappear, like the Cheshire cat, leaving only the grin behind. He will go on his own or the House Democratic Caucus—acting on the most complicated impulse its neurological system can handle: anxiety about reelection—will remove him."

**Chiaroscuro.** (kee-AHR-oh-SKOOR-oh) Italian. Literally, light-dark, it refers to the use of light and dark and shading in a painting or drawing that produces the effect of depth and distance. It was developed by Renaissance artists in the great change from earlier flat, one-dimensional painting. The term can be used in a broader sense, to suggest an atmosphere, style or mood created through the contrast of opposites.

The term in use, in *Spy* magazine, March 1989:

"So we crafted a manifesto, painting our prose with broad, flag-size strokes rather than the chiaroscuro and gossamer scumbling of delicate idiom that mark our usual manner."
[Ed. note: The word *scumbling* is an artist's term, meaning to lay a thin coat of color to soften the effect of other colors in a painting or drawing.]

**Children's Crusade.** A remarkable and tragic event in the Middle Ages in which thousands of French and German children banded together to conquer the Holy Land through love and purity, and perished in disaster.

The crusades—wave after wave of Christian pilgrims and armies seeking to oust the Moslems from Jerusalem—lasted for almost 200 years, from 1096 to 1274.

One of the saddest episodes of the era was the Children's Crusade, set in motion in 1212 by a French shepherd boy named Stephen inspired by a vision of Jesus. Stephen attracted a following of an estimated 30,000 children who decided to go to the Holy Land. A second group of at least 20,000 (some estimates are as high as 40,000) headed for the Holy Land under the leadership of a 10-year-old German boy.

The undertaking turned into a calamity. The French children

proceeded to Marseilles, expecting the seas to part as the waters had for Moses. Instead, the children fell into the hands of slave traders who offered them passage to the Holy Land only to ship them to the North African slave markets. The German children crossed the Alps into Italy, where they split into groups heading to various ports to find ships. Some were refused transport. Others were sold into slavery. A fortunate few were met by the pope, who took pity and released them from their vows so that they could return home. Their story may have been the inspiration for the tale of the Pied Piper of Hamelin.

The religious fervor generated by the children helped inspire the Fifth Crusade in 1218, a military disaster conducted by adults.

"Children's Crusade" has come to refer to any enterprise led by the inexperienced and idealistic young. Most notably, the name was applied to the grassroots political campaign undertaken by antiwar college students in support of presidential candidate Eugene McCarthy in 1968. McCarthy came close to upending President Lyndon B. Johnson in the New Hampshire primary; shortly after, LBJ decided not to seek reelection.

An example from *Time*, November 14, 1988, introducing an interview with McCarthy:

> "Eugene McCarthy, the low-key Pied Piper of the 1968 children's crusade against the war in Viet Nam, is a third-party candidate this year."

**Chimera** or **Chimaera.** (kuh-MIR-uh) A horrible or unreal creature of the imagination. A wild or crazy idea or illusion is called chimerical.

It comes from Greek mythology. A chimera was a monster: the front third was a lion, the midsection a goat, the rear end a serpent. Luckily it was slain by the legendary hero Bellerophon, riding the winged horse Pegasus. (Incidentally, the *Bellerophon* was a 74-gun British man-of-war of the Napoleonic era, which participated in the Battle of Trafalgar. And it was the captain of the *Bellerophon* to whom Napoleon made his final surrender after the defeat of Waterloo.)

The term in use, by Martin Peretz in *The New Republic*, November 28, 1988, "Why Dukakis Lost":

"Voices are already heard reproaching the Democrats for not having marched far enough left in this election. They hold out the chimera of seven or eight or ten million non-voters (any number will do) who are just waiting to respond to a party that will practice more believably the politics of class and race resentment."

**Chinese Wall.** An impassable barrier. From the Great Wall of China, probably the world's greatest public works project, a massive 1,500-mile rampart built on the border of ancient China to keep out barbarian invaders.

Today the Wall has come into figurative use, sometimes not capitalized, to suggest an impassable barrier.

The term in use, from *The New York Times*, November 16, 1984:

"The union had insisted on retaining the so-called 'Chinese wall' clause, which prohibits the sale in the metropolitan area of milk processed elsewhere."

The term is also used in the financial world, to describe the insulation required between the mergers and acquisitions departments of brokerage and financial houses on Wall Street and their stock trading activities. A "Chinese wall" separating the two divisions is intended to keep stockbrokers from picking up inside information about takeover attempts, information they could use to purchase stock before it rises in price as a reaction to the maneuverings over the acquisition or merger.

The term in use in the latter mode, applied this time to the avoidance of conflict of interest for law firms working with the savings and loan industry, by Marianne Lavelle, *The National Law Journal*, November 6, 1989:

"Because the agency [the Federal Deposit Insurance Corporation] needs a large pool of lawyers, Mr. Rosenberg says that it would be pragmatic for the FDIC to agree to the use of the 'chinese wall' shielding that law firms are accustomed to using."

**Chutzpah.** (KHOOTS-pah) A Yiddish word meaning audacity, brazen impudence, insolence, unmitigated gall. Leo Rosten gives the classic example of this quality in *The Joys of Yiddish:* someone who has killed his father and mother and throws himself on the mercy of the court pleading that he is an orphan.

The term in use, in an editorial in *The Wall Street Journal*, May 17, 1989:

> "It's real chutzpah for Members [of Congress] to use the excuse of the S&L crisis to put new burdens on the deposit insurance system. After all, there is a good case to be made that Congress created the problem in the first place."

Another example, from Arthur W. Wang, *The Wall Street Journal*, August 31, 1989, on the tax-evasion conviction of hotel "queen" Leona Helmsley:

> "Nor can most of us take much more of Leona's arrogant advertisements. They're no crime, either, but New Yorkers I know rub their hands in glee at the thought of her paying dearly for her chutzpah."

**Cinéma Vérité.** (see-nay-MAH vay-ree-TAY) A '60s movement in French filmmaking that emphasized realism and documentary-style film techniques. The phrase means cinema of truth.

Directors of this movement attempted to provide a film experience that closely resembled life rather than a make-believe image. Filmmakers would frequently record sound separately, taping actual conversations or interviews, and then put the audio and visual elements together in the cutting room. In television, this style was noted in such shows as "Hill Street Blues" with its grubby sets and action in background and foreground.

In current usage, the term sometimes is flipped back upon itself, describing real events that are viewed as drama. Art imitating life and vice versa, especially in TV news.

The term in use, by Maureen Dowd in *The New Republic*, August 1, 1988, describing "Tanner '88", a TV series on the campaign of a fictional candidate, Jack Tanner:

"[Creator and cartoonist Garry] Trudeau uses his *Doonesbury* technique of putting mythical characters in a real setting sprinkled with real people, and writes the show with his usual deft sense of the hip and the hypocritical. Mirroring the action of the campaign and piggybacking on as many real events, real candidates, and real celebrities as possible, [director Robert] Altman employs the choppy cinema verite style he made famous in "Nashville" and "M*A*S*H"—overlapping dialogue and plots that meander in a way that seems spontaneous. . . .

"The day Bruce Babbitt dropped out of the race, his staffers all took off their Babbitt for President buttons and put on Tanner '88 buttons. And Altman wasn't even shooting. That's verite."

**City on a Hill.** A place destined to be a shining example for all the world.

It's from the Sermon on the Mount in the Book of Mathew in the New Testament:

"Ye are the light of the world. A city that is set on an hill cannot be hid. Neither do men light a candle, and put it under a bushel, but on a candlestick; and it giveth light unto all that are in the house. Let your light so shine before men that they may see your good works, and glorify your Father, which is in heaven."

John Winthrop, rallying his band of Puritans crossing the Atlantic to found the Massachusetts Bay colony, turned to the phrase, suggesting they were conscious of founding a godly society that would be watched by the world: "We must consider that we shall be a City Upon a Hill, the eyes of all people are upon us."

Frances Fitzgerald chose the expression for the title of her 1987 book on American communities whose founding was based on an ideal—and whose members felt that the life and success of the community would be an example to the world.

The term in use, by television critic Tom Shales, in *The Washing-*

*ton Post*, December 7, 1988, bemoaning sleazy new television programs:

> "Perhaps American commercial television never was a shining city on a hill. But increasingly it seems a valley of slums."

**Cloud-Cuckoo-Land.** A dreamland, a foolish and fanciful place, taken from *The Birds*, a comedy by the Greek playwright Aristophanes (445–380 B.C.). Cloud-Cuckoo-Land (sometimes written Cloudcuckooland) was a city in the clouds which the birds were persuaded to create by two fugitives from Athenian taxes and litigation.

The term in use, by Arthur Frommer in his column "Dollar-Wise Travel," *Newsday*, April 30, 1989:

> "In short, to wander the airport car rental counters of America, looking for informed comment on third-party liability insurance, is to enter a cloud-cuckoo-land of ignorance and doubt, ranging from minimal knowledge to innocent deception ('the car is insured')."

**A Cloud Like a Man's Hand.** A small, faraway indicator of great turmoil yet to come.

It comes from the Old Testament (I Kings 18:44-45): "And it came to pass at the seventh time, that he said, Behold, there ariseth a little cloud out of the sea, like a man's hand . . . and it came to pass a great rain."

The term in use by economist Paul Samuelson in his column in *Newsweek*, August 13, 1973:

> "The reasons why the never-ending disclosures [of the Watergate scandal] have been so disquieting is that we begin to see, on the TV tube darkly, the face of Fascism. True, to use the vernacular of the King James Bible that has come so much into fashion, Fascism is still a cloud on the horizon no bigger than a man's hand. But if a George **Orwell** were alive to sniff out the signs of Fascism on the left or the right, he would be sounding the 1984 alarm."

**Cognoscenti.** (koh-nyoh-SHEN-ti) Italian, meaning experts; those in the know; sometimes used ironically.

The term in use, by Michael Pertschuk, former chairman of the Federal Trade Commission, quoted in *The Washington Post*, November 19, 1988:

> "Pertschuk said that, when Nader first began to speak years ago against insurance company efforts to resist regulation and [to] reduce vulnerability to citizen suits, prominent commentators announced that he 'had overreached and people were tired of him. The cognoscenti got bored.' "

Another example, from *The New York Times*, August 17, 1989, on the Cajun food fad in New York:

> "Things have changed along the Cajun chow line. Four years ago, when [chef Paul] Prudhomme was a buzzword only among the culinary cognoscenti, they flocked to his camp. Yet New York's free-floating anxiety seemed to hover over the chic crowd. The ones-who-would-always-be-first were reduced to being the ones-who-wait."

**Colonel Blimp.** See Blimp, Colonel.

**Colossus of the North.** The United States in its relations with the countries of Central and South America. The term sums up the overwhelming economic and military power of the United States and suggests—often in a negative sense—the use of these powers in a bullying and intrusive way.

The word "colossus," referring to a giant statue of the human form, was originally applied by the Greek historian Herodotus to the huge statues of ancient Egypt. But the most famous reference is to the Colossus of Rhodes, a statue of the god Helios (Apollo) and one of the Seven Wonders of the ancient world. The 105-foot-high statue stood at the entrance of the harbor of Rhodes and was completed about 280 B.C. Legends arose centuries later that the figure stood astride the harbor entrance so that ships sailed between its legs, and that the harbor was destroyed when it fell.

Shakespeare invoked this very image in *Julius Caesar* when Cassius says of Caesar:

> Why, man, he doth bestride the narrow world
> Like a Colossus, and we petty men
> Walk under his huge legs, and peep about
> To find ourselves dishonourable graves.
> Men at some time are masters of their fates:
> The fault, dear Brutus, is not in our stars,
> But in ourselves, that we are underlings.

"Colossus" is now used figuratively to describe anything vast, large or awesome, or someone of immense talent, power or influence.

*The Oxford English Dictionary* notes an example from 1831 of "Colossus of the North" referring to Russia. But today, the United States can claim the overwhelming majority of references.

The term in use, by Richard Cohen, *The Washington Post*, October 9, 1989, in a column on American attempts to topple Panamanian dictator Manuel Noriega:

> "The stupid indictment [of Noriega by U.S. authorities on drug trafficking charges] did something else as well: it turned a criminal-justice problem into a foreign-policy crisis. The consequences were predictable. Since the colossus of the North wanted little Noriega of even littler Panama, all he had to do was whip up existing anti-American sentiment."

**Comédie Humaine.** (com-AY-dee eyoo-men) The "human comedy" in French, the title 19th century novelist Honore de Balzac (1799-1850) gave to his works, which provide a sweeping, and realistic, view of France from many perspectives. Thus "comédie humaine" has come to mean the entire spectrum of human behavior.

Balzac's characters and plots are romantic, extreme, passionate and melodramatic. Like Dickens, he draws memorable pictures of human failings and virtues.

77

The term in use, by Max I. Dimont in the introduction to *Jews, God and History:*

> "This book attempts to portray the broad sweep of Jewish history, the grandeur and humor of the Jewish *comédie humaine*, and to present Jewish history through the eyes of a twentieth-century Western man rather than a sixteenth-century ghetto **Talmudist**."

## Comstockery. Militant prudery.

George Bernard Shaw is given credit for making a noun out of the name of Anthony Comstock, a famous American crusader against pornography, birth control and gambling in the late 19th and early 20th centuries. Shaw was quoted by *The New York Times*, September 26, 1905, saying, "Comstockery is the world's standing joke at the expense of the United States."

In 1873 Comstock was an organizer of the New York Society for the Suppression of Vice, and was personally credited with the destruction of 160 tons of dirty pictures and literature. He was a leader in putting pressure on Congress to enact laws against sending pornography through the mail—the "Comstock laws."

The term in use, by Steven Marcus in *The New Republic*, reviewing books on pornography in modern culture, June 16, 1987:

> "Kendrick is at least partly alive to this danger, and periodically gestures in the other direction. He writes that the principle of modernism, along with the pervasive influence of Freud and his followers, has resulted in a prevailing anti-Comstockery that is almost as oppressive as its defeated counterpart."

## Consent Decree. A judgment entered by the agreement of the parties to a legal action. It is in effect a contract by the parties, under the sanction of a court, and is enforceable by the court. It is a means of settling a legal action without a trial, and enables parties to settle a dispute without the express finding of fault that would come with a trial on the facts. Consent decrees typically result in a defendant

denying that he did the offensive activity, while agreeing not to do it again.

The term in use, by Dan Balz in *The Washington Post*, February 2, 1989, reporting on the controversial nomination of John Tower to be secretary of defense:

> "Tower offered his accusers the political equivalent of a consent decree. He denied any wrongdoing—'I am not an alcoholic nor have I ever been dependent on alcohol,' he said—but he promised not to do it any more."

**Conspicuous Consumption.** Spending for the sake of show; consumption intended as an ostentatious display of wealth.

The concept was introduced in 1899 by Thorstein Veblen in his book *Theory of the Leisure Class*. To test whether an expenditure fell within this classification, Veblen said one must merely ask "whether, aside from acquired tastes and from the canons of usage and conventional decency, its result is a net gain in comfort or in the fullness of life." By that standard, most of the consumer spending in the wealthy nations of the world would be conspicuous indeed.

Veblen maintained that spending for status and show exists in all classes of society, but his term is usually applied to truly flamboyant spending. At the time Veblen wrote, the wealthy constructed huge and ornate mansions, entertained lavishly, and competed in expensive excesses of all kinds. Reformers of the day loved to cite the Bradley Martin costume ball staged in the Waldorf Hotel at a cost of $368,000. It took place in February 1897 in the depths of an economic depression and was attended by guests wearing costumes costing as much as $10,000. That's the sort of showcase expenditure for status evoked by Veblen's phrase.

The term in use, by Staughton Lynd in his review of *Sparrows Point—The Rise and Ruin of American Industrial Might* by Mark Reutter (a history of the Bethlehem Steel plant near Baltimore, Maryland), *The Washington Post*, November 13, 1988:

> "The rigor required of the men contrasted with the institutionalized opulence of company executives . . . who did not see fit 'to pay for a decent R-and-D laboratory' dined in

chairs with their names affixed to gold-plated plaques; to the finding in 1957 that 11 of the 18 highest-paid corporate executives in the country worked for Bethlehem Steel; or to the 1980 retirement of chairman Lewis Foy, climaxed by a round-the-world airplane trip by Foy and his successor, Donald Trautlein, with their families, 'touching down at such important steel centers as Singapore, Cairo, and London'—the pattern revealed is a caricature of conspicuous consumption, passed on from generation to generation, regardless of the circumstances of the firm or the well-being of its workers."

Another example, from Paul Richard's profile of billionaire Walter Annenberg in *The Washington Post*, May 23, 1989:

"Even around Palm Springs, where consumption is conspicuous and awesome wealth a commonplace, no one lives as he does."

And from Playthell Benjamin, *The Village Voice*, November 8, 1988, describing the lifestyle of drug dealers:

"And they are prepared to commit bloody murder to attain the status symbols dictated by the amoral materialist ethos spawned by a uniquely American culture of narcissism. It is an ethos that prizes style over substance and thrives on conspicuous consumption."

**Cordon Sanitaire.** (KOR-don SAN-ee-TEHR) A group of neighboring, generally neutral, states forming a geographic barrier between two powers that harbor aggressive or ideological aims against each other. It is French, meaning an area quarantined to prevent the spread of disease. In contemporary usage, the term is still used to describe a zone that serves as a barrier to keep an unwelcome something in or out.

The term was applied to the ring of small states, from Finland to Rumania, that was created by the Paris peace conference along the borders of Russia in 1919 to contain Bolshevism.

The term in use, in "The Perils of Public Art" by Herbert Muschamp, *The New Republic*, August 8, 1988:

> "With its blank, fortresslike walls, its green *cordon sanitaire* of clipped golf course grass, the museum building embodies the idea of art as something isolated, set apart from its surroundings and from the history that produced it."

**Cotton Mather.** See Mather, Cotton.

**Coxey's Army.** A disorderly bunch. They were a protest group of unemployed men who marched on Washington in the spring of 1894 to demand the creation of jobs through public works programs. (The Panic of 1893 had caused enormous unemployment and hardship.)

Jacob S. Coxey was a well-to-do owner of a sandstone quarry and horsebreeder from Massillon, Ohio. He was also a populist and believed that a $500 million federal employment program of roadbuilding would alleviate the problem. When his plan was rejected by Congress, he vowed: "We will send a petition to Washington with boots on." His army was one of a number of groups of the unemployed to march on Washington in those difficult times.

Coxey's group marched peacefully from Massillon to Washington, picking up sympathizers along the way. They numbered several hundred when they arrived on May Day and marched to the Capitol, where they were assaulted by police. Coxey was arrested for walking on the grass and carrying a banner. He was not permitted to complete his speech.

Coxey lived until 1951; he had the satisfaction of completing his speech on the steps of the Capitol on May 1, 1944 and of seeing his concept of public works employment accepted as an orthodox solution for relieving cyclical unemployment.

The term in use, by Stan Isaacs in *Newsday*, September 4, 1988, on comments by tennis great/commentator Tony Trabert on TV coverage of tennis matches:

> "Trabert has some suggestions for CBS in its coverage of tennis. He says he doesn't like the network's Coxey's army approach of sometimes covering a match. 'Sometimes we

have three people in the booth and two people in the studio downstairs commenting on the same match.' "

**Cri de Coeur.** (KREE duh KUHR) A statement made from the heart, with the deepest of feelings. Literally, in French, a cry from the heart.

The term in use, in *The Washington Post*, July 9, 1989, in a review of *Conscience of a Conservationist: Selected Essays*, by Michael Frome:

> "The title, of course, is a play on Barry Goldwater's famous *cri de coeur. . . .* "

**Critical Mass.** The term comes from physics, where it refers to the point at which an atomic pile is capable of producing a sustained nuclear chain reaction. In broader use, the term is applied to situations in which the right elements come together to produce dramatic developments.

The term in use, by Christopher Hitchens, in *The Nation*, October 31, 1988:

> "Over the past month or so, the 1980 **'October surprise'** hypothesis has been striving to reach critical mass in the mainstream media. It is the story everyone has heard and that no one wants to print."

Another example, from an October 10, 1989 *New York Times* story quoting a report on hiring minority faculty members at Yale University:

> "The lack of a 'critical mass' of minorities on the faculty deprives undergraduates of role models, reinforces perceptions of minorities as marginal or tokens and reduces the opportunity for colleagueship, the report said."

**Crypto-** (KRIP-toh) From Greek, meaning hidden. For example, a crypto-communist would be a communist who hides his sentiments. Probably under the bed.

The term in use, by *Spy* magazine, March 1989:

> "Speaking of rich, smarmy, good-looking men who other people think are Nazis, almost-president Dan Quayle (whose father and in-laws do, in fact, subscribe to crypto-Nazi publications) remains a national pleasure."

**Cult of Personality.** A term made famous by Soviet leader Nikita Khrushchev in his 1956 "secret speech" denouncing the policies of the deceased dictator Joseph Stalin. Khrushchev accused Stalin of having created a "cult of personality" by making himself the central figure of government and superseding collective leadership in a betrayal of the Russian revolution and Communist party principles. The speech signaled the beginning of "destalinization" of the Soviet Union.

Now, at least in the West, the term has taken on a more casual meaning, describing someone who is building power in an organization by making himself the focus of attention and adulation rather than subordinating his personal image to that of the institution.

The term in use, in a *Wall Street Journal* editorial, March 28, 1989, on Soviet elections:

> "But there are folks like Mr. Yeltsin. Mr. Gorbachev first installed him as Moscow party leader and then threw him out when Mr. Yeltsin started worrying too publicly about a Gorbachev 'cult of personality.' "

And another example, by Burling Lowrey in *The Washington Post*, March 17, 1989, writing on foreign words and phrases in contemporary American usage:

> "*Charisma.* Greek (kar-IS-ma). We apparently needed a word to convey the chemistry that a public speaker exudes, and this seems to fit the bill. In America it has taken on an added significance because of the emphasis in the political realm placed on 'attractive' candidates and those who 'come across well on television.' It's the Cult of Personality reborn."

**-Cum-.** (kuhm) A Latin preposition meaning with, or together with, or along with. It is often seen in a hyphenated compound form.

The term in use, by Douglas Martin in *The New York Times*, December 14, 1988, writing about a well-known New York bar:

> ". . . the name of the place . . . is Chumley's—a cozy Greenwich Village saloon cum literary hangout at 86 Bedford Street. You will read some probably true stories in this column. But it is the ones made up and recited over time that somehow ring clearest: The night Fitzgerald made love to a woman in a booth, the days Hemingway spent sleeping off a mammoth drunk upstairs, the months Joyce spent at a corner table scribbling *Ulysses*."

Another example, from Meg Cox, *The Wall Street Journal*, November 16, 1989:

> "Here's a spook who makes old Smiley seem an artless plodder.
>
> "He's Clifford Stoll, astronomer-cum-spy catcher-cum-author, and his story involves computers, cookies, a penguin keeper, love and what you could call nuked Nikes."

# D

**Dada.** A movement in the arts that developed in the years after World War I with the goals of making fun of existing art, breaking all the rules, and seeking to shock the sensibilities of the middle class and the critics and pundits. It was a protest against the wastefulness and madness of the war.

Shock the Dadaists did. Exhibitions of dada art were anarchic, scenes of total confusion and nonsense, incorporating junk and common household items. Dada music was a deliberate cacophony of sound. And the critics and the squares reacted with gratifying apoplexy.

The movement ultimately self-destructed; when the only rule is "there are no rules" and when incoherence is a virtue, a legacy is unlikely. Dadaism's leaders quarreled or drifted off into other pursuits. Surrealism was founded by Dadaists and produced artists such as Salvador Dali. American artist Man Ray was a participant in both movements.

The movement was given its name by the poet Tzara and the artist Arp, who stuck a knife at random into a French dictionary and fortuitously struck upon "dada," French for hobbyhorse.

The term today generally is applied to deliberate nonsense.

The term in use, by Michael Hirschorn in *Spy*, February 1989, "Mr. Stupid Goes to Washington," on *Spy*'s list of the ten dumbest members of Congress:

> "[Congressman Joseph] Kennedy unscripted is hopped-up gibberish, an almost dadaist assortment of sentence fragments, expletives and exaggerated bonhomie that make Uncle Teddy's incoherent justification of his 1980 presidential bid to Roger Mudd look positively Periclean."

**Damascus, Road to.** See Road to Damascus.

**Damon and Pythias.** (DAY-muhn and PITH-ee-uhs) A metaphor for inseparable friends.

It comes from a Greek legend of the 4th century B.C. Damon and Pythias were devoted comrades. Pythias was condemned to death by Dionysius, the ruler of their city [see **Sword of Damocles**]. Pythias was released for one last visit to his family on condition that Damon take his place with the understanding that Pythias would return in a specified time. When Pythias' return was delayed, Damon was nearly executed, but Pythias arrived just in time to save his friend. So impressed was Dionysius with the strength of their friendship that he pardoned them both.

The term in use, by Janet Malcolm in *The New Yorker*, March 13, 1989:

> "In the summer of 1979, MacDonald and McGinniss were Damon and Pythias. In common with many other subjects and writers, they clothed their complicated business together in the mantle of friendship—in this case, friendship of a particularly American cast, whose emblems of intimacy are watching sports on television, drinking beer, running, and classifying women according to looks."

**Damon Runyon.** See Runyon, Damon.

**Dantesque.** An adjective meaning relating to Dante, or resembling his style, taken from the name of the great poet Dante Aligheri (1265-1321), the first important author to write in his native Italian. The scope and vivid detail of Dante's work give rise to the descriptive term. A Dantesque vision is one which is epic in scope but minutely detailed and richly allegorical.

Dante's greatest work is the epic poem *The Comedy* (1321, called *The Divine Comedy* after the 16th century) in which the poet is conducted through Hell, Purgatory and Paradise. Dante's picture of Hell (*The Inferno*) is the most famous. Over the door is written the legend: "Abandon All Hope Ye Who Enter Here." Hell has varying levels, to which sinners are assigned according to their transgressions. Those in the lowest circles are frauds, thieves, hypocrites and traitors.

The term in use, by Paul Gray in *Time,* September 26, 1988, on the appointment of A. Bartlett Giamatti to head organized baseball's National League:

> "He is convinced that major league baseball plays a **bardic,** mythic role in American society; the long, recurring seasons are an ongoing epic, **Homeric** or Vergilian or Dantesque, a vital locus of rapt assembly where enduring values are enacted and passed on."

**De Facto.** (day FAHK-toh) A Latin phrase meaning, literally, in fact or in deed. The phrase is used in the context of government and politics, to describe an existing situation that has not been sanctioned by government authority. Nevertheless, the situation exists and must be considered a reality.

The term can be applied to individuals exercising power as well as to the status of a government. [See **De Jure.**] Examples include descriptions of governments that have illegally seized power; in the United States, the term frequently arises in discussion of patterns of segregation in schools and housing, as in the first example below.

The term has also come into use in a broader context than government, to mean "in reality" as opposed to what the rules or official statements say.

The term in use, by *The Economist,* May 6, 1989:

> "Atlanta likes to call itself a city too busy to hate. . . . Yet the veneer is thin. Beneath the superficial harmony lies a powder keg of black deprivation as bad as in any northern city, along with a de facto segregation of everything from access to capital to housing."

Another example, from Tom Kenworthy, *The Washington Post,* December 6, 1989:

> "[House Banking Committee Chairman Henry] Gonzalez turned the Lincoln hearings into a de facto confirmation process for a man he accused of misleading Congress by repeatedly underestimating the cost of bailing out bankrupt thrifts."

And also from the *Post*, December 7, 1989, in a Michael Isikoff story on drug policy director William Bennett's nicotine addiction, the subject of a satiric series in Garry Trudeau's "Doonesbury":

> "One Bennett aide called the series 'nasty,' and noted that it ended with a de facto call for legalization of drugs—a position that polls show an overwhelming majority of the American public opposes."

**Defarge, Madame.** A character in Charles Dickens' 1859 novel of the French Revolution, *A Tale of Two Cities*, whose zealotry was so intense that her name became a synonym for the type.

Mme. Defarge's husband is keeper of a wine shop in the Faubourg St. Antoine district of Paris, a hotbed of revolutionary fervor. He is a revolutionary, but Mme. Defarge is the more terrible, an implacable and merciless fanatic for the Revolution. "Tell Wind and Fire where to stop," says she, "but don't tell me."

She attends the daily executions at the guillotine to gloat over the demise of aristocrats and enemies of the Revolution. The names of those marked out for her own vengeance are coded into her always-present knitting. She is a fictional example of the famous "tricoteuses," or knitters—Parisian women who attended revolutionary meetings and urged the crowds on to greater bloodshed, knitting all the while.

The term in use, by Tom Shales in *The Washington Post*, November 17, 1987, on the Federal Communications Commission decision to abolish the Fairness Doctrine (which required stations to air opposing viewpoints):

> "Some former FCC members do oppose the doctrine. They are mostly communications lawyers and lobbyists. Among them is definitive lightweight and former chairman Mark S. Fowler, the Mme. Defarge of deregulation."

Another example, from Nat Hentoff, *The Village Voice*, March 13, 1990:

> "In the Madame Defarge stage of the Red Scare (guillotine first, proof of guilt afterwards), the press in the 1950s did a

great deal to start the flames reaching toward the heretics at stake."

**Defenestration.** The act of throwing someone out a window. Today the word has come to be applied figuratively to any sudden and involuntary ejection from high office or prominent position.

A famous incident, known as the Defenestration of Prague, occurred in Bohemia in 1618 and was one of the aggravating elements of conflict leading to the Thirty Years' War. Bohemia was under the rule of the Hapsburgs, and discontent was widespread. In a fracas with a group of local citizens, two representatives of the government were thrown out of the window of Prague Castle. They fell fifty feet into the moat but weren't seriously hurt, and managed to escape with their lives.

Actually, defenestrations are "something of a Prague specialty," says David Binder, a *New York Times* reporter and old Czechoslovakia hand and our source on this subject. Binder says there was an earlier case in 1419, in which a mob of Hussites (followers of church reformer Jan Hus, who was burned at the stake in 1415) stormed the City Hall of Prague after someone there threw a stone at what apparently had been a peaceful demonstration. Once inside, the Hussites grabbed some members of the city council and tossed them out the window. The mob outside killed them.

In the modern era, Jan Masaryk, the foreign minister of post-World War II democratic Czechoslovakia, died in Prague on March 10, 1948 in a fall from his office window shortly after the Communist coup in his country. His death was explained as a suicide, but the circumstances remain mysterious to this day.

The term in use, by Hendrik Hertzberg in *The New Republic*, July 4, 1988, commenting on *Penthouse* magazine's publication of the photographs of the prostitute with whom televangelist Jimmy Swaggart dallied, leading to his downfall:

> "The big Swaggart-Murphree takeout was *Penthouse*'s revenge against *Playboy* for cornering the market, some months ago, on Jessica Hahn, the 'church secretary' who defenestrated Jim Bakker."

Another example, from *The Economist*, June 10, 1989, on the impact of Ayatollah Ruhollah Khomeini's rule in Iran:

"Many in the world, too, admired the way he took on the United States, defenestrating one American president and debunking another."

**Déjà Vu.** (day-JAH voo) The here-we-go-again sense of having previously experienced something, even though it is being encountered for the first time. French: literally, "already seen."

Yogi Berra, known for his malapropisms, is said to have exclaimed, "It's déjà vu all over again!"

It is commonly (and incorrectly) used for history repeating itself, as in both of these examples: first, by a New England Patriots football player after his team's defeat by the Buffalo Bills, quoted by *The Boston Globe*, October 24, 1988:

" 'Deja vu,' sighed offensive tackle Bruce Armstrong after watching the Bills' Scott Norwood beat New England for the second time this season with a last-minute field goal."

And in *The New York Times*, July 21, 1989, an article on the resurgent stock market climbing to levels attained just before the crash of October 1987, a headline asks, "Déjà Vu or a Different Story?"

The term in use, correctly, by singer Judy Collins, quoted by Robert Greenman, *Words That Make A Difference*:

" 'Send in the Clowns' was two years old when I first heard it," Miss Collins recalls, "and Sinatra had already recorded it. But as soon as I heard it, I knew it belonged to me. I have that feeling of déjà vu sometimes about a song. It's almost as though I knew it from another life."

**De Jure.** (day JUR-eh) Something sanctioned by law or created by legal processes. In Latin it means "of right."

Today the term appears most frequently in the context of racial discrimination. De jure discrimination is created by government, such as the laws that once prohibited blacks from serving on juries. **De facto** discrimination, by contrast, is discrimination which, like housing discrimination, exists in fact, though not mandated by law.

The term in use, in a *Wall Street Journal* editorial, July 31, 1989, rebutting criticism of William Lucas, a Bush administration nominee to head the civil rights division of the U.S. Department of Justice:

> "So now Mr. Lucas is being hung for the deadly phrase, 'I frankly do not understand the rest of the question.' This seems to us a perfectly intelligent commentary on the Senator's prose, but the lawyers at the Washington Post and so on profess to take it as proof that a 61-year-old lawyer had never encountered the terms **de facto** and de jure. Give us a break."

Another example, from the January 1990 issue of "Policy Consensus Reports," published by the Johns Hopkins Foreign Policy Institute:

> "The administration should press the South African government to take steps that will facilitate such an improvement in bilateral relations, including releasing Nelson Mandela. . . . President De Klerk appears to be moving toward meeting these conditions, if only in a **de facto** manner. He needs to be encouraged to follow through de jure as well."

**Delphic.** Ambiguous, obscure, sometimes double-edged in meaning.

In ancient Greece, the oracle at the shrine of Delphi delivered utterances that were so obscure or vague that more than one interpretation was possible. So "delphic" has come to describe statements that are ambiguous or enigmatic, headscratchers.

The term in use, from a movie review by J. Hoberman in *The Village Voice*, August 25, 1987 of "Where the Heart Roams," a documentary about romantic novels. Hoberman writes that the film's star is Barbara Cartland, author of 370 novels:

> "Shrouded in chiffon, wrapped in flowers, swathed in pearls, the turbaned Cartland resembles a female imper-

sonator and holds forth like the priestess of the Delphic oracle. Readers, she says, identify with a heroine 'from the position of being in her body,' romance fiction is 'what they want to believe,' for a marriage to work 'you have to make [a man's] prison really attractive.' "

Another example, from *The Economist*, March 4, 1989:

"For umpteen years everyone has known that Israel possesses nuclear weapons. For umpteen years Israel has denied it, intoning instead its Delphic promise to be neither the first country, nor the second, to introduce nuclear weapons to the Middle East."

**Dernier Cri.** (DAIR-nyay KREE) The very latest, most up-to-date, trendiest, most fashionable. French, it literally means, "the last cry" or "the last word."

The term in use, by Ann Conway in the *Los Angeles Times*, March 24, 1989:

"Leave it to billionairess Leona Helmsley of New York to wear le dernier cri in fashion at the Ritz-Carlton hotel last week when she and hubby Harry's Helmsley Palace received the Five Diamond Award from the American Automobile Association. The queenly brunette was all the rage in diamonds and rubies and a cloud of floaty chiffon. . . . "

**Deus Ex Machina.** (DEE-uhs eks MAK-in-uh) An artificial, forced or improbable device that intervenes to resolve an otherwise insoluble problem.

It's a literary device that solves the difficulties in a play or a plot by external means. Literally, it means the god from the machine; in classical Greek drama the god who sorted out the dramatic problem was lowered onto the stage by means of a crane.

The term in use, by Charles Krauthammer, *The Washington Post*, January 6, 1989, criticizing congressional willingness to avoid politically tough decisions by hiding behind blue-ribbon commissions:

"This Congress is willing to let Lloyd Cutler decide its salaries, Abraham Ribicoff close military bases, and some Gramm-Rudman *deus ex machina* cut the budget."

And from Molly Haskell, writing in *The New York Times Magazine*, September 24, 1989, about her husband's driving:

"These are perfectly normal, everyday, garden-variety accidents, the responsibility for which is legally and quite plainly his, but which he must dramatize by invoking a *deus ex machina* to exonerate the dummy in the machina."

**Deutschland über Alles.** (DOICH-lahnt oo-ber AHL-us) "Germany Over All"—the national anthem of Germany from 1922–45.

The anthem's association today is with Hitler's Germany and its title evokes a picture of goose-stepping Nazi troops. Both parts of postwar divided Germany, the Federal Republic of Germany and the German Democratic Republic, adopted different anthems. West Germany's anthem is "Deutschlandlied," the third verse of the 1848 hymn of which "Deutschland über Alles" is the first verse.

Frequently, in current usage, another idea is substituted for the word "Deutschland" to convey the suggestion of an undesirable or fanatical adherence to a dubious goal.

The term in use, from "Tyranny of the Couples" by Gerri Hirshey in *The Washington Post Magazine*, February 14, 1988:

"Call them coupleniks, these fortunate folks, these devotees to Coupledom Uber Alles. They tend to be between 30 and 45, married or cohabitating. They tend to 'dialogue' for hours on all details of their coupleness, their twin corduroys bulging with tile samples and paint chips."

Another example, from George Will, *The Washington Post*, December 3, 1989:

"The wall led to West Germany's Ostpolitik that fueled, through human contacts, explosive pressures behind the wall. That is why for years German foreign policy was 'deténte uber alles.'"

**Diaspora.** (digh-AS-puh-ruh) From Greek, meaning "a scattering" or "to scatter about." The unwilling dispersion of a community following a defeat or misfortune.

That's its general meaning. Capitalized, the word refers to the scattering of the Jews from Palestine following the Babylonian Captivity and unsuccessful Jewish revolts against Roman rule. "Diaspora" also refers to the body of Jews living in countries other than Israel.

The term in use, by T.R. Reid in *The Boston Globe*, August 22, 1987, writing about rumors that Gary Hart planned to reenter the race for the Democratic presidential nomination after he dropped out:

> "In the weeks after his bitter speech of withdrawal, there was a *diaspora* of Hart campaign workers and contributors to the campaigns of other Democratic contenders."

**Dickensian.** An adjective drawn from the name of novelist Charles Dickens (1812-1870), alluding to the stark scenes of injustice and deprivation or the memorable characters that appear in his novels.

Dickens, one of the great English novelists of the Victorian age, wrote books noted for their social outrage. Through his eyes, more than any other English writer of the time, we see the misery of the London slums, the harsh life of workers in the mills, the evils of child labor, the nonsensical and maddening toils of the law. His novels are filled with a multitude of characters memorable for unforgettable details of appearance or speech or personality—some notable for their kindness and virtue, others even more so for shocking cruelty, cloaked in pious statements of conventional morality. The names of his villains are wonderfully suggestive: Heep, Squeers, Merdstone, Bounderby.

The term in use, in Scott Turow's 1987 novel, *Presumed Innocent*, setting the squalid scene for his murder mystery:

> "Even in the best of times, the Office of the Kindle County Prosecuting Attorney has a dismal aspect. Most deputies work two to an office in a space of Dickensian grimness."

**The Die is Cast.** There's no turning back now.

The phrase comes from gambling with dice (one of a pair of dice is a die). Once thrown, the dice can't be taken back and the thrower must live with the results.

The statement (in Latin, "Jacta alea est") is attributed to Julius Caesar as he crossed the **Rubicon** with his army. As Plutarch put it in his *Lives:*

> "Using the proverb frequently in their mouths who enter upon dangerous and bold attempts, 'The die is cast,' he took the river."

Shakespeare used the phrase also in *Richard III* (1592):

> I have set my life upon the cast,
> And I will stand the hazard of the die:
> think there be six Richmonds in the field.

The term in use, by Mary McCarthy, *The New York Review of Books*, January 25, 1973, in a review of David Halberstam's **The Best and the Brightest:**

> "His [Halberstam's] determination to view Vietnam as an American tragedy means that the outcome is ineluctable, foreordained (cf. the 'would's and 'were to be's), and that all those **Rubicons** should be invisible to the participants; nobody ever says, 'Well, the die is cast.' "

Another example, by Jean Marbella, *The Los Angeles Times*, November 12, 1989, writing on gender differences in human beings:

> "The genetic die is cast at conception, but it takes a couple of months before the net result becomes apparent."

**Dienbienphu.** (dyen-byen-foo) The site of a disastrous military defeat.

Dienbienphu was a French military outpost in northern Indochina before the French colony became North Vietnam. In 1954 the garrison was besieged for 55 days by the Vietminh, the communist guerrilla army led by Ho Chi Minh. The French troops gave up in May 1954, and the fort's name became a symbol of arrogant military miscalculation.

French military strategists had devised what they thought was a trap to bring the elusive Vietminh into the open for a European-style battle in which superior French technology would destroy a primitive guerrilla force. The French established their position in a valley and left the high ground to the Vietminh in the serene conviction that the guerillas had no artillery; and if they did, they would not know how to use it. Both assumptions were false, and the French suffered the consequences.

The term in use, by Charles Paul Freund in *The New Republic*, "The **Zeitgeist** Checklist," January 25, 1988:

> "However long the siege of Khost lasts, Afghan rebels have won an important battle, a psychological Dien Bien Phu."

**Dionysian (Bacchic).** (DIGH-uh-NISH-ee-uhn, BAK-ik) An adjective taken from the name of Dionysus, the Greek god of wine and fertile crops (Bacchus was his Roman counterpart), meaning wild, frenzied, uninhibited and sensuous; orgiastic. According to mythology, he invented wine and encouraged cultivation of the grapevine. He was worshiped at festivals celebrating the return of spring. Greek drama is thought to have originated in the ceremonies performed in the god's honor.

The followers of Dionysus could take frightening turns in the frenzy of their worship: in Euripedes' play *The Bacchants* (or *The Bacchae*, 408-406 B.C.), the king of Thebes is killed, torn to pieces by his own mother during the rites. In Rome, the festivals (Bacchanalia) were notable for drunkenness and generally deranged behavior. So today Dionysian or **Bacchanalian** orgies are wild, licentious and drunken parties.

The term in use, by Lance Morrow in *Time* magazine, January 11, 1988, looking back on 1968:

> "In the great collision of generations, the young created their own world, a 'counterculture' as Historian Theodore Roszak first called it, and endowed it with the significances

and pseudo-profundities of a New World. No one had ever
had sex before, no one had ever had the Dionysian music,
the sacramental drugs, the world struggling back to its
protomagical state."

**Disinformation.** False information deliberately planted by a government or its intelligence services to manipulate public opinion or
fulfill some other political purpose. The word comes from the Russian "dezinformatsiya," part of the title of a special branch of the
Soviet secret service.

The United States has frequently accused the Soviet Union of
planting disinformation in the press of Third World countries to spur
anti-American sentiment. For example, the Soviets have circulated
stories that accused the Pentagon of creating the AIDS virus and other
bacteriological weapons designed to kill Cubans and Africans. But
the United States has also used the technique, and in some cases such
plants by American agents abroad have been picked up by American
reporters reading the local press. Such stories reported back to the
United States as fact are referred to as "blowback."

The term in use, as quoted in *The Washington Post*, December 18,
1989:

> "The U.S. military's Panama-based Southern Command
> accused the government of Gen. Manuel Antonio Noriega
> of engaging in a 'disinformation campaign' after it blamed
> four American officers for a shooting incident last night in
> which one of them was killed by a Panamanian soldier."

Another example, in a 1986 case in which the American government planted stories abroad that U.S. military action was imminent
against Libyan leader Gadhafi. In an article in *The Washington Post*,
October 5, 1986, Bob Woodward described the disinformation plan
and offered the following:

> "A former CIA officer said that the agency normally under-
> takes small, low-level disinformation campaigns in a few
> countries or a single country. But in the current anti-
> Gadhafi plan, the former officer said, 'the fire of disinfor-
> mation was supposed to sweep across the Middle East and

Europe . . . and no one was supposed to notice? They were kidding themselves.' "

**Disraeli, Benjamin.** (diz-RAY-li) A British statesman and novelist who championed expansion of the Empire. He lived from 1804 to 1881 and twice served as prime minister.

He was of Italian-Jewish descent, but his father's quarrel with a synagogue led to Benjamin's baptism as a Christian—making his political career possible, since Jews were excluded from Parliament until 1858. (This brings to mind a famous Disraeli riposte to a slur by Daniel O'Connell in 1835: "Yes, I am a Jew, and when the ancestors of the right honorable gentleman were brutal savages in an unknown island, mine were priests in the temple of Solomon.")

As the author of flamboyant novels, Disraeli cut quite a figure in London society with his extravagant dress and affected manners. His first four attempts to win a seat in Parliament failed, but he was finally elected as a Tory. His unconventional style and appearance were not popular with colleagues at first, but eventually he rose to positions of leadership; he became prime minister for the first time in 1867.

His rivalry with William Gladstone, leader of the Liberal Party, established the issues of the Victorian age. As James Morris put it in *Heaven's Command: An Imperial Progress*:

> "They might have been cast by some divine theatrical agency for their parts in the drama, so exactly suited were they to their roles. . . . They represented two complementary impulses in the British political genius: the idealistic impulse, which wished to make Britain the paragon of principle, [and] the urge for glory, which fed upon the exotic, the flamboyant, even the slightly shady."

Disraeli opted for the glory of imperial expansion. The English, he stated in 1872, had a choice: to be the subjects of an insular and comfortable England or of an empire that commanded the respect of the world. He charmed Queen Victoria and made her Empress of India, a title she relished.

An example of his swashbuckling political style—one that must bring groans of envy to today's would-be foreign policy buccaneers—

can be seen in one of his great triumphs, the acquisition by Britain of shares in the Suez Canal Company, purchased from the profligate Khedive of Egypt under the noses of the French. According to Morris, Disraeli sent his private secretary, Montague Corry, to Baron Edmund de Rothschild to ask for a loan of four million pounds for the purchase. Corry's report of the conversation:

Rothschild: "When?"
Corry: "Tomorrow."
Rothschild (pausing to eat a muscatel grape and spit out the skin): "What is your security?"
Corry: "The British government."
Rothschild: "You shall have it."

Political columnist Mark Shields invokes Disraeli's shrewdness (and ability to turn a phrase) in his column (*The Washington Post*, June 27, 1988) "The Disraeli Test":

"These candidate chronicles recall Benjamin Disraeli's formulation concerning the two requisites for political leadership: That a man (in spite of Queen Victoria, Ben was no feminist) know himself and that he also know his times. Four years ago, the Democratic presidential contest between Gary Hart and Walter Mondale, according to analyst Alan Baron, pitted one candidate who completely understood the times but didn't know how old he was against another who knew himself thoroughly but thought 1984 was 1936. This year, the question is, do Michael Dukakis and George Bush pass the Disraeli test?"

**DNA.** The abbreviation for deoxyribonucleic acid. It's an essential element of all living things—the building material of chromosomes, which control heredity, and are present in every cell.

Recombinant DNA is a product of laboratory tinkering—or genetic engineering—in which DNA is broken up and spliced with DNA from other organisms, to produce living things that have abilities or traits Mother Nature never thought of.

The DNA molecule is shaped like a double spiral, and when you see references to the "**double helix**" that is what is being referred to.

The term in use, by Ellen Goodman in the *The Washington Post*, November 24, 1988:

> "In America, families are spliced and recombined in as many ways as DNA. Every year our Thanksgiving tables expand and contract, place settings are removed and added. A guest last year is a member this year. A member last year may be an awkward outsider this year. How many of our children travel between alienated halves of their heritage, between two sets of people who share custody of their holidays."

**Doctors' Plot.** An alleged conspiracy by nine prominent Soviet doctors to murder high Soviet government and Communist Party officials and marshals in the Soviet army. It turned out to be a frame-up.

In January 1953, *Izvestia* reported nine doctors had been arrested and charged with the poisoning deaths of two officials and the attempted murder of others. The doctors, at least six of whom were Jewish, were accused of working for American and British intelligence.

These arrests presaged another of Stalin's bloody purges, but he died on March 5, before the doctors could be tried and his plans implemented. In April *Pravda* reported that the charges had been investigated and found to be false and that the confessions had been obtained through torture. The doctors were cleared and released, except for two who had died under interrogation.

In his secret speech before the 20th Party Congress three years later, Nikita Khrushchev accused Stalin of personally ordering the investigations of the doctors for the spurious plots.

Thus the term has come to mean an elaborate attempt to accuse antagonists of conspiring to do evil.

The term in use, by Charles Paul Freund in *The New Republic*, June 6, 1988:

> "Meese's firing of Terry Eastland, lest Eastland quit first, has a sad Doctor's Plot air about it. Even the *Washington Times* thinks the Justice Department is going down the drain."

**Dog in the Manger.** A spiteful character who prevents another from using or enjoying something, even though he has no intention of using it himself.

The expression comes from a fable about a dog who settled himself in the manger and would not let the ox eat the hay, even though the dog couldn't and wouldn't eat it himself.

The term in use, by James Grant in the December 1988 *Spy*, commenting on recent financial news:

> "You may remember the daggers-drawn battle for Federated Department Stores waged earlier this year by R. H. Macy & Co. and Campeau Corporation. After Robert Campeau won, Macy chairman Edward Finkelstein expressed relief. Given the weakness in retail sales, he said, 'I'm very pleased I don't have to deal with it and he does.'
>
> " 'It's the story of my life,' Campeau has said of his dog-in-the-manger critics. 'I like to take risks.' "

**Dooley, Mr.** See Mr. Dooley.

**Don Quixote.** See Quixote.

**Doppelgänger.** (DOP-pul-GENG-er) A ghost or spirit that is the double of a living person, representing another side of his nature— and usually an unpleasant one. An alter ego. From the German words doppel, meaning double, and gänger, meaning walker.

The term in use, by Terri Minsky in a July 1989 *Premiere* magazine profile of actor Michael Keaton and the movie *Batman:*

> "It [Gotham City] is the home of teeming masses, but more important, of two disfigured men—one physically (the Joker, formerly mob stooge Jack Napier, whose bizarre countenance is the result of falling in a vat of acid), and the other emotionally. They would be each other's doppel-ganger, and their confrontation would be the ultimate conflict between good and evil."

Another example, from Richard Brookhiser, *Time*, December 11, 1989:

> "A specter is haunting conservatives—the specter of the end of Communism. Our nightmare, our adversary, our dark doppelgänger for the past 40 years seems to be fading away."

**Dorian Gray.** One who leads a life of sin behind an outwardly innocent appearance.

The name comes from the central character of a novel by Oscar Wilde, *The Picture of Dorian Gray* (1891). A portrait is painted of the young Dorian Gray, an elegantly handsome man who leads a degenerate life. He expresses his wish always to remain as attractive and young as he is in the portrait. As he sinks deeper into a life of vice, his corruption shows on the face of the portrait, but his own face remains unblemished. In the end, the tormented Gray kills the artist and stabs the painting. But it is Gray who is found at the foot of his portrait with the knife in his heart, his face grotesquely aged. And the picture is once again that of a young and handsome man.

The term in use, by columnist Russell Baker in *The New York Times*, March 13, 1989, commenting on the behavior of major league baseball players:

> "Such things do not evoke visions of the boys of spring. They describe the lives of the rich, the arrogant and the corrupt. Dorian Gray stalks the diamond."

Another example, from Cathy Campbell, *The Village Voice*, November 7, 1989, on the updating of Quaker Oats' advertising icon, Aunt Jemima:

> "The mammylike image of Aunt Jemima—an immaculate deception [see **Immaculate Conception**]—has functioned as the inverse to Dorian Gray's portrait: never aging, never directly reflecting the sins of the master or the socioeconomic gains (however limited) of black Everywoman."
> [See **Everyman.**]

**Double Helix.** In its non-scientific meaning, two commingled strands or a complex intermingling.

In science, double helix describes the shape of **DNA,** the building block of human genes. The double helix was discovered by Francis Crick and James Watson in 1953, for which they received the Nobel Prize.

"Helix" derives from Latin and Greek, and means "spiral." The shape of the double helix is usually described as similar to a spiral staircase.

The term in non-scientific use, by Sharon Thompson in her review of Margaret Atwood's novel *Cat's Eye,* in *The Village Voice,* March 21, 1989:

> "A double-helix bildung [a German term meaning 'forma-
> tion,' as in the history and psychological development of a
> character], the novel combines adolescence and middle age
> to map two stories of development."

**Doublespeak.** The use of euphemisms and other obfuscations to avoid direct statements of fact. It is a hybrid of George Orwell's "newspeak" and "doublethink," from his novel 1984. Newspeak was the language created by the dictatorship, drained of historic meaning; doublethink was the ability to hold two conflicting ideas at the same time, a useful habit of thinking cultivated by Big Brother, the Sta-linesque dictator in Orwell's grim totalitarian vision.

The term "doublespeak" was coined at the annual meeting of the National Council of Teachers of English held in November 1971, according to Walker Gibson, Professor Emeritus of the University of Massachusetts at Amherst, who was in attendance. It is defined as "dishonest and inhumane uses of language" and was an outgrowth of concern expressed by delegates about lack of candor by the U.S. government in communicating with Americans about the Vietnam war. Clearly this was a problem crying out for a descriptive name, and doublespeak has come into wide use. Sometimes it is attributed mistakenly to Orwell himself. [See **-Speak.**]

*Doublespeak*, a book by William Lutz, chairman of the Committee on Public Doublespeak of the NCTE, cites examples from government, business, advertising and academia. Some gems from his collection:

—A company does not lay off or fire workers, they are "dehired" or "non-retained";

—People riding a roller coaster at the 1986 World's Fair would not get sick and throw up, but they might experience an "occasional protein spill";

—The U.S. military invasion of Grenada in 1984 was a "predawn vertical insertion."

The term in use, by Maud Lavin in *The Village Voice*, January 2, 1990, reviewing Nancy Reagan's memoir *My Turn*:

". . . Nancy claims over and over that (although she wanted Don Regan to go and said so to Ronnie) she really had little power and influence. This leaves her mired in vague doublespeak. . . . After recounting all the unfair flack she got for engineering Regan's departure, Nancy proudly describes the praise she got for it as well."

**Doyen, Doyenne.** (DWA-yeh, DWA-yehn) A French noun for the senior member or leader of a group or profession—the dean, or for women, the superior of a convent. Doyen is the masculine form, doyenne the feminine.

The masculine form in use, in *The Economist*, February 4, 1989:

"Satyajit Ray, the doyen of Indian film-makers, said recently that he would not be seen in the 'filth' and discomfort of a Calcutta cinema."

Another example, from Aram Bakshian, Jr., *The American Spectator*, May 1989, reviewing *The Lyre of Orpheus* by Robertson Davies:

"If you are among the growing number of readers who resort to fiction as a mental muscle relaxant, Robertson

Davies is not your kind of novelist. The doyen of Canadian authors refuses to succumb to the trite or trendy."

The feminine form in use, in a United Press International story, January 21, 1988, describing the efforts to preserve the **Art Deco** district of Miami Beach:

"Preservationists rediscovered the old hotels. Led by deco doyenne Barbara Capitman, a crusader with a knack for publicity, they were initially resented as outsiders trying to impede new development."

**Draconian.** (dray-KOH-nee-uhn) If capitalized, the adjective means pertaining to, or characteristic of, Draco's code. In lower case, it means particularly harsh, severe or punitive.

Draco was a lawgiver of Athens in the 7th century B.C. He was appointed to stop the practice of individual revenge for wrongs and replace it with public justice and punishment. His code was noted for its use of the death penalty for many offenses, and was said to have been written in blood, not ink. Most of Draco's code was abolished by another famous lawgiver, **Solon.**

The term in use, by *The New York Times* of August 15, 1988, in an editorial on air pollution control:

"Some 70 cities will fail to bring their ozone levels to Federal safety levels by the present deadline of August 31. Some will miss by a mile. Air in the New York region, breathed by 17 million people, sometimes contains 50 percent more ozone than permitted. The law provides for sanctions, but they are so Draconian that in practice Congress won't let them be applied."

Another example, from a *Wall Street Journal* editorial on the indictment of junk-bond king Michael Milken, March 31, 1989:

"We know that Mr. Giuliani was a politically ambitious prosecutor; he is after all currently running for Mayor of New York. We are entitled to suspect that his ambition played a part in his prosecutions. . . . We know he was a principal force in expanding the draconian RICO law beyond organized crime as commonly understood, applying it to financial figures, starting with Marc Rich in 1984."

**Dreyfus, Dreyfus Affair.** (DRAY-fuhs) A wrenching political scandal that dominated French politics and caught the world's attention at the turn of this century. The Dreyfus case stands as a metaphor for gross and cruel injustice, vicious bigotry and government malfeasance.

Alfred Dreyfus (1859-1935), a captain in the French army, was accused in 1894 of passing military secrets to the Germans. Although Dreyfus adamantly maintained his innocence and the evidence against him was thin, he was convicted of treason, stripped of his rank and honors in a humiliating public ceremony and imprisoned on Devil's Island. His persecutors found him easy to suspect because he was a Jew and the French army, like French society, was rife with anti-Semitism.

Gradually evidence built up clearly indicating the guilt of another officer, Major Ferdinand Walsin Esterhazy; Dreyfus gained adherents to his cause. After the army could no longer suppress the case against him, Esterhazy was court-martialed—but acquitted within minutes. At this point, the Paris newspaper *L'Aurore* published Emile Zola's famous open letter "**J'accuse**," in which the noted writer charged the government and military with covering up the truth.

The case broadly divided France. Royalist, militarist, nationalist and Roman Catholic elements of French society lined up in support of the army; republican, socialist and anticlerical forces lined up behind Dreyfus. New evidence caused Esterhazy to flee to England. Another court martial of Dreyfus was assembled; unable to admit error, the military court found Dreyfus guilty. Public outcry increased, and he was pardoned by the president. Public opinion in France and around the world demanded more, and Dreyfus was ultimately exonerated by the Supreme Court of Appeals in 1906 after years of suffering and political agony for France. (German documents published in 1930 established that Esterhazy was indeed the guilty party.)

The term invoked, by Robert C. Maynard in *The Washington Post Book World*, reviewing Taylor Branch's *Parting of the Waters*, November 20, 1988. Maynard discusses the allegations of Soviet influence made by the FBI against Dr. Martin Luther King's friend Stanley Levison:

> "To this day, the evidence on which Hoover based his allegations of Soviet influence on King associate Stanley Levison has never been released by the FBI, and Levison remains an American Dreyfus."

Another example, from Mark Silk, *The New York Times Magazine*, April 19, 1987, on a dispute within the history department of Princeton University:

> "As the German historian James Joll has pointed out, the case became 'a kind of historical Dreyfus affair . . . in which the original issues have often been obscured by the personal virulence and moral indignation with which Abraham has been attacked and the bitter and polemical tone of his replies.' "

**Droit du Seigneur.** (drwa doo say-NYUUR) French, meaning "the lord's right"; the term is used satirically to describe someone asserting rights or authority in a grandiose or overbearing fashion.

Originally, in medieval Europe, the right of the lord was the right to sleep with the bride of any of his vassals on their wedding night. But the custom appears to have existed on a theoretical basis, if at all; *Brewer's Dictionary of Phrase and Fable* suggests it may have been a revenue-raising measure, with the lord of the manor accepting payments instead of insisting on exercising his right.

The term in use, by Mary Battiata in an interview with British actor John Hurt, in *The Washington Post*, May 23, 1988, on his home in Kenya:

> "It's not unheard of for newcomers to this somewhat baronial way of life to feel a twinge of uneasiness at how far their First World dollars go in a country where high unemployment and crushing rural poverty still dovetail with a kind of post-colonial *droit du seigneur*. Hurt is no exception."

**Dunkirk.** A city on the northern coast of France near the French-Belgian border and a metaphor for the abandonment of a position under threat of total disaster.

Dunkirk was the scene of the greatest military evacuation in history. During World War II, from May 26 to June 4, 1940, the main body of the British army and the remaining French, Polish and Belgian troops, in full retreat before advancing German forces, abandoned the European mainland. About 340,000 men were rescued from the beach by a ragtag armada of Royal Navy ships, ferries, fishing boats and yachts while men and vessels were under attack by vast formations of German bombers.

The term in use, by David Stockman, the first budget director of the Reagan administration, in his 1986 book *The Triumph of Politics:*

> "This foreboding sense of being overtaken by events and economic conditions motivated the alarmist tone of my GOP economic Dunkirk memo. The split betweeen tax cutters and budget balancers was already gaining new intensity within the recently victorious conservative governing coalition. A Dunkirk-scale economic setback might be the final outcome by November 1982."

**Dybbuk.** (DIB-book) A Hebrew word meaning "evil spirit," or "a clinging thing." In Jewish folklore, it is a migrating demon or malevolent spirit of a dead person that enters the body of a human being and renders them mad or corrupt. Today it is used figuratively.

In pre-modern times, those unfortunates who went insane, became hysterical or suffered epileptic or other seizures were thought to have been entered by a dybbuk, just as Christians feared witchcraft or possession by the devil. Dybbuks can be cast out by holy men, in a fashion not unlike the procedures of the Roman Catholic Church to exorcise demons.

*The Dybbuk* is the title of a classic play of Yiddish literature; the more recent *The Tenth Man* (1959), by Paddy Chayefsky, is about a dybbuk.

The term in use in a contemporary political context, as quoted by *The New York Times*, November 6, 1989:

"Jews, says Albert Vorspan, senior vice president of the Union of American Hebrew Congregations, 'do not have to support Jesse Jackson out of some misconceived Jewish guilt,' but nor should they reflexively judge Mr. Dinkins guilty of associating with Mr. Jackson without assessing his own record.

" 'There is a name for that—it is racism,' Mr. Vorspan said. 'It is time to exorcise that dybbuk, lest Jesse Jackson become our excuse for racial stereotyping and hatred.' "

# E

**East Lynne.** To say "Tonight we play East Lynne" is to suggest that one is about to be treated to a tear-jerking display of bathos and purple prose. It comes from *East Lynne*, a hugely popular English novel by Mrs. Henry Wood published in 1861, which became a hugely popular play. The story was a sentimental, multiple-hanky weeper in which the heroine abandons her husband for another man but returns in disguise to care for her children.

The term in use, by Thomas M. Disch in *The Nation*, April 23, 1988, in a review of a made-for-TV movie on homelessness:

> " . . . they sink to ever more fearful and life-threatening depths of the welfare system, until the mother is faced with a final soul-crushing choice: to save her daughter's life she must seem to abandon her. The last scenes rival East Lynne for their capability of putting a lump in the throat, but a drama about homelessness that did not invite pathos would be an act of cowardice."

**Echt.** (ekt) A German word meaning the real thing; typical, true, genuine.

The term in use by Jonathan Yardley in *The Washington Post*, September 14, 1988, reviewing P. J. O'Rourke's *Holidays in Hell*:

> "His [O'Rourke's] pose—his journalistic persona—that of the tough, cynical man of the world: the *echt* foreign correspondent."

**Eddie Haskell.** A character in the popular American TV series "Leave It to Beaver" who was a neighbor boy notable for smarmily obsequious behavior to adults.

The term in use in a *Time* heading in its "Grapevine" column, November 7, 1988:

> "Eddie Haskell Lives. Dan Quayle knows that manners matter. When he found that he was on the list of Veep prospects, a job he deeply desired, he made a point of calling the Bush campaign and asking for permission to acknowledge that he was under consideration. He was the only prospect to do so."

**Edwardian.** Refers to English life and letters during the reign of King Edward VII (1901-1910).

The period followed the Victorian era and was characterized by a relaxation of the conservatism that marked the old queen's reign. The king himself symbolized the era: he was charming and fond of good food, good company, yachting and horse racing. He supported philanthropic causes, traveled widely to promote peace, and was popular with his people. Edward's reign was a period of opulence and elegance, at least for the wealthy few, and is viewed nostalgically as a time of ease and tranquility before the horrors of World War I.

But changes were afoot. Writers like George Bernard Shaw and H.G. Wells were challenging old ideas and values; expansion of the vote was bringing the Labour Party increasing representation in the House of Commons; and militant women were demonstrating for the vote. Abroad, the rising power of Germany and the United States was leading to great changes in the international order established in the Victorian period.

The term in use, by Gore Vidal in his essay "What Robert Moses Did to New York City" (from *Matters of Fact and Fiction: Essays 1973-1976*, Random House, 1977):

> "From Yale Moses went to Oxford where he succumbed entirely to the ruling-class ethos of that glamorous place. For young Moses the ruling class of Edwardian England was the most enlightened the world had ever known, and its benign but firm ordering of the lower orders at home and the lesser breeds abroad ought, he believed, to be somehow transported to our own notoriously untidy, inefficient and corrupt land."

Another example, from *The New York Times*, January 18, 1982, in Phil Gailey's profile of Washington insider Craig Spence:

" . . . Mr. Spence, who is something of a mystery man who dresses in Edwardian dandy style."

**Élan.** (ay-LAHN) French: dash, spirit, impetuous ardor.

An example of the idea of such spirit raised to an almost mystical level is presented in Barbara Tuchman's history of World War I, *The Guns of August*. The French army, rebuilding its pride after the disastrous defeat of the Franco-Prussian War of 1870, embraced the idea of "élan vital," the French spirit, "the idea with a sword," which would give France the winning edge even when faced by the superior numbers and equipment of the German army. In military terms, this meant reliance on attack; a defensive strategy was deemed to be alien to the French soul.

The term in use, by Tom Mathews in *Newsweek*, May 1, 1989, in writing about the revival of *Vanity Fair* magazine by editor Tina Brown:

"With uptown élan and Front Page gusto, Brown has taken a heavy little dumpling from Condé Nast and turned it into a real magazine."

Another example, from Vincent Canby's review of the film *Casualties of War*, *The New York Times*, August 18, 1989:

"Mr. [Sean] Penn plays Meserve with terrific élan. There is plausibility in every movement and gesture, and especially in his crafty handsomeness."

**Elmer Gantry.** The title and central character of a 1927 novel by Sinclair Lewis. The name has become a metaphor for corrupt, manipulative evangelical preachers. Gantry is a handsome and charming ex-football player who becomes a successful evangelist. He is also an unscrupulous cheat who plagiarizes his sermons, deludes his innocent followers and steals their donations to his church.

The term in use, as quoted by *The New York Times Magazine*,

April 23, 1989, in a profile of Boston University president John Silber:

> "Silber is quick to deride 'Elmer Gantry' fundamentalism, but what he calls 'religious literacy' is so basic to his understanding of education that, as an ethics professor, he would quiz his students on central points in the Bible and church history *before* they studied Christianity—to illustrate their 'ignorance.' "

**Éminence Grise.** (AY-mee-nonce greez) A powerful, shadowy figure who exercises power through influence with another, rather than in any open, official capacity.

French, it literally means "gray cardinal." The term originated with Father Joseph, confessor and confidential agent of Cardinal Richelieu, the powerful minister of King Louis XIII. Father Joseph wore a gray habit, and his influence on Richelieu earned him the nickname of "Éminence Grise."

In American politics, the expression has been applied to backstage operators such as Mark Hanna, an Ohio businessman who retired in 1895 to devote himself exclusively to putting William McKinley in the White House. Once he succeeded, he held great influence over the president.

The term in use, by John Homans in *The New York Times Magazine*, March 13, 1988, "The Lure of the Political Road," about the young men and women who do advance work in presidential campaigns:

> "At the age of 35, he is the *éminence grise* of the advance world, and indeed, there's some gray in his hair, a fact that was not left unremarked-upon by the advance people from the other campaigns who saw him sitting there."

Another example, also from *The New York Times*, August 6, 1987, describing the unofficial influence exerted by Britain's Prince Charles on contemporary architecture:

> " 'The Prince has become the éminence grise of British architecture,' says Martin Pawley, another critic, who con-

tends that Charles displays 'vast lacunae of ignorance' in speaking out 'uncannily' as a **Luddite** echo of the man in the street but one who regularly overlooks, critics complain, the special design and economic technicalities of a chip factory and low-cost housing."

**The Emperor's New Clothes.** A metaphor for human credulity and folly, from a fairy tale of that title by Hans Christian Anderson.

In the tale, the emperor was given a set of clothes that he was told was visible only to people who were not fools. Word got around. Since no one wanted to admit he could not see the clothes, and thus admit he was a fool, both emperor and subjects praised the wonderful new duds for their elegance and beauty. Finally an innocent child piped up and spoke the truth—that the emperor had no clothes on—and the pretense collapsed.

The term in use, by Brock Yates in a review of *Alice Roosevelt Longworth*, by Carol Felsenthal, in *The American Spectator*, October 1988:

> "How could a woman with such breeding, intelligence, and connections within the inner circles of power have been so impotent? Moreover, why in the fashion of the emperor's new clothes, did so many movers and shakers consider her imprimatur so critical?"

Another example, from *The Economist*, December 9, 1989, discussing democratic reform in Czechoslovakia that began when ordinary people took a stand:

> "Mr. [Vaclav] Havel has long argued that westerners never understood what it meant to live under a regime of hypocrisy, a government which signs human-rights declarations and then jails its critics, says it rules with popular support but simultaneously destroys public life. Once all the greengrocers stood up, Mr. Havel predicted, the seemingly invincible regime would be 'an emperor without clothes.'
> "Events showed that he was right."

**Enfant Terrible.** (ahn-FAHN teh-REE-bluh) A French expression for an outspoken, often talented, individual who does outrageous things, often embarrassing his friends.

The classic example is Oscar Wilde, who said and did indiscreet, outrageous and irresponsible things. In latter-day America, David Stockman was an enfant terrible of the Reagan administration, in which he served as budget director. (Or was he a **wunderkind** who became an enfant terrible?)

Literally, it means a terrible child, unruly, incorrigible, a spoiled brat.

The term in use, by Jonathan Yardley in *The Washington Post*, April 24, 1989:

> "Whittle Communications is the creation of Christopher Whittle, the prodigious *enfant terrible* who rescued *Esquire* magazine by turning it into a survival guide for yuppies and who currently is producing a series of magazines produced to be read in doctors' offices."

And by Richard Berendzen, *The Washington Post*, October 22, 1989, reviewing Harry S. Ashmore's biography of Robert Maynard Hutchins, who became dean of the Yale Law School at age 28:

> "Meteoric Hutchins made his mark. He proposed raising admissions standards and reducing the number of students. He hired impecunious William O. Douglas, who considered Yale students rich, spoiled brats. Soon, the Yale Law School became the *enfant terrible* of legal education."

**The Enlightenment.** Roughly, the 18th century, also called the Age of Reason.

The name is apt. The leading thinkers and politicians of the Enlightenment believed in the idea of human progress, welcomed skepticism, free thinking and science, and possessed an abiding confidence in the power of reason. Their outlook was in part a reaction to the religious wars and persecutions of the 17th century, and they turned their minds away from spiritual matters to the practical.

Religious tolerance grew and the absolute power of the clergy waned. While leading philosophers did not deny the existence of God, they often saw an awesome Creator, a great watchmaker who set the universe in motion rather than the personal, all-knowing deity of the medieval church.

Some of the Enlightenment's major figures were radical. Voltaire assaulted the traditional Christian concept of the world and wrote his "Universal History" from a purely secular point of view. He viewed Christianity as a social phenomenon, and observed, "If God did not exist, it would be necessary to invent him."

The leaders of the American Revolution and of the infant United States were products of this age: Thomas Paine, Thomas Jefferson and John Adams eloquently stated their belief in reason and their commitment to freedom of thought. Jefferson's words are carved around his memorial in Washington: "I have sworn upon the altar of God, eternal hostility against every form of tyranny over the mind of man."

The term in use, by Robert Orsi in his review of *People of God: The Struggle for World Catholicism* by Penny Lernoux, the *Voice Literary Supplement*, June 1989:

> "With *People of God*, Lernoux joins the circle of post-modern political tragedians who, decrying the desiccation of liberalism, look to religion as the hope of a new political culture. Lernoux believes that Enlightenment traditions are dead. In the 'developed' countries, she argues, the liberal mainstays of 'tolerance and freedom' have emptied out into materialism, consumerism, and conformity."

**Epicenter.** The focal point or central point.

When it is earthquakes that are being talked about, the epicenter is the point on the earth's surface that's closest to the point of origin of the quake.

The term in use, by Guy Trebay, in *The Village Voice*, September 15, 1987:

> "After 18 years on Broadway, Speakeasy Antiques is closing shop. One hundred and fifty boxes into the departure, the

store is still packed to the rafters. 'Can you believe we're supposed to be leaving in five days?' asks Bob Brand, surveying a sales floor that makes Fibber McGee's closet seem spare. . . . Proprietors of New York's **kitsch** epicenter, the Brands are natural collectors who met and fell in love over a $3 oak bucket in Vermont."

And from television critic Tom Shales, writing in *The Washington Post*, November 29, 1989 on viewer apathy about television coverage of events in Eastern Europe:

"America isn't the news epicenter it was, and Americans may even subconsciously resent that the big stories are happening elsewhere. Despite the everyday wonders of the satellite link, the **Global Village** may still be a long way off. A National Village prevails. It's one wall that has not fallen."

**Epiphany.** (ih-PIF-uh-nee) Greek: "to show forth."

As a religious term, it refers to a Christian festival commemorating the revelation of Jesus as the Christ during the visit of the Magi. Epiphany is celebrated on January 6.

As a literary expression, it refers to a sudden revelation or understanding. James Joyce coined the term, according to the *Reader's Encyclopedia*, to describe a sudden realization of the essential nature of a thing, person or situation. It is the moment in which " 'the soul of the commonest object . . . seems to us radiant' and may be manifested through any chance word or gesture."

The term in use, in a *New York Times* book review, August 19, 1987, by Michiko Kakutani, of *Herself in Love* by Marianne Wiggins:

". . . the heroine experiences a bizarre epiphany while strolling on the shore: she comes to see a dying, beached whale as a symbol of her own mismanaged life, and she begs, with nearly religious fervor, that it (and presumably she) might be granted a second chance."

And by film critic Vincent Canby, *The New York Times*, December 7, 1984:

> " '2010' is not, however, very mysterious, and although it has its own little epiphanies, they are—is it possible to say?—rather conventional epiphanies."

**Eton, Playing Fields of.** See Playing Fields of Eton.

**Et Tu, Brute?** (et too, BROO-teh) A cry of reproach for an act of treachery or betrayal by a friend or ally.

It's Latin, meaning "And you too, Brutus?" and was Julius Caesar's cry when he saw his friend Brutus among his assassins. The phrase is best known from William Shakespeare's *Julius Caesar*, but is quoted by the Roman historian Suetonius in his *The Lives of the Caesars*.

The term in use, by Bob Lauterborn, *Advertising Age*, November 13, 1989, commenting on the predominance of women working as advertising representatives for magazines:

> "Not long ago I was teasing Don Barr, publisher of *Sports Illustrated*. 'How's it feel to have the last male-dominated sales force in America?' I asked. 'Not so fast,' he said. 'Count again.' Et tu, Brutus?"

The phrase often shows up as "Et tu, ————?" with the writer filling in the blank with the name of a false friend—as Marjorie Williams did in a *Washington Post* essay, August 3, 1988, decrying *Ms.* magazine's decision to print a beauty advertising supplement: It may be smart advertising, argued the disillusioned Ms. Williams, but had *Ms.* forgotten its origins? She asked, "Et tu, *Ms.* magazine?"

Another example, from Kathy O'Malley and Hank Gratteau, the *Chicago Tribune*, November 12, 1989:

> " . . . Et tu, Bruce? Anti-establishment comedy writer Bruce Vilanch, known for the edgy one-liners he writes for people like Bette Midler and Cher, is collaborating with (you may want to sit down) The Osmonds!"

**Everyman.** The ordinary person, John Q. Public, the man in the street, not rich or brilliant or exceptional—just one of us.

The term comes from the title of one of the morality plays of the 15th century, allegorical dramas that served as popular entertainment as well as religious and ethical instruction for the unlettered public. Everyman, the central character, is, of course, the ordinary person. Other characters are virtues, vices and good and bad influences.

In the play, Everyman receives a summons from Death and calls on his friends—Beauty, Fellowship, Kindred and Worldly Goods, among others—to accompany him. Only Good Deeds agrees to attend Everyman to the grave. Not too subtle, but neither was the audience. And today the term "morality play" is used to describe a situation or event that teaches a plain, clear lesson in basic right and wrong.

The term in use, in *The Washington Post*, October 30, 1988:

> "The Bush family reveled in the middle-class life of Midland, Tex. Bush seemed to be Mr. Everyman: YMCA founder and fund-raiser, church elder, Sunday school teacher, baseball coach, bowling team member, community theater promoter."

Another example, from Thomas Boswell, *The Washington Post*, April 19, 1989, on scandals in baseball:

> "Baseball may have to pay a price for marketing Rose as an Everyman symbol of the entire sport."

**Ex Cathedra.** From a position of authority. In Latin, it literally means "from the seat," and was originally applied to the decisions of popes from their seats, or thrones. Thus it means speaking in an official capacity, and not necessarily (as the phrase seems to suggest) shouting out the cathedral door.

In Catholic doctrine, when the Pope speaks ex cathedra, he is addressing matters of Church doctrine on faith or morals, and speaks with infallibility. In general usage, the phrase is applied to statements uttered by authority and may be used ironically to describe dogmatic, self-certain statements.

The term in use, by J. M. Coetzee, *The New Republic*, January 8 & 15, 1990, reviewing Alan Paton's *Save the Beloved Country*:

> ". . . Paton was turned, not wholly unwillingly, into a sage and oracle. . . . The effects can be seen not only in the increasingly ex cathedra tone of his pronouncements, and in his tendency to think, speak, and write in brief, easy-to-chew paragraphs, but in his failure to break new ground and to develop as a writer."

# F

**Fabulous Invalid.** That's Broadway, the New York theater world, whose health and future seem forever to be on the verge of collapse. For all its death notices, New York's legitimate theater manages to survive year after year.

The term in use by Jay Carr in *The Boston Globe*, November 18, 1988, reviewing "The Land Before Time," an animated feature movie:

> "Animation, the movies' Fabulous Invalid, gets a real boost from 'The Land Before Time.' "

Another example, from the headline of a February 11, 1990, *New York Times* story on the latest effort to abolish the House of Lords of Britain's Parliament:

> "That Fabulous Invalid, the British House of Lords"

**Fall on One's Sword.** To take full responsibility—and pay the price—for a disastrous turn of events; the ultimate gesture of sacrifice. For example, to acknowledge a grave error by resigning from office.

The term comes from the literal act of penance by those ancient Romans who failed in a grand way. Frequently they were generals who felt honor-bound to take their lives if they were responsible for a defeat in battle.

Distinguished examples from history include Brutus, who is best known for his part in the stabbing assassination of Julius Caesar. He was subsequently defeated by Octavian and Mark Antony at the battle of Philippi in 42 A.D. Recognizing that all was lost, he threw himself on a friend's blade.

During the reign of Augustus, the Roman general Varus led three legions into a trap while attempting to quell a revolt in the German provinces of the Empire. The Roman army was massacred and Varus paid the price: he fell on his sword.

Nowadays, when someone falls on his sword, he usually does so figuratively, as illustrated below.

The term in use, quoted by Hobart Rowen in *The Washington Post National Weekly Edition*, October 12, 1987, discussing a disagreement between Secretary of the Treasury James Baker III and Federal Reserve Chairman Alan Greenspan:

> "When Baker learned from the Fed chairman on Sept. 3 of Greenspan's plan to boost the Federal Reserve discount rate the next day—the first increase in three years—he tried unsuccessfully to persuade Greenspan to ask the Japanese and the Germans to lower their rates in a coordinated action.
>
> " 'It was not a big deal; not something that Baker was going to fall on his sword about,' as one official put it."

Also, by Robert Kuttner in *The New Republic*, December 5, 1988:

> "Representative Barney Frank observes that ACLU-type liberals would have the Democratic Party fall on its sword over issues where liberals have the moral high ground, but ultimately matter less than the big question of economic justice."

**Falstaff, Falstaffian.** Those with the characteristics of jolly Sir John Falstaff, who shows up in William Shakespeare's plays (*Henry IV: Parts I and II, The Merry Wives of Windsor,* and his death is treated in *Henry V*). He's fat, engaging, witty, a rogue who takes robust enjoyment in drinking, wenching and other sins. He is shamelessly self-indulgent and a monumental liar, but his zest for life makes him irresistible.

The term in use, from Howell Raines, *The New York Times*, November 19, 1989:

> "Bobby Bryan struck me as a throwback to the kind of mythic characters one encountered in the hunting camps and fishing lodges of the region. He has a grizzled beard and is built along Falstaffian lines."

Another example, by Peter J. Boyer on National Public Radio's "Morning Edition" program, February 28, 1989, describing the "Today" show's ebullient weatherman Willard Scott as "the Falstaff of morning television."

And by George Will, *Newsweek*, December 4, 1989, on Robert Bork's *The Tempting of America:*

> "Writing well is the best revenge and Bork brings Falstaffian zest to the cheerful fun of making his adversaries look foolish."

**Faulknerian.** Resembling the characters, themes or settings of the works of William Faulkner, the American novelist and short story writer (1897-1962) who won the Nobel Prize for Literature in 1949 and two Pulitzer prizes.

His characters are prisoners of their pasts, their society, their personalities. As Malcolm Cowley noted in his introduction to *The Portable Faulkner* in 1946: "They also carry, whether heroes or villains, a curious sense of submission to their fate. . . . They are haunted, obsessed, driven forward by some inner necessity. . . . Even when they seem to be guided by a conscious purpose . . . it is not something they have chosen by an act of will, but something that has taken possession of them. . . . "

Faulkner was born and lived in Mississippi most of his life. His writing explored the Southern past, the burden of slavery and the catastrophe of the Civil War, as well as conflict between the old ways and modern life and relations between the races.

The setting for his stories is the imaginary Mississippi county of Yoknapatawpha, where he created a rich and detailed variety of characters: decaying aristocrats and cunning, avaricious and unscrupulous rubes. His novels and stories are characterized by tragic themes and bizarre and melodramatic violence.

The term in use, from the *Voice Literary Supplement*, June 1989, in Bill Marx's review of *Sort of Rich*, by James Wilcox:

> "Crazy as life gets in James Wilcox's fictional patch of Southern soil, Tula Springs, Louisiana, the goings-on don't match the lusty or tragic stuff of Yoknapatawpha

County. 'It doesn't seem as Faulknerian as I had hoped,' observes former New Yorker Gretchen Dunbar, the addled heroine of Wilcox's latest expert farce, *Sort of Rich*. 'People don't seem really weighed down by the Civil War and all that.' But what the suburbanized nouveau crackers [See **Nouveau Riche**] lack in weightiness they make up in wry absurdity."

**Faustian Bargain.** (FOWST-ee-uhn) A bargain with the Devil. Selling one's soul in order to gain power, knowledge, wealth, beauty, eternal youth or other similarly desirable attribute.

It is an age-old theme: one may gain short-term delights, but the Devil always comes to collect in the end.

It comes from a body of literature about a quasi-legendary 16th century German magician who became the subject of numerous literary and musical works. In 1587 *The History of Dr. Faustus, the Notorious Magician and Master of the Black Arts* appeared and became popular; Christopher Marlowe used him as the central character in his *Tragical History of Dr. Faustus* in the late 16th century. In the 19th century, Goethe developed the theme of the struggle between the best and worst elements of man's nature and Wagner, Berlioz, Gounod and others wrote operas on the subject, the best known of which is Gounod's *Faust*.

The term in use, by Godfrey Hodgson, *All Things to All Men: The False Promise of the Modern American Presidency*:

> "With this electronic **Mephistopheles,** presidents have made a 'Faustian deal' because the same instrument that elects them so often has turned out to be the engine of their destruction."

**Fawkes, Guy.** See Guy Fawkes.

**Feet of Clay.** A weakness or hidden flaw in a greatly admired person.

The term comes from the Book of Daniel in the Old Testament. Nebuchadnezzar, king of Babylon, dreamed of an image which had a head of gold, breast and arms of silver, belly and thighs of brass, legs of iron and feet of iron and clay. According to Daniel's prophecy the feet were the image's weakness and the dream foretold the fall of Nebuchadnezzar's empire.

The term in use, by Tom Callahan, *The Washington Post*, November 12, 1989, on banned-for-gambling baseball great Pete Rose:

> "Clay feet and other body parts aside, Charlie Hustle's baseball honor was always absolute, and in fact was on display that same week in Chicago."

Another example, from *The Washington Post*, December 8, 1989, quoting reaction to racist and antisemitic statements in the recently published diaries of H.L. Mencken:

> " 'This hero has not only feet of clay, but feet of mud,' said Laurence M. Katz, president of the Baltimore Jewish Council. 'Any respect I ever had for him is shattered.' "

And as the title of an article by Roger Williams, in *Sport*, June, 1986. In "Feet of Clay," Williams observes:

> "American men have not won the French Open in 30 years, despite the likes of Connors and McEnroe. The [clay court] surface is too soft—and so are the Americans."

**Felliniesque.** Fantastic, surreal. An adjective derived from the name of the Italian film director Federico Fellini. As *Readers Encyclopedia* puts it, his films, for which he writes his own screenplays, are "characterized by obscure, intensely personal fantasies" (and for his casting of physically grotesque, non-professional extras to enhance the bizarre context of his stories).

Some of his most famous films are: *La Strada* (1954); *La Dolce Vita* (1959); *8 ½* (1963); *Satyricon* (1969); and *Amarcord* (1973).

The term in use, by John Mintz and Saundra Saperstein Torry in *The Washington Post*, December 8, 1987, describing the scene in Washington during the visit of Soviet leader Mikhail Gorbachev:

> "It was a Felliniesque scene: a woman clad in a garbage bag over her full-length fur coat pacing Lafayette Park from

rally to rally, a man calling himself 'Mr. Wake-Up America' hiring a plane with banner to take his message to the skies, and an outraged Afghan in a curbside argument with a top D.C. police official yelling, 'You will be Soviet slaves.' "

**Fifth Column.** A secret group of traitors or sympathizers with an outside enemy who seek to assist it from within.

The term comes from the Spanish Civil War. In an interview, rebel General Emilio Mola described the four columns of troops advancing on Republican-held Madrid in October 1936. When asked which column would take the city, he said, "The fifth," referring to sympathizers within the city who would rise up when the time was right.

*The Fifth Column* was the title of Ernest Hemingway's only play (1938). The phrase was applied to Nazi sympathizers in Western Europe, and is now used in the broader sense of hidden traitors.

The term in use in a *Washington Post* story, April 18, 1988, on the troubles of Continental Airlines:

"[Continental president Frank] Lorenzo complained about the difficulty of 'trying to run an airline when you have two 'fifth columns' within your airline,' whom he identified as the pilots and the mechanics."

**Film Noir.** (film nwahr) A film **genre** that developed out of the American crime/mystery/thriller movies of the 1940s. Frequently filmed in black and white in seedy urban settings, these films make use of flashbacks and voice-over narrations, usually by the cynical, world-weary hero. The phrase is now used to suggest the atmosphere, style or characters typical of these films.

The term, literally "black film" in French, was coined by French film devotee Nino Frank in 1946. Classics of the genre include *The Maltese Falcon* (1941), *This Gun for Hire* (1942), *Laura* (1944) and *Out of the Past* (1947).

The endings in these movies are not always happy and the hero does not always unambiguously overcome. Leading men such as

Humphrey Bogart, Dana Andrews, Robert Mitchum and Alan Ladd made their mark in these movies, portraying tough, laconic characters clad in rumpled trenchcoats with cigarettes dangling from their lips. They roamed the night streets, which always gleamed with fresh rain in the harsh light of street lamps. These flawed heroes struggled to unravel, but frequently became snared by, the schemes of bad men and wicked women.

Sometimes reference is made simply to "noirish" as in a Joel Siegal review of *Who Framed Roger Rabbit* in Washington's *City Paper*, June 24, 1988: "Cast in the role of Eddie's noirish girlfriend, Joanna Cassidy lacks the wit she displayed so abundantly on the much-missed TV sitcom 'Buffalo Bill.'" The same review speaks of the "LAnoir" of the '50s television series "Peter Gunn" and "Mr. Lucky."

The term in use, by Vic Sussman in a *Washington Post Magazine* description, September 18, 1988, on the horrors of dealing with the Motor Vehicle Division of the District of Columbia government:

> "Sometimes people begin with a little story. My car was stolen, or booted, or my permit went through the washing machine, or my dog ate the title. The clerk, leaning on the counter like a film noir bartender, listens, then ships them out to other rooms: 1063, 1065. . . . "

Another example, from Howard Wornom, writing in *Premiere*, July 1989, on the movie *Batman*:

> "But the big event for Batman took place in 1986, when readers spent nearly $16 for the four-part *The Dark Knight Returns*, the violent, *film-noir*-like saga, set in the future, of an aging Batman coming out of forced retirement."

**Fin de Siècle.** (FAN duh see-EH-kluh) In French, it literally means the end of the century, but in general use it has come to refer to the end of the 19th century. While the phrase once referred to progressive ideas and customs, it now connotes decadence, fatigue, the end of an era.

The term in use, by Tom Mathews in *Newsweek*, May 1, 1989, in a profile of *Vanity Fair's* editor, Tina Brown:

"But as things stand, having so exuberantly glossed the
'80s, Brown now has the chance to define *fin de siecle*
America the way Frank Crowninshield's Vanity Fair captured the '20s, to be to the '90s what Harold Hayes's Esquire
was to the Kennedy years and the Age of Aquarius."

**Final Solution.** The euphemism for Hitler's plan to exterminate the
Jews through a systematic program of mass murder in concentration
camps. According to Robert Leckie in *Delivered from Evil: The Saga
of World War II*, the term was coined by Reinhard Heydrich, the Nazi
leader given by Hitler the "housecleaning" assignment of deciding
the fate of three million Jews in the portion of Poland that Hitler
shared with the Russians. "Heydrich began with the Jews by deport-
ing them to German labor camps, but in his first report to Hitler he
used the now notorious and chilling phrase, 'the final solution,' of the
Jewish problem," Leckie writes.

With its ghastly associations, the term is the definitive attack phrase
for characterizing as reprehensible schemes to eliminate those of
opposing views or values.

The term in typically vitriolic use, by conservative activist James
Garrett in the alternative Dartmouth College student newspaper, *The
Dartmouth Review*, October 19, 1988, likening Dartmouth president
James Freedman to Hitler:

"*Der Freedman* would need such a weapon to carry out his
most precious dream—the 'Final Solution' of the Conservative Problem at Dartmouth."

**Fire and Brimstone.** It's a biblical description of Hell, from the
New Testament's Book of Revelation: a lake of fire and brimstone in
which the damned suffer. Brimstone is sulfur, so picture a volcanic
lake of molten lava.

To preach a fire and brimstone sermon is to threaten the congrega-
tion or others with damnation in hell for their sins, to send a message
in a passionate, fiery style.

The term in use, by Mark Potts in *The Washington Post*, May 22,
1988:

"John F. Welch Jr. has been preaching a fire-and-brimstone philosophy of change since he became chairman of General Electric Co. in 1981."

**Fire When Ready, Gridley.** Actually, the quote is, "You may fire when you are ready, Gridley." These deathless words were uttered by then-Commodore George Dewey, commanding the American fleet at the Battle of Manila Bay on May 1, 1898. (Gridley was the captain of Dewey's flagship.)

The outcome of the battle was a foregone conclusion; the Americans won a glorious victory over a vastly inferior force without losing a single man. Dewey's statement has since become a catch phrase, used in various forms.

An example, from Michael Dolan, writing in Washington, D.C.'s *City Paper*, May 5, 1989:

"Nobody goes into journalism to *work*; if all a newshawk has to do to avoid having to open all those envelopes is pay out some money, then fire when ready, Gridley."

**Fleet Street.** A street in London on which British newspapers have historically located. Today it is used as a synonym for English journalism and newspapers.

The term in use, by Tom Mathews in *Newsweek*, May 1, 1989, in a profile of *Vanity Fair* editor Tina Brown:

"A general-interest magazine can only be as interesting as the mind of its editor. Brown's is quick and eclectic; she may have learned how to read at Oxford; but she learned how to write on Fleet Street; she knows what sells."

Another example, from Richard Corliss, in *Time*, June 19, 1989:

"*Batman* sure has consumer anticipation—in Hollywoodese, 'wanna-see.' Last fall Fleet Street sent out helicopters to get photos from the film's closed London set."

**Flotsam and Jetsam.** In general, useless debris or wreckage, odds and ends, lost people and things.

The terms are from admiralty law, which pertains to ships, their cargoes and the sea. In law, flotsam and jetsam have specific meanings.

Flotsam (derived from the same root as "float") refers to floating goods from a ship that wrecked or sank; jetsam (it is a variant of jettison, from the Latin word meaning "to throw") refers to goods deliberately thrown overboard in an attempt to stabilize and save a ship in distress.

The term in use, by Jonathan Yardley in *The Washington Post Book World*, December 4, 1988, "Looking Back on a Year's Reading":

> " . . . new books, as it turns out, were not the ones that gave me the greatest pleasure or the most delightful surprises. Those came, instead, from three books that for one reason or another had for many years escaped my attention; discovering them, in the midst of 1988's flotsam and jetsam, was a pleasure—not to mention a relief."

Another example, from Nick Ravo in *The New York Times Book Review*, March 3, 1989, on novelist Bobbie Ann Mason:

> "These are somewhat surprising admissions considering that Ms. Mason's fiction is as well known for its pop-culture flotsam as for its western Kentucky setting and hard-luck working-class cast."

**Foggy Bottom.** The neighborhood in Washington, D.C. where the State Department is located, and now a nickname for that institution.

Lower reaches of the area were marshy and flat, generating the mists that gave the place its name. While historians and geologists insist the area was not completely a swamp before, enemies of the Department of State bureaucracy would undoubtedly contend that it is now. The name is irresistibly suggestive of obscure language, muddled thinking and bureaucratic lassitude.

The term in use, by William Safire, in a column on diplomatese, *The New York Times Magazine*, September 10, 1989:

"As previously reported here, *feckless* is the vogue word in the spookspeakeasies for 'ineffective, helpless'; now the word on everybody's lips in Foggy Bottom is *otiose*, 'idle, indolent, lazy.'"

**For Whom The Bell Tolls.** The phrase, from John Donne's *Devotions*, eloquently expresses a powerful concern for his fellow man in one of the most frequently quoted passages in the English language:

"No man is an Island entire of itself; every man is a piece of the Continent, a part of the main; if a clod be washed away by the Sea, Europe is the less, as well as if a promontory were, as well as if a manor of thy friends or of thine own were; any man's death diminishes me, because I am involved in Mankind; and therefore never send to know for whom the bell tolls; it tolls for thee."

Donne (1572?-1631), an English metaphysical poet and dean of St. Paul's Cathedral, wrote satirical and love poetry in his youth ("Go and catch a falling star"). In 1614 he converted from Catholicism to the Anglican church, and became an eloquent and influential preacher.

"For whom the bell tolls" was adopted by Ernest Hemingway as the title of his 1940 novel set in the Spanish Civil War. *Death Be Not Proud*, a book by John Hersey about the death of his child, takes its title from another famous Donne quotation:

Death be not proud, though some have called thee
Mighty and dreadful, for thou art not so. . . .

This is powerful stuff, and puts Donne in the front rank of the—if we may be permitted to create a word—literarily alluded to.

The term in use, by Ralph Ellison in *The New York Times*, March 12, 1989, in a collection of statements by writers on behalf of Salmon

Rushdie in hiding as a result of death threats by Muslim religious leaders objecting to Rushdie's book, *The Satanic Verses:*

> "This story of a man alone against worldwide intolerance, and a book alone against the craziness of the media, can become the story of many others. The bell tolls for all of us."

**Force Majeure.** (fawrs mah-JUHR) French: an irresistible force. In insurance law, an act of God or unavoidable accident.

The term in use by *Publishers Weekly,* October 21, 1988, in a review of *Radical by Design: The Life and Style of Elizabeth Hawes* by Bettina Berch:

> "Seldom heard of today, Hawes was a force majeure during most of her life (1903-1971). . . ."

**Four Horsemen of the Apocalypse.** They're allegorical figures in the New Testament's Book of Revelation, in which St. John envisions the end of the world. Personifying the horrors of war, the riders are Conquest astride a white horse, Slaughter riding a red horse, Famine on a black and Death mounted on a pale horse.

The Spanish novelist Vicente Blasco Ibañez entitled his 1916 book on World War I *The Four Horsemen of the Apocalypse.* But the phrase's most famous application was the handiwork of sportswriter Grantland Rice (1880-1954), describing a football victory by Notre Dame over Army in *The New York Tribune,* October 18, 1924:

> "Outlined against a blue-gray October sky, the Four Horsemen rode again. In dramatic lore they were known as Famine, Pestilence, Destruction and Death. These are only aliases. Their real names are Stuhldreher, Miller, Crowley and Layden." (The cast of characters is a little off, but Rice probably had forgotten to take his New Testament with him to the game.)

Contemporary use of the term is generally jocular. Keying off Rice, the term is applied to any four characters united in an enterprise.

The term in use by Hendrik Hertzberg in *The New Republic*, February 27, 1989, on a book of memos from the Nixon White House:

> *"From: The President* contains pungent memos by H.R. 'Bob' Haldeman, John Ehrlichman, Pat Buchanan, and Chuck Colson—the Four Horsemen of the Nixonian apocalypse—but the best are from the master himself, alone and hunched over his dictaphone far into the night."

**Fragging.** The practice of assassination of American officers by their own troops.

The term originated in the Vietnam war. It comes from fragmentation grenades, the favored instrument for these killings; the grenade would be tossed under the bed or into the tent of the target while he was asleep.

Fraggings frequently involved efforts to get rid of individuals who were considered threats to the rest of their unit due to incompetent or overzealous leadership. Estimates of deaths from fragging vary widely, from about 1,000 officers and non-commissioned officers, to the less than 100 confirmed by the Pentagon.

Now the term is applied figuratively in the sense of a sudden, sneaky and devastating attack.

The term in use, in *The Washington Post*, February 2, 1988, quoting an Iowa politician on the power of *The Des Moines Register* in the Iowa precinct caucuses:

> " 'The Register is capable of fragging you,' says Iowa's Democratic speaker of the House, Donald Avenson, who is working in Missouri Rep. Dick Gephardt's campaign. 'They can open the door, throw in the grenade, and boom, you're finished.' "

**Full-court Press.** An all-out effort, especially in politics and government.

Like many political terms, this one comes from sports, in this case basketball. The term refers to a defense tactic designed to apply intense pressure to keep the offense from moving the ball downcourt or to cause them to lose the ball. Players are covered throughout the full court—as opposed to just the defense's half of the court—in hopes of forcing a turnover. The defense's use of every fair means to do this is a full-court press.

In use in politics and other applications, the phrase seems to have lost its connotation as a defensive measure; it is simply a no-holds-barred, all-out effort. Political lexicologist William Safire notes that the term became part of the lingo of the White House in the Nixon years.

The term in use, quoted in *The Washington Post*, September 8, 1989:

> " 'The word we're getting back from our informant is that the cartels have made a full court press to obtain assault weapons,' said Keith Prager, group supervisor of Operation Exodus, a Miami-based U.S. Customs Service program designed to stop the illegal flow of guns to South America."

A play on the term by Michael Lewis, author of *Liar's Poker*, excerpted in *The Washington Post*, January 28, 1990, describing competition in the training program at the Wall Street brokerage house of Salomon Brothers:

> "The odds of making it into the Salomon training program had been 60:1 against. The winners of the interviewing process were pitted against one another in the classroom, competing for jobs. Thus was born the Great Divide. Those who chose to put on a full-court grovel found seats in the front, where they sat, lips puckered, through the entire five-month program."

**Future Shock.** The stress caused to people and society by the velocity and scope of social and technological change.

The term was coined by Alvin Toffler and used as the title of his 1970 book, which offered strategies for coping with the phenomenon. Toffler said he coined the term in 1965 "to describe the shattering stress and disorientation that we induce in individuals by subjecting them to too much change in too short a time." He based the idea on "culture shock," the sense of disorientation one feels when plunged into a radically different culture in which familiar reference points and norms of behavior are completely changed.

The term in use by Henry Allen in *The Washington Post*, February 27, 1989, in a piece entitled "Nothing's Happening," exploring the problems of future shock withdrawal:

"What future? What shock?

"These are dog days in America. Nothing seems to be happening. This is not to say that nothing is, in fact, happening—one assumes the rough beast of the future is always slouching around [see **Slouching Toward Bethlehem**] out there somewhere. But nothing *seems* to be happening. After lifetimes of shock and/or delight at upheaval and invention, we are putting our ears to the ground and hearing little more than our own heartbeats."

# G

**Gang of Four.** A term of opprobrium first applied by Chinese Communist authorities to four leaders held responsible in 1976 for the excesses of the Cultural Revolution and accused of trying to seize power following the deaths of Mao Tse-tung and Cho En-lai. The best known of the group was Mao's widow, Chiang Ching.

Today the term can be pejorative, but is also often jocular, and applied to any group of four people engaged in a joint enterprise or strongly advocating a point of view. We also frequently see references to Gangs of Three, Five, etc.

The term in use, by Susan F. Rasky, *The New York Times*, July 27, 1989:

> "First there was the Gang of 17, a bipartisan group of House members, Senators and officials of the Ronald Reagan Administration who brokered a deal on taxes and spending that got the 1982 budget through Congress.
>
> "Now there is the Gang of Six, half a dozen Democrats on the House Ways and Means Committee who have created a political crisis for their party leaders by joining the panel's 13 Republicans to support a capital gains tax cut favored by President Bush."

**Gantry, Elmer.** See Elmer Gantry.

**Gatsby.** The central character of *The Great Gatsby*, a 1925 novel by F. Scott Fitzgerald, which offered a devastating picture of wealthy society in the 1920's, a society of greed, tinsel extravagance and what H.L. Mencken called "glittering swinishness." Critics have judged it one of the most finely constructed novels in American literature.

Mysterious Jay Gatsby moved into a luxurious mansion on Long Island and entertained at lavish parties. He was once simply Jay Gatz of a poor family in the Midwest, but with his ill-gotten millions he created a new past for himself. He spent lavishly to impress rich friends and win the love of Daisy Buchanan, but they brought about his downfall. Gatsby was shot and killed by the husband of a woman killed by Daisy's careless driving.

To the raising of literary eyebrows, Ronald Reagan's chief speechwriter, Anthony Dolan, wrote an article for *The New York Times* in 1986 which offered the hypothesis that Reagan is Gatsby. Dolan found admirable qualities in Gatsby—a sense of vision and hope, of steady self-assurance—and found them, too, in Reagan.

A Reagan critic, columnist Anthony Lewis, seized the opportunity.

Wrote Lewis in *The New York Times*, August 6, 1986:

> "Could Anthony Dolan have remembered the book when he compared President Reagan to Jay Gatsby? Had he read it? No matter. We can be grateful for the insight, no matter how inadvertent it may have been.
>
> "Of course Ronald Reagan is not Jay Gatsby. The comparisons are not to be forced. But there are themes— values—that echo.
>
> "When Mr. Reagan fixes on an end, like Gatsby he is indifferent to means. . . . Like Gatsby, too, Mr. Reagan has created his own world. In it facts yield to fantasy and obsession."

Another example, from Molly O'Neill, *The New York Times*, September 13, 1989:

> "Chicago's premier caterer, John Calihan, still remembers the nightmare. It was to be a dinner party à la Gatsby, a black-tie evening for 20 of the local Jays and Daisys. The hostess, a Chicago socialite, had enlisted Mr. Calihan to prepare her family bouillabaisse recipe. Spare no expense!"

**Gemütlichkeit.** (guh-MOOT-li-kight) Good-fellowship, a feeling of well-being, coziness and homey comfort. It's German.

The term in use, by *Newsweek*, February 9, 1987, quoting an authority on beer:

"In the old days taverns were like clubs where people gathered to drink beer and talk. We're coming back to that. People come to brewpubs for Gemütlichkeit—and good beer."

And from *Time*, November 23, 1987:

"How did Americans manage to forget for so many years that downtowns are invigorating and old cities grand? That the dignity and *Gemütlichkeit* of 18th century buildings and 19th century streets are incomparable."

**Genius Loci.** (JEE-ne-uhs LOH-sigh) Latin, meaning the spirit or deity of a place.

The ancient Romans believed that protective spirits were assigned to watch over people and places. Thus, the term came to mean the unique character of a place. (Only later did "genius" come to mean extraordinary intellectual ability or creativity.)

The term in use, by Henry Allen in *The Washington Post*, June 24, 1987:

"On a really hot day in Washington . . . in the kind of Washington heat when the flesh inside your elbow hisses unstuck as you straighten your arm and people on the streets move through the glare as if they're blind . . . the kind of heat when Washington's streets stretch out, the whole city seems to shrug, smog sits on the horizon like a rotten rind and everything seems lost, preoccupied, provisional, endless . . . it's on that kind of day that Washington is Washington.

"This is why true Washingtonians love the heat. Heat is a kind of local god, a guardian angel, a genius loci. We love our heat the way San Francisco loves its fog or New York loves its neurosis. . . . Paris is the City of Light, Washington is the City of Heat."

**Genre.** (JHON-ruh) A type, or style, of a school of literature, art or cinema. It's French; its Latin root word is "genus."

The term in use by Carolyn Banks in a review in *The Washington Post Book World*, December 18, 1988:

> "Bruce Cook's mystery, *Mexican Standoff*, is a standout example of good genre fiction."

In use again, by Charles Paul Freund in *The Washington Post*, January 3, 1989:

> "Leaving the White House with a word of warning for the American people has been a subgenre of presidential speechmaking since George Washington cautioned against 'the insidious wiles of foreign influence' in 1796."

And by Peter C. Marzio in his book, *Rube Goldberg: His Life and Work*:

> "His brilliant satire was a positive genre, aiming to cleanse and refresh rather than discourage or destroy."

**Gestalt.** (guh-SHTALT) A German word without an exact English equivalent, but meaning a unified whole; a form or structure or entity in which the whole is greater than the sum of its parts.

It has given its name to a field of psychotherapy that rejects the Freudian approach of analysis of the past, and concentrates instead on the senses and complete experience of the present.

The term in use, by former Assistant Attorney General Arnold Burns, testifying before the Senate Judiciary Committee on July 26, 1988, on the impact on the Justice Department of the numerous allegations made against then-Attorney General Edwin Meese:

> "But you've got to understand that you've got a picture here, a gestalt, of allegations, not bare, spurious allegations, but allegations of impropriety. . . . "

Another example, from P.J. O'Rourke, *Holidays in Hell*, describing his visit to Poland as a reporter for *Rolling Stone*:

> "I said, 'Zofia, there's only one way to cover this story. We have to get inside it, we have to experience it in the social

context. We have to capture the gestalt, get the big picture.
We've got to go out and drink too much and boogie.'
" 'Your magazine *pays* you for this?' she said."

**The Gilded Age.** The title of a novel published in 1873 and, from it, the name of an era.

The novel, jointly written by Mark Twain and essayist-editor Charles Dudley Warner, describes speculators and their greedy schemes in post-Civil War America. The book captures the excesses of its day, and its title came to sum up the vulgar extravagance of the era.

The phrase is particularly apt—"gilded" suggesting excess, as in "gilding the lily" as well as the idea of superficial splendor; a gilded age, after all, is not a truly "golden" one, but merely a cheap imitation.

The term in use, by Laurence I. Barrett in *Time*, January 23, 1989, discussing the political legacy of Ronald Reagan:

"Looser ethical standards and the adoration of capitalism led to a wave of scandals in and out of government that rivaled the excesses of the Gilded Age."

**Gladstonian.** An adjective used to describe a politician of great ability and rectitude. It was coined from the name of William Ewart Gladstone (1809-1898), four times prime minister of Great Britain, known as the "Grand Old Man" or "G.O.M." He was one of the most capable men of his age, and one of its leading orators. As leader of the Liberal Party, he is remembered for his decades-long rivalry with Benjamin **Disraeli,** leader of the Tories.

Gladstone originally intended to follow the Church of England as a vocation, but instead moved into politics, where he strove throughout his life to serve the principles of his religious faith. He was regarded throughout his career as a man of unfailing integrity and courage. Courage was needed for the causes he espoused—reform in Ireland, extension of the vote and opposition to Britain's imperial expansion in the late 19th century.

One of the supreme moments of his career came late in his political life, during the so-called "Midlothian campaign." Gladstone had retired from politics in 1874, but in 1879 he made a comeback. In a series of great speeches to his Midlothian constituency in Scotland, he addressed not only the electors but the nation at large—something new in political campaigns. Gladstone's sincerity and argumentative skill not only won his seat but carried the Liberals into power, and returned him to the post of prime minister.

Unlike Disraeli, Gladstone was never able to charm Queen Victoria, and as the years passed, her aversion grew. In 1892, she described him as "an old, wild, and incomprehensible man of 82½." (She, of course, was a glum and reclusive 73.)

The Grand Old Man invoked by *The Economist*, April 8, 1989, in a discussion of the U.S. budget deficit:

> "If the federal budget were in balance, not counting social security, the federal government would be in overall surplus and this would be a form of national savings. The government would reduce its outstanding debt, freeing capital for private investment. But there are two crucial provisos—besides the political impossibility of such Gladstonian rectitude."

**Glick, Sammy.** See Sammy Glick.

**Global Village.** The concept, forwarded by communications theoretician Marshall McLuhan, that electronic communications have made mankind citizens of a single community. [See also **The Medium Is the Message.**]

McLuhan's idea was that reading the printed page is a very private and isolated form of communication that brought to an end the earlier communal forms of oral communication. He believed that radio and television would restore the old sense of community, but on a worldwide basis, linking mankind in a "global village."

The term in use, by John Rockwell in *The New York Times*, October 11, 1987:

> "We really do live in a 'global village' where nearly everyone—or at least the more sensitive among us, mean-

ing our artists—is affected by everyone else. . . . This is the
era of international artistic cross-fertilization."

## Goldberg, Rube. See Rube Goldberg.

## Golden Parachute. From the world of business, an apt term for a
settlement that cushions the landing of an executive after ejection
from a high-level position. "The Barnhart Dictionary Companion"
speculates that the "parachute" may come from the 1982 job-
changing handbook *What Color Is Your Parachute* by Richard Bolles.
As Bolles put it, "I hate to tell you this, but the time to figure out
where your parachute is, what color it is, and to strap it on, is *now*—
and not when the vocational airplane that you are presently in is on
fire and diving toward the ground."

Another version is the "golden handshake," a lucrative severance
deal given to a high-salaried executive who has been fired, forced into
retirement or bought out as part of a corporate power play or takeover.

An example, from a May 26, 1988 report in *The Washington Post*
on congressional reaction to U.S. government efforts to coax Panamanian strongman Manuel Noriega to step down from power:

> ". . . Senate Minority Leader Robert J. Dole (R-Kan.) ap-
> peared to sum up the dominant sentiment when he said:
> 'Noriega must go if we are to achieve our goals in Panama.
> But sending Noriega into retirement with a legal golden
> parachute . . . would have been the wrong step at the
> wrong time.'"

And by Brooks Jackson, *The Wall Street Journal*, August 4, 1989,
on an exception to rules of the U.S. House of Representatives that
permits certain retiring members to keep surplus campaign funds for
personal use:

> "Those golden parachutes leave some people sputtering. 'It
> is ludicrous that conversion [of campaign funds to personal
> use] is breaking the law for some members but perfectly OK
> for others,' says Fred Wertheimer, president of Common
> Cause."

**Gonzo.** A style of journalism that mixes fact and fiction. It is produced, or allegedly produced, by a writer in a crazed state, sometimes induced by the excessive consumption of drink and/or drugs.

The term comes from the Italian word for simpleton.

The preeminent practitioner of gonzo journalism is the quasi-legendary Hunter S. Thompson, the political reporter for *Rolling Stone* magazine in the 1970s, who was famous for producing his copy while under the influence of Wild Turkey bourbon and a variety of drugs. Thompson's works include *Fear and Loathing in Las Vegas* and *Fear and Loathing on the Campaign Trail 1972*. His writing is characterized by outrageously false allegations about public figures and grotesque and exaggerated descriptions of events. His legend has been taken further through the character of Duke in the comic strip *Doonesbury*.

The term in use, by R.Z. Shepard, *Time*, October 17, 1988, in a review of P.J. O'Rourke's *Holidays in Hell*:

> "The papa of gonzo is, of course, Hunter S. Thompson, who at 49 seems to have lost his bite. . . . For true spite and malice one must now turn to P.J. O'Rourke, 40, a baby boomer who seems to have teethed on brass knuckles and suckled on bile."

**Gordian Knot.** An especially complicated (and knotty) problem. "Cutting the Gordian knot" means decisive and swift action to resolve a complicated problem or situation.

It comes from a Greek tale. Gordias was a peasant who became king of Phrygia, an ancient country in central and northwestern Asia Minor. He did so in fulfillment of a prophecy that whoever drove up to the temple of Zeus in a wagon would become king. Gordias, in gratitude, dedicated his wagon to Zeus. The wagon was secured by an intricate knot, and it was said that whoever could undo it would rule Asia. Alexander the Great arrived on the scene and cut the knot with a single stroke of his sword. Thus, a quick resolution to a difficult problem.

The term in use, by Turkish Prime Minister Turgut Ozal, referring to the long history of bitter disputes between Greece and Turkey, quoted in *The Washington Post*, June 14, 1988:

> "While searching for solutions to problems, we have above all to be patient. This is a task which falls on all of us. The nature of our existing problems is not of a kind that can be undone with a single stroke of the sword like the Gordian knot."

**Gothic.** A type of novel or event or scene, characterized by horror, violence and bizarre or supernatural effects. Also frequently applied in a jocular way to describe lurid, peculiar, mysterious, primitive people or goings-on; also, pertaining to the Middle Ages.

The term also applies to the architecture of Western Europe in the 12th-16th centuries, which was chiefly characterized by the pointed arch, soaring high ceilings and flying buttresses, as seen in such great cathedrals as Chartres and Notre Dame de Paris.

Gothic novels often have a medieval setting; gloomy castles and wild landscapes are almost mandatory. Indeed, Horace Walpole's *The Castle of Otranto* (1764), the first of the **genre** in English, was subtitled *A Gothic Story*, reflecting its themes of dark passions and cruelty. Mary Shelley's *Frankenstein* (1818) is perhaps the most famous example. Gothic elements are also found in the works of the Brontë sisters, and continue to appear in fiction today. The term also is frequently applied to the modern romance novel genre known as "bodice rippers."

Tania Modleski, in *Loving with a Vengeance*, a study of soap operas and paperback Gothic novels, writes: "Gothics can be identified by their cover illustrations: each portrays a young girl wearing a long, flowing gown and standing in front of a large, menacing-looking castle or mansion. The atmosphere is dark and stormy, and the ethereal young girl appears to be frightened. In the typical Gothic plot, the heroine comes to a mysterious house, perhaps as a bride, perhaps in another capacity, and either starts to mistrust her husband or else finds herself in love with a mysterious man who appears to be some kind of criminal."

But why are the novels or the architecture called Gothic, anyway? The Goths were a barbarian tribe that invaded Europe in the declining days of the Roman Empire, sacking and pillaging. So "Gothic" as an adjective came to mean primitive and barbarian. The adjective was attached to medieval architecture during the Renaissance (the 14th through the 16th centuries); the bright stars of the new era applied the term retroactively and pejoratively, to let the world know that the old styles were backward. You can bet that the master builder of Chartres did NOT call the cathedral Gothic.

At any rate, the adjective has spread beyond novels and architecture, as shown by this example, from a table of contents teaser in *Spy* magazine, February 1989:

> "The Mystery of Albemarle Farms: Avery Chenoweth spins a true Gothic tale of America's second-wealthiest man (John Kluge), his exotic British wife (Patricia Kluge), their instant-aristocratic southern estate (Albemarle Farms) and the Transylvanianesque goings-on (luxurious crypts, mass graves brimming with the bones of neighbors' pets) and unbridled social lust that have the local townspeople spooked."

Another example, from Tom Shales in *The Washington Post*, April 13, 1989, in a profile of communications mogul Ted Turner:

> "Turner's plans to colorize 'Kane' fell through when lawyers for the Welles estate managed to block it. 'The tests looked great,' Turner insists. But doesn't he concede that 'Citizen Kane' has a dark, stark Gothic look that makes it an extremely poor candidate for what Welles on his deathbed allegedly called 'Ted Turner's crayons'?"

And from *Washington Post* movie critic Rita Kempley's review of *The War of the Roses*, December 8, 1989:

> "Under director Danny DeVito's evil eye, a blushing comedic romance becomes a rarefied bedroom Gothic, as black as a witch's mood."

**Götterdämmerung.** (GUH-ter-DEHM-er-ung) The day of doom, the end of the world, total destruction.

In Norse mythology, the destruction of the world is preceded by a battle between the good and evil gods and the good gods all die heroically. Afterward, a new world is to be born. In German, the term literally means "twilight of the gods."

The term in use, from columnist Mary McGrory in *The Washington Post* of March 2, 1989:

> "Bush seems determined to turn the Tower nomination affair into Valley Forge and the Cuban missile crisis. High strategy meetings are held at the White House, Gotterdammerung-strength warnings are issued. Bush's presidency is on the line."

And from Jeanne Basinger, writing in *The New York Times*, July 3, 1989:

> "The new police movies reflect the fear the average citizen feels, and the helplessness. The screens show an operatic panorama of explosion, death, destruction and blood, a Gotterdammerung removal of crime."

And a play on the term: when *The New Republic* ran a contest to find an appropriate name for the Iran-contra scandal in December 1986, someone nominated "Gipperdammerung" as in "the twilight of the Gipper" (a nickname the president acquired from a movie character he once played) suggesting that the scandal was so cataclysmic as to be the end of Reagan, the fall of a political idol.

**Grand Guignol.** (gron GEE-nyol —pronounce Guignol with a hard g, as in "good") In today's use, an adjective meaning gruesome, macabre and bloody. The expression comes from the plays of that type that were performed in Paris in a theater called the Grand Guignol. That name apparently springs from an 18th century puppet theater in France that was similar to Punch and Judy in England and was frequently violent. The main character was named Guignol.

The term in use, by David Falkner, *The New York Times*, August 4, 1989, writing about the Baltimore Orioles baseball team:

> "The current edition of the Orioles has no business being anywhere near first place. There are all rookies on the team; 33 different players have gotten playing time this

year, and 18 of those have had two or fewer years of major league experience.

"Only eight of the players currently on the roster were there for the Grand Guignol losing streak last year."

And another example, from Terri Minsky, *Premiere*, July 1989, on the 1989 movie *Batman:*

"[Director Tim] Burton approached Warner production chief Mark Canton with yet another notion. He saw the story of Batman as a kind of Grand Guignol opera: Gotham City as an oppressive metropolis, crammed with urban decay and decadence, besieged by crime—what Hell would look like if it were a city."

**Gray, Dorian.** See Dorian Gray.

**Great Leap Forward.** An enormous, painful and unsuccessful campaign in China from 1958 to early 1960 to promote rapid economic development. Today, the term is used—often sarcastically or negatively—to describe great and dramatic changes in policy.

In China, unreachable goals were set for increasing industrial output, often with impractical means. One example: an effort to increase iron and steel production through the use of small backyard smelters. Simultaneously, China's rulers sought to combine cooperative farms into large agricultural communes—and after another disaster the government was forced to swallow its early optimistic food production predictions. Serious economic problems followed from the strains and dislocations caused by the Great Leap Forward.

Failure of the Great Leap led to conflict among China's Communist Party leadership. The power struggle eventually led to Mao Tse-tung's launching of the Cultural Revolution to restore revolutionary purity. In 1966 Mao created the Red Guards, youthful fanatics whose rampages led to beatings, public humiliation, imprisonment or death for those seen to be opposing the dictates of Chairman Mao. Chaos reigned until 1970, when the authorities began to move toward **normalcy.**

The term in use, by David Margolick, *The New York Times*, August 4, 1989:

> "In the past decade, China's legal system, largely shut down during the Cultural Revolution, has experienced a Great Leap Forward. The number of law students has grown from 50 to more than 15,000. . . . "

A play on the term, on the cover of *Business Week*, June 19, 1989 (and in many other news stories), reporting the suppression in China of student advocates of democracy in the spring of 1989: "China: The Great Leap Backward."

And in *Newsweek*, June 19, 1989, also in a report on the turmoil in China:

> "The great leap backward sent reverberations through financial centers around the globe."

**Great White Fleet.** From American naval history: at the direction of President Theodore Roosevelt, a force of 16 battleships and four destroyers of the U.S. Navy's Atlantic fleet—all painted a dramatic white—took a 14-month global cruise starting in 1907. The journey was a public relations triumph, alerting the world to America's arrival as a major power. The show of strength, recalled the *National Journal* of April 21, 1984, also intimidated Japan (at least for the next 35 years) into observing the status quo in the Pacific. The phrase is now invoked in descriptions of contemporary flexings of American naval muscle.

The term in use, in an editorial in *The New York Times*, July 28, 1983:

> "There is a cold-blooded case for sending a great white fleet to the Caribbean. It is a comparatively low-cost way of sending a message to the Managua Marxists and their friends in Havana and Moscow."

And more whimsically, by David W. Dunlap in *The New York Times*, December 2, 1981:

"The New York Transit Authority's 'great white fleet,' the first of the Flushing-line subway trains to be painted completely white, suffered a minor graffiti attack Monday."

**Great White Hope.** A contender, a hoped-for victor, the champion of a cause.

The term first came into use after Jack Johnson, a black man, won the world heavyweight boxing championship. White supremacists couldn't abide the notion and launched a search for a "great white hope" to take the crown away from Johnson. Their first candidate was Jim Jeffries, a former champ lured out of retirement. Johnson knocked him out as well as disposing of other hopefuls (including Victor McLaglen, who later did better as an actor).

Johnson further infuriated his enemies with a flamboyant way of life outside the ring, including marriages to white women. Prosecutors went after him; he was convicted of violating the Mann Act for transporting a woman (who later became his wife) across a state line, spent several years in exile in Europe and eventually served a year in Leavenworth Prison. In 1915 another great white hope, Jess Willard, finally dethroned Johnson, although Johnson was later to claim that he threw the fight.

Today we see the phrase frequently used without the racial connotation and not reflecting the ugliness of its origins.

The term in use, by movie director Phil Robinson, quoted in *The New York Times Magazine*, April 23, 1989, in a profile of actor Kevin Costner:

> " 'I've heard the phrase "Great White Hope" applied to him,' says Phil Robinson, 'not in a racial sense but in the sense of someone who has a classic kind of strength to him but is still exciting. It's what the movie business has been looking for a long time.' "

Another example, from William Gildea, *The Washington Post*, January 15, 1990, on the upcoming boxing match between overweight oldtimers Gerry Cooney and George Foreman:

> "Cooney's been advertised as the Great White Hope so long

he's just about killed the phrase from the language—his major accomplishment."

And a play on the phrase from the *National Review*, August 28, 1987: a letter to the editor extolling the virtues of Congressman Jack Kemp as presidential candidate is given the headline "The Great Right Hope."

**Greek Chorus.** Originally, in the theater of ancient Greece, an organized group of singers and dancers who appeared in religious festivals and dramatic performances associated with them. In the tragedies, the chorus functioned as interested spectators commenting on the ideas and emotions evoked by the play.

Through the ages, playwrights have continued to use the device. In *Henry V*, Shakespeare reduced the chorus to one person to speak the prologue and epilogue and to explain and comment on events. Today the term is used figuratively to describe those who function in a similar role outside the theatrical setting.

The term in use, in a *Wall Street Journal* editorial, December 27, 1989:

> "Some Latin American leaders may indeed fear reprisals from their local narco-terrorists, but we are also witnessing a sort of Greek chorus swaying to the grand myth that people can never support a liberation from the north."

**Greenhouse Effect.** The warming of the earth's atmosphere that many scientists say is occurring because pollutants in the air, such as carbon dioxide and other gases, are trapping heat, keeping it from escaping into the upper atmosphere.

The result is comparable to the experience that awaits one inside a greenhouse—intensified warmth because the sun's heat is held in by the glass of the walls and roof. In the same way, carbon dioxide in our atmosphere permits heat from the sun to pass through the shell of gases above the earth, but traps heat from the earth which usually escapes through the atmosphere. Thus the average temperature of the atmosphere rises over the years. Among the feared consequences:

the melting of the polar ice caps, the swelling of the oceans and the disappearance of coastal land.

The term in use, in a review of the film *The Accidental Tourist*, *The Washington Post*, March 3, 1989:

> "Lawrence Kasdan doesn't adapt Anne Tyler's popular novel so much as create a greenhouse effect around it. He bottles the characters in tight shots and constricting angles so that it stifles the bittersweet comedy 'Tourist' might have been."

**Gresham's Law.** Bad money drives out good.

It was named for Sir Thomas Gresham (ca. 1519-1579), English financier, merchant and adviser to Queen Elizabeth I. He noted that when coinage was debased or when cheaper metals were used as currency, the more valuable coins and metals would disappear from circulation because they were being hoarded or exported. Gresham was credited with authorship by economist H.D. MacLeod in 1857, who did not know that the same observation had been made earlier by others, including Copernicus.

In a broader sense, Gresham's law means the inferior substitute will always replace the superior predecessor.

The term in use, by Democratic pol Ann Lewis, quoted in an article about negative political ads in the 1988 presidential campaign in *The Washington Post*, October 28, 1988:

> "They [the Republicans] realized that debating the policies to be addressed in 1989 was not a winning stage for them . . . so they built this whole other stage of peripheral issues and said, 'Here, this is what this campaign is going to be about.' The result is you have a candidate running to be commissioner of prisons. What we may be seeing this time is a sort of Gresham's law of politics, where bad issues drive out good ones."

And from Michael Kinsley, *The New Republic*, November 13, 1989:

> "Twenty years of Gresham's Law—the bad politics driving out the good—brought us to last year's George Bush cam-

paign. That is now the model and standard for political campaigns at every level."

And from *Village Voice* film critic J. Hoberman, December 12, 1989:

"There is a Gresham's law of images: the facile ones drive the tougher ones out of circulation."

**Gridley.** See Fire When Ready, Gridley.

**Grub Streeter.** A hack writer.

The term comes from Grub Street in London, where, in the 18th century, writers of trashy stuff seemed to congregate. Samuel Johnson's definition was: "Much inhabited by writers of small histories, dictionaries, and temporary poems; whence any mean production is called grubstreet."

The term in use by Francis Russell in *The American Spectator*, March 1988, commenting on the use of ghost writers for the memoirs of prominent politicians:

"So Tip O'Neill is 'with' the political tradition. He talks, a grub-streeter records and then fills in the gaps and interstices with scraps from other books."

**Gulag.** A prison camp or, more specifically, the system of prison camps in the Soviet Union. Often the term is used as a metaphor for horrible, isolated, oppressive or otherwise grimly prison-like conditions.

The term gained notoriety in the English-speaking world with the publication of Alexander Solzhenitsyn's 1973 novel, *The Gulag Archipelago*. "Gulag" is a Russian acronym for the administration of labor camps in the Soviet Union. "Archipelago" means a group of islands, or a sea with many islands. Thus the image of the archipelago is of a chain of camps—like islands in the vast ocean of the Russian landscape.

The term in use, by Leonard Shapiro, writing in *The Washington*

*Post*, February 17, 1988, about the amenities of Calgary during the Winter Olympics there:

> "They've put the press corps in prefabricated housing in a vacant lot on the outskirts of town—some people are calling it the gulag."

Another example, from Michael Willrich, writing in Washington, D.C.'s *City Paper*, September 8, 1989:

> "Once a bastion of D.C.'s counterculture, today Adams Morgan [a gentrifying Washington neighborhood] is a yuppie gulag."

And from Paul A. Gigot, writing in *The Wall Street Journal*, September 22, 1989:

> "An American visitor to Moscow asked recently to use a Xerox machine. He was led, with Fort Knox-like ceremony, behind a locked door into a backroom, where a Soviet made the precious copies. The question of the week is: What can the U.S. possibly do to help a nation that treats Xerox machines as a controlled substance? . . .
>
> "The Bush administration has proposed Open Skies, and yesterday it offered Open Lands, but why not 'Open Minds'? Liberating the Xerox machine from its Gulag would do more for *perestroika* than all of the arms control ever dreamed of."

**Guy Fawkes.** One of the conspirators in the famed Gunpowder Plot of 1605.

A small group of Roman Catholics planned to murder the King of England, James I, and members of Parliament by exploding a large cache of gunpowder in the cellars under the House of Lords on November 5, when the king would appear at the opening of Parliament. Fawkes was in the cellar, ready to strike the match, when he was arrested. (Historians suggest that the king's intelligence network had discovered the plot much earlier, but let it go to the last minute in order to achieve the maximum political advantage.)

Fawkes was tortured to obtain the names of his co-conspirators, and executed in front of the Houses of Parliament before a large crowd. Parliament established a day of thanksgiving for its deliverance. The British now celebrate Guy Fawkes night on November 5 with fireworks and bonfires in which "guys," or effigies of Guy Fawkes, are burned.

The name invoked, by *The Economist*, March 11, 1989, in a story on corporate mergers:

> "Yet the only sputter so far is an 8% stake in America's Cummins Engine, acquired at the end of 1988. Capturing Cummins might cost $1.2 billion—a good rocket, perhaps, but hardly Guy Fawkes night."

# H

**Habeas Corpus.** (HAY-bee-uhs KOR-puhs) A legal document requiring that a prisoner be brought before a court or a judge for investigation into whether detaining him is warranted.

It's been called "the great writ of liberty" (a writ is a document issued by a court ordering or prohibiting some action); its function is to determine that a prisoner being held has received due process (it is not a determination of guilt or innocence) and to require the release of prisoners from unlawful imprisonment. Habeas corpus is a fundamental premise of English and American law, created by the British Parliament in 1679.

Literally, in Latin: "You have the body."

*Washington Post* columnist Richard Cohen refers to the writ March 23, 1989, in discussing a Supreme Court decision on drug tests for government employees:

> "When the left (Marshall) and the right (Scalia) combine, the muddled middle (the rest of the court) ought to pay heed—and so should the nation in general. The war on drugs is not, for all the rhetoric, a real war. When Abraham Lincoln suspended habeas corpus during the Civil War, he was facing an insurrection and conditions in certain areas (Baltimore, for example) where juries would not convict sympathizers with the South, or even traitors. The drug problem is different."

**Haiku.** (HIGH-koo) A form of Japanese poetry, which in contemporary American use describes brief, cryptic, sometimes highly polished writings or utterances.

Haiku demands a rigid form and has specific rules of composition set forth by its master, Matsuo Basho (1644-1694). A haiku is composed of seventeen syllables in a 5-7-5 pattern in three lines, and frequently describes a spiritual moment precipitated by contact with nature.

The term in use, by Michael Dolan in *City Paper*, May 5, 1989, describing the "daybook," a daily listing of events in Washington prepared by and distributed to the media over the wires of the Associated Press and United Press International:

> "Like the classifieds, the daybooks can be read as haiku, minimalist illuminations of universes inane and heartbreaking. How else to look at a day's listing that ranges from a chance for reporters to burn rubber in a turbocharged Bentley to a memorial concert for an Environmental Protection Agency worker stabbed to death on the job with a pair of scissors?"

**Half-life.** A scientific term which means the time period in which the quantity of a sample decreases by half. Most often it is employed in physics and refers to the decay of radioactive substances. Used figuratively, the term describes the period of flowering, growth or prosperity before decay or decline sets in.

The term in use, in *Time*, December 11, 1978:

> "Alas, in the mercurial cosmetics business, almost all products have short half-lives, and Charlie sales have started to decline. But before they did, Bergerac and Revlon were ready with both an explanation and a new product."

And from *The Economist*, December 9, 1989, in a description of prospects for German reunification:

> "It is becoming plain that East Germany's half-life is shorter than anyone thought, and that, unless something serious happens in Moscow, fusion with West Germany is going to occur sooner rather than later."

**Hamlet.** Anyone displaying characteristics of the Shakespearean character—tortured, even immobilized, by indecision.

The central character in *Hamlet, Prince of Denmark* is torn by suspicions over the death of his father and the remarriage of his mother to his uncle, the usurping king. He hesitates to act on his mistrust but cannot find peace in inaction. He doubts himself and contemplates suicide.

The term in use, by Blaine Harden and Mary Battiata, *The Washington Post*, December 3, 1989, on the anti-communist revolution in Czechoslovakia:

> "The government could not, however, prevent the formation within two days of a new group called Civic Forum. It was headed by playwright [Vaclav] Havel, a shy, Hamlet-like dissident who for years had agonized about how great a role he should play in leading the opposition."

**Hardball.** Rough and tough political tactics.

The term became popular in the Watergate era. It originates, no doubt, from the differences between the games of baseball and softball. Baseball is played with a harder, faster ball and thus is often called hardball to distinguish it from the slower, more widely played version of the sport. Hardball is a tougher game and is played in the big leagues, though its political counterpart is as often practiced on the local level as it is on the national one.

The term in use, in *Man of the House*, by Tip O'Neill with William Novak, in which the former speaker of the House complains of the tactics employed by the Nixon White House:

> "I thought I knew all about political hardball. Hardball was ballot-stuffing in Illinois during the 1960 presidential election. Hardball was when you pressured somebody to make a donation on the basis of your friendship. Hardball was when organizations feuded and tried to destroy each other. Hardball was repeat voters being run in and out of the polls in Boston. In 1972, I learned about a new kind of dirty politics in the Republican camp."

**Harpy.** In Greek mythology, ravenous predatory creatures with the bodies of birds but the heads of women. The legend is they snatched food from the blind king Phineus until they were frightened away by the mythological heroes, the Argonauts, who sailed with Jason to recover the Golden Fleece.

In contemporary usage, usually (but not always) a woman who is grasping, scolding, nagging and bad-tempered; a shrew.

The term in use, by *The Sunday Telegraph* of London, September 17, 1989:

> "Closer to home, but infinitely further removed from thinking at No. 10 [Downing Street, the residence of the British prime minister], the French have allowed Mrs. Thatcher to develop into a creature of myth—La Dame Fer, a combination of Harpy and **Red Queen** constantly blocking the moves of the rest of the Euro chess pieces and ready to savage her opponents."

Another example, from Rick Marin, *The Washington Times*, September 20, 1989, reviewing the TV comedy series "Nutt House":

> "With grossly exaggerated breast and buttock padding, Ms Frick is really just another variation on the Frau Blucher-style harpies Miss Leachman has played before for Mel Brooks, in movies such as 'Young Frankenstein,' and 'High Anxiety.'"

And from *The Economist*, October 7, 1989:

> "Ms. Peggy Pascoe of the University of Utah challenges the myth that frontier women were either the non-beings their absence from the history books would imply, or the harpies and angels that western films have painted them."

**Haskell, Eddie.** See Eddie Haskell.

**Hastings, Battle of.** A battle between the armies of King Harold of England and Duke William of Normandy. The Norman victory changed the course of world history.

The battle took place in 1066 near the English seaport of Hastings on the English Channel. It was the culmination of a dispute over the succession to the crown of England, King Edward the Confessor having died childless.

On one side: Harold, Earl of Wessex and greatest nobleman in the kingdom, who had apparently been designated heir by Edward on his deathbed; the selection was confirmed by the parliament of Saxon nobles. On the other: William, Duke of Normandy (a region in northern France on the English Channel), who thought that Edward had promised him the throne. There was also the matter of an oath Harold made to William two years before. (Keep in mind that historians are *still* arguing about these events.)

The outcome: While Harold was watching England's south coast in anticipation of an invasion by the Normans, his rebellious brother and the king of Norway landed 200 miles to the north with an army of Vikings. Harold marched his army north in four days and defeated these ferocious invaders. But during his absence William and his army landed in the south.

Harold's battered army raced south to fight William's forces. The battle was joined on the morning of October 14 and remained indecisive until late afternoon, when Harold's line was broken by waves of Norman arrows.

Legend says Harold fell dead or wounded with an arrow in his eye, and his army collapsed in confusion and defeat. William moved quickly to consolidate his hold on the kingdom. The Norman version of the dispute, invasion and battle is told in the Bayeux Tapestry.

With William's control of Normandy, England became a power on the continent of Europe. The struggles of English kings to maintain, expand or regain territories in France set up centuries of war and diplomatic rivalry.

The battle brought a new Norman ruling class to England and a more centralized and organized feudal government. Thus from an early date England had a strong monarchy which promoted order (not always successfully, but consider the time), the growth of towns, merchant classes and other institutions with less disorder than on the Continent.

The outcome would also produce a new language, English, which possesses the largest vocabulary in the world, thanks to the confluence of French (based on Latin) and Anglo-Saxon.

The term in use, by Nat Hentoff in *The Village Voice*, March 21, 1989:

> "For years after the previously unimaginable horrors of Hiroshima, the print and broadcast press carried stories about American children afraid they would be incinerated before they grew up. I have seen no such stories for a long time. To today's kids, Hiroshima and Nagasaki are as remote as the Battle of Hastings, and most of them never think of that historic turning point either."

**Hat Trick.** Three repeated successes.

The term comes from sports, particularly ice hockey in the United States, as well as soccer and baseball. But where it originated in British-born cricket it means the taking of three wickets one after another. A player accomplishing this feat is entitled to a new hat at the expense of the club, rather like earning a letter in sports in the United States. In hockey and soccer, a player who scores three goals in one game achieves a hat trick. Broadcasting's baseball announcers refer to a player who gets three hits in three times at bat as having achieved a hat trick.

The term in use, by Lois Romano in *The Washington Post*, February 24, 1988, in a profile of Arizona's acting governor, Rose Mofford:

> "No one would have paid much attention to her sudden rise to Democratic 'acting governor' if it hadn't been for the fact that the man she is entitled by law to at least temporarily replace—Republican Evan Mecham—has become something of a national joke. He is desperately hanging onto his political life and will need nothing short of a political hat trick to survive. He faces a state Senate impeachment trial next week, a criminal prosecution next month and a May recall election."

**Heart of Darkness.** The primitive subconscious that lurks within human nature.

The term comes from the dark jungle into which the narrator of Joseph Conrad's 1902 story, *The Heart of Darkness*, goes in his search for Kurtz, a mysterious and powerful white trader who lives deep in the jungle. Marlow, the narrator, who ran a river boat in what was then the Belgian Congo, recounts his search and also describes the cruelties of the colonial regime. The story was adapted for the 1979 film *Apocalypse Now*, with the scene changed to the Vietnam War.

The term in use by Bruce Bawer, in *The American Spectator*, May 1989, reviewing the film *Dangerous Liaisons*:

> "Neither [of the leading characters] brings us anywhere near the heart of his character's particular darkness."

In use again, by William McGurn, also in *The American Spectator*, March 1989, on travel in the Third World:

> "Yet there exist lands where an L.L. Bean knapsack only singles one out as a likely mark, places where credit ratings are unknown and life (human, at least) is cheap. Here in the heart of darkness, with no Arthur Frommer to clear the way, the adventurer stands alone."

And by Alan Barra, *The Village Voice*, August 22, 1989:

> "Brian DePalma is experiencing his own heart of darkness. Seated in the open-air restaurant of a luxury hotel at the edge of Thailand's densest jungle, he puts down his cup with a grimace. 'You can't,' he says, 'get decent cappuccino here.' "

**Hearts and Minds.** A phrase that came into currency in the Vietnam era, describing how the people of Vietnam had to be wooed away from communism. As President Lyndon Johnson put it in 1965, " . . . so we must be ready to fight in Vietnam, but the ultimate victory will depend on the hearts and minds of the people who actually live out there."

William Safire, in his *Political Dictionary*, attributes the origin of the phrase to Theodore Roosevelt, who explained his popularity to his young aide, Douglas MacArthur, this way: "To put into words what is in their hearts and minds but not in their mouths." James S. Olson's *Dictionary of the Vietnam War* attributes the phrase, albeit reversed, to John Adams' description of the American Revolution:

"The Revolution was effected before the war commenced. The Revolution was in the minds and hearts of the people. . . . " (Letter to Hezekiah Niles, 1818)

The term in use, by George Lardner Jr., in *The Washington Post*, April 12, 1989, writing about the dramatic confrontation between defendant Oliver North and prosecutor John Keker, as Keker cross-examined North on the witness stand:

> "Throughout the day, the two men, both Marine Corps veterans of the Vietnam War, battled head-on for the jurors' hearts and minds. Keker, more accustomed to being a defense lawyer in San Francisco, has a penchant for rapid-fire questions and unexpected shifts from one point to another. North tends to respond with rambling answers and mini-lectures about the underlying morality of what he was doing."

**Hegemony.** (hih-JEM-uh-nee) Dominance or leadership, especially that of one nation over another. Suzerainty, if you'd like another word for it. The term comes from the Greek hegemon, or leader.

In contemporary use in international politics, it has a negative bias. The term was especially favored in diatribes between the Russians and Chinese, when the communist superpowers had little good to say for each other. William Safire calls it "the dirty word for leadership."

The term in use, by Fred Barnes in *The American Spectator*, May 1989, discussing Republican failure to increase their strength in the House of Representatives:

> "Not surprisingly, Republicans grew dispirited, which further enhanced Democratic hegemony. Why else would Dick Cheney trade the certainty of becoming House Republican leader in a few years for an undetermined future as George Bush's defense secretary?"

**Hegira.** (hih-JIGH-ruh) Arabic, meaning departure or flight to a more congenial place. In Islamic theology, the Hegira (with a capital H), refers to the flight of Muhammad the Prophet from Mecca to Medina with his followers on July 2, 622 to escape persecution, the event that marks the opening of the Moslem era. In a general sense, the word is applied to long and arduous journeys.

The term in use, by Mark Muro in *The Boston Globe*, December 15, 1988, reviewing John Feinstein's book *One Year in College Basketball*:

> "But even so, this 464-page hegira plods on with little of the elegance and still less of the junkie's religiosity that might make it transcend numbing logistics."

Another example, also from the *Globe*, from David Nyhan, October 27, 1988, writing on presidential candidate Michael Dukakis' appearance on ABC's "Nightline":

> "Koppel elicits a telling admission: 20 months into his hegira, Duke's greatest regret is that he didn't give the people enough of a sense of who he is."

**Heisenberg Uncertainty Principle.** A scientific term, the understanding of which is beyond the capacity of many laymen, including the authors. Nonetheless, it has entered the world of allusions where it is usually—and questionably—employed to describe situations in which the act of observing something changes that which is being observed.

In quantum mechanics the only way to observe an atomic particle is to measure it. The process of measuring the particle disturbs it, therefore producing a minimum uncertainty in the state of the particle. It is this uncertainty that was formulated in 1927 by the German mathematical physicist Werner Heisenberg (1901–1976). It is important to remember that outside of quantum mechanics observing something does *not* alter it.

This usually does not appear to be fully understood by non-scientific writers and commentators who employ Heisenberg as an allusion, as seen in this use of the term, from Caryn James's review of *Charades*, a novel by Janette Turner Hospital, *The New York Times*, February 18, 1989:

> "She knows enough about Heisenberg to realize that the act of observation alters the object observed; or in literary terms, telling a story alters the story being told."

Probably a better allusion for laypersons to use when they want to point out the impact of observation on objects, or people, is the Hawthorne Effect. During a human relations study conducted between 1960 and 1965 at the Hawthorne Works plant of the Western Electric Co., in Cicero, Illinois, researchers noted that workers who perceived they were being observed demonstrated a temporary increase in productivity.

**Hemlock, To Drink.** To kill oneself, especially by taking poison.

That's how death came to the Greek philosopher Socrates. In 399 B.C., he was tried and sentenced to death on charges of corrupting the morals of youth and committing religious heresies. Resisting all efforts to save his life, he willingly drank the cup of the poison hemlock given to him. His life and death were recorded by his most famous student, Plato.

Today the phrase is used figuratively to describe an act which is deliberately destructive of one's interests.

The term in use, by Barbara Tuchman in *The Proud Tower*, setting the scene for the historic vote in 1910 in which the British House of Lords gave up its power of veto over the House of Commons:

"On August 10, the day for drinking the hemlock, the temperature reached a record of a hundred degrees and tension at Westminster was even higher, for, unlike previous political crises, the outcome was in suspense."

Another example, from Mary McGrory, *The Washington Post*, September 14, 1989, on difficulties confronting Democrats in the House of Representatives:

"While they were groaning though this silly exercise, the Democrats were sipping hemlock on the capital gains tax, an issue on which their position has been dramatically different from that of the Republicans."

**Herodotus.** (hih-ROD-uh-tus) This Greek historian is called "the father of history."

He was the first to research the past and to treat events as history rather than myth. He lived circa 480-425 B.C. He is famous for his highly readable chronicles of the wars between the Persian Empire and the Greek city-states. George Seldes in his *The Great Thoughts* notes that the first historian was also the first muckraker, exposing bribery of the oracle at Delphi [see **Delphic**] by military men seeking favorable predictions for the outcome of battles.

Employed as an allusion, he appears in *The Village Voice*, "Jock-beat," February 21, 1989, in a quotation of A. J. Liebling to the effect that writer Pierce Egan was "the Herodotus of pugilism."


**Hindenburg.** The president of the weak German republic that preceded Hitler, and whose name was given to a German dirigible. The crash of the airship *Hindenburg* has made its name a metaphor for disaster, for the total failure of ideas and projects.

Field Marshal Paul von Hindenburg was chief of staff of the German armies during the first world war and was elected president of Germany in 1925. The aged Hindenburg's attempts to resist the takeover of power by Hitler were feeble; Hitler became chancellor in 1933 and assumed the presidency after Hindenburg's death the following year at age 87.

The airship *Hindenburg* successfully crossed the Atlantic but exploded on May 6, 1937, as it approached its mooring mast in Lakehurst, N.J., at a cost of 36 lives.

The term in use, by *The Boston Globe*, August 22, 1987, describing the reaction of former Hart-for-president staff members to rumors that Gary Hart, politically crippled by personal scandal, might try for redemption by reentering the race for the 1988 Democratic presidential nomination:

> "Former policy chief David Dreyer said of reentry, 'It's absurd. If this is a trial balloon it's the Hindenburg of trial balloons.' "


**Hit the Wall.** The point in a marathon in which the runner feels utter mental and physical exhaustion—usually around the 20-mile mark. This unpleasant state of affairs is probably brought about by the body's running out of its fuel, muscle glycogen.

Bill Rogers describes it this way in *Marathoning:* "When you hit the wall, you suddenly catapult into a whole new world. When I talk about the wall, I mean the psychological impact you encounter when you start to fall apart. Sometimes it hits you very suddenly. Usually you can feel it building up. There is a tightening in your legs and a dizziness. You are mentally fatigued and your perspectives and your goals change very drastically."

The term in use, by columnist and marathoner Colman McCarthy in *The Washington Post*, November 7, 1988:

> "The marathon has become an athletic rite of passage, the personality's run-in with mediocrity. It is the metaphor of choice in the presidential race now stumbling in hit-the-wall and hit-the-fan exhaustion to Election Day's 26.2 mile finish line."

**Hobson's Choice.** In reality, though often misused, no choice at all.

The expression comes from Thomas Hobson, a livery stable operator in England. His fame is based on his rigid policy of never allowing his customers to choose the nag they wanted to hire; no horse could be taken out of turn.

The term in use, by columnist Andy Grundberg in *The New York Times*, March 13, 1988, discussing the properties of a new type of color film:

> "For such customized information and delivery one has to pay a premium, of course, which is why pro films generally cost more than their non-pro equivalents. But since the beauties of Ektachrome 100 Plus currently only come in a professional version, the choice is Hobson's."

**Hoi Polloi.** (HOY puh-LOY) In Greek, literally, the many, but in popular use a sneering term for the common people, the rabble.

The term in use, in *The Village Voice*, November 8, 1988, by John Derevlany discussing the candidacy of former Army general Pete Dawkins in the New Jersey race for the U.S. Senate:

"Dawkins so loved the Garden State that he initially reached out over the Hudson and touched it with call-forwarding from New Jersey to his Madison Avenue apartment [in Manhattan]. His unabashed affinity for New Jersey, where three-fourths of the hoi polloi live in communities of 50,000 or less, was best captured when he declared, 'I'd blow my brains out if I had to live in a small town.'"

## Hoist With One's Own Petard. (PAY-tar) Caught in one's own trap, or destroyed by the very weapon that you were to employ against someone else.

Petard is French for a mine-like device used in medieval times. It was packed with gunpowder and attached to doors and gates to blow them up. Just the thing for breaking into an enemy's castle to end those tiresome sieges, when the science of warfare was getting acquainted with guns and gunpowder. The problem with these primitive contrivances was that they tended to blow up the unlucky person assigned to touch them off. As Shakespeare put it in *Hamlet:*

For 'tis sport, to have the engineer
Hoist with his own petar . . .

The term in contemporary use, by James K. Glassman in *The New Republic*, April 11, 1988:

"A year ago, at a *New Republic* editorial meeting, I predicted that Ronald Reagan would run for a third term and win (I still think that if the ridiculous 22nd Amendment, passed by vengeful Republicans now hoist with their own petard, were repealed Reagan could win this time around)."

## Holy Grail. The object of an idealistic quest, an all but unattainable goal.

A grail is a cup or chalice. The one that tradition says Jesus used at the Last Supper vanished and became the subject of numerous legends and romances of the Middle Ages. Versions differ, but the tale goes like this: Joseph of Arimathea (who offered the tomb built to house his own remains for Jesus' burial) took the cup to what is now England, where he founded Glastonbury Abbey and worked to convert Britons to Christianity. The Grail disappeared, and the search became all-important—and part of the legend of King Arthur and his Knights of the Round Table.

The term in use, by Joel Garreau in *The Washington Post*, June 20, 1988:

> "The Houston Galleria is more than a mall. . . . it is beginning to feel like a community. Hotels and office skyscrapers connect intricately with shopping areas and promenades in dense combinations never before achieved in America outside a downtown. Ages and occupations mix in a fashion approaching that Holy Grail for urban planners: the 24-hour city."

**Homeric.** Larger-than-life; mythic; of heroic dimensions.

This adjective comes from the name of Homer, the ancient Greek bard who is commonly accepted as author of the *Iliad* and the *Odyssey*, epic poems relating the stories of gods and heroes in the Trojan War, and the adventures of Odysseus.

Little is known of the real Homer—not even whether he actually lived, or if so, when. According to legend, he was blind. The poems are among the Western world's greatest literary works.

The term in use, by Russell Baker, *The New York Times*, March 13, 1989:

> "There has been a gaudier baseball show than usual this spring, with players carrying on like nasty rich kids. . . . The story of Wade Boggs' adulterous romantic life on the road for the Red Sox has titillated even readers of Penthouse, whose tastes cannot be easy to titillate. From the Yankees, stories about Homeric boozing."

**Horatio Alger.** A prolific 19th-century writer of books for boys about boys whose honesty, perseverance and cheerfulness inevitably led to material success.

The pattern was repeated so endlessly in Alger's books that "a Horatio Alger story" has become a synonym for a rags-to-riches saga. And the author is so identified with the **genre** that "Horatio Alger" is often applied to someone who has achieved such success, thus confusing the author and his creation. Alger's heroes invariably were newsboys or bootblacks. Pluck worked for them, but luck figured in prominently; a worthy lad would stop a runaway carriage and wind up marrying the rich banker's daughter whose life he had saved.

In contrast to his grindstoney heroes, Alger was somewhat of a youthful rebel. After a brilliant academic career, he spent several years trying to make a living as a magazine writer rather than taking the path chosen for him by his family—the ministry. Eventually he returned from a sojourn to Europe to attempt, unsuccessfully, to enlist in the Union Army during the Civil War and then enrolled in a seminary. He continued writing and his first success in the genre he was to make his own—*Ragged Dick: or, Street Life in New York* — was published in 1867. He ultimately wrote some 120 books, most indistinguishable from each other.

Intriguing, too, is the odd life Alger led in New York. He never married and fled from women who seemed interested in him. He lived alone and became increasingly eccentric in appearance and behavior. He spent a good deal of time at a home for newsboys (which sheltered the otherwise homeless street urchins of the day who hawked newspapers). It was his charity as well as the source of inspiration for his novels.

The term in use, by Ira Berkow, writing in *The New York Times*, May 22, 1989, on the New York Mets team of 1969:

> "You'd read that the Mets had pumped optimism into the lives of the downtrodden, the working stiff; these people, said some social observers, could now grasp a straw of hope. The Mets were the ragamuffins of baseball until then. It was Horatio Alger revisited, but with a bedsheet flapping from the mansion window. The sheet was inscribed: 'Macy's Long Island Warehouse Loves the Mets.' "

Another example, from *The Economist*, May 20, 1989, on the

nomination of William Lucas as assistant attorney general for civil rights in the Bush administration:

> "He is a black Horatio Alger: orphaned at 14, he won a track scholarship to college and attended law school at night while working as a New York city police officer."

**Horatius at the Bridge.** Someone who conducts a valiant defense against overwhelming odds.

Horatius Cocles was a legendary hero of the ancient Roman republic. Tradition has it that he saved Rome when the city was attacked by the Etruscans, led by Lars Porsena of Clusium, in the 6th century B.C. There are several versions of the story, but the predominant one says Horatius and two companions held off the entire invading army while the Romans chopped away at the wooden bridge behind them to cut off the enemy's access to the city. Horatius then swam to safety, having sent his two companions back earlier.

That's the version popularized in Thomas Babington Macauley's *The Lays of Ancient Rome*, which immortalized these exploits for the Victorian era in verses of ringing doggerel like this:

> Then out spake brave Horatius,
> The Captain of the Gate:
> To every man upon this earth
> Death cometh soon or late.
> And how can man die better
> Than facing fearful odds,
> For the ashes of his fathers,
> And the temples of his Gods.
>
> "Horatius," quoth the Consul,
> "As thou sayest, so let it be."
> And straight against the great array
> Forth went the dauntless Three.
> For Romans in Rome's quarrel
> Spared neither land nor gold,
> Nor son nor wife, nor limb nor life,
> In the brave days of old.

And even if you are not fixated on poetry read in your high school literature class, you have probably heard this refrain somewhere, as Horatius prepares to swim to safety:

"Oh, Tiber! father Tiber!
To whom the Romans pray,
A Roman's life, a Roman's arms
Take thou in charge this day!"

While the traitor Sextus mutters:

"Curse on him," quoth false Sextus,
"Will not the villain drown?"

The term in use, in *Time*, November 20, 1989:

"Hoping to revive Bush's cherished reductions in the capital-gains tax, Senate Republicans considered attaching it to the debt-ceiling legislation. Majority Leader George Mitchell, increasingly playing the role of an unyielding Horatius at the Bridge, blocked them."

Another example, from Barbara Tuchman's *The Guns of August* (1962):

" . . . sudden peril loomed when it was found that the bridges could not be destroyed for lack of an exploder to fire the charges. A rush by the Germans across the canal in the midst of the retirement could convert orderly retreat to a rout and might even effect a breakthrough. No single Horatius could hold the bridge, but Captain Wright of the Royal Engineers swung himself hand over hand under the bridge at Mariette in an attempt to connect the charges."

Horatius is sometimes confused with another fictional character, the Shakespearean pal of Hamlet, Horatio. (As in, "Alas, poor Yorick. I knew him well, Horatio.")

*The New Republic*'s "**Zeitgeist** Checklist" of June 6, 1988, for example, put Horatio at the bridge, not in Denmark where he belongs:

"*Drug legalization.* More mayors, some congressmen, and few governors now favor a legalization debate. Well, there is a debate, and it's on page one. But now what? Representative Rangel, who heads the narcotics committee, thinks he's Horatio at the bridge; he dismisses anti-prohibition arguments out of hand."

One final point. Many historians now agree that the story of Horatius was something cooked up by the Romans to rationalize, if not cover up, their own aggression and total conquest of the Etruscans. Alas, poor Lars Porsena, but it's the winners who write the history.

**Hors de Combat.** (or deh COHM-bah) French; it means out of action; disabled.

The term in use, in the gossip column of *The Chatham Courier*, Chatham, New York, September 15, 1988: "A prominent Kinderhook ladies' man will be hors de combat for the next two weeks. He checked in Monday at a Boston hospital for the works—hernia, vasectomy, hair transplant. . . . "

Another example, from Martin Pave, *The Boston Globe*, January 21, 1989:

> "Losers of three straight and with three of last year's starters rendered hors de combat, the Celtics needed somebody to step forward in crunch time—which lately had resembled crumble time in Chicago, Detroit and Philadelphia."

**Hot Stove League.** All talk, no action in this league. The baseball season is over, snow is on the ground, there is nothing else to do but sit with other fans around a hot stove, real or imagined, and talk about seasons ancient, the season past or the season soon to come.

The origin is uncertain. The expression was applied to baseball around the turn of the century. *The Dickson Baseball Dictionary* also reports references to horse racing's off-season.

The term in use, by Dan Shaughnessy of *The Boston Globe* sports section, October 25, 1988, discussing post-season player moves:

> "Here's more cordwood for New England's ever-blazing Hot Stove League. Red Sox catcher Rich Gedman was granted

immediate, second-look free agency by arbitrator George Nicolau."

Another example, also from the *Globe*, by Paul Hirshson, September 12, 1989:

"The party is expected to attract the political junkies and lots of talk from the hot stove league of presidential politics."

**Hubris.** (HYOO-bruhs) This is the pride that goes before the fall. It is an excessive, overweening, I-can-make-the-Red-Sea-part, arrogant pride.

In Greek tragedy, hubris is a prideful refusal to accept the authority of the gods. When the central character begins to believe that his achievements result from his own powers and virtue rather than the favor of the gods, he is laid low.

An example, from *The New Republic*'s "Washington Diarist" of May 18, 1987, talking about the author's reluctant sympathy for insider-trading wheeler-dealer Ivan Boesky:

"I have to admit that there was something exhilarating about Ivan in the old days. He had so much hubris, was so outrageous that it was fun watching him, whispering behind his back. Almost everyone suspected that he was due for a fall. . . . "

And another example, in Melvin Maddocks' review of David Halberstam's **The Best and the Brightest**, in *Time*, November 27, 1972:

"Like all proper tragedies, *The Best and the Brightest* begins with *hubris*: the certainty of a young and ebullient President Kennedy and his New Frontiersmen that they constituted an elite, 'a new breed of thinker-doers' who could handle the world, to say nothing of what President Johnson was to refer to as 'a raggedy-ass little fourth-rate country.' "

# I

**Iago.** (YAH-goh) One of the most purely malevolent characters in literature, a clever and scheming provocateur.

He makes his appearance in Shakespeare's *Othello*. Iago is an aide to the Moorish general Othello and is bitterly disappointed when Othello instead chooses Cassio as his lieutenant. Iago plots to avenge himself on both. Although maintaining a show of being a good friend, Iago cunningly manipulates Othello and fosters suspicions that Othello's wife, Desdemona, is two-timing him with Cassio. Mad with jealousy, Othello kills his wife and then himself when he realizes her innocence.

The term in use, by Gore Vidal, quoted in Garry Wills' book *Nixon Agonistes*, describing Kennedy assistant and speechwriter Richard Goodwin:

> ". . . his established pattern of showing up where the action is hottest had even taken him to the Pierre Hotel when Nixon was choosing his administration. Men were beginning to feel Goodwin was not trustworthy. As Gore Vidal said of him, 'Goodwin is forever an Iago in pursuit of an Othello.' "

And from David Denby, writing in *Premiere*, October 1989, on Alfred Hitchcock's 1943 film, *Shadow of a Doubt*:

> "Uncle Charlie [Joseph Cotten], however, has not only a cruel temperament but a cruel point of view. Genial and sociable, he is nevertheless tormented by the awfulness of existence. 'Do you know the world is a foul sty? Do you know if you ripped the fronts off houses you'd find swine? The world's a hell,' he rants in the extraordinary, Iago-like aria that he delivers to his niece in a cheap bar."

**Icon.** (IGH-kahn) Someone who has achieved such fame and authority in his field of endeavor that he is accorded reverent respect.

Literally, in Greek, the term means image. In the Eastern Orthodox Church, it refers specifically to a sacred representation of Jesus, a
saint or an angel. These icons may be mosaics, paintings or low-relief
sculpture. They range from simple to richly ornate and are accorded
the burning of candles and incense.

(The opposite of reverence for icons is iconoclasm, Greek for
image-breaking, or the opposition to the religious use of images, out
of fear that the practice leads to idol worship. In contemporary
language, an iconoclast is one who tears down popular figures,
cherished beliefs or traditional institutions.)

The term in use, by Michael Milstein in *National Parks*,
November-December 1988, writing about the forest fires that summer in Yellowstone National Park:

> "At the end of July, the charring of an American icon had
> become national news."

Another example, from Anne Taylor Fleming, writing in *The New
York Times*, May 10, 1989, on a palimony suit against actor Clint
Eastwood:

> "The current target is none other than Dirty Harry himself,
> a.k.a. Clint Eastwood, who, at age 58, with his laconic
> sneer and tough-guy epithets, has become a virtual Ameri-
> can icon. A recent Esquire cover story noted that in 1985
> young Americans put Mr. Eastwood at the top of their list
> of heroes, ahead of Ronald Reagan, the Pope and Mother
> Teresa."

In use as an adjective, by Katherine Dieckmann in *The Village
Voice*, November 15, 1988, reviewing the movie *Far North*, written
and directed by Sam Shepard:

> "Predictable but true, Sam Shepard's increasing iconic
> popularity has paralleled the dwindling of any edge in his
> writing."

And from Deirdre Donahue, *USA Today*, December 18, 1989, on
cooking and entertainment writer Martha Stewart:

> "This radiant blond icon beams at us from 45 K-Mart
> commercials and the pages of 2.5 million cooking and

entertaining books. We hear her mellifluous voice on TV specials that allow us a peek into the sacred shrine of her perfect 1805 Connecticut home."

**Id.** Coined by Freud to name the unconscious or instinctive impulses, such as the sex drive and aggression present at birth, which motivate individuals. In Freudian theory, the id is one of three agencies of human personality. The other two are the ego (the conscious) and the superego (the externally imposed standards or regulations that humans live by).

The term in use, by Jim Hoagland in *The Washington Post*, September 20, 1988, discussing Zbigniew Brzezinski's joining the presidential campaign of George Bush:

> "You will recall Brzezinski as the id of the Carter administration's divided foreign policy brain, constantly battling the superegos in Cyrus Vance's State Department. Those battles created the shambles that helped bring Ronald Reagan and George Bush to the White House nearly eight years ago. Now Bush has named Brzezinski a member of his team of senior campaign foreign policy advisers, presumably so Brzezinski can help attack the shambles he helped create in the first place."

Humorist Dave Barry explains it all this way in *The Washington Post Magazine*, February 19, 1989:

> "Psychologically, the most important parts of your brain are the 'id,' a small, slime-covered organism that hardly ever gets to leave your subconscious and consequently thinks about nothing but sex; and the 'ego' (in women, the 'egress'), which oversees all of your mental activity until your fourth beer and which, because it is very strict, is sometimes referred to as 'the Rev. Jerry Falwell of the Brain.'"

**Idée Fixe.** (EE-day FEEKS) An obsession or preoccupation. Literally, in French, a fixed idea.

The term in use, in *The New Republic*, December 5, 1988, quoting Eric Auerbach on Don Quixote and his mania for chivalry, that once the "idealism of Don Quixote's idée fixe takes hold of him, everything he does in that state is so incompatible with the existing world that it produces only comic confusion."

**Idiot Savant.** (ID-ee-uht sa-VAHNT or SAV-ahnt) A person of below-normal intelligence who nevertheless shows brilliance in one particular, narrowly-defined activity. These people usually demonstrate their extraordinary ability in music, mathematics, feats of memory or extrasensory perception.

The term is of French origin. "Idiot" originally meant someone living a reclusive life, in a private world, and "savant" meant a knowledgeable person.

Idiots savant should not be confused with prodigies, who frequently show signs of genius at an early age. Mozart, who was composing at age 5, was one.

The term in use, by Stanley Kauffmann in *The New Republic*, May 9, 1988, reviewing a movie:

"Mess though it is as a total experience, 'The Moderns' is worth discussing for two reasons. First, [director Alan] Rudolph has become (if it's possible to become one) an idiot savant of cinematics."

**Immaculate Conception.** A doctrine of the Roman Catholic Church that the Virgin Mary was free of sin from the moment of her conception ("immaculate" meaning free from spot or blemish). Contrary to popular misconception among non-Catholics, this does not refer to the Virgin Birth, the birth of Jesus, but to the conception of the Virgin.

The immaculate conception of Mary had been a widespread belief for centuries, although argued about by scholars in the Middle Ages. Thomas Aquinas didn't accept it; Duns Scotus did (and doctrinal disputes being bitter then as always, adherents of Duns Scotus were called "dunsers," which then became "dunces").

The Pope finally settled the issue (so to speak) in 1854 with the **papal bull** *Ineffabilis Deus*, agreeing with the dunsers.

In contemporary use, the term refers with sarcasm to something which is brought into being in an unconventional manner, or with no apparent author—something that miraculously appears.

The term in use, by Richard Darman in *The Washington Post*, October 26, 1987, discussing the need for an agreement to reduce the budget deficit in the aftermath of the stock market crash of October 19:

> "Now what's needed is to arrange the political equivalent of an immaculate conception: a compromise that materializes without any politician having to take the blame."

**In Flagrante Delicto.** (in flah-GRAHN-teh dih-LIK-toh) Literally, in Latin, it means "in the heat of the crime," or caught in the act, red-handed. It's frequently applied (perhaps because of the insinuating richness of the phrase) to those caught in an illicit sexual act.

The term in use, in Carolyn Banks' review of Michael Korda's *The Fortune*, *The Washington Post*, March 14, 1989:

> "This novel opens with the man who handles legal matters for the legendary Bannerman family traveling to a dusty airstrip in Uganda to announce the death of Arthur Aldon Bannerman to Cici, his daughter. Well, Cici and the rest of the family don't know what is worse: that Bannerman, 65, died *in flagrante delicto* in an apartment inhabited by a ravishing 24-year-old woman. . . . "

Another example, from Christopher Buckley in his review of *From: The President, Richard Nixon's Secret Files*, edited by Bruce Oudes, *The New York Times*, February 26, 1989:

> " 'From: The President' is pretty much everything you would expect it to be: fascinating, appalling, boring every now and then, but mostly fascinating, showing human beings caught in the act of being themselves, or rather, laboring with considerable lack of success *not* to be themselves; history *in flagrante delicto*."

**Invisible Hand.** Adam Smith, the *laissez faire* economist, gave this name to his doctrine of enlightened self-interest.

Smith, writing in 1776, argued that individuals, seeking to further their self-interest, will be led, "as if guided by an invisible hand," to achieve the best for all.

Smith opposed government interference with free competition and foreign trade, arguing that a policy of "laissez faire" (French—"allow to do" or "to let things alone") would promote individual freedom, the best use of economic resources and economic growth. Critics of the invisible hand proposition say it might work under conditions of perfect competition, but those conditions do not exist in the real world.

The term in use, in a headline in *The Washington Post*, December 29, 1988, over an article by Joel Garreau about street-corner markets for illegal drugs in the District of Columbia and analysis of crime according to free-market principles:

> "The Invisible Hand Guides D.C.'s Visible Menace."

And reporter Jerry Knight explains his **leveraged buyout** of a BMW, *The Washington Post*, December 6, 1988:

> "Car salesmen are just investment bankers with white shoes, the way I figure it. Undercoating, underwriting, it's all the same. The invisible hand of the free market gets into your pocket one way or another. . . .
>
> "So I offered this guy the same kind of deal that Kohlberg Kravis Roberts & Co. made to RJR Nabisco—you know, where they bought $25 billion worth of company with $15 million of their own money. I said I'd give him $15 down on a $25,000 car."

**Iron Lady.** A nickname of British Prime Minister Margaret Thatcher, applied to her in a fit of pique by *Krasnayazvesda*, the Soviet defense ministry newspaper, in January 1976. The paper was irked by hardline Thatcher speeches contending the Soviets were bent on world domination.

Perhaps *Krasnayazvesda* in applying the term to Mrs. Thatcher had other famous Iron types in mind, such as the Iron Duke (the Duke of Wellington) or the Iron Chancellor (Otto von Bismarck, who, to unite Germany, provoked wars with Denmark, Austria and France).

The Russians' attack and the appellation proved to be a political boon to Mrs. Thatcher with only one pitfall: occasionally someone (sometimes a newsman in a former colony) slips and calls her the Iron Maiden, thus likening her to the heavy metal rock group or a medieval instrument of torture—a coffin-like box large enough to contain a man and full of spikes that impaled the occupant when the lid was closed.

The term in use, by Karen DeYoung in *The Washington Post*, January 4, 1988, profiling Mrs. Thatcher's husband:

"Far from causing outrage, Denis Thatcher's caricatures have brought him no small measure of public affection. One theory is that his alleged lapses make him a welcome antidote to his wife, the nation's Iron Lady."

Another example, from U.S. News and World Report, August 28/ September 4, 1989, on Thatcher's political troubles:

"The Iron Lady's corrosion at home is paralleled overseas."


**Iron Triangle.** One of those expressions dear to Washington, it refers to the friendly/incestuous/sometimes corrupt mesh of communication and support among lobbyists, government agencies and the members of Congress who oversee the affairs of the agencies.

A classic example is the linkage of defense contractors, officials of the Department of Defense and members of Congress who sit on committees with jurisdiction over the department or that recommend its appropriations. Also part are other members of Congress who have important contractors or a significant military installation in their districts. Many times Defense Department employees, and sometimes former senators or representatives, go to work for the contractors. They provide each other with information useful to win or keep a contract. Or they might provide inside information on budget cuts under consideration so that opposition can be mounted even before the decisions have been made. The upshot is that changes in policy, especially spending cuts, are made very difficult.

Iron triangles work the same way throughout the government, from agriculture to banking regulation to health care to transportation.

The term in use, by President Ronald Reagan in a speech 37 days before leaving office:

> "Administrations come and go, but the members of the iron triangle endure." (Reagan, in keeping with his own views of government, had his own version of the triangle: he took the executive branch out and put the news media in.)

# J

**J'accuse.** (Ja-KOOZ) A dramatic and impassioned accusation of wrongdoing and cover-up. The French phrase, which means "I accuse," comes from a celebrated open letter by writer Emile Zola, expressing outrage and protest at government actions in the infamous **Dreyfus affair.** "J'accuse" is one of the most famous and successful polemics ever written.

Publication of the letter on the morning of January 13, 1898 electified Paris. The newspaper *Aurore*, in a special edition, printed it in bold letters under the headline "J'accuse," a title taken from the litany of charges in the conclusion of the letter, each beginning "I accuse. . . ." Publication of the letter marked a turning point in the epic struggle that had gripped France.

Zola accused the government and army of convicting Dreyfus on the basis of a secret document which Dreyfus had no opportunity to rebut, conducting an elaborate and criminal cover-up, and misleading the press and people to conceal these actions. He denounced the "odious anti-Semitism from which the great liberal France of the rights of man will die if it is not cured."

Zola was successfully prosecuted in the courts and forced to flee the country. He was vilified as a foreigner who took up the cause of Dreyfus for mercenary reasons, when in fact it nearly ruined him financially. But his role was pivotal in turning the tide toward eventual justice for Dreyfus and in forcing the public and government to confront the truth.

The term in use, by Charles Paul Freund in *The Washington Post*, January 3, 1989:

> "Characteristically, Reagan's effort was less another version
> of the usual 'Beware!' farewell than it was his familiar
> 'J'accuse!' approach of finding someone to blame."

Another example, from T.R. Reid, in *The Washington Post*, July

23, 1989, commenting on press coverage of the previous summer's fires in Yellowstone Park:

> "If the first job of the media is to convey accurate information, then we failed in our job. I offer this assessment not as a j'accuse, but rather as a nostra culpa [see **Mea Culpa**]. I played a small role in the *Post's* coverage of Yellowstone last summer, and there are definite evocations of moonscape in some of my own copy."

**Jacobean.** (jak-uh-BEE-uhn) Referring to the literature and architecture, as well as the darkening mood and style, of the reign of James I, king of England from 1603 to 1625. The adjective comes from "Jacobus," the Latin form of the name James.

It was a period of great achievement, producing some of the finest writing in the English language: Shakespeare's great tragedies, the poetry of John Donne and Ben Jonson, the essays of Francis Bacon and the King James Version of the Bible.

The period was a cautious and somber one in contrast to the booming optimism of the Elizabethan years. This reflected the growing tensions in English society over religion and values. **Guy Fawkes** and the other members of the Gunpowder Plot tried to blow up Parliament and the king; growing quarrels over the king's authority and the divergence of values between the pleasure-loving court and its Puritan critics in Parliament would ultimately lead to the Civil War and the execution of King Charles I in 1649. "Jacobean melancholy" shows up in the tragic themes of the plays of the period, which provide some of the most memorable portraits of evil in the history of drama. Today plots or dark scenes of bloody murder and vengeance are frequently characterized as "Jacobean."

The term in use, by Joel E. Siegal, reviewing the Blake Edwards movie *Sunset* in Washington, D.C.'s *City Paper*, May 6, 1988:

> "In his comedies, Edwards has revealed a preoccupation with pain and physical cruelty, an obsession that is grotesquely indulged in *Sunset*. From the opening reel crotch-twistings and beatings, the punishment escalates to

Jacobean proportions, ending in an ocean of blood and an uncommonly high body count."

In use again, by Mel Gussow, reviewing Caryl Churchill's play, *Serious Money*, in *The New York Times*, February 10, 1988:

"This is a **neo**-Restoration comedy crossed with a Jacobean revenger's tale. As the author indicates, with all malice intended, there is no end to the greed."

**Jacobins.** (JAK-uh-buhns) A group of French intellectuals who started out as relatively moderate democrats in 1789, but became the radical leadership of the French Revolution, ushering in the Reign of Terror. Their name is synonymous with extreme radicalism and revolutionary zeal.

The group, formally the Society of Friends of the Constitution, was one of many political clubs active during the Revolution. They met in a former Dominican convent; the nickname Jacobins comes from Jacobin, the Parisian name for the Dominicans. (Because the Dominicans had first been established in the Rue St. Jacques, because the Latin for Jacques is Jacobus—hence Jacobins.)

The club's members included some of the most influential leaders of the National Assembly: Mirabeau, Danton, Marat and **Robespierre** among them.

Initially they sought to limit the powers of the king but grew increasingly extreme. The Reign of Terror, in 1793-94, was a wartime dictatorship to preserve the republic against counter-revolutionaries, and sent thousands to the guillotine. Ultimately, popular discontent led to the overthrow of the government installed by Robespierre and others.

The term in use, by Matthew Cooper in *The Washington Monthly*, December 1988:

"The idea of Jacobin-style revolution haunted Dickens, who poured his fears into prose in A *Tale of Two Cities*."

In use again by Walter Lippmann, as quoted by Erik v. Kuehnelt-Leddihn in the *National Review*, October 24, 1986:

"The democratic ideas of the French Revolution, so despised by the Founding Fathers, have, since 1828, deeply
affected the American political climate. Walter Lippmann
told us that 'Jacobinism becomes the popular creed of
American democracy.' "

William Safire in his *Political Dictionary* reports a dust-up that
arose from a misunderstanding of the term. John P. Roche, a White
House official in the Johnson administration, referred in an interview
to "the West Side [of New York City] Jacobins." This was reported in
the *Partisan Review* as "jackal bins," causing, as Safire puts it, "a mild
furor in the intellectual community."

**Jihad.** (jee-HAHD, jee-HAD) An Arabic word meaning crusade or
holy war, referring to a war by Muslims against infidels (unbelievers).
In English usage the word is used figuratively to refer to bitterly-
fought conflicts.

The term in use, in a *Wall Street Journal* editorial, August 9,
1989, railing against the activities of Democrats in Congress:

"Their current jihad against a capital-gains tax cut is an
attempt to revive 1930s-style attacks on 'economic royal-
ists,' i.e. the rich."

**Jingoism.** Cocky, pugnacious, shrill, chauvinistic, xenophobic,
chest-thumping patriotism.

The term originated in British politics. In 1876, Disraeli threatened the Russians with war if they continued interfering in Turkey.
The London music halls rang with the refrain:

We don't want to fight,
But by Jingo, if we do,
We've got the ships,
We've got the men,
We've got the money, too.

The song and theme made their appearance in the United States in
the late 19th century as the country experienced its own taste of
imperial exuberance. James G. Blaine, secretary of state (1889-92)

under President Harrison, earned the nickname "Jingo Jim." The jingle made an appearance in this period during a fishing dispute with Britain and Canada in this Americanized version:

We don't want to fight,
But by Jingo, if we do,
We'll scoop in all the fishing grounds
And the whole Dominion too.

The term in use, by Norman Chad in "Sportswaves" in *The Washington Post*, September 20, 1988, discussing television coverage of the Olympics:

"NBC largely has steered away from the jingoism, brought us admirable camera work and presented a balanced picture of the proceedings."

# K

**Kafkaesque.** (kahf-kuh-ESK) Scenes that are grotesque and surreal and in which individuals are frustrated by a mindless bureaucracy.

It comes from the name of author Franz Kafka (1893-1924) whose work was characterized by nightmarish settings in which individuals were crushed by nonsensical, blind authority. Kafka's work foreshadowed the horrors of the modern police state and expressed vividly the 20th-century emotions of alienation, powerlessness and fear. In *The Trial*, an innocent man is deprived of the means of defending himself and, condemned, is stabbed to death by polite executioners; in *Metamorphosis*, a young man wakes up to find that he has turned into a gigantic cockroach.

The term in use, by Richard Conniff, *Time*, October 3, 1988, reviewing a study of public bathrooms in Washington, D.C. by architecture professor Alexander Kira:

> "The tour adjourns to the Martin Luther King Memorial Library downtown, a large, gloomy building in the soul-crushing modernist style. Here the search for a rest room takes on a literary character, mainly Kafkaesque: a visitor finds the men's room down a darkened corridor on the third floor, just past the security cameras, but it's locked and a sign on the door says AFTER 5:30 USE MEN'S ROOM ON A-LEVEL.
>
> "A librarian supplies directions: take that elevator there, cross the lobby, take another elevator to A-level, and bingo, you're there. But the second elevator has a sign on it: OUT OF SERVICE. PLEASE USE ELEVATOR AT OTHER END OF BUILDING. The stairs are handier, but they lack directional signs and so lead the uninitiated to an underground garage. Back up one flight, through a vast, empty room, into another room containing only a security desk (unattended), just in time to see the ostensibly broken elevator arrive. . . . "

**Karma.** (KAHR-muh) In Hinduism and Buddhism, this Sanskrit word refers to the cumulative effect a person's actions will have through his many lifetimes. The accumulation of good and bad deeds will control his destiny in the next stage of existence. Wrongful actions may go unpunished in one life, but the moral debt remains and payment is exacted in the future.

The word came into vogue in the United States in the 1960s as part of the period's fascination with Eastern religions. Today, in our culture, the term is used loosely to mean fate or destiny, or to explain events or circumstances, or to refer to the aura felt to emanate from persons, places or things—good (or bad) vibrations.

The word in use, by R. Emmett Tyrell Jr., in *The American Spectator*, August 1988, decrying certain elements in the Democratic Party:

> "These zealots want something other than power from politics. . . . They want a sense of existential well-being, good Karma, a pleasant sense of oneness with the Cosmos, the Revolution, the Movement—that sort of flapdoodle."

Another example, from Dennis Drabelle, reviewing Susan Sontag's *AIDS And Its Metaphors* in *The Washington Post Book World*, January 15, 1989:

> "The very word cancer has lost some of its bad karma."

And from David Margolick, *The New York Times*, December 1, 1989:

> "After seven years of litigation, there is still some dispute over whether toxic solvents dumped at a tannery in Woburn, Mass., found their way into the municipal water supply and caused six deaths from leukemia. But there is no denying that bad karma from the case has seeped even further than the chemicals, crossing the Charles River and into Boston's blue-blooded bar."

**Kitsch.** (kich) German: literally, junk, trash. A word applied to objects or culture deemed to have no aesthetic value, produced for the vulgar popular taste. For all that, it is possible to love kitsch— sometimes for its very kitschiness.

The term in use, by *The Economist*, January 21, 1989, on the change in presidential style between Reagan and Bush:

> "One flaw in the argument that Mr. Reagan's kitsch will be replaced by Mr. Bush's class is to be found in the list of musicians entertaining the guests at various inaugural celebrations. Mr. Bush's taste in music is if anything worse than Mr. Reagan's."

And from *The New Republic*, December 4, 1989:

> "FREEDOM OF KITSCH: Two years after the Constitution's 200th birthday, the commission on its bicentennial is still spending $14 million annually on festivities. Although McDonald's is no longer using bicentennial trayliners for its burgers, the commission's chairman, ex-Chief Justice Warren Burger, has been keeping the marketing spirit of 1787 alive. Besides T-shirts, hats, and key chains, the commission has licensed the use of its official logo to makers of 'heirloom quality furniture,' crystal, and replicas of George Washington's wine coaster."

**Know-Nothings.** The popular name for an anti-foreign movement that developed in the middle of the 19th century in the United States in opposition to immigration and immigrants. Today, the term is applied somewhat more broadly, incorporating those who take a reactionary political position based on bigotry, ignorance and emotion.

Dislike of immigrants was rooted in fears of cultural dilution, economic competition and the immigrants' growing political power, but the chief element was anti-Catholicism. Agitation started in the 1830s with the publication of anti-Catholic newspapers and books, the stonings of Catholic institutions and the burning of the Ursuline Convent School in Charlestown, Massachusetts, in 1834.

By the 1850s, aliens constituted half the population of New York City and outnumbered native-born Americans in Chicago, Milwaukee and St. Louis. The great Irish famine, from 1845 to 1847, sent millions of Irish to America.

Secret groups sprang up to resist the perceived menace. The Sons of America, the Druids and others united to form the Order of the Star Spangled Banner. Because members were sworn to secrecy and refused to answer questions about their activities, they were called Know-Nothings.

In 1854 and 1855, the movement captured several state legislatures, elected several governors and claimed the allegiance of at least 75 congressmen. In 1856, as the American Party, it won a quarter of the popular vote for the presidency under the candidacy of former President Millard Fillmore (he had been Zachary Taylor's vice-president and held the presidency for two years after Taylor died in 1850.) The movement faded as the nation became embroiled in the slavery issue and the idea of America as a place of religious refuge reasserted itself.

Today charges of "know-nothingism" surface periodically when xenophobia and anti-intellectualism arise. The term in use, by Lance Morrow in *Time*, October 24, 1988, on the presidential campaign:

> "Bush used to be a moderate Republican. Now, inheriting the Reagan legacy, he is constrained to run as a right-winger. He trumpets right-wing 'values'—and panders unapologetically to the Know-Nothing instincts in the crowd, but one listens to him always with a smudge of doubt: Does he really believe that?"

And, from Alex Heard, on a protest concert during the Bush inauguration festivities, *The New Republic*, February 13, 1989:

> "Inside was ample evidence as to why, no matter what stylistic mistakes the right makes, the left is still losing. Kristofferson, the lumpy balladeer of left-wing know-nothingism, came out and said, 'Are they really spendin' $40 million on this inaugural thing? Hell—' *twang twang*—'that don't surprise me. Navy shot down two Libyan jets the other day. Seems they mistook them for two Iranian airbuses fulla *tourists*.' "

**Kristallnacht.** In German, the Night of Broken Glass. It was the night of November 9, 1938, when the windows of thousands of Jewish shops and homes were shattered across Germany and Austria.

The attack on Jewish homes, businesses and synagogues was planned and carried out by the Nazis. The pretext was revenge for a fatal attack two days earlier by a 17-year-old Polish Jew, Herschel Grynszpan, on Ernst von Rath, a third secretary in the German embassy in Paris.

Researchers estimate that about a thousand Jews died that night, at least 1,118 synagogues were vandalized or destroyed and approximately 30,000 people were taken to concentration camps.

The event was a prelude to the Holocaust, and is seen with horror today not only for the violence of the Nazis against people guilty of nothing except being who they were, but also for the failure of the rest of the population—or the world—to protest. While there are many individual stories of aid being given the victims, there are many more of bystanders watching passively or joining in the violence.

The term in use, by Senator Albert Gore, Jr., in a guest editorial on the environmental crisis in *The New York Times*, March 19, 1989, entitled "An Ecological Kristallnacht." Gore goes on to invoke not only Kristallnacht but **Munich** and the Holocaust to dramatize the urgency of the problem.

Another example, from Herbert Muschamp, writing in *The New Republic*, August 28, 1989, on the relationship of architecture to society and the construction of the Holocaust Museum in Washington, D.C.:

> "If we think of glass in connection with the Holocaust, the image most likely to arise is the shattered glass of smashed shop windows sparkling in German streets. Like Columbus Prison, the memory of Crystal Night also mocks the belief that exposing the darker recesses of life can . . . 'raise our culture to a higher level.' . . .
>
> "Now, 50 years after Crystal Night, we have a flourishing type of architecture nurtured by the belief that visibility can defeat denial."

**Kulturkampf.** (KUL-toor-KAHMPF) a German word meaning, literally, struggle for civilization.

It was the name given the conflict in the 1870s between Germany's Chancellor Otto von Bismarck and the Roman Catholic hierarchy.

The clash was touched off by an encyclical issued by Pope Pius IX in 1864 laying down what he didn't like about the 19th century (just about everything): asserting church control over culture, science and education; denouncing freedom of conscience and of worship and religious tolerance; and maintaining that the church was free of all state control. In 1870, to top things off, the pope also asserted the doctrine of papal infallibility.

His actions, needless to say, caused ripples among secular governments. In Germany, they set off a struggle between the newly formed empire and the church. Bismarck would admit no exceptions to the sovereignty of the German state and took measures to make his point clear. These included expelling the Jesuits, dissolving Catholic religious orders and imposing state controls to assure that church activities in secular matters were strictly supervised. Bismarck abolished the church department for spiritual affairs, saying, "Have no fear—to Canossa we shall not go, either in body or spirit." (This was an allusion to an episode in January 1077, when Henry IV, emperor of the Holy Roman Empire, stood barefoot in the garb of a penitent at Canossa, a castle in northern Italy, for three days awaiting the absolution of Pope Gregory VII in another church-state dispute. "Going to Canossa" has come to mean humiliation, being forced to eat humble pie, a dish definitely not in the diet of Otto von Bismarck.)

The crisis eventually was resolved when Pius died and was replaced by a more diplomatic and liberal pontiff, Leo XIII.

The term in use, by Susan Sontag in her book, *AIDS And Its Metaphors*:

> "Although these specialists in ugly feelings insist that AIDS is a punishment for deviant sex, what moves them is not just, or even principally, homophobia. Even more important is the utility of AIDS in pursuing one of the main activities of the so-called **neo**-conservatives, the Kulturkampf against all that is called for short (and inaccurately) the 1960s."

Another example, from Hendrik Hertzberg, writing on President Bush's inaugural address in *The New Republic*, February 13, 1989:

"One of the subtexts of Bush's speech was an effort to declare peace in the Kulturkampf of the past 20 years—a laying down of arms made weirdly explicit the next night, when Ron Wood of the Rolling Stones ceremonially presented his guitar to Lee Atwater, chairman of the Republican National Committee, after Atwater had played and sung with the likes of Percy Sledge and Joe Cocker at an inaugural rhythm-and-blues bash."

# L

**Last Hurrah.** The last campaign, valedictory speech or act of a veteran politician before leaving the political scene, either in victory or defeat.

The term comes from the title of Edwin O'Connor's 1956 novel of the same name, based on the life of James Michael Curley (1874-1958), mayor of Boston. (John Ford directed and Spencer Tracy starred in the 1958 movie.)

The term in use, by the *National Journal*, November 5, 1983:

> "Stockman's Last Hurrah? In a series of briefings for President Reagan, Office of Management and Budget Director Dave Stockman is presenting key conclusions of an intensive, computerized study of the federal budget. . . . Some at OMB think that Stockman's ultimate conclusion will be that he has completed his task and should move on."

Another example, from Michael White, *The Village Voice*, May 16, 1989, on the career of Britain's Margaret Thatcher:

> "When her economic policies led to recession, a vainglorious Argentinian general named Galtieri saved her with his bid to seize the Falkland Islands. Not since the Venetian Republic's final struggle against the Barbary pirates has a moribund empire enjoyed such a Last Hurrah."

And from Kathy Sawyer, *The Washington Post*, August 20, 1989, on the Voyager space probe:

> "The Neptune encounter is a last hurrah of sorts for the extended bionic family of people and machines that make up the Voyager expedition. And it is the last element of Earth's first wave of interplanetary reconnaissance."

**Lazarus.** (LAZ-uhr-uhs) A New Testament figure, he was raised from the dead by Jesus. Lazarus fell ill and his sisters, Mary and

Martha, sent for Jesus. On his arrival, Jesus found that Lazarus had died. Reproached by Martha, Jesus responded: "I am the resurrection and the life; he who believes in me, though he die, yet shall he live, and whoever lives and believes in me shall never die."

Jesus went to the tomb, ordered the stone rolled away and commanded Lazarus to come out. And Lazarus emerged, still wrapped in his burial shroud.

His name is now a metaphor for a remarkable recovery or return from defeat or disaster, either professional or personal.

The term in use, from *The Proud Tower*, by Barbara Tuchman, a description of the return of Captain Alfred Dreyfus from imprisonment on Devil's Island to be retried on charges of spying. As the judge summoned the accused, all eyes turned to the door:

> "Every gaze fastened on it with a kind of shrinking awe as if fearful to look upon a ghost. . . . For five years he had been present in all their minds, not as a man but as an idea; now he was going to walk through the door and they would look on Lazarus."

Another example, from Terri Minsky, *Premiere*, July 1989, on the revival of the career of actor Michael Keaton:

> "Indeed, Hollywood is paying Keaton the sort of homage worthy of Lazarus; since returning from *Batman's* London set in late January, he has been approached by John Boorman, David Mamet, Mike Nichols and Martin Scorsese."

And from *Washington Post* columnist Colman McCarthy, January 7, 1990:

> "One of the early victims of the pope's no-politics rule was Robert Drinan, the Boston Jesuit priest who served in the House from 1971 to 1981. Rising like Lazarus, Drinan, currently a law professor at Georgetown University, has returned to political life as the founder and chairman of Peace PAC."

**Lebensraum.** (LAY-benz-ROWM) German: literally, it means "living space."

The word was used by Hitler to justify Germany's aggressive policy of territorial expansion, the rationale being that Germany was crowded and, as the national home of the master race, was entitled to take what it needed.

The term in use, by Steven L. Spiegel, writing in *The New Republic*, April 10, 1989, on the case for opposing a Palestinian state:

> "It [a Palestinian state] might move against Jordan and/or Lebanon, attempting by subversion to emerge with a sympathetic or subservient regime in these countries. Such a Palestinian thrust toward *lebensraum*, motivated also by a desire to integrate the surrounding Palestinian **diaspora** into the new society, would pose an immediate concern to any Israeli government, and tensions would heighten."

**Leitmotiv.** (LIGHT-moh-TEEF) A German word meaning "leading motive." It refers to a recurring theme or idea in a literary or dramatic work; these reappearances become meaningful in the context of the work. The concept was developed by German composer Richard Wagner, who attached musical themes to the characters in his operas. Recurrence of the themes was used to heighten the dramatic effect.

The term in use, by Lance Morrow in *Time*, January 11, 1989:

> "In Paris, what began as protest over sex-segregated dormitories ended in a general strike and very nearly brought down the government of Charles de Gaulle. Hallucination again, the decade's leitmotiv of illusion: now you see it, now you don't. For some days it looked as if France were in the grip of a revolution, everyone manning the barricades. The country came to a boil and then, just as quickly, cooled down to the status quo."

Another example, from Michael Newman, *The New Republic*, February 6, 1989:

> "One leitmotiv that ran through orientation [of freshman Congressmen] was the matter of re-election. Not that Jones—or anyone else—needed reminding."

**Lèse-majesté.** (LEHS-MAH-jhest-ay) Literally, injured sovereignty, in French. The term originated in days when kings could be weakened by acts of high treason, rebellion or an affront. Now it has a lighter and more ironic meaning, describing an act of impudence to a pompous or self-important figure, or grandiose offense taken to an inoffensive act.

The term in use in that latter sense by David Puttnam, the former head of Columbia Pictures, describing Aljean Harmetz, *The New York Times* Hollywood correspondent, in *Spy*, September 1988:

> "Deposed Columbia Pictures boss David Puttnam received a withering rebuke from Harmetz when a big *Vanity Fair* story on him appeared in April. 'She felt she should have had the story first,' he says. 'I said, "The other magazine called me and you didn't." But she made it very clear that I committed some reprehensible, if vague, act of lèse-majesté.' "

Another example, from Michael Dirda, *The Washington Post Book World*, August 27, 1989, reviewing Gary Taylor's *Reinventing Shakespeare:*

> "No bardolater, Taylor maintains that Shakespeare's privileged status derives as much from social and political forces as from his virtuosity as a wordsmith, play doctor and theatrical jack of all trades. He hopes that his book-length work of lèse majesté will free readers from culturally conditioned responses of awe, humility, even downright sycophancy."

And from Michael Kinsley, *The Washington Post*, December 14, 1989, describing Question Time in the British House of Commons:

> "Thatcher, world-renowned for her haughtiness, undergoes a twice-a-week ritual of humiliation-by-questioning that would be an unthinkable act of *lèse majesté* if inflicted on our jes' folks president."

**Let a Hundred Flowers Bloom.** An invitation to an outpouring of diverse opinion.

The invitation was extended by Mao Tse-tung in a speech in 1957, signaling that views that contradicted the party line would be acceptable in the power structure of the People's Republic of China. "Let a hundred flowers bloom," said Mao, "and a hundred schools of thought contend."

This is just what happened for a brief period after Mao's speech, but repression followed in the ensuing years of the Cultural Revolution. This was a reign of terror in the 1960s in which those perceived as opposed to the revolution were subjected to public humiliation, mob action, imprisonment, exile to collective farms and sometimes were even killed.

In American politics (and other aspects of life), the term is used today to put the best face on embarrassing public disagreements among members of an administration or other organization.

The term in use, in a George Scialabba review of books on American politics in 1968, in *The Village Voice's Literary Supplement*, December 1988:

> "Victories had been won; more would soon follow, as the women's movement, the environmental movement, the welfare-rights movement, and consumer movement were born and flourished.
>
> "By now, most of those hundred flowers have withered. The American economy and polity are turning into a **vast wasteland**."

**L'État, C'Est Moi.** (lay-TAH seh MWAH) French; it means "I am the state." A term used to sum up someone's pumped-up notion of grandeur, in politics and elsewhere. The term is attributed to Louis XIV (1638-1717), called the Sun King and the Grand Monarch, who sat on the throne of France for 72 years.

Whether he said it or not, Louis certainly acted the role. As Judy Jones and William Wilson's *An Incomplete Education* puts it, he was "the greatest repository of personal power in an age that was crawling with absolutist, divine-right monarchs. He spent vast sums on wars and domestic extravagances such as the enlargement of the palace and gardens of Versailles, ultimately bankrupting his country."

A play on the phrase, by Andrew Ferguson in *The American Spectator*, December 1988, on the wave of recollections by associates of John F. Kennedy stimulated by the 25th anniversary of his assassination:

> "So, now, when they celebrate Camelot, they celebrate themselves; the tears they cry are for their own 'golden times,' surely not the country's. 'Le Camelot, c'est moi.' When the encomiums swell to tidal levels on this sad anniversary, as they certainly will from Sorenson and Galbraith and MacNeil and Manchester and the rest of **the best and brightest**, we should remember that John Kennedy, a graceful and witty man if nothing else, deserves more, not less."

The term in use, in a July 27, 1989, *Wall Street Journal* editorial on Congressional perks:

> ". . . accustomed to the bowing and scraping of huge staffs, intimidated bureaucrats and favor-pleading lobbyists, many Congressmen assume an almost royal arrogance. . . . The egotism verges on: *l'état, c'est moi.*"

**Level Playing Field.** A term used in business, politics, sports and elsewhere to describe even-handed regulations and criteria assuring that all competitors receive equal treatment.

The term in use, by sportswriter Tony Kornheiser in *The Washington Post*, January 15, 1989, on attempts to impose, through national Collegiate Athletic Association rules, stricter academic standards on college athletes:

> "Prop. 42 is a bad rule because it seeks to insidiously level the playing field, to solve the problem of the academically at-risk athlete—often the best athlete—by effectively barring him from college."

Another example, from *The New York Times*, September 6, 1989, quoting a New York lawyer on setting limits on the amount of money law firms spend to recruit top law students:

> " 'There's a feeling that we should start fostering the right attitudes in students from the beginning by keeping expenses reasonable. . . . This would bring back a sense of reason to the process, and it's a good way of having all the firms in New York play on a level playing field.' "

**Leveraged Buyout.** According to *Barron's Dictionary of Business Terms*, the "takeover of a company using borrowed funds. Most often, the target company's assets serve as security for the loans taken out by the acquiring firm or investors, who repay the loans out of cash flow of the acquired company."

LBOs, as they've come to be known, are a growing phenomenon in today's corporate world. An LBO is usually the key instrument in a hostile takeover of a corporation.

Often, after a leveraged buyout occurs, the new owner sells off components of the company to reduce the debt acquired in buying back the public's shares; they hope to pay off the rest through more efficient operations or by using money that would otherwise be earmarked for stockholder dividends. And frequently more money is made on these sales than was paid for the whole company—thus demonstrating that here, at least, the sum of the parts is greater than the whole.

The term in use, by Thomas Boswell of *The Washington Post*, describing Super Bowl hype, January 22, 1989:

> "This Sunday's Super Bowl XXIII for the National Football League Championship is not a game. Like its self-parodying forebears, it is a week of guiltless, gaudy, Bunyanesque Americana that dwarfs any mere athletic contest. Long before Trump and Reaganomics there was the Super Bowl—a leveraged buyout of dull good taste, predicated on absolute faith that **conspicuous consumption** begat growth."

And from William Safire, *The New York Times*, February 16, 1990:

"In what was dubbed 'the Trump Scuttle,' the *New York Daily News* gossip columnist Liz Smith revealed that the nation's most celebrated deal artist is working on a leveraged throwout of his wife, who betrayed his trust by turning 40."

**Leviathan.** (luh-VIGH-uh-thuhn) A Hebrew word, meaning something really big, a monster.

In the Bible there are references to such a creature: "Canst thou draw out Leviathan with a hook?" (Job 41:1). These references spring from an ancient myth in which the Creator conquers a monster who represents chaos. Modern scholars speculate that it was a whale, maybe a crocodile.

*Leviathan* is also the title of a treatise on government, written in 1651 by Thomas Hobbes—a plea for a strong, absolute ruler. Hobbes considered that without a controlling authority, individuals would always follow their self-interest, leading to social conflict. Without absolute government authority to maintain stability, there would be "war of man against every man" and "no arts; no letters; no society; and which is worst of all, continual fear, and danger of violent death; and the life of man, solitary, poor, nasty, brutish and short."

Thus Hobbes' *Leviathan*—government—was also vast and powerful.

The term in use, by Gregory Fossedal, "George Bush, Politician," *The American Spectator,* July 1988:

". . . the impromptu photo opportunity was broken up by some aide just as we began to press for a little more specific answer about slashing the federal leviathan."

**Libido.** (luh-BEE-doh) Lust, the sex drive. The word was coined by Sigmund Freud to refer to pleasure-seeking as a motivating force in human activity, a source of psychic energy. It is one of the drives that all are born with, like hunger and thirst. [See **Id.**] Although the concept in psychoanalysis is more complex, the term commonly is used in its literal sense, to mean sexual desire. Winifred Gallagher describes it as "the cranial software of sex," in "Sex and Hormones," *The Atlantic,* March 1988.

The term in use, by Robert Darnton in *The New York Review of Books*, January 19, 1989, in a piece entitled "What was Revolutionary About the French Revolution?":

> "The violence itself remains a mystery, the kind of phenomenon that may force one back into meta-historical explanations: original sin, unleashed libido, or the cunning of a dialectic."

And in a May 1989 *Vanity Fair* profile of fortyish model-actress Lauren Hutton by Maureen Orth:

> "Hutton is back, taunting the libidos of the newly middle-aged."

**Lilliputian.** (LIL-luh-PYOO-shun) An adjective describing something as small or miniature, and often in the context of the power of the small to control giants.

The word derives from Lilliput, the name of the fictitious country in Jonathan Swift's satire, *Gulliver's Travels* (1726). The inhabitants, Lilliputians, are tiny, about one-twelfth human size, and also small in their lives, outlook and politics. They are able to subdue Gulliver by tying him down in his sleep with hundreds of tiny ropes. Although he cooperates with his captors at first, he decides to make his escape when they begrudge him food and contemplate blinding him.

The term in use, by Richard Cohen in *The Washington Post*, December 8, 1987:

> "The Soviet Union and the United States, for all their raw military power, have less control over world events than they ever did. Once the twin kings of the postwar mountain, both now have to deal with a world where brute military power means less and less. Militarily weak Japan has a gross national product equal to that of the Soviet Union. Afghanistan eludes Soviet control and Vietnam went communist, U.S. B-52s notwithstanding. Gulliver has met the Lilliputians."

And from David Stockman, *The Triumph of Politics*, on the early days of the Reagan era in Washington:

"It was evident that Meese was the acting President. But it was also obvious that the Lilliputians already had him tied down on the mat. They had him thrashing around with everything."

**Lingua Franca.** (LEEN-gwa FRAN-ka) Italian, meaning Frankish language. An informal, standard language that serves as a general means of communication; it is applied to the specialized jargon and terms of reference of particular professions, technical fields or other subcultures.

Originally, lingua franca referred to a hybrid language which developed in Mediterranean ports in the 17th century. It was a mixture of French, Spanish, Greek, Italian, Arabic and maybe more; lingua franca became the language of commerce in the lively trade in the region.

A similar language is "pidgin," which originated in the English-Chinese trade in the 17th century.

The term in use, in *The New York Times*, as quoted in *Words That Make A Difference*, by Robert Greenman:

"Collage as a way of making great art has been around for 70 or so years. Not only is it part of the lingua franca of 20th century art, but it also seems almost to have been bred into us, like table manners or brushing our teeth. For this reason, the fallacy is now widespread that almost anyone can make a good collage if he puts his mind to it."

Another example, from *The Economist*, February 4, 1989, in an article on the status of British Gibraltar:

"But according to a recent history of Gibraltar, Spanish would have been the language of the territory in any case: 'It was the lingua franca of the whole of the Western Mediterranean.' "

And from Robert Reinhold, writing in *The New York Times*, December 13, 1987, an illustration as well as a usage:

"The proposal was an explosive one for Hawaii. Ey, the

Board of Education wen go max out trying to ban pidgin English speaking in school. Fo' real!

"Once again, the issue of Pidgin English, the lingua franca of the Hawaiian Islands, is sweeping this state whose real face is obscured by the aloha veil it presents to tourists.

"Pidgin, a spare, direct and often delightfully irreverent patois in which even 'aloha' becomes 'howzit' is for many Hawaiians a crucial link to a rich past that is quickly being bulldozed for tourist and commercial developments."

**Literati.** (lee-tuh-RAH-tee) Educated and well-read people. It refers to an intellectual elite, and it is sometimes used sarcastically. From Latin, meaning "learned."

A glib corruption is glitterati, a reference to "the beautiful people" of glitz and glitter.

Both terms in use, from Robert Greenman's *Words That Make A Difference*, quoting *The New York Times*:

"Northern New Mexico has been an oasis for writers, artists and photographers since D.H. Lawrence and Georgia O'Keefe settled here in the 20's. The literati have been well-established for decades, but now the glitterati are moving in and much to Santa Fe's dismay, the town is fast becoming an open secret. The most notable new arrivals are probably the Duke and Duchess of Bedford. . . ."

**Loaves and Fishes.** From the New Testament, one of the miracles of Jesus. Thousands of people followed Jesus into the wilderness to hear him preach. There was very little food for the great crowd, and the disciples nervously suggested that the people be sent away. But Jesus said to feed them and blessed the few loaves of bread and fish that they had among them. The food was miraculously multiplied and the huge multitudes were fed.

The phrase comes up in praise of resourceful and bountiful hosts or cooks who provide satisfying meals out of seemingly little. It is also seen in the phrase "having an eye to the loaves and fishes", that is, having an eye on physical and material needs rather than the spiritual. As Jesus said, " . . . Ye seek me, not because ye saw the miracles, but because ye did eat of the loaves and were filled. . . . " and urged his followers to labor not for food which perishes, but for the spiritual nourishment which endures.

The term in use, by Phyllis Richman in *The Washington Post*, April 19, 1989:

> "On April 27, the more you eat, the more there will be for the poor to eat. Call it the modern version of loaves and fishes—the miracle of the pates and mousses. It's the second annual Taste of the Nation, a 50-city feast organized by Share Our Strength, a nonprofit network of chefs and restauranteurs dedicated to fighting hunger."

**Lochinvar.** (LOK-in-VAHR) According to *The Oxford English Dictionary*, a man who elopes with a young woman; but also used in the broader sense of a romantic suitor, a bold and handsome young hero.

The original is the hero of a ballad in *Marmion*, a lengthy narrative poem by Sir Walter Scott (1771-1832) set in 16th century Scotland. Lochinvar's lady love, the fair Ellen, enters a loveless marriage with another suitor ("a laggard in love, a dastard in war"). Lochinvar appears at the wedding feast and asks for one last dance with the bride. The young knight then sweeps her out the door and sets her on his horse ("through all the wide Border his steed was the best") and dashes away with her.

The term in use by J. Anthony Lukas in *The New York Times Magazine*, March 12, 1989, on Harvard's Kennedy School of Government:

> "What liberated Harvard's governmental studies from this cul de sac was the death of the university's young Lochinvar. Twenty-seven days after John F. Kennedy's assassination in 1963, his brothers convened a small group of present and former Harvard professors . . . to devise a 'living memorial.' "

**Loman, Willy.** See Willy Loman.

**Long March.** An incredible trek undertaken in 1934–35 during the Chinese civil war by 90,000 embattled men and women who constituted the Red Army of the Chinese Communist Party under Mao Tse-tung.

Mao and his followers marched from southwest to northwest China, covering 5,000 miles, crossing 18 mountain ranges and 24 rivers in about a year. It was a great hardship and more than half of the participants perished, but the survivors who arrived in Shensi Province in 1935 were toughened and unified behind Mao's leadership. From this crucible they emerged to eventually take control of all China.

Nowadays, a "long march" describes any bitter or difficult period of exile from which an individual emerges stronger and ready for a comeback; a long and audacious journey.

The term in use, in *The Village Voice*, March 28, 1989; writer Leslie Savon describes the career of publisher Chris Whittle:

> "It's a tactic he used on his first project, 'Knoxville in a Nutshell,' a single-sponsor campus shopper aimed at his fellow students at the University of Tennessee. 'Nutshell' sprouted onto other campuses, other publications were whipped into the mix, and 10 years after graduating Whittle and former partner Phillip Moffitt made the Long March to New York to buy *Esquire*. Remaking the fading rag in their own image, they saved it from bankruptcy."

Another example, from B. Drummond Ayres Jr. in *The New York Times*, July 27, 1989, describing an unusual incident in which Washington, D.C. police officers required prostitutes to walk from downtown Washington to the Potomac River bridge crossing into Virginia:

> "By Mao's standards, it did not qualify as a Long March. But Mao never tried to hike a couple of miles in translucent three-inch spike-heeled shoes and a thigh-high leather miniskirt spangled with glitter beads."

**Loose Cannon.** Someone who is out of control and a possible hazard to himself, his colleagues or his cause.

The expression comes from naval warfare and predates fixed-turret guns aboard ships. In earlier days, muzzle-loading cannons were mounted on wheeled carriages so they could be run in and out of gunports for loading and firing. When not in use they were lashed down. If a cannon came loose, that huge mass of metal rushing to and fro with every roll of the ship was a hazard to everyone and everything in its path and to the ship itself.

The term in use, by Lt. Col. Oliver North in his testimony to the congressional committees investigating the Iran-contra affair, as reported in *The Washington Post*, July 8, 1987:

> "I don't want you to think, counsel, that I went about this all on my own. I realized, there's a lot of folks around that think there's a loose cannon on the gun deck at the NSC. That wasn't what I heard while I worked there. I've only heard it since I left. People used to walk up to me and tell me what a great job I was doing."

Judge Robert Bork offers a lawyer's play on the term in his book, *The Tempting of America*, as quoted in a *Wall Street Journal* review, November 15, 1989:

> "Yet the right to privacy became what Mr. Bork calls a 'loose canon in the law' in 1965, when Yale law professors and the ACLU concocted a legal challenge."

And some variations on the theme, from Maureen Dowd, *The New York Times*, September 10, 1989, writing about Bush administration drug czar William Bennett:

> "He rubbed other administration officials the wrong way, jumped too far out ahead on a couple of initiatives, and seemed about to fulfill predictions by White House advisors that he would be a black sheep, a bull in a china shop, a loose cannon, a Lone Ranger, 'Mr. Aggressive Steam Roller,' or, in a moniker Mr. Bennett was given when he

was appointed to head the National Endowment for the Humanities, a 'fat boy in a canoe.' "

**Lord Acton.** See Acton, Lord.

**Lounge Lizard.** A cheap lothario, someone who will lurk around to prey upon the susceptible with oily charm. Picture him in a shiny suit, pointy-toed shoes, with every hair slicked into place.

It's an American slang term from the early 20th century. William Safire says the expression was coined around 1912 to describe cheap-skates who wanted to pet in a girl's parlor without first taking her out for a soda and movie. The *OED*'s earliest use is 1918.

The term in use, quoted by Lou Cannon in *The Washington Post*, November 5, 1987, in anticipation of the appointment of Lt. Gen. Colin Powell as national security adviser to President Ronald Reagan:

> "He is similarly valued by former Pentagon colleagues. 'He's not a guy who's come up as a Pentagon lounge lizard,' an Army official said. 'He's got a lot of field time.' "

And Alex Heard, writing in *The New Republic*, February 13, 1989, refers to "oil-soaked lounge iguana Julio Iglesias."

**Loyal Opposition.** In two-party systems such as those in the United States or Britain, the out-of-power political party.

The phrase suggests that the out-of-power party remains loyal to the country while disagreeing on policy matters with the party in power. In Britain, the outs have official status and are described as "His (or Her) Majesty's Loyal Opposition." The leader of the Opposition receives a salary, and has a "shadow cabinet" of members with expertise who put forth the Opposition's views on matters relating to specific government ministries. The public has the advantage of hearing what the other side would do with a given issue and knowing in advance who would hold key government positions should the Opposition win a majority and take over the government.

Wendell Wilkie, FDR's Republican opponent in 1940, popu-larized the concept in this country. Following his defeat, he described the role of the GOP in the face of war in Europe: "A vital element in the balanced operation of democracy is a strong, alert and watchful opposition. . . . Let us not, therefore, fall into the partisan error of opposing things just for the sake of opposition."

The idea lacks official status in the United States, and doesn't work as well outside a parliamentary structure. Things become complicated in this country when one party controls the presidency and the other the Congress.

The term in use, from *The New Republic*, January 23, 1989, on French political history since the Revolution:

> "The ideas of representation, a stable party system, and a loyal opposition developed very slowly. Revolutionary and postrevolutionary regimes alike had difficulty distinguishing opposition from treason. . . ."

**Luddites.** Bands of craftsmen in industrial England, 1811-16, who smashed textile machines that were displacing them from their jobs. They were named after their semi-mythical leader, Ned Ludd.

The movement had its casualties: one band was shot in 1812 at the order of a manufacturer who felt threatened; he in turn was murdered. At one point, Parliament debated the death penalty for destroying textile machinery. A period of prosperity, laying the workers' worst fears to rest, put an end to the movement.

Luddites nowadays are those who worry about the impact of new technology on jobs or suspect that the march of progress may run over some innocents.

The term in use, from *The Economist*, June 3, 1989, on automated trading at the Chicago Board of Trade and the Chicago Mercantile Exchange:

> "Both the Merc and the CBOT are still daytime Luddites, insisting that floor trading, using open outcry, is the only way to trade—and provide liquidity—during America's waking hours. Yet, for night-time, they espouse high-tech automation."

**Lumpenproletariat.** (LOOM-pen-pro-leh-TAH-ree-aht) Coined by Marx to describe the poorest and most ignorant, the lowest class in society, even below the working class proletariat.

It combines the German "lumpen" (rags, tatters) with the Latin-based "proletariat" (from "proletarius," someone of the lowest class).

The term in use, by Margo Howard, in *The New Republic*, May 18, 1987, reviewing *Vanna Speaks* by Vanna White, a sex object in television's **vast wasteland**:

> "It is therefore a fair question to ask, who is Vanna White, and why is she saying anything at all?
>
> "The stock answer is that she is the designated hostess of a television show called 'Wheel of Fortune,' offering her life story because, presumably, millions of her fans are interested. The real answer is that Vanna White is the pinup girl of the lumpen proletariat, and this rambling collection of you-name-it is an odd and strangely honest reply to fan mail."

# M

**Machiavellian.** (MAHK-ee-ah-VEL-ee-uhn) An adjective meaning ruthless, unscrupulous and cunning, especially in a political context. The word derives from the name of Niccolo Machiavelli (1469-1527), the Italian statesman and writer often praised as a pioneer of modern political science because he attempted to report clearly and realistically about what heads of state really do and why.

Machiavelli's most famous work is *The Prince* (1513), which closely analyzed the princes reigning over the warring city-states of Italy. Machiavelli observed that human beings were basically corrupt. A successful ruler did not hesitate to act to keep this base nature under control, even if it meant being "ruthlessly despotic as well as cunningly magnanimous," in the words of *Benét's Reader's Encyclopedia*.

In fairness, we should report that Machiavelli himself had ideals—he believed in a republican form of government, favored using citizen armies instead of the customary mercenaries and opposed senseless cruelty. Historians recognize these virtuous sentiments, but nothing will shake Machiavelli's identification with ruthless, cold-blooded politics.

The term in use, by Anna Quinlen in her "Life in the 30's" column in *The New York Times*, October 6, 1988, on male reaction to her very apparent pregnancy:

> "I have even used this effect to my advantage—the Machiavellian madonna. Each time I was visibly pregnant before, I was a manager in the company of mostly male executives. Along with the world of baggage any woman brings to such a role, I was happy to be toting 35 pounds of one-time weight. . . . I felt desexualized then, too, but it worked: clearly a woman here, gentlemen, but of the most nonthreatening variety. . . . My belly was my shield, and I used it."

**Madame Defarge.** See DeFarge, Madame.

**Magic Bullet.** In medicine, where it originated, and by extension elsewhere, a treatment or drug that goes directly to its target and destroys the disease without damaging anything else.

Sometimes the same meaning is assigned to "silver bullets," which have the legendary power of killing vampires. The Lone Ranger, a hero of radio serialization and television, fired bullets made of silver.

The term in use, by Dr. James Cleeman, on the benefits of a high fiber diet, quoted by Carole Sugarman in *The Washington Post*, August 1, 1989:

> "James Cleeman, a physician and coordinator of the National Cholesterol Education Program, is concerned about focusing too narrowly on psyllium and other soluble fibers. They are 'not a magic bullet,' he said."

Another example, from *The Arizona Republic*, February 21, 1990:

> " 'We no longer have a magic bullet,' said Dr. Marilyn Roberts, a pathologist at the University of Washington, where studies have found tetracycline-resistant bacteria prevalent even in women who have no recent exposure to the drug."

**Maginot Line.** (MA-jhuh-NOH) The line of fortifications France built along its border with Germany in the years between World War I and World War II, and which the French sadly discovered was not the barrier they had imagined. It is now a synonym for obsolete defenses or technology that's easily overcome by innovative strategy. Or for blind reliance on a passive defense rather than an offense.

On the basis of the experience of World War I, the French thought the line of heavily fortified barriers and gun emplacements—named after André Maginot, the minister of war, who conceived the idea—would be a foolproof protection against the power of resurgent Nazi Germany. In the First World War, heavily fortified positions were successfully held and, after the slaughters of that war, technology that could protect manpower had a powerful appeal.

So the line was the best that modern technology could produce: the thickest concrete walls, biggest guns and even air conditioning for the troops, who were moved about on underground railway lines. A perfect strategy for winning World War I.

Unfortunately, this was not the war the French would fight. The Maginot Line was rendered irrelevant by the new, highly mobile style of warfare adopted by the Germans. Instead of attacking France through the Maginot Line, the German army simply moved through the "impassable" Ardennes forest in southern Belgium and Luxembourg and swept south into France behind the helpless fixed defenses.

The Line has its defenders, however. They argue that it succeeded because the Germans were forced to go around it.

The term in use, by Howard Rosenberg, in *The Baltimore Sun*, February 14, 1988, discussing the heavy press coverage of the Iowa precinct caucuses:

> "Major media are journalistic Maginot lines—rigid, immovable and unalterable once committed and in place. By the time TV began wondering aloud about this year's overcoverage, the major media had already spent so much energy and money on the coverage that they had a vested interest in the process. In fact, they had become part of the process."

**Main Street.** The title of a famous novel by Sinclair Lewis published in 1920 and, as an outgrowth, a reference to provincialism and boosterism at their least attractive, as portrayed in the book.

*Main Street* gives us the fictional town of Gopher Prairie, Minnesota, and tells of the efforts of Carol Kennicott, spirited wife of the local doctor, to introduce culture to the townsfolk. She fails, leaves for a time to pursue her own life, and finally returns.

Gopher Prairie was modeled on Lewis' home town of Sauk Centre, Minnesota, which knew it and didn't like it. In fact, it took many years for the town to forgive and honor Lewis for his portrayal of a dull, isolated and inward-turning town.

"Main Street" has come to refer to insular attitudes of small-town middle America, a state of mind as well as a place, where conventionality reigns. The term is also sometimes used in the broader, nonpejorative sense of typical or ordinary American communities—

"Middle America," as in the use by presidential candidate Michael Dukakis, quoted in *Newsweek*, November 7, 1988:

> "George Bush wants to help people on Easy Street. I want to help the people on Main Street."

The latest word from Sauk Centre, as reported by the Associated Press and published in the *Omaha World Herald*, May 31, 1989, is that the town is considering restoration to give the place more of the ambience of Lewis' time. An architect from the Minnesota Historical Society described the town as "a mess of plastic and **kitsch**. They've got some pretty well-preserved buildings behind all that tin and plastic, but downtown is kind of a void."

The local newspaper publisher sums it up: if enough business owners go along with the restoration project, "we can give the tourists something unique so someone from Omaha will want to come."

**Major-domo.** Someone—like the chief steward or butler—who is in charge of a great household, or, as is more often the case when the term is used nowadays, an establishment. It comes from Latin: "major" meaning greater, and "domo" meaning house.

The term in use, in "Dollars and Scents" by Stephanie Mansfield, *The Washington Post Magazine*, March 6, 1988, in a profile of Ilona Domotor, long-time perfume saleswoman at Garfinckel's department store in Washington, D.C.:

> "She is Ilona, the Ayacologna. The Major Domo of Aroma."

**Malthusian.** (mal-THOO-zhuhn) Pertaining to the theory of Thomas Malthus holding that poverty and distress are unavoidable because population increases faster than the means of subsistence.

In 1798, Malthus (1766-1834), an English clergyman, economist and pioneer in population studies, published *An Essay on the Principle of Population as it affects the Future Improvement of Society, with Remarks on the Speculation of Mr. Godwin, M. Condorcet, and other Writers,* setting forth his grim doctrine that since population grows in a geometric ratio while food increases in an arithmetic ratio, population will always outstrip food production. Malthus had so little faith in human nature that he could not imagine men solving the problem. Balance, he contended, would be achieved through inevitable war, famine and disease. In an 1803 revision, Malthus offered self-imposed sexual restraint as another means of controlling population (in addition to his previous list of afflictions and catastrophes).

(The Godwin of his title was William Godwin, an English radical who believed that men could be persuaded to rational action, and therefore could live without laws and government. Marie Jean Nicolas Antoine de Caritat, Marquis de Condorcet, was a French philosopher who also believed in the perfectibility of mankind. He was rewarded for his optimism by being forced into hiding during the French Revolution when his faction of relative moderates was overthrown by radicals in 1793. He died in prison under mysterious circumstances in 1794, but had managed to write *Progress of the Human Mind* before his capture.)

The term in use, by P. J. O'Rourke in his 1988 book, *Holidays in Hell*:

> "This is the main thing the next quarter century will bring to the Third World—the same thing the last quarter century brought—lots and lots of colorful death. What with famine, war, genocide, sexually transmitted diseases and general dirty habits, we can expect the next twenty-five years to be a veritable feast of Malthusianism."

**Mandarin.** (MAN-duh-rin) A member of an elite; in modern bureaucracies, a high-ranking official. Often, he's clever and well-educated, but resistant to reform. The term is frequently used derisively to suggest pompous self-importance. (See **Nabob** and **Pooh-Bah**.)

In old China, the mandarin class wielded great power throughout the government. Students aspiring to join the class had to follow a rigorous course of study and pass examinations to qualify.

Interestingly, the term is not Chinese but has several possible roots, from Portuguese, Malay or Sanskrit words meaning "counsel."

The term in playful use, by Benedict Nightingale, reviewing a biography of British critic Kenneth Tynan, *The New York Times Book Review*, January 3, 1988:

> "Tynan was an elitist egalitarian, a mandarin crusader for radical causes, a romantic realist, a libertine puritan and, as some unkindly said, a champagne socialist."

Another example, from Vic Gold, in *The American Spectator*, September 1989:

> "Of the mandarin historians of the American left, few suffer the ongoing **angst** of James MacGregor Burns; or, at least, the torment visited upon him during this past decade of the Reagan terror."

**Man For All Seasons.** A person with a great breadth of talent and accomplishment as well as courageous adherence to principle.

The phrase was first applied to Sir Thomas More (1477-1535), English humanist, statesman, scholar, poet and martyr of the Roman Catholic Church. He wrote *Utopia*, describing an ideal state governed entirely by reason, a contrast to his own time, the reign of Henry VIII.

More served Henry as chancellor but was imprisoned and executed for resisting Henry's order establishing himself as the head of the church of England to facilitate his shedding of his first wife so he could marry Anne Boleyn. More was willing to acknowledge Anne as queen but would not take an oath repudiating the pope as head of the church. More was canonized 400 years after his death.

More's friend Desiderius Erasmus, a great Dutch humanist, described him as "omnium horarium homo" ("a man for all time"). This was later rephrased as "a man for all seasons" and given currency today as the title of a 1960 play and popular film (1966) about More by British playwright Robert Bolt.

The term in play, in a headline over a profile of versatile American musician Gunther Schuller in *The Boston Globe*, April 30, 1989:

> "At 63, Gunther Schuller remains a man for all tempos."

**Manichean** or **Manichaean.** (man-uh-KEE-uhn) A viewpoint which sees things as black or white, good or bad, and caught in a struggle of absolutes.

It comes from a religion founded in the 2nd century in Persia by a prophet named Mani who saw the universe governed by a struggle between Good and Evil.

The term in use, by historian Paul Kennedy in his review of Richard Nixon's 1988 book *1999: Victory Without War* in *The Washington Post*, April 17, 1988:

> "Thus described, the book might still appear to be purely Manichaean, a world-view not unlike that of the early Reagan years which saw international politics as a struggle between the forces of good (the U.S.A.) and the forces of evil (U.S.S.R.) for the rest of the world."

Another example, as quoted by Christopher Lehmann-Haupt in his review of *Destructive Generation*, written by former 60s radicals-turned-Reaganites Peter Collier and David Horowitz, and *Second Thoughts*, edited by Collier and Horowitz:

> "Finally, they force one to agree with Susan Sontag, who shows up in an anecdote near the end of *Destructive Generation*. When taxed by Mr. Collier and Mr. Horowitz for insufficiently appreciating American culture, Ms. Sontag responds: 'You're just projecting your own Manichean politics onto the world. I don't want to enter your world, where you push everything to extremes.'"

**Manifest Destiny.** The slogan applied in American history to a drive for U.S. domination across the entire North American continent to the Pacific Ocean.

The phrase made an early appearance in 1845 in an editorial by John L. O'Sullivan in *The United States Magazine and Democratic Review*, which declared that it was America's "manifest destiny to overspread and to possess the whole of the continent which Providence has given us for the development of the great experiment of liberty and federated self-government entrusted to us."

That same year Texas was admitted to the Union; the United States settled a dispute with Britain, ending up with that part of the Oregon Territory below the 49th parallel; and war with Mexico in 1846 led to the possession of California and New Mexico. Manifest destiny so enthralled some Americans that President James Polk was criticized by more ardent **jingoists** for not seizing all of Mexico and a huge chunk of western Canada. For all that, the United States grew by more than a half million square miles during his presidency.

The doctrine had a revival in the late 19th century to accommodate a growing American appetite for status as a world power. As a result, Hawaii was annexed in 1897, and the U.S. Navy grew from the world's 12th largest to the third. The Spanish-American War, meanwhile, brought about the acquisition of Puerto Rico, Guam and the Philippines.

The term in use, by Henry Allen in *The Washington Post*, June 15, 1988, describing a gathering of devotees of Harley-Davidson motorcycles, that most American of vehicles:

> "Instead of vaulting into the future, Harley is dedicated to preserving a past, manufacturing copies of old motorcycles with the great thick tires and mammoth mudguards like Spartan helmets, Wide Glides with Fat Bob gas tanks, that sense of inexorable heft, manifest destiny on wheels."

**Man on Horseback.** An individual—often a military figure with an authoritarian bent—who comes forward in a time of unrest and political confusion to restore order. Napoleon's emergence from the French Revolution is the classic example.

There are exceptions to the rule that the man on horseback has to be a dictator: France's wartime hero Charles DeGaulle (whose height and sense of grandeur probably made the horse unnecessary) returned to power in the late 1950s to restore political order without jeopardizing democracy.

William Safire, in his *Political Dictionary*, notes that the expression was introduced to American politics by General Caleb Cushing in 1860, who expressed fear that an impending civil war could lead to a danger for democracy—"a man on horseback with a drawn sword in his hand, some Atlantic Caesar, or Cromwell, or Napoleon."

Safire points to a more recent usage, from an angry letter by E. M. Dealey, chairman of the *Dallas Morning News*, to President John F. Kennedy in 1961:

> "We need a man on horseback to lead this nation, and many people in Texas and the Southwest think that you are riding Caroline's bicycle."

The term in use, by sportswriter Jim Murray, *The Los Angeles Times*, November 19, 1989:

> "The trick of leadership is to project confidence, unflappability. The man on horseback has to look in control. Panic is contagious. Coach Shell is the least panic-stricken looking individual in the game."

**Mano a Mano.** (MAH-noh ah MAH-noh) A man-to-man, one-on-one confrontation or fight. In Spanish, literally, hand to hand.

The term in use by Charles Krauthammer in his column in *The Washington Post*, March 27, 1987:

> "In other democracies, the leader of the opposition directly confronts the prime minister during a parliamentary question period. . . . in the United States, the role of inquisitor has devolved upon the press. And devolved almost constitutionally—if the president goes too long without a prime-time *mano a mano*, the clamor for another ritual matchup begins."

**Manqué.** (mon-KAY) Refers to someone who would have achieved more in another capacity; or someone who fancies himself or postures in another role—a would-be. The word is French, meaning missed or lost.

The term in use, by Jonathan Yardley in *The Washington Post*, December 5, 1986, writing about designer Ralph Lauren:

> "His influence has grown so large that at this Christmas season the Manhattan shopping district has been transformed into a virtual museum in his honor . . . where gentry manqué can purchase all the necessary accouterments of false status."

**Mantra.** (MAN-truh) In Hinduism and Buddhism, a sacred mystic word or verse repeatedly chanted or sung as part of devotions and meditation. "Om"—said over and over—is considered to be the greatest mantra, embodying the essence of the universe.

For many Americans in the 1960s, when interest in Eastern religion soared and meditation went secular, the mantra became a private word or sound chanted repeatedly as part of the meditative effort. Further secularized in the commercial 1980s, the mantra is transformed into a formula or slogan that's repeated frequently, almost as an article of faith.

The term in use, by *Forbes* magazine, November 15, 1976:

> "There's the story of the Scarsdale matron who decided she wanted to try transcendental meditation. She needed a mantra: the essential secret word that would make her feel relaxed and comfortable, perhaps even elated. After due deliberation, she selected the obvious: '**Bloomingdale's**.'"

Another example, from *The Economist*, February 4, 1989:

> "It is an established routine. After every widely publicised gun massacre, gun-control advocates renew their call for legislation and the gun lobby repeats its mantra that if guns are made criminal only criminals will have guns."

And from Robin Toner, *The New York Times*, November 14, 1989, covering a meeting of the Democratic Leadership Council:

> "Today's conference was one long mantra to mainstream America, reflecting a party still reacting to a 1988 campaign that saw its nominee hammered for being 'out of the

mainstream' on issues from national security to reciting the Pledge of Allegiance."

**Mark of Cain.** A stigma; the mark or brand of a criminal or outcast.

In the Book of Genesis in the Bible, Cain, first child of Adam and Eve, murdered his younger brother, Abel, and became a fugitive.

The Bible tells the story: "And the Lord said unto Cain, where is Abel thy brother? And he said, I know not; Am I my brother's keeper? And He said, what hast thou done? The voice of thy brother's blood crieth unto me from the ground." The Lord put a mark upon Cain so that he would be protected in his wanderings, but would also be identified as the killer of his brother. As the term is used today, the idea of a protective mark has been lost; it is now used in the negative sense of a mark of shame or criminality.

The term in use, by Washington lawyer Leonard Garment, quoted in *The New York Times*, August 23, 1988, on the political hazards in seeking psychiatric care:

> "Even the fact of having consulted a psychiatrist on an intermittent basis or after some kind of tragedy becomes a label. It is among a number of things that Washington punishes people for that make no sense. Almost anything these days can become a mark of Cain."

**Mather, Cotton.** An American clergyman and writer (1663-1728) often invoked, a bit unfairly, as the embodiment of extreme Puritanism.

Little Cotton was a child prodigy who entered Harvard at age 12. He became a historian, folklorist and writer on a broad range of subjects—as well as an ardent Puritan. He was inclined to believe in witchcraft, but he upheld the rational teachings of Isaac Newton, and he supported inoculation against smallpox when this was the subject of great fear. Nevertheless, his name is now synonymous with fanatic, intolerant Puritanism.

The term in use, by Andrew Ferguson, reviewing P.J. O'Rourke's *Republican Party Reptile* in *The Wall Street Journal*, April 28, 1987:

> "Far funnier were the self-satisfied targets on the left, whether it was Sen. Kennedy lecturing, without a trace of

irony, on public morality . . . or the lugubrious Ralph Nader, a man so Puritanical as to make Cotton Mather think twice, intoning gravely about the need for airbags—a fitting subject since he was so obviously one himself."

Another example, from Hendrik Hertzberg in *The New Republic*, February 13, 1989, writing on President Bush's inaugural address:

"The door to the future opened into 'a room called Tomorrow' and other rooms called Freedom, Prosperity, and Moral and Intellectual Satisfaction—it sounded like the convention facilities at the Hotel Cotton Mather."

**Mau-mau.** (mow-mow—say "ow" as in cow) A verb meaning to use threatening, harassing, aggressive and intimidating, but not physically violent, behavior.

In that meaning, the term is the invention of iconoclastic journalist Tom Wolfe, adopted from the name of the Mau Mau, a secret society of the Kikuyu tribe of Kenya, which rebelled against British colonial rule in the 1950s. The Mau Mau advocated violent resistance to white rule. Mau Mau leader Jomo Kenyatta was jailed in 1952—and became prime minister of an independent Kenya 10 years later.

Wolfe adopted the term and made it a slang verb in his 1970 essay, *Radical Chic and Mau-Mauing the Flak Catchers*, writing about the manipulation of white federal poverty workers by black hustlers:

"Going downtown to mau-mau the bureaucrats got to be the routine practice in San Francisco. . . . They sat back and waited for you to come rolling in with your certified angry militants, your guaranteed frustrated ghetto youth, looking like a bunch of wild men. Then you had your test confrontation. If you were outrageous enough, if you could shake up the bureaucrats so bad that their eyes froze into iceballs and their mouths twisted up into shit-eating grins, so to speak—then they knew you were the real goods. They knew you were the right studs to give the poverty grants and community organizing jobs to."

The term in use, by John B. Judis in *The New Republic*, January 23, 1989, in a profile of U.S. Surgeon General C. Everett Koop:

"His liberal supporters say he has 'grown in office.' His right wing critics think he sold himself out to the liberal and homosexual lobbies. 'He was mau-maued by the confirmation process,' one former Reagan administration official explained."

Another example, from Timothy Noah in *The New Republic*, September 11, 1989:

"In earlier years Jesse Helms mau-maued the NEA [National Endowment for the Arts] for funding Erica Jong's *Fear of Flying* ($5,000). . . . "

**Maven.** (MAY-vehn) A Yiddish word, meaning an expert, a connoisseur.

"Media mavens," for example, are the experts brought on to the television news shows to pontificate on the events of the day. A pickle maven, according to an advertisement, is one who can tell a great pickle from a not-so-good pickle.

The term in use, by Hobart Rowen in *The Washington Post*, September 22, 1988, in a tribute to the late Henry Wallich, former member of the Federal Reserve Board of Governors:

"Over a sandwich, a beer or a glass of wine (he was a world-class wine maven who entertained at home with elegant tastings) Wallich would exercise his role as educator."

**Mc-.** A prefix, inspired by the immensely successful McDonald's restaurant chain, that is attached to words to suggest values associated with fast-food franchises: sameness, speed and the nagging knowledge that they offer food that tastes good but is laden with calories and fats.

*USA Today*, the nationwide newspaper started by the Gannett chain in 1982, quickly was dubbed "McPaper," a criticism by non-Gannett journalists for its shallowness and relentlessly upbeat tone. Surrendering to the inevitability of the nickname, Gannett adopted it, as reflected by the title of the paper's authorized biography by Gannett editor Peter Prichard: *The Making of McPaper: The Inside Story of USA Today.* The book quotes Jonathan Yardley of *The Washington Post* using the junk food theme to describe the paper:

> "Like parents who take their children to a different fast-food joint every night and keep the refrigerator stocked with ice cream, *USA Today* gives its readers only what they want. No spinach, no bran, no liver."

The term in use, by Harry F. Waters in *Newsweek*, September 14, 1987, in a review of Bill Cosby's book, *Time Flies:*

> "At 176 pages (for $15.95), it's two pages shorter (and $1 more) than its predecessor, which was not exactly a **Proustian** read itself. *Time Flies* could easily be consumed by an airline passenger between the salted almonds and the after-dinner mints—even allowing for a trip to the lavatory. But if Cosby has cooked up a sort of McBook, he's also delivered exactly what his legions of admirers treasure. . . . "

In use again, by Jennet Conant in *Newsweek*, September 28, 1987:

> "People want simple, comfortable, honest clothes that they can be reasonably sure look OK, and they want to be able to purchase them with the same ease they pick up dinner at McDonald's. . . . What people want these days, and what they're spending billions on, is McFashion."

And by *The Washington Post Magazine*, April 30, 1989, in the headline over a piece by Richard Cohen decrying the loss of regional distinctions:

> "McAmerica the Beautiful."

**Mea Culpa.** An admission of guilt. Latin, it literally means, "I am guilty." To speak of someone's "mea culpa" refers to a public confession of guilt or admission of responsibility for a wrongful act.

The term in use, by Vic Gold in his tribute to the late and legendary Big Jim Folsom, one-time governor of Alabama, in *The American Spectator*, February 1988:

"It followed that this sort of *mea-culpa*-with-a-wink (*Yes*, I had a drink with a black Congressman; *Sure*, I was arrested in Birmingham; *You bet* I spent the night with a blonde) only compounded Big Jim's image problem with 'the damned decency crowd.' He wasn't merely guilty-as-charged, they said, but brazen about it. And they were right, of course, to the extent that a healthy dose of cynicism is part-and-parcel of the populist **Weltanschauung**."

And from *The Economist*, May 6, 1989:

"A recent episode involving the Gridiron Club, an elite clique of Washington journalists, shows how elaborate anti-discrimination etiquette can become. The formerly all-male Gridiron has been open to women for a number of years. It held an officers' meeting at a business club in Baltimore. That club is also open to women guests at lunch, but does not have women members. Therefore, the women officers of the Gridiron refused to attend the lunch, and the men who arranged the lunch wallowed in *mea culpas*."

**The Medium Is the Message.** The catchphrase coined by Marshall McLuhan, a Canadian scholar of modern communications.

McLuhan (1911-1980) contended that the medium of communication itself, such as radio or television, has the power to shape the information being communicated and the audience to which the information is transmitted. The viewpoint summarized in a nutshell: "The medium is the message."

McLuhan coined other terms to characterize the impact of the media: "**global village**," and "hot" and "cold" media.

The term in use is often a playful variant of the original. Howard Rosenberg, in *The Baltimore Sun*, February 14, 1988, for example, discussed the intense news coverage of the Iowa precinct caucuses in an article headlined: "Which Came First? The Media or the Message?" He quoted a former Iowa Democratic chairman on the beginnings of this event: "First we had to convince the candidates they had to be here because the national press was going to be here. Then we had to convince the national press to be here because the candidates were going to be here."

*The New York Times* ran a front page article March 1, 1988, about efforts to communicate with illegal aliens so as to inform them about the government's amnesty program; it included putting information inside packages of tortillas. The story was headlined:

"Amnesty Sale: The Medium Is the Tortilla."

**Meltdown.** A catastrophe of immense and uncontrollable dimensions, associated today with nuclear power plants. Its original meaning, however, was more agreeable. It was originally coined in 1937 by a writer for the *Ice Cream Trade Journal* to describe what happens to ice cream in the taster's mouth.

The word began to appear in the nuclear power industry in the 1960s. A meltdown in this context is the melting of the core of a nuclear reactor, which can occur when the controlled use of nuclear reaction to generate power or for another purpose goes out of control, causing the release of radioactivity in dangerous amounts. The disaster at the **Chernobyl** reactor in the Soviet Union underscored just how devastating such an event can be.

Inevitably the term has come to be applied to other disasters, such as the October 19, 1987 plunge of the stock market, about which a *New York Times* editorial asked:

"Must the market undergo another meltdown before the Administration accepts the urgent need to raise taxes by an extra few billion dollars or spend a few billion less on the military?"

**Ménage à Trois.** (men-ahdj ah TWAH) Literally, in French, a household, or domestic situation, of three. The term refers to a three-sided relationship in which husband-wife-mistress or husband-wife-lover live under the same roof. The three parties know and tolerate what is normally considered to be an irregular arrangement. Now we also see it applied figuratively to unusual alliances or cooperation among three individuals whose interests should not coincide.

The term in use, by Martin Amis in his essay "Mr. Vidal: Unpatriotic Gore" from *The Moronic Inferno*, describing author Gore Vidal's years as a screenwriter in Hollywood in the 1950s:

> "At one point there was surprising talk of a romance and engagement between Vidal and Joanne Woodward. They ended up living *à trois* for a time in California, the third member of this curious *ménage* being Paul Newman."

Another example, from *The Washington Post*, March 2, 1989, recounting Margo Adams' revelations of her extramarital relationship with baseball player Wade Boggs:

> "But it was her graphic descriptions [in *Penthouse* magazine] of the sexual high jinks of other Red Sox players—some of whom were said to have teamed up in *ménages à trois*, while others entertained girlfriends in the same hotels where their wives were staying—that stunned the team's training camp in Winter Haven, Fla."

**Mensh.** Yiddish, meaning someone who is really admirable, noble, a good person. A mensh doesn't have to be important; the critical element is fine character.

Leo Rosten in *The Joys of Yiddish* says, "As a child, I often heard it said: 'The finest thing you can say about a man is that he is a mensh' or 'Be a mensh!' This use of the word is uniquely Yiddish in its overtones."

A cross-cultural application of the term from writer Nat Hentoff, self-described Jewish atheist and author of a biography of Cardinal John O'Connor, quoted in *The New York Times Book Review*, July 10, 1988:

> "Yeah, I like him. . . . Whatever disagreements I have with him, I guess what I like most about O'Connor is that he is a mensh."

**Mephistophelean.** Like Mephistopheles, the demon of legend who tempts Faust to sell his soul. (See **Faustian Bargain**.) The origin of the name may be Greek—"not loving the light"—or Hebrew—"destroyer and liar." Both seem apt.

In legends, Mephistopheles appears in various forms—as one of the chief devils, or a mischievous spirit, or as an urbane demon who sneers at virtue. He is not the devil himself, but clearly is devilish in actions and intent.

The term in use, by Anthony Lewis in *The New York Times*, October 27, 1988, deploring the tactics used by the presidential campaign of George Bush:

> "But the facts have been overwhelmed by the Mephis-tophelean skill of Messrs. Baker, Atwater and Ailes [Bush's campaign aides] in playing on emotions in their advertis-ing."

**Mess of Pottage, to Sell One's Birthright for a.** Giving up something of great value for something worth little, or for some transitory comfort or advantage. "Mess" comes from the Latin "missus," which means a course, a serving at a meal. "Pottage" is a thick soup or stew.

The allusion is biblical, from the story in Genesis of brothers Esau and Jacob. Esau came back from hunting, faint with hunger. Jacob, his younger brother, was cooking but wouldn't give Esau anything to eat until he agreed to give up his rights as the oldest son. Thus Esau sold his heritage for something of little value.

The term in use, by conservative Patrick Buchanan in *The Washington Post*, November 1, 1987, bemoaning what he saw as the takeover of the Reagan Administration by despised moderate Republicans:

> "Like Esau, Reagan was persuaded to trade his birthright for a mess of pottage. The president is paying a heavy price for having deeded over so generous a slice of his political inheritance to a party establishment whose disenfranchise-ment, after all, was supposed to be the first order of busi-ness of the Reagan Revolution."

**Micawberesque.** (mi-KAW-buhr-esk) Unrealistic and never-failing optimism.

It is an adjective taken from the name of Mr. Wilkins Micawber, a memorable character created by English novelist Charles Dickens [see **Dickensian**] in his semi-autobiographical novel *David Copperfield* (1849-1850).

Mr. Micawber, who is thought to be based on Dickens' own n'er-do-well father, is always impoverished and frequently unemployed, cherishing schemes that will lead to wealth but that always fall apart. Nevertheless, Mr. Micawber is always certain that "something will turn up" to help him out of his pecuniary difficulties. He is feckless but kind, and eventually helps to defeat the schemes of the villain Uriah Heep.

The term in use, by Jack Beatty in *The Atlantic Monthly*, February 1989, on the legacy of Ronald Reagan in arms control:

> "Events might thrust crises before President Bush from which he could try to extract a 'win.' But this Micawber-esque vision of foreign policy—something might turn up—is a formula for drift, not mastery."

**Mickey Finn.** A drug or knockout drop which, slipped into an unsuspecting victim's drink, renders the drinker helpless. It is a gangster slang term left over from the 19th century.

The term in use, by movie critic Desson Howe, *The Washington Post*, panning *Arthur II: On the Rocks*, July 8, 1988:

> "But most of the time he's flat on his face—the victim of this comedic Mickey Finn."

And from Jane Bryant Quinn, writing on the bond market in *Newsweek*, February 23, 1981:

> "The Mickey Finns: Companies leave you alone with your folly when interest rates rise. But they hate to see you collecting high payments on older bonds when interest rates fall. So they're pouring Mickey Finns into the sub-clauses, to knock out high-yielding issues as soon as it suits them."

Interestingly enough, this term has been picked up and used in the Soviet press to describe capitalist propaganda (in the past, anyway; as we write, all bets and allusions are off). Try this example, from a BBC broadcast of April 18, 1983, quoting *Pravda*:

> "The Americans are being actively exposed to militarist propaganda in an effort to make them into submissive consumers of chauvinistic Mickey Finns. The Administration officials have not forgotten the aversion to war that was produced in American **hearts and minds** by the Indochinese adventure, which resulted in a protracted 'Vietnam syndrome.'"

Another example, from a BBC report of a Soviet Telegraph Agency broadcast commentary of December 15, 1982, entitled "Madness in Oklahoma":

> ". . . he cranked up a self-propelled howitzer and tore off shouting 'The Russians are coming'. . . drove seven miles into the centre of town where he broke through a restaurant wall, knocking down a lamp-post. The crazy 'warrior,' high on vicious anti-Soviet Mickey Finns and the Pentagon's chauvinistic manuals, would have run amok till Doomsday if the police had not cut the rampage short."

**Mirabile Dictu.** (mee-RAH-bi-leh DIK-too) A Latin phrase meaning marvelous to say; wonderful to relate. Frequently used sarcastically.

The term in use, by Jonathan Yardley in *The Washington Post*, May 16, 1988, on excessive zealotry in the anti-smoking movement:

> "Yes, I am all in favor of banning smoking in airplanes and restaurants and even, *mirabile dictu*, the news room of *The Washington Post*; it is a vile habit indeed, and anything we can do to discourage it should be welcomed. Anything, that is, within the bounds of decency and civilized discourse."

**Miranda, Mirandize.** A shorthand reference to the Miranda Rule, enunciated by the United States Supreme Court in 1966 in the case of *Miranda v. Arizona*. In this controversial decision, the Court held that prior to any questioning by law enforcement officers after a person is taken into custody, the person must be informed:

1. That he has a right to remain silent;
2. That any statement he does make may be used as evidence against him;
3. That he has a right to the presence of an attorney;
4. That if he cannot afford an attorney, one will be appointed for him prior to any questioning if he so desires.

Unless these warnings or a knowing and intelligent waiver of these rights are demonstrated, no evidence obtained in the interrogation may be used against the accused.

Miranda was convicted of kidnaping and rape on the basis of a confession obtained after two hours of questioning during which he was not told of his right to counsel or to remain silent. The Court held that the privilege against self-incrimination can be jeopardized when the accused is in custody and deprived of his freedom, seeing the danger that someone in police custody could be intimidated into making a confession.

The decision caused significant controversy when issued, and the controversy continues to this day. Reagan administration attorney general Edwin Meese, for example, called the decision "infamous."

Like it or not, the term has entered our language. Those involved in law enforcement may say that someone has been "Mirandized," meaning that the warnings have been given. And thanks to television cop shows, most of us are familiar with the litany—"you have the right to remain silent," and so on, as the bad guys are handcuffed.

The term in use, by George F. Will, *The Washington Post*, October 12, 1989, on a failed coup in Panama:

> "The president's philosophy is, 'Hey, we were not sent here to bicker.' So he seems to have vaguely sagged into a policy of encouraging Panamanian coups—but only those in which the toppled dictator will be read his Miranda rights and kept intact."

Another example, from *Newsweek*, March 19, 1990, reporting on the changing role of the U.S. military:

"Not only have the services dropped their aversion to the drug war ('Vaporize, not Mirandize,' went the credo), they are undertaking their mission with a new sense of purpose."

**Mise en Scène.** (mee zahn SEN) In movies, the arrangement of space and setting, the relationship between components such as lighting, the placement and movement of actors, the camera perspective. Literally, in French, "placing the scene."

The term in use by Brendan Gill, author of *Many Masks*, a biography of Frank Lloyd Wright, discussing Wright's famous work, the Johnson Wax building in Racine, Wisconsin, in a public broadcasting radio interview on December 3, 1987, with host Studs Terkel:

"There's nothing wrong with the *mise en scène* of Racine. It's a perfectly nice city."

Another example, by Bruce Bawer, movie reviewer of *The American Spectator*, October 1989:

"More than a decade ago . . . [Rob] Reiner wrote, directed and starred in one of the worst TV movies of all time. It was called *More Than Friends*, and it owed a great deal to *Annie Hall*, which had come out only a year or so earlier. Reiner borrowed with great care but little understanding: he appropriated a plot point here, a detail of character there, and emphasized the metropolitan *mise en scène* in a big way."

**Mitty, Walter.** See Walter Mitty.

**Möbius Strip.** (MOH-bee-uhs) A continuous strip with only one edge, named after the German mathematician and astronomer who discovered it, August Ferdinand Möbius (1790-1868). The discovery was made virtually simultaneously with that by Johann Benedict Listing in 1858.

The strip is a "topological space" obtained by pasting together the ends of a rectangular strip, after having given one of the ends a half twist. It looks as if it has two edges, just as it did before the ends were connected, but if you trace around one side with a pencil, you find there is only one. The strip retains the same property when cut down the middle.

The term in use, by Jerry Knight in *The Washington Post*, May 14, 1984:

> "When the company that owns The Limited boutiques tried to buy the Carter Hawley Hale department store chain last month, CHH responded by secretly buying back half its own stock, leaving little for Limited to buy.
>
> "Like a snake swallowing its tail, Carter Hawley Hale's Mobius strip maneuver put a new twist in takeover defenses."

Another example, from *Autoweek*, August 14, 1989, by Satch Carlson:

> "Which brings to mind an interesting thought: When they complete the tunnel from England to France, will the Brits enter it driving on the left, while the Frenchazoids enter on their right? Will there be some sort of interesting interchange in the middle, sort of like an underground Mobius strip, so they can all keep going?"

And from Vic Sussman, *The Washington Post Magazine*, January 22, 1989:

> "And when I turn the page again I see a picture that directly confronts my existential Tupperware questions: here are Tupperware containers designed to hold Tupperware containers! A Mobius strip of endlessly compulsive neatness— Tupperware nestled inside Tupperware nestled inside Tupperware."

**Moby Dick.** Invoked as the object of a mystical quest or to describe something awesomely monstrous.

The term comes from the name of the great white whale pursued by the fanatical Captain Ahab in Herman Melville's 1851 novel,

*Moby-Dick, or The Whale.* This complex work is viewed as one of the greatest novels in American literature. Many theories of the symbolism of the whale are offered—Moby Dick is thought to be the incarnation of evil, the symbolic victim of modern man's destruction of nature or the embodiment of knowledge and understanding of reality.

Ahab, maimed by the creature, pursues the whale with an obsessive hatred, sweeping along to their deaths all in the crew except the narrator Ishmael.

The whale invoked, by James M. Markham in *The New York Times*, May 1, 1989, writing from Paris on the construction of the architecturally controversial Bastille Opera:

> " 'It's surprising looking,' said Maurice Solignac, the owner of the Tour d'Argent restaurant, which flanks the new opera, melding into its mass. The gentle, 68-year-old Mr. Solignac was doing his best to sound polite about the architectural Moby Dick beached on his doorstep."

Another example, by William L. Vance, author of *America's Rome*, describing the widely-varying responses of American visitors to the Colosseum:

> "The Moby-Dick of architecture, a sublimely multivalent symbol, ravaged and enduring."

**Modus Operandi.** (MOH-dus op-uh-RAN-dee) Latin; literally, it means "method of operation."

It's a term much favored in cops-and-robbers movies and television shows to refer to distinguishing quirks in the behavior of criminals: their style of operation is their "m.o."

The term in use, in a somewhat different context, in an anonymous description of corporate raider Carl Icahn, quoted in *The Wall Street Journal*, June 16, 1989:

> " 'People really don't understand Icahn any more,' one money manager says. 'He started out as one kind of animal—a greenmailer. But his investment in steel and TWA are long term, and he's operating TWA. His modus operandi has changed.' "

**Modus Vivendi.** (MOH-dus vih-VEN-dee) A working arrangement, or understanding in which adversaries—they can be people, groups or nations—manage to coexist without open hostilities.

Literally, in Latin, it means method or mode of living. One could say that the "balance of terror" or the doctrine of "mutually assured destruction" have served as a modus vivendi between the United States and the Soviet Union.

The term in use, by Norman Cousins, writing in *The New York Times*, August 27, 1989:

> "If the future of Israel depends on a modus vivendi with Israel's Arab citizens, to say nothing of Israel's neighbors, then the importance of creative and fully functional Arab communities within Israel itself cannot be overestimated."

Another example, from David Richards, *The Washington Post*, October 13, 1989, reviewing a production of *The Glass Menagerie*:

> "Tom (Jonathan Earl Peck) of course is a thinly disguised portrait of playwright Williams himself as a young man. . . .
>
> Most of Peck's scenes are opposite [Ruby] Dee, however, and it is hard to avoid the impression that the two are still working out a modus vivendi."

**Mr. Dooley.** A fictional Irishman invented by American journalist and humorist Finley Peter Dunne (1867-1936) in the *Chicago Tribune*. In Dunne's writings, Mr. Dooley presided over a small saloon on Chicago's West Side and made biting comment on the events and personalities of the day from the Spanish-American War to World War I.

As Gene Shalit notes in his humor anthology, *Laughing Matters*, "Dunne never could have jabbed the rich and powerful men and the mores of his time in his own voice—the *Tribune* would not have published it. But to have it from Mr. Dooley—who could take seriously anything said by an Irish bartender on Chicago's Archer Road? Everybody, that's who."

Samples of Mr. Dooley's drollness, in the Irish brogue Dunne gave him:

"A man can be right an' prisident, but he can't be both at th' same time."

"No matter whether th' constitution follows th' flag or not, th' supreme court follows th' iliction returns."

"Histhry always vidicates th' Dimmycrats, but nivir in their lifetime. They see th' thruth first, but th' trouble is that nawthin' is iver officially thrue till a Raypublican sees it."

"A fanatic is a man that does what he thinks th' Lord wud do if He knew th' facts iv th' case."

Dooley invoked, by Robert Kuttner in *The New Republic*, March 6, 1989, reviewing Brooks Jackson's book, *Honest Graft: Big Money and the American Political Process:*

"Jackson's tone, though serious, manages to avoid the dreary indignation characteristic of reformist tracts. This is a good tale, wise to the folkways of American politics, chock full of delightful anecdotes, and, in the spirit of Plunkitt of **Tammany Hall** and Finley Peter Dunne's Mr. Dooley, not without a storyteller's appreciation of a good rogue."

**Mullah.** (MUL-uh) A Muslim teacher or scholar. In Arabic, literally, master.

In the United States in the 1980s, however, the term came to stand for a hate-filled religious fanaticism, a view arising from the bitter crisis in which mullah-led Iranians held 52 Americans hostage in their embassy in Tehran for 444 days during the Carter Administration.

The term in use, by Sean Wilentz, in *The New Republic*, April 25, 1988, in an article about fundamentalist Jerry Falwell:

"Not too long ago, after all, many people thought of Falwell as an American mullah in the making, a clear and present danger to democracy—fears that Falwell fed with his fiery rhetoric about putting the nation back on a biblical footing."

**Munchkin.** A minor player, someone who is diminutive, eccentric, weak or unimportant.

That's its current usage. Originally, the munchkins were small, kind, elf-like people in Frank L. Baum's *The Wizard of Oz*. As Dorothy's adventures begin, her house falls on the wicked witch who had ruled over the Land of the Munchkins, and they are very grateful to her for liberating them. They set Dorothy on her way, following the yellow brick road, and the rest is history.

When Barbara Honegger, hired in the Reagan administration's Justice Department to analyze women's status under state laws, resigned, calling the project a sham, administration spokesman Thomas DeCair responded by calling her "a low-level munchkin," as quoted in *The Washington Post*, August 25, 1983. Ms. Honegger held a press conference and responded by displaying a picture of herself with President Reagan. Said she, "This is the munchkin with the Wizard of Oz" (*The Washington Post*, August 26, 1983).

**Munich.** A German city whose name has become a metaphor for catastrophic appeasement of tyrants.

On September 30, 1938, British Prime Minister Neville Chamberlain, French Premier Edouard Daladier, German dictator Adolf Hitler and Italian dictator Benito Mussolini signed an agreement ceding to Germany the Sudetenland, an area in western Czechoslovakia inhabited by ethnic Germans, in an attempt to finally satisfy Hitler's demands for more territory. The Czechs were there only to sign, not to negotiate. They signed "to register their protest before the world against a decision in which they had no part."

Chamberlain returned to London and read to an ecstatic crowd a pledge of everlasting Anglo-German friendship signed by himself and Hitler. With his familiar umbrella (now itself a symbol of appeasement) in hand, waving the document in the other, he uttered a phrase that has become famous for its historic misreading of a situation, declaring that the accord meant "peace for our time."

So Munich has come to stand for a policy that seeks to appease an aggressor nation, particularly at the expense of small or weak nations, a policy that can lead only to failure and ultimately to war.

An example of the term in use comes from then-Congressman Jack Kemp during his unsuccessful run for the 1988 Republican presidential nomination, who turned to the analogy in attacking the Intermediate Nuclear Forces treaty. As quoted by *The Washington Post*, November 25, 1987, Kemp warned that the INF accord could bring about a "nuclear Munich."

# N

**Nabob.** (NAY-bahb) A corruption of the Hindi word, "nawab," which means deputy governor, a title used for provincial governors in the Mogul Empire. These men usually became wealthy and powerful. Today, the word has a mocking tone, suggesting self-importance and/or vulgar raw wealth.

The term worked its way into English in the early days of British occupation of India. English merchant adventurers who made their fortunes and returned home to enjoy their wealth were derided as "nabobs," similar to the implication of "**nouveau riche**."

Journalist William Safire confesses to having rejuvenated the word when he was a speech writer for Vice President Spiro T. Agnew who, on September 11, 1970, attacked the press as "nattering nabobs of negativism." The speech's notoriety egged Agnew down an alley of alliterative allusions.

The term in use, by Bob Mack, *Spy*, July 1989, on possible successors to conservative icon William F. Buckley:

> "At best, he offers a **regency** while an heir matures, an heir who must achieve not just the intellectual heft that Buckley possessed in his prime but also the style, wit and gregariousness that helped make him palatable to the media nabobs who helped promote him over the years."

**Neo-.** New, in Greek, but in English it is attached as a prefix, usually without a hyphen, to indicate a modern form or practice of a doctrine, inclination, language or art form; a new version of something already known.

For example, "neoconservative" came into use in the 1960s to describe those who reacted against what they saw as the excesses of modern liberalism. Unlike traditional conservatives, who believe government is at its best when it governs least, neoconservatives were willing to use the full force of government to solve social problems. The term is often applied to former Democrats, conservative Democrats and conservative-on-some-things-but-not-others Democrats.

Neoconservative thinker Seymour Martin Lipset, quoted in *The New Republic*, January 23, 1989, proclaimed neoconservativism not so much a movement as a "tendency." When Senator Paul Simon announced for the presidency in 1987, he aroused amused appreciation from other traditional Democrats by declaring: "I'm not a neo-anything."

"Neocolonial" describes the control which former colonial powers can exert over their independent ex-colonies. Often the neocolonialism takes the form of economic rather than political power when trade ties remain after political ties are cut. The term also describes the dominance exerted by a great power over a small one even if there never had been a colonial relationship.

"Neoclassical" is applied to works of art and architecture inspired by those of ancient Greece and Rome, such as the Supreme Court building in Washington.

The term in use, by *The Economist*, March 4, 1989, discussing the behavior of British soccer fans:

> "Seasoned observers of football insist that Mr. Moynihan [the British minister of sport] is behind the times; that the game has calmed down, that the police (aided by video-cameras) have a better grip on things, and that the neofascist psychopaths who follow the English national team abroad would not necessarily follow clubs there."

**Ne Plus Ultra.** Latin: literally, "nothing more beyond." It means the ultimate, the highest or furthest possible point attainable, the acme; sometimes an obstacle to further advance.

The term in use, in *Publishers Weekly*, March 3, 1989, in a review of *William Faulkner: American Writer* by Frederick R. Karl:

> "It's tempting to consider these 1200 pages the *ne plus ultra* of Faulkner studies, not only for the book's comprehensiveness but for its depth."

**Night of the Long Knives.** In the history of Nazism, it was June 30, 1934, when Hitler had assassins kill possible rivals to his recently acquired power. Hundreds of real or suspected adversaries, including old friends and collaborators, were brutally murdered.

The term is used to refer to vicious and ruthless struggles among rival factions, including non-bloody power struggles or purges among bureaucrats and ideologues.

The term in use, from *The New Republic*, April 10, 1989, by Fouad Ajami:

> "The Arab Rebellion has become the stuff of legend. But it was an unmitigated disaster for the Palestinians. It was an act of self-immolation. After the fury came the hunger and the deprivation. Then came the Night of the Long Knives, when Palestinian society turned on itself and began the search for collaborators, for sacrificial lambs."

A variation, from Tom Kenworthy and Don Phillips in *The Washington Post*, March 20, 1989, describing turmoil in the House of Representatives over ethics charges against the Speaker of the House, Jim Wright:

> "Speculation is mounting that Wright will not survive as speaker. The corridors are full of the sound of long knives being sharpened."

**NIMBY.** An acronym, standing for "Not in my backyard"— shorthand for the objections heard from neighbors of proposed public facilities (prisons, half-way houses, trash incinerators, power plants, nuclear waste dumps) which they believe will have an unpleasant or value-degrading effect on their property and surroundings.

"We heartily endorse the building of this (fill in the blank)," say objectors, "but as public-spirited citizens, we believe a more suitable site exists elsewhere."

The term in use, by *Time*, December 26, 1988, in a headline on disputes between Colorado and Idaho on disposal of nuclear waste: "Playing Atomic NIMBY."

And the *Omaha World Herald*, May 26, 1989, editorializes on neighborhood opposition to a recycling plant:

> "The question is whether a place exists anywhere where the facility could be placed without generating a campaign to send it elsewhere. The danger is that the city will eventually run out of back yards without having found a place for the facility. Either that or the NIMBY syndrome will have to give way to the common good."

**Ninety-five Theses.** The fundamental document of the Protestant Reformation, nailed by Martin Luther on the door of the castle church in Wittenberg, Germany, in 1517. Now, generically, any set of controversial ideas boldly set forth.

Luther, a professor at the University of Wittenberg, had been provoked by a visit to the area of a monk selling indulgences to finance the construction of St. Peter's in Rome. (In the Roman Catholic Church, an indulgence is a remission of punishment for sins and is supposed to save the sinner from purgatory.) Luther believed that souls could not be saved in such a way. His theses contended that the sinner was freed of his burden not by confession but by faith; that the priest was not a necessary intermediary between man and God.

Although Luther did not set out to break with the pope, as time passed he became increasingly reformist in his views. He was excommunicated in 1521 but continued his work and began to translate the Bible into German. In 1522, he introduced services in German. Lutheranism—or anti-Romanism—swept through Germany and spread throughout the Western world.

The term in use, by automobile columnist Brock Yates, having set forth his program as imaginary czar of the auto industry in *The Washington Post Magazine*, November 6, 1988:

> "There you have it. You will recall that Martin Luther nailed 95 theses to the door of the Wittenberg Cathedral,

but I have managed a certain triumph of brevity by limiting mine to 58."

Another example, from B. Drummond Ayres Jr., *The New York Times*, July 9, 1989:

"The Rev. George Augustus Stallings Jr. says he is no Martin Luther, no renegade Roman Catholic with a fistful of heretical theses to nail to a church door.

"But if he is no Luther, this maverick among Catholic priests has nevertheless defiantly embarked on a course that is forcing the 53-million-member church to consider anew whether it is adequately addressing the needs of its 1.5 million black parishioners."

**Noblesse Oblige.** (noh-BLES oh-BLEEZH) The moral obligation of the rich or the well-born to display honorable or charitable conduct. It is French, and means literally, "nobility obliges." In other words, rank has its obligations.

The term in use, by Timothy Noah, *The New Republic*, February 13, 1989:

"In the spirit of noblesse oblige, the new president declared this 'the age of the offered hand.' "

**Nom de Guerre.** (nom duh GAIR) An assumed name under which one paints, performs or fights; a stage name. It's French, and literally means "name from war." It dates from the days of chivalry, when knights were known by the symbols on their shields. Nom de plume, or pen name, is specifically a writer's pseudonym.

The term in use by Loren Jenkins in *The Washington Post*, April 17, 1988, discussing the assassination of Khalid Wazir, the military chief of the Palestine Liberation Organization:

"Wazir, better known by his nom de guerre, Abu Jihad, was known to be responsible for coordinating the continuing Palestinian uprising in the Israeli-occupied West Bank and Gaza Strip."

**Normalcy.** A word made current in our time by Warren G. Harding, 29th president of the United States. Harding was picked for the office in the original smoke-filled room when the Republican convention of 1920 deadlocked. Harding promised, popularized and epitomized "normalcy"—a time of retrenchment and consolidation at the end of a period of great endeavor, sacrifice, controversy and turmoil. In Harding's case, blissful normalcy followed the upheavals of World War I, the bitter national debate over participation in the League of Nations, and domestic social conflict.

Harding was mocked for allegedly creating the word, but he claimed he found it in the dictionary, and it does turn up as far back as the mid-19th century.

The term in use, by Fred Barnes, in *The New Republic*, August 28, 1989, on White House handling of the death of an American hostage in Lebanon:

> "Faking normalcy was a superficial problem."

Another example, from Richard C. Carpenter, in *The Wall Street Journal*, October 16, 1989:

> "For those hoping to see a modicum of political normalcy restored—in view of Greece's eight-year misadventure under autocratic pseudosocialism and subsequent three-month hitch with a conservative-communist coalition government—there is but one bright sign: The scandals still encircling former Prime Minister Andreas Papandreou and his fallen socialist government are like flies buzzing around a rotting carcass."

**Nostalgie de la Boue.** (noh-stahl-gee duh la BOO) French: literally, yearning for the mud. More broadly, it means seeking degradation and depravity, particularly among those people who seem to be above such things.

The term in use, by Tom Wolfe, in *Radical Chic and Mau-Mauing the Flak Catchers*:

> "**Radical chic**, after all, is only radical in style; in its heart it is part of society and its traditions. Politics, like Rock, Pop,

and Camp, has its uses; but to put one's whole status on the line for *nostalgie de la boue* in any of its forms would be unprincipled."

Another example, from architecture critic Ada Louise Huxtable, *The New York Times*, June 29, 1980:

"To want the Museum of Modern Art to stay the way it is today, even under much less strain than the Picasso spectacular imposes, can only be put down to *nostalgie de la boue*, or a fondness for primordial mud. More kindly, this attachment to the status quo can be attributed to remembrance of things past [see **Proust, Proustian**]."

**Nouveau Riche.** (noo-voh REESH) The new rich. A French term for the possessor of new wealth. The term suggests a tendency toward vulgarity, ostentation—that those with "new money" do not enjoy their wealth as discreetly or graciously as those who are born to a more aristocratic tradition. The plural form is "noureaux riches."

The term in use, by Sidney Blumenthal in *The Washington Post*, January 15, 1989, on the images of Reaganism:

"The small-town life [artist Norman] Rockwell depicted in all its foibles was the one Reagan promised to restore. . . .

"But in the Reaganite aesthetic as it was lived, the realities of the *nouveau riche* clashed with the projections of the traditional village."

Another example, aimed at the same target, from Timothy Noah, *The New Republic*, February 13, 1989, on President Bush's inaugural address:

". . . Bush criticized the notion that we are 'the sum of our possessions,' which struck me as less a call for equality than an upper-class sneer at the tacky nouveau-riche couple that preceded him in the White House."

**Number-crunching.** Doing intricate mathematical computations to reach conclusions from masses of numbers.

The expression calls up the image of some busy person chomping his way through piles of statistics or budget figures to analyze things most people are happier not to think about—and that is what gives those talented crunchers their power.

A less-innocent application of the term suggests that the numbers are bent to lead to a predetermined conclusion. Thus the term sometimes suggests manipulating data to deceive the unwary—cooking the books.

The term in use by Ellen Benoit in *Forbes*, May 6, 1985, discussing computer software:

> "No sooner do accounting programs such as Lotus 1-2-3 enable middle managers to crunch numbers in more imaginative ways than a need arises for computerized help with the more conceptual process of making decisions."

**Nuremburg Defense.** "Just following orders"—the defense unsuccessfully offered by Nazis put on trial at Nuremburg, Germany for war crimes following World War II. Now the term is used contemptuously to characterize this excuse when offered by someone who has carried out orders to perform what he knows to be a criminal or reprehensible act.

The term in use, by James Glassman in *The New Republic*, May 29, 1989, commenting on the trial of Marine Lt. Colonel North:

> "I had always thought of North as a Gordon Liddy/jump-on-that-grenade type. I asked an ex-CIA friend about the phenomenon, and he had an interesting explanation—a guess, but a plausible one: [North's attorney] Brendan Sullivan had painted a nasty picture of prison for Ollie and told him that the only way to get off was to pull a Nuremburg. So Ollie, follower of Bill Casey's orders (or Ronald Reagan's, or John Poindexter's, or whoever's), followed Sullivan's. A good Marine, willing to drag a president or two down with him."

# O

**October Surprise.** A last-minute political bombshell timed to affect the outcome of an election.

The Ronald Reagan camp put the term into the political lexicon in 1980 by talking ceaselessly of its expectations that President Jimmy Carter would exercise the power of his office to produce an event—perhaps the release of the American hostages in Iran—timed to derive maximum political benefit for the Democratic ticket. The Reagan camp hoped to undercut the impact of any such surprise by warning of it in advance and calling into question the motives behind it. No surprise materialized.

As reported by Abe Melnikoff, *The San Francisco Chronicle*, October 16, 1980:

> "Voices are tense and there is a hushed air these days at meetings of the October Surprise Committee. This is a little-known secret operation being run by Reagan National Headquarters.
>
> "It was set up to figure out what surprise Jimmy Carter might pull this month to turn the election around. And prepare plans to defuse it once Jimmy struck."

The term in use, by Christopher Hitchens in *The Nation*, October 31, 1988 (referring to rumors that representatives of Reagan's 1980 campaign negotiated with the Iranians to assure that the hostages would not be released before the election):

> "Over the past month or so, the 1980 'October surprise' hypothesis has been trying to reach critical mass in the mainstream media. It is the story everyone has heard and that no one wants to print."

**Oedipal.** (ED-uh-puhl) Describing a child's sexual attraction (usually not recognized by the child) for his or her parent of the opposite sex, linked with jealous hatred of his or her sexual rival, the parent of his or her own sex. Freud originated the concept and gave it the name "Oedipus complex."

The term springs from Greek mythology. When Oedipus was born to King Laius of Thebes and Queen Jocasta, an oracle warned that the child would kill his father and marry his mother. To avert such a turn of events, the parents left him on the mountain to die. He was found by a shepherd, who brought the child to the king of Corinth. Oedipus was raised believing the king and his wife were his true parents. When he learned of the prophecy, he left Corinth seeking to avoid his fate. On the road he unknowingly met Laius, his true father, quarreled with and killed him. Oedipus then went to Thebes, saved the city from the Sphinx by solving her riddle, and was offered the throne of the city and the hand of Laius' widow, Jocasta. He accepted both, not knowing, of course, that Jocasta was his mother. After many years, he learned the truth and, in horror, blinded himself. Jocasta killed herself. The story has been the basis for many literary works, most notably Greek playwright Sophocles' *Oedipus Rex*. It is clear how Freud would have chosen the name he did for the complex he discovered, one which arises in the psychosocial development of the personality around ages 3 to 5.

The term in use, by Timothy Noah in *The New Republic*, April 3, 1989, on the career of the late Senator Prescott Bush, father of President George Bush:

"And most puzzling of all is that the leader of the free world should have such a diminished view of himself in comparison to this particular father. In the great Oedipal footrace, George Bush has lapped Prescott Bush several times over."

A somewhat more elaborate use, by Lance Morrow, in *Time*, January 11, 1988, describing the student takeover of Columbia University 20 years earlier:

"With some of the student movement's talent for converting disrespect to symbolic desecration, the occupation forces moved into [university president Grayson] Kirk's office, smoked his cigars (one student with his feet perched on Kirk's desk, an act of smirking and virtually Oedipal **lese** majeste—O.K., Dad, whatcha gonna do about it, huh?) and, after six days of occupation, left the place a mess."

**Offending Adam.** See Whip the Offending Adam.

**Old Guard.** The old-fashioned, conservative element of a political party, particularly the Republican Party. Or, used nonpolitically, the conservative, orthodox, establishment members of any group or movement. [For the opposite of the Old Guard, see **Young Turks.**]

The term comes from the elite imperial guard of Napoleon, a unit of towering prestige. Their imposing presence was enhanced by long coats with broad epaulets at the shoulder and tall bearskin hats. They were devoted to their emperor, and were always relied upon in the most desperate circumstances. But not even they could save Napoleon at **Waterloo.** Late in the day the Emperor hurled them at the Duke of Wellington's battered formations. The Old Guard charged valiantly, but for the first time in their history they were broken.

The term in use, by Tom Kenworthy and Don Phillips in *The Washington Post*, March 20, 1989, describing the race for the Republican whip position in the House of Representatives:

> "Gingrich's reputation as a bombthrower so bothers some old-guard Republicans that there has been an extraordinary effort to defeat him."

**Orwellian.** (or-WELL-ee-uhn) An adjective drawn from the name and works of British novelist George Orwell (real name Eric Blair, 1903-1950), and most particularly his 1947 novel *1984*. Orwell fought on the Republican side of the Spanish Civil War but came away disillusioned by communism. His books reflect that disillusionment by depicting the horrors of a totalitarian society in which individuality counts for nothing and, indeed, is viewed as a detriment to the overall good. In Orwell's frightening vision, truth is turned on its head by a pervasive, intrusive government and its relentless propaganda machine.

"Orwellian" suggests that grim world: oppressive bureaucracies and spying governments ("Big Brother is watching" comes from Orwell); propaganda campaigns that say love is hate and war is peace, in which language is rewritten [see -**Speak**] to change its meaning, history is rewritten to serve the state and truth is blotted out.

The term in use, by *The Washington Post*, June 27, 1988, in an editorial:

> "The Senate Appropriations Committee has found a new way of controlling the government that is spread before it. It has gone into the Orwellian business of rewriting history."

Another example, in *The Washington Post*, January 3, 1989. Charles Paul Freund reports on reaction to President Reagan's farewell speech:

> "Reagan's redefinition of the **Iron Triangle** also alters its original meaning significantly, and self-servingly. When Myron Moskovitz, a law professor at Golden Gate University, pointed this out recently in *The New York Times*, he went so far as to accuse Reagan of 'Orwellian Newspeak.' "

Another example, from Simon Leys, writing in *The New Republic*, June 19, 1989 on turmoil in China:

> "Following the Orwellian convention that generally requires that cannibal kings be called 'Wise Leaders,' that gangs of thugs be known as 'Liberation Fronts,' and that every murderous despotism should always carry the title of 'Democratic Republic,' the Chinese Communist regime used to affix 'People's' labels on virtually every institution and organ of the state, as if better to indicate that the *real* people were to be effectively evacuated from the entire political system."

**Outré.** (oo-TRAY) A French adjective meaning overdone, exaggerated, excessive.

The term in use, by *The New York Times*, September 27, 1988, describing Democratic Sen. Frank Lautenberg of New Jersey:

> "His white hair and dark eyebrows lend distinction to his appearance, even if his brown suit and burgundy tie seem a

touch rumpled and outré in a season when politicians seem to be sporting a uniform of dark pinstripe suits and red 'power' ties."

Another example, from Bob Mack, *Spy*, July 1989:

"In 1971, however, when [William F.] Buckley was still ideologically outré, he could get away with it. But by 1983 Buckley's act had got old, and his description of the custom Jacuzzi in his basement as 'the most beautiful indoor pool this side of Pompeii' was as tired as it was appalling."

**Ozymandias, Ozymandian.** (oh-zee-MAN-dee-uhs) A sonnet by English poet Percy Bysshe Shelley, published in 1818, with a line ("Look on my works, ye Mighty, and despair") that's often put to use in other works, mighty and otherwise, to illustrate the short staying power of self-aggrandizing monuments. "Ozymandian" appears now as an adjective to describe something huge or grandiose.

The poem describes the colossal ruined statue of an ancient king in a barren desert, like the gigantic monuments of ancient Egyptian pharaohs. ("Ozymandias" is the Greek name for the Egyptian pharaoh Ramses II.) Shelley was commenting on the futility of power and of the foolish arrogance of tyrants that their grandeur will never fade:

I met a traveller from an antique land
Who said, "Two vast and trunkless legs of stone
Stand in the desert. Near them, on the sand,
Half sunk, a shattered visage lies, whose frown
And wrinkled lip, and sneer of cold command,
Tell that its sculptor well those passions read
Which yet survive, stamped on these lifeless things,
The hand that mocked them and the heart that fed.
And on the pedestal these words appear—
"My name is Ozymandias, king of kings:
Look on my works, ye Mighty, and despair!"
Nothing beside remains. Round the decay
Of that colossal wreck, boundless and bare
The lone and level sands stretch far away.

The term in use, in *Time*, February 8, 1982:

> "Federal Reserve Board Chairman Paul Volcker charges that by letting the deficit run up toward $100 billion, the White House has all but abandoned its fight against inflation. This has left the struggle to be waged singlehanded by the Federal Reserve, and that, Volcker feels, is asking too much of the American central bank. It is those Ozymandian budget deficits that are soaking up private capital, depriving the economy of productive investment."

And a play on the sonnet by Martin Amis, in his essay "Norman Mailer: The Avenger and the Bitch" in *The Moronic Inferno*, 1987:

> "His name is Norman Mailer, king of kings: look on his works, ye Mighty, and—what? Despair? Burst out laughing? In secure retrospect, Mailer's life and times seem mostly ridiculous . . . only towards the end, perhaps— with no more drink and 'no more stunts,' dedicated to his work and to a noncombatant sixth wife—has he struck a human balance. As for the past, nothing beside remains."

# P

**Pale, Beyond the.** See Beyond the Pale.

**Panglossian.** (pan-GLOSS-ee-an) Foolishly optimistic: Taken from Dr. Pangloss, a character in Voltaire's *Candide*. His name is Greek, meaning "all tongues." Dr. Pangloss is notable for his incurable and absurd optimism, regardless of circumstance, and his constant refrain "All is for the best in this best of all possible worlds."

The term in use, in *The Economist*, January 14, 1989, on Ronald Reagan's farewell address:

> "It would be churlish, while pausing on Mr. Reagan's Panglossian cloud, to question whether government has grown less greedy in the past eight years. For while the president is modest in his way of putting things, and self-deprecating in his humor, his view of his political achievements are wonderfully immodest."

Also from *The Economist*, October 21, 1989:

> "This Panglossian view is not shared by Fred Halliday, who is professor of international relations at the London School of Economics. As far as most third-world countries are concerned, the idea that peace and prosperity are round the corner is an illusion."

**Papal Bull.** An edict, decree or command issued by the pope. In non-ecclesiastic usage, an authoritative statement: the law, as laid down by someone from on high.

The term "bull" comes from the Latin word "bulla," or seal, after the lead seal that was attached to such documents.

The term in use, by Stacy Jolna, *The Washington Post*, May 19, 1979:

> "[Harvard University President Derek] Bok also answered critics of his earlier academic 'papal bulls' like Georgetown

University President Timothy S. Healy, who attacked the Harvard president's call for universities to maintain a neutral stance and remain above campus political scuffles."

Another example, from Garry Ray in *PC Week*, March 15, 1988:

"It is an **icon** in the company's theology, a step into the world of tomorrow, a fundamental change from the way things are to the way they will be. It is one more step in Microsoft's journey to its highest vision: The Automated Office.

"You may think this is a spoof, but it is precisely the papal bull issued by Mr. Letwin in the first two chapters of his entertaining encyclical on OS/2."

**Parkinson's Law.** An observation laid down in 1955 by British historian C. Northcote Parkinson in his book of the same title. It holds: "Work expands so as to fill the time available for its completion."

Following the enunciation of his law, writes Paul Dickson, author of *The Official Rules*, "Parkinson became famous and his law has become a permanent tenet of organizational life." [See also **Peter Principle**.]

The term in use, in *The Economist*, March 11, 1989, referring to delays in filling key posts in the new Bush administration:

"The White House personnel director, Mr. Chase Untermeyer, claims that more presidential nominations are in train than at the same stage of the 1981 Reagan administration—and there is anyway less urgency about a friendly than a hostile takeover. Despite (or, following Parkinson's law, because of) a growing staff, the Federal Bureau of Investigation is taking two or three times longer to clear nominees than it did 20 years ago. . . ."

**Parvenu.** (PAHR-vuh-noo) Newly arrived, in the literal French; the term refers to someone who is newly rich or powerful or important, an upstart not yet accepted by those more established. [See **Arriviste, Nouveau Riche**.]

The term in use by Robert H. Williams in *The Washington Post*, December 14, 1988, commenting on the manners shown by drivers new to four-wheel-drive vehicles:

> "They will run you down, these parvenus of dangerous terrain, and they will honk their horns at you and cut you off and force you into a snow bank and snarl at you, and if you can admit your powerlessness over them you will finally wind up at home, safe and sound."

Another example, by Sidney Blumenthal, also in *The Washington Post*, January 15, 1989, "Goodbye To All That," on Reagan-era **kitsch**:

> "But more than money was involved in setting value. The dominant Reaganite aesthetic was built upon the older generation's pop-cult memories, which included Reagan. The new was almost exclusively a pastiche of the old. And yet, while a quasi-official premium was placed on 'cheerful sociability' (George Will's standard for literature), the only original characters in the pantheon of Reaganite culture were the uncheerful parvenus from 'Dynasty' and the unsociable heroes from the movies like 'Rambo.' "

**Pas de Deux.** (pah deh duh) Intricate maneuvering by two individuals, who may be partners or opponents. Literally, in French, step for two, or a dance for two. In ballet, the most famous pas de deux is for a ballerina and her male partner.

The term in use, by Tom Carter in the December 1988 *Bicycle Guide*, describing the neck-and-neck competition of two cyclists in the 1988 Race Across America:

> "With about 700 miles to the finish line, Fedrigon and Templin were still engaged in their pas de deux. Fedrigon led through Effingham, Illinois, and Terre Haute, Indiana. Templin wanted the seven day's white jersey, so he jammed and caught Fedrigon about ten minutes before the

two o'clock deadline. Templin then backed off, and Fed-
rigon led into Indianapolis."

And from Elsa Walsh, *The Washington Post*, October 2, 1989,
reporting on the trial of an alleged Washington drug kingpin:

"The judge's order was only the latest in an almost daily
series of outbursts and unexpected events that have often
overshadowed the courtroom testimony. At the center of it
has been a tense pas de deux between two of the principals
in the drama, U.S. District Judge Charles R. Richey and
William H. Murphy, Jr., a former judge who is one of
Edmond's attorneys."

**Patois.** (PAT-wah) A French word meaning jargon, the indigenous
local dialect.

The term in use, by Arthur M. Schlesinger in *One Thousand
Days*, his memoir of the Kennedy presidency, discussing the State
Department:

"The intellectual exhaustion of the Foreign Service expressed itself in the poverty of the official rhetoric. In
meetings the men from State would talk in a bureaucratic
patois borrowed in huge part from the Department of Defense. We would be exhorted to 'zero in' on 'the purpose of
the drill' (or of the 'exercise' or 'operation') to 'crank in' this
and 'phase out' that. . . ."

Another example, from *The Economist*, January 14, 1989:

"By the end of the nineteenth century, the rich sent their
sons to 'public' boarding schools so that they would lose
any local burr. All the same, the 15th Earl of Derby (Rugby
and Cambridge), who was foreign secretary in the 1860s
and 1870s, spoke in 'a Lancashire patois,' according to
**Disraeli**."

And from Maureen Dowd, *The New York Times*, March 9, 1990:

"Once upon a campaign, many people thought George
Bush would never be elected President because he was a

disjointed speaker who favored the odd patois known as Ivy-
speak."


**Pavlovian.** Describes an automatic, conditioned, knee-jerk and utterly predictable response to a signal or a provocation. The adjective
comes from the experiments of Russian physiologist Ivan Petrovich
Pavlov (1849-1936, winner of the Nobel Prize, 1904), who rang a bell
when he fed dogs. After a while, he found that the dogs would salivate
when the bell rang, even though there was no food in sight. He
discovered the "conditioned reflex."

Thus someone who acts like Pavlov's dogs, or is Pavlovian, is
reacting in a completely predictable, automatic fashion to a particular
stimulus.

The term in use, by Bill Rodgers in *Marathoning*; the famous
runner discusses press reaction when runners drop dead of heart
attacks:

"The automatic Pavlovian response was to call me."


**Pax Americana.** From the Latin word for peace, modified by the
Latinized adjective "Americana"; "American peace." The expression
is the etymological grandchild of Pax Romana, and the child of Pax
Britannica.

The Pax Romana refers to the period of peace and civil order that
prevailed within the Roman Empire. In the 19th century, many
British enjoyed likening their colonial rule and the worldwide economic and political power they wielded to that of Rome, and both
terms gained currency.

After World War II, with British power diminished and the Empire
breaking up, many Americans thought the United States should step
into the role of world banker and policeman previously played by the
British. We continue to hear today arguments about the judiciousness
of those decisions and whether or not the period of American ascen-
dancy has ended.

The term in use, by Leonard Silk in *The New York Times*, January

27, 1987, referring to the effect of the federal deficit on the fluctuating value of the American dollar:

> "But this indirect method of financing the Pax Americana makes an extremely volatile dollar inevitable, with dangerous consequences for the United States and the world economy."

*The Oxford English Dictionary* notes that a variety of similar constructions are made using Latinized adjectives on this model (including "pax atomica"), referring to the peace imposed by a great power. An example from *Time*, August 29, 1977:

> "Bell-bottom denims, miniskirts and platform shoes have turned Ulan Bator's girls into the prettiest within the Pax Sovietica."

And also in *Time*, September 25, 1989, Charles Krauthammer writes:

> "Germany was conquered, then divided into two states designed to remain forever in a state of permanent, if cold antagonism. Pax Americana and Pax Sovietica solved the German problem."

**Peck's Bad Boy.** Anyone whose bad, mischievous or tasteless behavior is a source of embarrassment or annoyance. It comes from the 1883 novel *Peck's Bad Boy and His Pa* and years of humorous sketches by George Wilbur Peck, an American journalist and aphorist who served twice as governor of Wisconsin. Hennery, the bad boy in question, was given to playing tricks on his boozy father, such as lining pa's hatband with limburger cheese.

The term in use, by Tom Shales, in a profile of communications magnate Ted Turner in *The Washington Post*, April 13, 1989:

> "He's a major player and a legend among oddballs, and never too busy to become Peck's Bad Boy. He's a maverick, an upstart, a rogue and a swashbuckler. The last of the red-hot moguls. A Frank Capra hero."

Another example, from Maureen Dowd in *The New York Times*, June 19, 1989, on the activities of Republican National Committee chairman Lee Atwater:

> "Reports began circulating recently in Washington that the First Lady was displeased with Lee Atwater's second career as an impersonator of Elvis Presley. . . . she felt that his Peck's Bad Boy behavior was 'trivializing' the image of the party her husband heads."

## Pecksniff, Pecksniffian. A moralizing hypocrite.

It is taken from the character Seth Pecksniff in Charles Dickens' 1844 novel *Martin Chuzzlewit*. Pecksniff is notable for uttering pious moral statements while acting heartlessly.

The term in use, by Leo Rosten, in *The Joys of Yiddish:*

> "In the United States, the social-prestige scale was sensitive and exact: first-generation Jews envied second-generation Jews; and German Jewish families . . . became an elite of remarkable influence and social cohesiveness. The 'pecking order' of this Establishment, its pride, philanthropy, snobbery, and Pecksniffian patronage of Russian and Polish Jews—all this is described by Stephen Birmingham in *Our Crowd: The Great Jewish Families of New York.*"

## Persona Non Grata. (per-SOH-na nohn GRAH-tuh) Latin, literally, it means a "person not welcome"; an unacceptable person.

It is chiefly used in international law or diplomacy. A person who is objectionable to a government to which he is to be sent or has been sent as an ambassador or minister may be rejected as *persona non grata*. Sometimes someone enjoying diplomatic immunity who is caught spying is expelled without any further formalities through the device of declaring him *persona non grata*. In retaliation the country caught red-handed then expels a diplomat in a tit-for-tat game that is accepted as routine.

Sometimes the expression is used at a personal level, too: an individual who has offended another person or committed a gross social error as someone's guest (such as setting fire to the tablecloth, or the cat) could be said to be *persona non grata* with the person so affronted.

The term in use, by George Lardner, Jr. in *The Washington Post*, April 12, 1989, reporting on testimony in the trial of Iran-contra defendant Oliver North:

> "North said the deal [for a ship to be purchased by the CIA] never went through, partly because of the involvement of Thomas C. Clines, a former CIA officer described by other witnesses as 'persona non grata' at the agency."

Another example, from Howard Kurtz, *The Washington Post*, December 6, 1989, in a profile of controversial *Boston Herald* columnist Howie Carr:

> "One would think such attacks would make Carr *persona non grata* among politicians. Two months ago, Carr posed the following question in print to State Treasurer Robert Q. Crane: 'How many politicians, ex-politicians and politicians' relatives—all the genus known as hackus Craneus— how many of these layabouts are infesting your various state payrolls on this day of days, Mr. Crane?' "

**Peter Principle.** A theory advanced by educator and author Laurence J. Peter. To wit: "In a hierarchy every employee tends to rise to his level of incompetence." It was proclaimed in Peter's 1969 book, *The Peter Principle: Why Things Always Go Wrong*.

Do a good job, contended Peter, and you'll be promoted; keep doing well and you'll move up until you're finally assigned to work you can't do, and there you'll stay. The principle explains why so many supervisors are in over their heads. If you don't think so, ask their underlings.

The term in use, by Joe Queenan and Tatiana Pouschine, *Forbes*, July 10, 1989. In an article entitled "The Peter Principle," the authors offer a thesis as well as a play on the name of its subject:

> "In what appears to be a classic example of overreach, Peter Cohen [head of Shearson/American Express] has inflated a highly profitable retail brokerage outfit into a full-service

investment house that does absolutely everything but does not excel in anything."

**Peyton Place.** (PAY-tuhn) A term that's applied to an innocent-appearing small town that turns out to have lots of sin behind the scenes.

It comes from *Peyton Place*, a 1956 bestselling novel by Grace Metalious (1924-1964) about a small New England town (actually Gilmanton Iron Works, New Hampshire). Prepublication stories alleged that the author's husband had lost his job because of the beans she spilled in the novel, and that sent hordes of tourists and reporters to Gilmanton Iron Works. The novel purported to represent the secret life of violence and illicit sex lurking beneath the respectable surface.

In its day, the racy sex scenes shocked and outraged many readers and assured the success of the novel. "A horny book," says Grace Slick, **icon** of rock, who read it as an 18-year-old college student.

The term in use, by a resident of tony Southampton, L.I., quoted in *The New York Times*, November 5, 1989, on the arrest and conviction for prostitution of a local doctor and his wife:

> " 'There's a lot of curiosity, quite frankly, about someone who is a doctor and has another life,' said Trudy Kramer, director of the Parrish Art Museum. 'This is a small town and, like any small town, sort of a Peyton Place.' "

**Pharisees.** (FA-ruh-sees) These may have been the original hypocrites. They are sanctimonious folk who observe the letter, but not the spirit, of the rules.

The Pharisees were a Jewish religious party, first noted in the first century B.C., and known to us chiefly through the writings of the historian Josephus, the collection of Jewish law and tradition known as the Talmud, and the New Testament. The Pharisees were laymen, noted for their exacting interpretation of Jewish law and their strict adherence to it.

In the New Testament, the Pharisees appear as the chief opponents of Jesus, whom they attacked for such violations of religious law as breaking the Sabbath and consorting with sinners.

Jesus rebuked the Pharisees for their self-righteousness and only outward conformance with the letter of the law. This view of the Pharisees led to the contemporary meaning: hypocrites, outwardly pious and conforming to the rules, but lacking compassion.

The term in use, by Robert Runcie, Archbishop of Canterbury, as quoted in *The Economist*, October 7, 1989:

> "The Archbishop of Canterbury, Robert Runcie, caught the headlines twice. He warned that Britain is turning into a nation of self-interested, self-righteous 'Pharisees' ('very much on target,' agreed high-priest [Labour Party leader Neil] Kinnock; Fabian clap-trap, retorted Thatcherites); and he attended mass in St. Peter's, embracing a puzzled pope."

**Philistine.** (FIL-uh-steen) (also frequently seen in lower case: philistine) Someone who is ignorant, ill-mannered and materialistic, or who is hostile or smugly indifferent to culture or aesthetic refinements.

But why is that so? The Philistines in the Old Testament days were a people who lived in Palestine and fought with the Israelites, who naturally took a dim view of them, as reported in the Bible. The Philistines produced the gigantic Goliath, and Samson's seductress Delilah. Archaeologists say they had a significant culture and valued hard work. The Philistines were no philistines.

But the story doesn't stop there. As *Brewer's Dictionary of Phrase and Fable* elaborates, the term came to be used as an epithet in Germany in 1693. It seems there was a dispute between the townspeople and university students at Jena in which a number of people died. The university preacher took for his text "The Philistines be upon thee" from Judges, using it as a play on "philister," a German term for outsiders. Matthew Arnold used the term in *Culture and Anarchy* (1869), criticizing those whose sole interest was the accumulation of wealth.

The term in use, by Tom Wolfe in *The Bonfire of the Vanities*, Farrar, Straus and Giroux, 1987:

" 'Aubrey Buffing,' said Sherman lamely. It was really a question.

" 'The poet,' said Mrs. Rawthrote. 'He's on the short list for the Nobel prize. His father was the Duke of Bray.' Her tone said, 'How on earth could you not know that?'

" 'Of course,' said Sherman, feeling that in addition to his other sins he was also a philistine. "

Another example, from George Will, *The Washington Post*, November 27, 1988, on the retirement of Senator William Proxmire:

"Proxmire knows how to get noticed, as with his monthly Golden Fleece award, ridiculing what he considers foolish government spending. Some of his awards have been Philistine, but populism often is. "

**Philippics.** (fuh-LIP-iks) Generally (and in lower case), bitter diatribes or verbal attacks.

Specifically (and capitalized), the term refers to the speeches (Phillippics) in which the orator Demosthenes tried to rouse the Athenians to resist the advancing power of King Philip of Macedon. (Rhetoric failed; King Philip completed his conquest of Greece in 338 B.C.) The orations of Cicero against Mark Antony are also called "Philippics."

The term in use, by Jonathan Yardley of *The Washington Post*, reviewing *At Home*, a volume of essays by Gore Vidal, November 20, 1988:

"But Vidal has, as he always does, other fish to fry, and fry them he most certainly does. Ronald Reagan, the Israel lobby, fundamentalist right-wingers, Hollywood, Oliver North—on these and other subjects of public interest Vidal writes sardonically, if not as crisply as his previous philippics have led us to expect. "

**Phoenix Rising from the Ashes.** Someone who makes a dramatic recovery from defeat or adversity.

The phoenix, a bird the size of an eagle with scarlet and gold feathers, was a mythological creature in the legends of ancient Egypt, Greece and the early Christian era. Only one lived at a time; its life span was about 500 years. When it was about to die, the bird would build a nest and set it on fire. The phoenix would be consumed by the flames and would rise anew from the ashes.

The bird thus was associated with immortality and seen as an allegory of resurrection and life after death.

The term in use, by *Washington Post* film critic Rita Kempley, September 15, 1989:

> " 'Shirley Valentine,' a tale of a phoenix risen from the frying pan, reaffirms that most hopeful of notions: It's never too late to start over again."

Another example, in a photo caption in a September 21, 1988, *Washington Post* story on a former Redskins kicker called upon to try out for the Phoenix Cardinals, in a double play on the term:

> "Former Redskins kicker Ali Haji-Sheikh is hoping to rise from the ashes in Phoenix."

**Photo Opportunity.** An event that exists so that it can be photographed.

The term describes a phenomenon of White House news management (although it has crept beyond the Executive Mansion). The stage-managed event produces for news broadcasts flattering photographs or videotape showing the president and his visitor or staff or Cabinet officials doing things that will impress the public.

The name comes from the White House press office announcement that photographers will be given an "opportunity" to record a moment at a time and in a manner dictated by the president's PR staff. Whatever happens is done for the cameras. Words are not supposed to be part of the event, but sometimes reporters accompanying the cameramen turn the "photo op" into a 30-second-or-so news conference. And often, to further complete the picture of news manipulation, the president is rehearsed to handle the "unexpected" questions, so both words and photos are as unspontaneous as the hand of man can devise.

The term in use, by Alan K. Lecker in an editorial reprinted in the *Omaha World Herald*, March 16, 1990, on Jesse Jackson's decision not to run for mayor of Washington, D.C.:

> "Which brings us to the Jackson Free Will Doctrine: Jackson doesn't have to do anything he doesn't want to do. If he prefers to speechify, fine. If he prefers to trot around the globe for photo opportunities, fine."

## Pickett's Charge. A dramatic, even romantic, gesture or action that's doomed.

Pickett's charge was the climax of the battle of Gettysburg, fought July 1-3, 1863, during the American Civil War. After two days of unsuccessful assaults on Union positions, Confederate commander Robert E. Lee made a last desperate gamble. On July 3, Major General George Pickett was ordered to lead his 15,000 troops against the center of the Union line. Witnesses said it was an unforgettable sight as the Confederate troops emerged from the cover of woods and marched in battle order across open fields under the deadly fire of Union forces. The attack failed, with terrible losses; Lee, forced to withdraw, never came close again to administering a decisive blow to the Union army.

The term in use, by Patrick Buchanan, a conservative and controversial aide in the Nixon and Reagan administrations, who toyed with the idea of running for president in 1988, as quoted in *The Washington Post*, January 21, 1987:

> "Some of the oldest friends I have in politics have said pointedly that a Buchanan campaign would be the Pickett's charge of the American Right, that its only certain and predictable consequence would be to mortally wound the campaign of Congressman Jack Kemp, whose service to the [conservative] cause has earned him an unimpeded shot at the nomination."

## Pilgrim's Progress. The struggle of a simple person to reach salvation, as told in the prose allegory by English writer and preacher John

Bunyan. Published in the late 1600s, its full title is *The Pilgrim's Progress from This World to That Which Is to Come*.

Bunyan, a Puritan, tells the tale of Christian, who goes on a pilgrimage and eventually reaches the Celestial City after overcoming many dangers, hardships and temptations. Along the way he is helped by such persons as Evangelist, Mr. Good-will, Hopeful and Faithful, and is distracted and tempted by Mr. Legality, Mr. Worldly-Wiseman, Simple, Sloth and Presumption. The book gave many expressions to the language, including Vanity Fair, the **Slough of Despond**, Doubting Castle and House Beautiful.

The term in use, by Gene Degrussen of Pittsburgh State University in Kansas, interviewed on National Public Radio's Weekend Edition, September 4, 1988, he described Upton Sinclair's *The Jungle* as hero Jurgis Rudkus' "Pilgrim's Progress."

Another example, from director Robert M. Young on his film *Triumph of the Spirit*, based on the true story of a Jewish prisoner, a boxing champion who survived the Auschwitz concentration camp by winning boxing matches against Nazi opponents, *The Washington Post*, August 20, 1989:

> " 'There are moral choices involved,' said Young, who described *Triumph* as 'kind of a pilgrim's progress. By that I mean a journey that a man takes where he becomes witness to the human spirit in torment—where people become more than they ever were and people become less than they ever imagined they could be.'"

**Plato's Cave.** (PLAY-toh) An allegory used by Plato (c427-c348 B.C.), the Greek philosopher, to illustrate how perceptions can be false and misleading.

In the allegory, men chained in a cave are held in a way that permits them to see only the back of the cave by the light of a fire burning behind them. They can see only their own shadows and those of other men as they go by. Knowing nothing else, the men in the cave assume the shadows they see are reality.

The term in use by Anthony Lewis in *The New York Times*, November 10, 1988:

"Madison's vision was of an informed electorate 'examining public characters and measures': the voters would be active participants in a public policy debate. Today the voters are passive figures in a process utterly removed from public policy, watching shadows on the wall of Plato's cave."

An oblique reference, by U.S. Senator Bob Kerrey of Nebraska, quoted in *The New York Times*, September 3, 1989, speaking to constituents on the flag-burning controversy:

"When you're all done arguing, what have you got? Have you built a house? Have you helped somebody? Have you fought a battle worth fighting? Or are you banging into shadows on the wall of a cave? It seems to me there's nothing produced from it and you've divided the nation."

**Play in Peoria.** A term which probably originated in vaudeville when acts were tried out on audiences in Peoria before going on to Chicago or St. Louis. It's usually used inside a question posed by a political operative or observer: "Will it play in Peoria?" meaning, "Will ordinary folks buy it?"

The expression gained currency in the Nixon administration, which claimed to be in touch with the heartland, or, in another Nixonian term, "the silent majority," the people who don't picket or protest—as distinct from the media centers on each coast, or the supercilious elites inside the **Beltway**.

The term in use, by Jack Beatty in *The Atlantic Monthly*, February 1989, discussing arms control issues facing the Bush Administration:

"Overshadowing these negotiations are the domestic politics of treaty ratification. These are themselves so complicated and exigent that the administration must always have one eye on them. Indeed, it must frame its proposals to the Soviets with a criterion of dual negotiability in mind: How will this play with the Soviets, and how will it play in the Senate? Peoria it can take for granted."

Another example, from Richard Morin, quoting Robert Lichter of the Center of Media and Public Affairs, in *The Washington Post* "Outlook" section, March 26, 1989:

> " 'Last year, it [a political humor study] kind of started because we found out that Lee Atwater [the Bush campaign manager] watched "The Tonight Show" to see how George Bush was playing in Peoria,' Lichter said."

**Playing Fields of Eton.** That's where the Duke of Wellington is said to have said that the battle of Waterloo was won. The implication is that British officers had acquired the leadership, character and competitiveness which won the victory through their education in the elite system of "public" (meaning private) schools of England, of which Eton is the most famous.

The expression is used today not only to suggest the character-building virtues attributed to sports, but to describe the privileged environment of elite private schools both in Britain and the United States.

It is doubtful that Wellington ever said it. Elizabeth Longford, one of his biographers, says there were no organized games at Eton during his three unhappy years there. She also notes that the quotation did not make its appearance until 3 years after the duke died. A French writer quoted the duke as saying during a visit to the school, "It is here that the battle of Waterloo was won." No mention of playing fields; that was added by later writers. (Eton's headmaster, Robert Birley, made a gallant attempt to recover the situation for the academic side, saying "here" meant the classroom.)

The term in use, by Malcolm Cowley in *The New York Times Magazine*, December 12, 1988:

> "And if you wanted to be a pop singer or a hippie—and who in the 60s didn't?—it hardly mattered whether you were reared on the playing fields of Eton or on the tarmac yard of a Liverpool comprehensive school."

And a play on the expression, by Jonathan Yardley, *The Washington Post*, November 14, 1988, referring to Andover, the prep school attended by George Bush:

"What, if anything, does it mean that for the first time since 1945 the country is to be led by a man whose 'values,' as he insists on calling them, were shaped on the playing fields of Andover and in the sanctuary of the Episcopal Church? . . ."

## Plus Ça Change, Plus C'Est la Même Chose. (ploo sah shahnj, ploo seh lah mehm shohs) French, meaning the more things change, the more they stay the same. Sometimes used in the abbreviated form, "plus ça change," to suggest the thought, as below.

The term in use, by *The Economist*, November 21, 1987:

"The French, trust them, have the phrase for it. If the latest trade figures and a Soviet official's visit to Tokyo this week are any guide to Japan's relations with Russia, *plus ça change* sums it up. If there were nervous people in America and Europe who had feared that a geopolitical change was in the making, they can relax again."

A play on the term, by television critic Tom Shales in *The Washington Post*, January 6, 1989:

"And as if to prove it really was all for nothing and that we've come full circle and back again, 1989 began with Jim and Tammy Faye Bakker back on the air. And Joan Rivers was busily readying another daily talk program. *Plus ça change, plus c'est la même shows.*"

## Pogrom. (poh-GRAHM) An organized, officially tolerated massacre or gang violence directed at a specific group, usually Jews, and usually taking place in Christian Europe, particularly in Russia. The word is Russian, meaning "desolation." According to *The Oxford English Dictionary*, the root word, "grom," means thunder or thunderbolt; thus, to strike down as if by a thunderbolt, to destroy without pity.

The term in use, by Robert Leckie in *Delivered from Evil: The*

*Saga of World War II,* in which he writes of the days in Germany that served as a precursor to the Holocaust:

> "Gradually the pogrom against the German Jews escalated, culminating on November 9, 1938, in **Kristallnacht,** or Night of Broken Glass, so called because of the shattering of thousands of Jewish shops across the country."

**Poison Pill.** A stratagem employed by corporations to ward off hostile takeover attempts.

If you swallow a poison pill, you will also poison whoever swallows you. That's the theory behind such corporate ploys as requiring that shareholders receive special shares at one price which a successful corporate raider must instantly buy back at twice the price. These and other tricks are constantly being tested in the marketplace and the courts; the goal is to make a company unpalatable, too difficult or expensive to gobble up. The company fighting the takeover may void the pill if it gets a better offer.

The term has expanded beyond the business world to describe similar tactics in other arenas.

The term in use, by *The Economist,* March 11, 1989:

> "The budget deficit looms over and paralyses most conceivable policy initiatives. Some cynical Democrats think this is why it was created: Ronald Reagan's poison pill that for years to come guarantees a welcome inertia in Washington."

And from Jay Mathews, writing in *The Washington Monthly,* July/August 1989, on repression of pro-democracy demonstrations in China:

> "I thought the Tiananmen Square encampment was too large, too public, too much of a thumb in the leadership's eye. What I said out loud was that I was amazed at how far things had gone. Then again, I thought: Why should I worry? If Deng Xiaoping seemed ready to tolerate Hong Kong, a capitalist poison pill of unequalled potency, why not this?"

**Polonius.** A character from William Shakespeare's tragedy *Hamlet*. Polonius is a garrulous old courtier, famous for his pompous maxims. He is lord chamberlain to the king of Denmark and agrees to spy on Hamlet, who kills him by running his sword through the arras (tapestry) behind which the old man is hiding.

Pomposity aside, one of the most famous speeches in Shakespeare is the advice Polonius gives to his son:

> This above all: to thine own self be true,
> And it must follow, as the night the day,
> Thou canst not then be false to any man.

The term in use, by Alan Abelson in *Barron's*, January 16, 1989:

> "Early reports show a certain tentativeness in Corporate America in following the Borden lead. We suspect that they have heeded Polonius's sage advice and they know themselves all too well. More specifically, they realize that should management adopt the 'Don't shoot me or I'll jump' approach on any significant scale, it would touch off the greatest purge of hostile takeovers in history."

**Pooh-Bah.** A big cheese; somebody important, or who pompously thinks he is, or who holds many jobs at the same time.

In Gilbert and Sullivan's "The Mikado" (1885), Pooh-Bah was the Lord High Everything Else, a self-important bureaucrat.

The term in use, by Paul Gray in *Time*, September 26, 1988:

> "Many sports fans believe the Pooh-Bahs of professional athletics—the commissioners, presidents, team owners, the whole briefcase brigade—should play a role similar to background music at the movies. They are doing their jobs most successfully when no one notices them at all."

Another example, from Alan Abelson in *Barron's*, June 5, 1989, commenting on disclosures of questionable investments by employees of the Securities and Exchange Commission:

> "The new SECers scorn such fainthearted commitment in favor of racy ventures befitting a member of the Specula-

tors' Exclusive Club. Thus one bold pooh-bah, the Journal disclosed, is the proud (and increasingly affluent) owner of a number called Blockbuster Entertainment."

## Portmanteau Word. (port-MAN-toh) A term invented by Lewis Carroll to describe a word made up from the parts of others. It comes from portmanteau, a suitcase that opens into two compartments. Smog—a combination of smoke and fog—is a portmanteau word; another is brunch.

In *Through the Looking Glass*, Alice has a conversation with Humpty Dumpty and asks him the meaning of the poem "Jabberwocky," which is filled with strange words like "slithy." Humpty explains that slithy is a combination of slime and lithe: "You see, it's like a portmanteau—there are two meanings packed up into one word."

The term in use, by Mike Wyma, *The Los Angeles Times*, February 20, 1987:

> "Both varieties work the same way as a mobile phone. The unit's transceiver (portmanteau word for transmitter and receiver) communicates via FM radio waves with a system of cell sites established by a 'carrier.' . . ."

## Potemkin Village. (puh-TEM-kuhn) A village with false facades, named after just such a place created by Prince Grigori Aleksandrovich Potemkin, chief minister (and lover) of Catherine the Great, who ruled Russia from 1762 to 1774.

Catherine invited Emperor Joseph II of Austria to join her in 1774 on a tour of Russia's newly acquired Black Sea provinces. Potemkin arranged for the construction of artificial, one-street, one-dimensional villages along the route, complete with cheering crowds of happy peasants. He thus qualifies as one of the most creative political advance men in history.

The term has come to stand for a phony, bogus image, a false front used to fool people into thinking a fake proposition or situation is real.

Columnist Richard Cohen, *The Washington Post*, March 27, 1987, writing about the sex-blackmail scandal involving television evangelist Jim Bakker in 1987, referred to "Potemkin village theme parks in which a contrived past is recreated in the synthetic present."

On September 24, 1987, President Reagan suggested that the Nicaraguan government's steps toward democratization might turn out to be "mere show" and "Potemkin reforms."

**Pour Encourager les Autres.** (poor en-COO-rahj-ay layz oht-ruh) Literally, in French, "to encourage the others" but it is used in a pointed, ironic sense to refer to going to extremes to make an example of someone. The expression comes from a reference in Voltaire's *Candide* to the execution of Admiral Byng in 1757: "In this country [England], it is well from time to time to kill an admiral to encourage the others."

Byng's downfall came about in this way: During the Seven Years' War (1750-1757) between Britain and France, Byng was sent with a naval force to raise a French siege of the island of Minorca. His force was inadequate, so he made only a half-hearted attempt before withdrawing to leave the island to the French. In the ensuing uproar at home, the prime minister, the Duke of Newcastle, promised that the errant admiral would be "tried immediately and hanged directly." Byng was tried and found guilty of neglect of duty, but he was spared a hanging: they executed him by firing squad instead.

The term in use, in *The Economist*, March 31, 1984:

> "Should Miss Sarah Tisdall, leaker of one **Whitehall** document that plainly did not concern national security and another that conceivably did, have been given six months in prison pour encourager les autres? That, Mr. Justice Cantly last Friday made clear, was the reason for the jail sentence; and both the reason and the sentence have aroused much uproar and some nonsense ever since."

Another example, by Duncan Spencer in *The Washington Post Book World*, August 6, 1989, reviewing *The Court-Martial Of Clayton Lonetree*, by Lake Headley with William Hoffman:

> "The trial of Lonetree [arising out of security breaches at the U.S. embassy in Moscow] was a way for the services to close the matter of lax security at the . . . Embassy without

embarrassing the higher-ups. It was a way of warning the troops, just as the French were wont to do in World War I and before, by executing a man simply 'pour encourager les autres.' It was an expedient, and a nasty and brutal one."

**Praetorian Guard,** or **Praetorians.** The household guard of Roman emperors, from Augustus to Constantine, who acquired great political power and sometimes were able to make (and unmake) emperors. Nowadays, they're powerful hangers-on.

One example of an emperor who was manipulated into office by his guards was Claudius, who ruled from the year 41 to 54. Following the assassination of Caligula, the Praetorian Guards, knowing that without an emperor they'd be out of work, squelched a fledgling effort in the Roman Senate to restore the republic. The Praetorians discovered Claudius, a neglected grandson of Augustus who was regarded as a mental defective, and declared him to be the emperor. (Claudius surprised everyone by doing a decent job.)

The power of the guards finally was broken in A.D. 312 when they were dispersed among Rome's armies.

The term is applied figuratively to functionaries who surround and serve, and sometimes manipulate, powerful officeholders; also, **apparatchiks** whose interest is in defending the established order, especially a corrupt military system.

The term in use, by William R. Doerner in *Time,* January 8, 1990:

> "According to Ion Pacepa, a Rumanian lieutenant general who defected to the U.S. in 1978, the Securiatate under Ceausescu had various functions. One was to serve as a kind of Praetorian Guard for members of the Communist Party's Central Committee and specifically the Ceausescu family."

**Preux Chevalier.** (pruh shev-AH-lee-ay) Peerless knight; a knight in shining armor. It's French.

The term in use, by William Manchester in his review of Rhodes James' *Anthony Eden, The Washington Post Book World,* July 12, 1987:

"Anthony Eden *looked* like a prime minister, as Ronald Reagan looks like a president—slim, elegant, with a clipped mustache and gift for rallying followers. As Neville Chamberlain's foreign secretary, he was the 'preux chevalier' of the House of Commons—'the one fresh figure of the first magnitude,' wrote Winston Churchill, 'arising out of a generation which was ravaged by the war.' "

**Pro Bono.** The work lawyers do free for indigent or non-profit clients.

It is the shorthand form of a Latin expression, "pro bono publico," "for the good of the public." In recent years the term has gone beyond legal matters, and is sometimes employed to characterize services (usually professional) that are provided free of charge to individuals or groups for altruistic reasons.

The term in use, by Martha Sherrill in *The Washington Post*, May 1, 1989, describing the White House Correspondents' Association dinner:

"Bush was scheduled to yuck it up at the microphone for 10 minutes or so, but he pulled a stunt of his own—surprising everyone, his staff included. After seven minutes of joking, Bush yanked TV comedian Garry Shandling from behind a curtain and had him work the crowd pro bono."

**Procrustean.** (proh-KRUS-tee-uhn) A rigid or absolute standard of ideas or behavior.

It comes from the robber Procrustes who, according to ancient Greek legend, would take prisoners and place them on an iron bed. If they didn't fit, he would either stretch them or amputate until they did. Thus a procrustean standard produces conformity by arbitrary means.

The term in use in *The Washington Post*, February 25, 1988, by columnist Mary McGrory, commenting on American politicians' generally indecisive statements about Israel's use of violence to suppress bloodshed on the West Bank:

"We self-righteously apply to Managua procrustean standards of proper 'democratic' behavior. But when Israel does the indefensible, we turn away."

Another example, from Wendy Doniger O'Flaherty's review of Paul Johnson's *Intellectuals*, in *The New York Times Book Review*, March 12, 1989:

"Paul Johnson's definition [of an intellectual] is equally idiosyncratic: an intellectual is someone who wants to re-fashion the world, politically, in accordance with principles of his own devising. Moreover, a 'disregard for truth and [a] preference for ideas over people . . . marks the true secular intellectual.' Of the people whom Mr. Johnson forces to lie on this Procrustean bed, a dozen are given a chapter apiece: Rousseau, Shelley, Marx, Ibsen, Tolstoy, Heming-way, Brecht, Bertrand Russell, Sartre, Edmund Wilson, Victor Gollancz and Lillian Hellman."

**Promethean.** (pruh-MEE-thee-uhn) An adjective alluding to the Greek mythological deity Prometheus—his bold creativity and ge-nius, his defiance of authority and the dreadful punishment he suffered for that defiance.

As the story goes, Prometheus modeled man from clay and then taught him agriculture and how to tame horses. He also stole fire from the gods and gave it to man. In retaliation, Zeus chained him to a rock, where an eagle tore out his liver by day; by night, it was restored so the torture could begin again.

The Greek dramatist Aeschylus (525-456 B.C.) treated Pro-metheus as a hero. So did the Romantics, who liked his anti-establishment rebelliousness. Prometheus is variously portrayed as a rebel against tyrannical power, a Christ-like figure who sacrificed himself for man and a symbol of man's creativity and independence.

Prometheus invoked, by Tom Wolfe, "Starting from Zero," *The American Spectator*, December 1987:

"But above all they will look back upon the 20th as the century in which their forebears had the amazing confi-dence, the Promethean **hubris**, to defy the gods and try to push man's power and freedom to limitless, godlike extremes."

In use again by Janet Malcolm, writing about journalists' ethics in *The New Yorker*, March 13, 1989:

"For what the incident is about, what lies below its light surface, is the dire theme of Promethean theft, of transgression in the service of creativity, of stealing as the foundation of making."

And again by computer hackers, described by Roger Lowenstein and G. Pascal Zachary in *The Wall Street Journal*, June 9, 1989:

"A group of high-tech Robin Hoods—possibly including employees of Apple Computer Inc.—apparently is trying to disseminate the super-secret source code of Apple's Macintosh computer.

"Various people have gotten copies of a floppy disk with the closely guarded Macintosh code, along with a letter signed by 'the New Prometheus League (Software Artists for Information Dissemination).' "

**Protean.** An adjective describing someone who can readily effect change within himself, or who is inconstant, equivocal. It comes from the name of Proteus, a figure in Greek mythology. He was the herdsman of Poseidon, the god of the sea. Proteus' fame arose, however, from his ability to change himself into different forms at will.

The term in use, by David Hoffman, *The Washington Post*, August 13, 1989:

"Bush is a protean figure. . . . He adapts readily to the shifting demands of politics and public opinion; he transformed himself from last year to this and will evolve again."

**Proust, Proustian.** (PROOST, PROOST-ee-uhn) He's the 20th century French novelist, Marcel Proust (1871-1922), one of the great, if hardly read, literary figures of modern times. His name became an adjective to describe the complexity of his style as well as elements of his life's work, *Remembrance of Things Past,* a novel in seven volumes.

The difficulty of reading Proust is legendary. The 3,000-page novel is filled with long, complicated sentences, digressions, metaphors, imagery and analyses packed into dense paragraphs. He frequently employed a stream-of-consciousness technique.

The narrator of the story is also called Marcel. The taste of tea and a madeleine cake (a feather-light French tea cake in an elongated petal shape, perhaps the most important cookie in world literature) stimulates a recollection of his childhood and memories of holidays spent by the sea in the village of Combray. After recounting the complex events of his life and that of his friends, Marcel comes to the realization that he must record the beauty he has experienced and sets out to write the novel the reader has just completed.

A theme of the work is the link between external and internal reality found in time and memory. In the Proustian world, the individual is isolated, society is false and ruled by snobbery while artistic endeavor is raised to a religion.

Proust, afflicted with asthma and nervous ailments, mingled as a youth in Parisian society but later became increasingly withdrawn. After 1907, he lived mainly in a cork-lined room, to prevent attacks of illness and to avoid distraction, and worked at night on his monumental novel.

The term in use, by David Denby in *The New Republic,* May 22, 1989, reviewing John Updike's autobiography *Self-Consciousness:*

> "The reminiscing sidewalk tour which turns, by degrees, into an interior journey, marvelously combines a Proustian caressing of the frayed crib-coverlets of childhood with flinty O'Hara-like Pennsylvania class distinctions."

And Proust invoked, by Amy Hempel in *The New York Times Magazine,* November 27, 1988, in a profile of cartoonist Lynda Barry:

> "Over the years, reviewers have likened her to Mark Twain, James Thurber, Knute Rockne ('the baby boomers' Proust')."

And parodied by John Thorne, reviewing a collection of Italian cookbooks in *The Washington Post Book World*, March 12, 1989, under the headline:

"Remembrance of Things Pasta."

**Ptolemaic Universe.** (TOL-uh-MAY-ik) A theory that the Earth remains stationary at the center of the universe while the sun, planets and stars revolve around it. The theory was devised by the astronomer-mathematician-geographer Ptolemy (Claudius Ptolemaeus, c. A.D. 85-165) and his idea was accepted until the 16th century when Polish astronomer Nicholas Copernicus laid the foundation for modern astronomy. Copernicus' concept, that the Earth and the other planets rotate around the sun, was resisted by church leaders since it removed man from the center of creation.

The term in use, by Lance Morrow in *Time*, October 24, 1988, on the presidential campaign of 1960:

> "One man who helped transform that election campaign into instantaneous myth was Theodore H. White. . . . The premise that gives his narrative its dramatic drive is a broad foundation of certitude about the rightness and preeminence of American power and, therefore, the absolute centrality of the presidential race in the drama of the world. It was then a Ptolemaic universe, revolving around the White House. What higher story to tell? Americans did not then lose wars. Presidents did not get assassinated, or lie, or have to barricade themselves in the White House."

**Pumpkin Papers.** Microfilmed documents hidden in a pumpkin patch in an incident that caught the attention of Americans during the Red-hunting days of the Cold War—and opened a door to bigger things for one Richard M. Nixon, novice congressman.

Whittaker Chambers, former communist and an editor of *Time*, alleged in August 1948 before the House Un-American Activities Committee that he had known State Department official Alger Hiss in the 1930s as a fellow communist. Hiss denied it; the case turned on whether Hiss perjured himself in denying even knowing Chambers.

279

Young Congressman Nixon (whose internal frettings about how active a role he should play in the case became one of the crises in his autobiography, *Six Crises*) decided to pursue the case and subpoenaed papers that Chambers told him would be a "bombshell." Chambers led HUAC investigators into the pumpkin patch of his farm in Westminster, Maryland, and pulled out some microfilm. When examined, it showed classified documents, which Chambers alleged he got from Hiss.

Bombshell it was. Hiss was indicted for perjury. His first trial ended in a hung jury; he was found guilty in a second trial in January 1950 and served a prison term. He has spent the years since seeking to restore his reputation. Nixon went on to other things.

The term in use, by Victor S. Navasky, in a review of David Halberstam's **The Best and the Brightest,** *The New York Times Book Review,* November 12, 1972:

> "It [U.S. involvement in the Vietnam war] happened, Halberstam concludes, because 'they had, for all their brilliance and **hubris** and sense of themselves, been unwilling to look and learn from the past. They ignored Hanoi history and misunderstood **Munich** history. And they had been swept forward by their belief in the importance of anti-Communism (and the dangers of not paying sufficient homage to it.)' The Age of the Pentagon Papers is, in reality, the Age of the Pumpkin Papers."

**Putsch.** (pooch) In German, a revolutionary attempt; William Safire defines it as a failed insurrection.

One of history's most famous occurred on November 8, 1923, when Adolph Hitler and 60 of his storm troopers tried to overthrow the government of the state of Bavaria and install Hitler at the top— the so-called Beer Hall Putsch. Learning that the state's ruling triumvirate in Munich had called a meeting of 3,000 officials at a hall known as the Burgerbraukeller, Hitler and his thugs stormed the gathering.

The attempt failed. Hitler was imprisoned and used the time to write *Mein Kampf (My Struggle)*. Although sentenced to five years, he was released in less than one and was able to resume his career with his reputation enhanced.

The term today is applied to rebellious activities more generally, such as attempts to take over organizations, clubs, companies and the like as well as governments. Wordsmith William Safire calls the term an "attack word" because of its association with Nazism, giving a negative character to the insurgencies it is used to describe.

The term in use, by James M. Markham in *The New York Times*, March 19, 1989, describing a walking tour of Paris landmarks of the French Revolution:

> "At No. 286 (Rue St.-Honore) is the church of St.-Roch, where on October 5, 1795, Napoleon massacred more than 200 royalists who had hoped to stage a putsch against the Convention installed in the nearby Tuileries; it was a turning point in his fast-rising career."

**Pygmalion.** (pig-MAY-li-uhn) A figure from Greek mythology. Today it is used figuratively to refer to someone who remakes another individual by teaching skills or accomplishments, and falls in love with his or her protege.

Pygmalion was a sculptor who spurned the love of all women and instead created a statue of the ideal woman. The goddess Aphrodite was offended, and punished him by causing him to fall in love with his own cold and lifeless creation. Pygmalion prayed for the statue to be brought to life; the goddess relented and transformed the sculpture into a living woman, Galatea, who could return the sculptor's love. A frequent mistake applies the name "Pygmalion" to Galatea, the pupil or protege, rather than the teacher/creator.

The story has been retold in various forms, the most famous being George Bernard Shaw's 1912 play, *Pygmalion*, which was in turn the basis for the 1956 musical *My Fair Lady*, by Alan Jay Lerner and Frederick Loewe, in which Cockney flower girl Eliza Doolittle is taught to speak English properly by the irascible Professor Henry Higgins. Shaw shaped the story to make his own comment on society, of course—Higgins transforms the guttersnipe into a lady, but she cannot return to her old life and he does not marry her.

The *Facts on File Dictionary of Classical, Biblical & Literary Allusions* says the legend is also a cautionary tale against the consuming pursuit of an ideal that can leave the seeker caring only for a cold and lifeless work of art.

The term in use, by *People* magazine, May 22, 1989, reviewing the movie *Scandal,* a recounting of the Profumo affair, a British politics-and-sex scandal:

> "To his credit, [director] Caton-Jones has created a fascinating reconstruction of a sensibility as well as a scandal. In 1958, [Christine] Keeler met society osteopath and alleged pimp Dr. Stephen Ward. Through Ward, with whom she lived out a perverse *Pygmalion,* she mingled in high society, and her brief encounter with Profumo crescendoed into a tabloid intrigue."

**Pyrrhic Victory.** (PIHR-ik) A hollow victory, one won at too great a cost.

Pyrrhus, king of Epirus, defeated the Romans in battle in 279 B.C. but with such heavy losses that he said, "One more such victory and we are lost." Prophetically, too. Says *The Concise Columbia Encyclopedia:* "His [Pyrrhus'] sole accomplishment was the ruin of Epirus." The expression is now applied to quarrels or contests in which the damage inflicted on the winner is greater than the fruits of victory.

The term in use, by Michael Ledeen, *The American Spectator,* February 1988:

> "The two best assessments of the summit that I found were a charming op-ed piece by David Aaron in *The New York Times* . . . and an upbeat article by Zbigniew Brzezinski in *The Wall Street Journal* which proclaimed Reagan the winner 3 to 1. He's right, but the victory may be pyrrhic; any President who believes that a new era is at hand, and that Gorbachev doesn't believe in the eventual triumph of Communism might make some serious mistakes down the road a bit."

Another example—Janusz Bagajski comments on Solidarity's rise to power in Poland, *The New Republic,* September 11, 1989:

"According to a contrary assessment, the Party has in fact outsmarted Solidarity in a maneuver even Lenin would have been proud of. Solidarity's capture of the Cabinet will turn out to be a Pyrrhic victory. . . . Solidarity has been caught in a carefully prepared trap."

# Q

**Quantum Leap** or **Quantum Jump.** Commonly used to describe a dramatic change that's great in scale. Although borrowed from physics, this is not the scientific definition of quantum jump (there is no quantum leap in physics). Quantum comes from the Latin, meaning "how much."

In quantum mechanics the smallest change that can occur in the energy of an atom is a jump to the nearest neighboring allowed energy value. The important thing to remember is that in going from one value to another the atom cannot take on intermediate values. This is the quantum jump. The jump is always abrupt but it is not necessarily large.

Popularly, the expression is used in a wide variety of contexts and almost invariably to suggest a mammoth change, as illustrated by the gossip columnist "Suzy" in the *New York Post*, May 8, 1989:

> "Wozencraft, who at one time thought of becoming a nun, took instead a quantum leap and became an undercover narcotics agent in Texas."

**Queeg, Captain.** He is a character in Herman Wouk's *The Caine Mutiny*, a 1951 novel about the American navy in World War II. Queeg commands the destroyer minesweeper *Caine*, whose officers rebel against him. Queeg is a solitary, querulous, suspicious man who compulsively pursues small issues, such as the theft of strawberries from the officers' mess, but who is unable to effectively lead or to gain the trust of his men. He blames his failures on the incompetence and conspiracies of others.

Thus, "a Queeg" is someone in authority who is a martinet about petty rules, small-minded, arbitrary and defensive, even paranoid.

The term in use, in a May 8, 1988, column by *Washington Post* ombudsman Richard Harwood, discussing the paper's story about congressional aide Tom Pappas, who committed suicide the day the story ran:

> "As the office manager for Rep. Roy Dyson, an Eastern Shore [of Maryland] Democrat, Pappas behaved as a petty tyrant, a sort of Captain Queeg, placing unreasonable and sometimes irrational demands on his staff."

And by Tom Shales, *The Washington Post*, January 12, 1988, in a profile of anchorman Dan Rather:

> "It was bandied about in New York media circles that Rather was taking medication for clinical depression, and was holed up in his office like some sort of Captain Queeg waiting for the Caine to founder."

**Queen of Hearts.** A character from Lewis Carroll's *Alice's Adventures in Wonderland* (1865). She is best known for her screams of "Off with his (her) head!" at anyone who crosses her. During the trial of the Knave of Hearts (for stealing tarts), she says: "Sentence first—verdict afterwards." [See **Red Queen.**] Given her impatience with due process, the Queen of Hearts is often invoked by those complaining of unfair treatment at the hands of authority.

The term in use, by Paul Perito and Robert Plotkin, writing in *The New York Times*, October 15, 1989, decrying the treatment of their client by a congressional subcommittee:

> "The subcommittee has, while piously declaring its respect for the Fifth Amendment, linked Mr. Pierce to the infamous **Teapot Dome** scandal and dared him to return Oct. 27 to play the same game by the same rules. As the Queen of Hearts in *Alice in Wonderland* bellowed at her topsy-turvy courtroom: 'Sentence first; verdict afterwards!' "

**Quisling.** (KWIZ-ling) A collaborator with the enemy, a traitor.

It comes from Vidkun Quisling, a Norwegian fascist leader whose name had the dishonor of becoming a synonym for traitor. Quisling, founder of the fascist Nasjonal Samling (National Unity) Party, served as the advance agent for Hitler's invasion of his country in 1940 and was installed by the Nazis as the puppet premier until the German defeat in 1945. After the war he was tried for high treason and shot.

The term in use, in *The Economist*, October 16, 1974:

> "But for years the government has used them [moderate leaders of South African blacks] only to put on a front of 'consultation,' while paying scant regard to their views. It is this which has left them feeling like quislings whose only purpose is to give the system a look of respectability."

**Quixote, Quixotic.** (key-HO-teh) The central figure (and title) of a famous 17th century novel by Miguel de Cervantes whose character is so distinct that his name has become an adjective: quixotic (kwik-SAHT-ik). It is applied to someone who is idealistic but unrealistic.

That Don Quixote is. His real name is Alonso Quijano, a kindly country gentleman who becomes so crazed by reading chivalric romances that he believes he must redress the wrongs of the whole world. He takes the name of Don Quixote de la Mancha, and is knighted by an innkeeper. After a series of misadventures (see **Tilting at Windmills**), he wearily returns to his home and gives up chivalric novels.

The term in use, by Jay Matthews in *The Washington Post*, November 19, 1988:

> "Over the years, however, [Ralph] Nader has developed a Don Quixote reputation for dogged pursuit of wrong-headed causes, the staff member said."

In adjective form, by Barbara Toman, *The Wall Street Journal*, December 5, 1989, on a challenge to Britain's prime minister Margaret Thatcher from within her own party:

> "While Sir Anthony [Meyer] almost certainly won't win his quixotic battle, it's possible that Tory MPs could vote for him—or, more likely, abstain—in sufficient numbers to embarrass Mrs. Thatcher."

# R

**Rabbi.** (RAB-igh) A Jewish clergyman or woman and, in American vernacular, a protector or mentor.

In Hebrew, it means "my teacher." Rabbis, ordained teachers of Jewish law, fulfill many of the same functions as other clergy: performing the ceremonies that attend birth, confirmation, marriage and death; and serving as counselors. But the origins of the role are different from those of Protestant or Catholic clergy. Rabbis were primarily scholars. Leo Rosten, author of *The Joys of Yiddish*, says traditionally rabbis had no hierarchical status or power other than the authority which rested on character and learning.

In politics and elsewhere, "rabbi" has taken on the meaning of someone in a position of power who takes a less senior person under his wing and helps advance his interest. This rabbi is a patron and sponsor, and the employee with a rabbi upstairs will enjoy a big advantage over his colleagues.

The term in use, by Andrew J. Glass in his review of *Guts and Glory: The Rise and Fall of Oliver North* by Ben Bradlee Jr. in *The New York Times*, July 3, 1988:

> "Over the years, Mr. North invariably has had such a rabbi at hand. At Annapolis, it was Emerson Smith, the Naval Academy's famous boxing coach. . . . For most of his years at the White House, Mr. North's rabbi was Robert (Bud) McFarlane. . . ."

And from David Stockman's book *The Triumph of Politics*, on his tenure as Director of the Office of Management and Budget in the Reagan administration:

> "All my mentors and rabbis had been intellectual power-houses: Morrison, Moynihan, Anderson, Kemp. Even Gampa Bartz. They had all burned with ideas, curiosity.
> "Now my greatest rabbi of all, the President-elect of the United States, seemed so serene and passive."

**Radical Chic.** (sheek) The taking up of radical causes by the fashionable and/or wealthy as the latest proof of trendiness. Chic is a French word that has entered the English language and means stylish elegance.

"Radical chic" was coined by writer-journalist Tom Wolfe in a famous 1970 essay about fundraising events for the revolutionary Black Panthers. Specifically Wolfe used his acid pen to describe a party held in the Manhattan home of composer-conductor Leonard Bernstein:

> "The very idea of them, these real revolutionaries, who actually put their lives on the line, runs through Lenny's duplex like a rogue hormone. Everyone casts a glance, or stares, or tries a smile, and then sizes up the house for the somehow delicious counterpoint . . . Deny it if you want to! but one does end up making such sweet furtive comparisons in this season of Radical Chic. . . ."

Wolfe's term is now a sneering reference to leftish political fads taken up by the trendy wealthy for whom fashion is conviction.

The term in use, by Alan Fotheringham writing of Canadian politics in *MacLean's*, June 23, 1980:

> "The Liberals (unlike those stubborn Tories and idealistic Socialists) always go outside for their leaders. Rented MacKenzie King from the Rockefeller family. Rented St. Laurent from corporate law. Recruited Lester Pearson from diplomatic world. Scouts plucked Pierre Trudeau from radical-chic ranks of academe."

And a play on the expression, by Peter P. Swire, in *The New Republic*, January 30, 1989, on the rush by the fashionable to take up the cause of preserving the world's rain forests:

> "Tropical chic is particularly evident in Washington, D.C. The Smithsonian is featuring a major exhibition on rain forests, the National Zoo is raising money to start its own tropical forest, and environmental groups are staffing up on lobbyists and grass-roots activists in the area."

**Raison d'Être** (ray-ZON DET-ruh) Reason for being, in French. A justification, or purpose.

The term in use by Paul Kennedy in *The Rise and Fall of the Great Powers*, describing the Marshall Plan:

"... it took no genius to see that the raison d'être for the plan was to convince Europeans everywhere that private enterprise was better able to bring them prosperity than Communism."

Another example, from Palestine Liberation Organization adviser Bassam Abu-Sharif, writing in *The New York Times*, November 8, 1989:

"As Prime Minister Yitzhak Shamir and several colleagues have said in unguarded moments, Israel will not talk to the P.L.O. because the organization's raison d'être is the achievement of the Palestinian people's right to self-determination."

**Rara Avis.** (RAH-ruh AY-vihs) Latin: rare bird; something unusual or rarely encountered. Popular with crossword puzzle creators.

The term in use, in *The Los Angeles Times*, March 26, 1989:

"Dr. Rosenthal was personally a charmer; he was also that rara avis, a scientist who was essentially a humanist, which often created problems in academia."

**Rashomon.** A 1951 Japanese film that teaches that absolute truth in human experience is impossible to attain, that the truth lies in the perceptions of each individual.

The film was directed by the distinguished Japanese director Akira Kurosawa and based on a short story by Akutagawa Ryunosuke. The story takes place in 10th-century Japan and recounts the varying recollections of a crime—a murder and rape—by the characters: a samurai, his wife, a woodcutter and a bandit. Each has a distinctly different version.

The term in use, by David A. Koplan in *The New York Times*, July

16, 1989, reviewing a television program on the murder of a Chinese-American in Detroit in 1982:

> "Two New York film makers, Christine Choy and Renee Tajima, subsequently made a *Rashomon*-style documentary that explores the legal and social ambiguities of the case. 'Who Killed Vincent Chin?,' which will have its television premiere this week on the Public Broadcasting Service [sic], allows the real-life characters—the killers, the witnesses, the lawyers, the Asian-American activists and relatives of Vincent Chin—to tell their stories in a way that proves reality is not a fixed point."

**Realpolitik.** (ray-AHL-poh-lee-TEEK) Politics based on shrewd and unsentimental calculations of national advantage and interest.

The word—German—came into use in the years after the failed revolutions of Europe in 1848. It was coined by Ludwig von Rochau in 1853, in criticizing the lack of realism on the part of German liberals during this period.

The term was subsequently popularized in application to the policies of Otto von Bismarck as he worked toward German unification. Bismarck's actions were based on "a scrupulous attention to what is possible, a shrewd estimation of what one's opponent really wants, rather than what he says he wants, and a preparedness to assert force when necessary," says Roger Scruton in A *Dictionary of Political Thought*. In pursuit of this goal Bismarck made and broke political alliances, made war or insisted on peace as these suited his needs. As he said: "Not by speeches and majority votes are the great questions of the day decided—that was the great error of 1848 and 1849—but by blood and iron."

The term in use, by R.W. Apple, Jr., writing in *The New York Times*, May 24, 1989, on President Bush's response to the suppression of the pro-democracy movement in China:

> "Ever since Richard M. Nixon's opening to China, Washington has asked less of the leaders in Beijing on human rights than it has asked of others. That point was noted forcefully this week by Chinese students attending Ameri-

can universities in asking for more palpable signals of support for their brethren at home.

"Perhaps they are wrong. Perhaps Realpolitik dictates that the Chinese regime be treated with kid gloves, lest the advances of two decades be lost."

Another example, from a *Wall Street Journal* editorial, December 12, 1989:

"We agree that the Nixon-Kissinger opening to China was a triumph of *Realpolitik.*"


**Red Queen.** She's a chess set piece come to life in Lewis Carroll's *Through the Looking-Glass,* and she follows few of the rules of logic. In the book, Alice and the Red Queen rush off together running as fast as they can. After running for a spell, they find themselves at exactly the place where they were before. "Well, in our country," says Alice, "you'd generally get to somewhere else—if you ran very fast for a long time as we've been doing."

"A slow sort of country!" responds the Queen. "Now, here, you see, it takes all the running you can do, to keep in the same place. If you want to get somewhere else, you must run at least twice as fast as that."

The term in use in a *Washington Post* article, February 18, 1987, about the closing of Quill & Brush, a bookstore specializing in literary first editions. The store had a devoted clientele, but:

"When it came to money, Quill & Brush was running a Red Queen's race. In its decade of operation, it consistently did better each year, but not well enough to outpace the soaring rents."

The Red Queen should not be confused with the irritable **Queen of Hearts** of *Alice's Adventures in Wonderland,* but even the mighty can get their Lewis Carroll queens mixed up. The bitterly disputed nomination of Robert Bork to the Supreme Court provided a field day of such errors.

On August 12, 1987, *New York Times* columnist and word maven William Safire accused Senator Joseph Biden of "exhibiting the open-mindedness of Lewis Carroll's Red Queen" in announcing his opposition to Bork before confirmation hearings took place.

Anti-Bork pundit Michael Kinsley repeated the error in his retort in *The New Republic*, August 24, 1987:

> "So now conservatives are comparing Biden to the Red Queen of *Alice in Wonderland* and demanding that, having prejudged the issue, he should stand aside during the Senate confirmation process." (Kinsley noted no similar criticism of those Senators who had prejudged in Bork's favor.)

Both gentlemen have graciously conceded the error.

**Reductio ad Absurdum.** (ri-DUK-tee-oh ad uhb-SUR-duhm) Literally, in Latin, reduction to absurdity. It is a method of disproving a principle by showing that it leads to an absurd result when followed through to its logical conclusion.

The term in use, by Charles Krauthammer, *The Washington Post*, May 12, 1989, mocking the romanticization of baseball in current books and movies:

> " . . . 'Field of Dreams' . . . marks the limits of baseball cliche. The movie is visually arresting, evocative and ingratiating. It is also the *reductio ad absurdum* of baseball worship."

**Redux.** (REE-duhks) Latin; meaning brought back, returned.

The word was popularized in contemporary times by John Updike in the title of his 1971 novel, *Rabbit Redux*, a sequel to *Rabbit Run*, the saga of Harry Angstrom ("Rabbit"). In the 19th century, Anthony Trollope chronicled the revitalized parliamentary career of his hero, Phineas Finn, in *Phineas Redux*.

The term in use by *The Washington Post* in a January 15, 1989, headline on the return to power of old-line elites in the Bush Administration:

> "Establishment Redux: New Jobs for the **Old Guard**."

**Regency.** Rule by someone appointed to fill in because a monarch is ill, too young or absent and thus unable to fulfill the responsibilities of office.

When you see the word with a capital "R," it usually* refers to the period in English history during the reign of King George III when his son George, the Prince of Wales, served as regent during his father's spells of mental disability between 1811 and 1820. The period is noted for its distinctive styles in architecture, decoration and fashion and also for its naughtiness—Lord Byron [see **Byronic**], Lady Caroline Lamb, Beau Brummel, gambling clubs and all that. Perhaps something was let loose in the aftermath of the wars with Napoleon or the influence of the French Revolution, or maybe the period looked racier in contrast to the Victorian period.

These days the period has inspired a sub-genre of romance novels in which rakes are regularly reduced to romantic gelatin by perky and virtuous heroines. [See **Gothic**.]

The term in use, by Henry Allen in *The Washington Post*, November 22, 1988, writing about President John F. Kennedy on the 25th anniversary of his assassination:

> "Much has been made of authenticity, Camelot, Weberian concepts of charisma and so on: the wit, the cool, the Irishness, the aristocracy, the family man, the Regency rake, the war hero, the media manipulator, and our nostalgia for an era when everything was possible and nothing was quite real."

**Road to Damascus.** (duh-MAS-kuhs) The point at which a dramatic change in viewpoint or a conversion to a sharply different opinion occurs.

Saul of Tarsus was a rabbi on his way to Damascus to persecute Christians there. As described in the New Testament (Acts), Saul suddenly saw a great light, and Jesus spoke to him, saying, "Saul,

---

* In French history, the Regency refers to the period 1715-1723, when the Duke of Orleans served as regent for Louis XV.

Saul, why persecutest thou me?" Saul was immediately converted to Christianity and, as Paul, became the great apostle and missionary of Christianity. He traveled through the Roman world and his writings, the Epistles, are the most influential of early Christian documents.

The term in use, by Peter Carlson in *The Washington Post Magazine*, March 20, 1988, in a profile of anti-abortion activist ChristyAnne Collins:

> "One day, a friend invited her to an Episcopal church service. Collins, a lapsed Catholic and a confirmed skeptic, went reluctantly. It turned out to be her road to Damascus. 'I heard the pastor speak and it couldn't have been more earth-shattering if God had spoken to me himself.' "

In use again, by mystery writer P. D. James in her novel, *A Taste for Death*. A government intelligence official responds languidly to Scotland Yard's complaints about withholding evidence on the death of a Cabinet official in the vestry of a London church:

> "There's a rumour that it could have been suicide. After all, he was hardly normal at the time. This habit he'd developed of sleeping in church vestries. . . . And such a very curious church to choose. . . . a Romanesque basilica in Paddington is surely an improbable choice for a good night's sleep, let alone one's personal road to Damascus."

**Robber Barons.** Used generically to describe unscrupulous and ruthless business tycoons.

They were a particular feature of the economic landscape in the second half of 19th century America. The growth and industrialization of the new country led to the creation of great fortunes through economic buccaneering unrestrained by government regulation. The period saw the rise of empires in railroading, steel, banking and oil.

The reference undoubtedly originates from earlier times, when rogue noblemen of medieval days defied the authority of kings, made war and took plunder as they saw fit. In 1896, E. L. Godkin, editor of *The Nation*, described rapacious tycoons as "medieval barons"; Henry Demarest Lloyd and Carl Schurz referred to "robber barons" in

1882. Lloyd described the atmosphere in 19th-century America in his 1894 book, *Wealth Against Commonwealth:* "If our civilization is destroyed . . . it will not be by . . . barbarians from below. Our barbarians come from above. Our great money-makers have sprung in one generation into seats of power kings do not know. . . . They are gluttons of luxury and power, rough, unsocialized, believing that mankind must be kept terrorized." Matthew Josephson's 1934 book *The Robber Barons: The Great American Capitalists 1861-1901* brought the expression into contemporary times.

The term in use: A local describes the social geography of the tony horse country community of Middleburg, Virginia, in *The Washington Post,* May 1, 1988:

> " 'There are three tiers to its society—the old families, the robber baron set, and the retired airline pilots,' said the scion of an area family with deep roots in the land. . . .
>
> " '[Paul] Mellon is definitely part of the Robber Baron set. There are people in that set who have been here two or three generations, who are superb citizens, generous with their money and time, low key, there when they're needed. They are real assets in that respect.
>
> " 'But they're **arrivistes**. They are not the Old Families.' "

**Robespierre.** (ROHBZ-pyair) A zealous leader of the French Revolution whose name today is synonymous with ruthlessness and revolutionary extremism.

Maximilien Francois Marie Isidore de Robespierre (1758-1794) was one of the most radical of the radical **Jacobins** and virtual dictator of France during the Reign of Terror, 1793-1794. An icy, priggish intellectual with considerable powers of oratory and a reputation for incorruptibility, Robespierre was fanatically dedicated to the revolution. He instigated the executions of fellow revolutionaries, most notably Danton, who predicted on the way to the guillotine that Robespierre would soon follow.

Danton was right; the Terror ultimately consumed itself. Robespierre was overthrown on July 27, 1794 by deputies in the National Convention who disagreed with his policies and feared they might be next to be shaved by the "national razor." He was guillotined the next day with several associates.

The term in use, by George Will, *The Washington Post*, June 1, 1989, on internecine warfare in the House of Representatives:

> "[House Republican Whip Newt] Gingrich, who relishes his bicentennial role as Robespierre, thinks the sulfurous smoke sweeping from the Capitol dome denotes civil health and (in his words) 'tougher standards.' "

In use again, by Jack Kroll in a review of the movie *The Adventures of Baron Munchausen* in *Newsweek*, March 13, 1989:

> "This 18th century SWAT team defeats the Turks and discomfits the city's boss, the puritanical, Robespierre-like Horatio Jackson (Jonathan Pryce) who hates fantasy and fun."

And from *The New Republic*, May 9, 1988:

> "The conservatives' overexcitement has made agitators of them. The apparent calm of Elliot Abrams' arrogant bearing is that of a fanatic, a Robespierre of the right."

**Rogers, Will.** See Will Rogers.

**Roman à Clef.** (roh-MAHN ah CLAY) A novel in which real people are characters. They're usually given fictitious names. Literally, in French, it means novel with a key.

The term in use, by Delia Ephron in her review of Maureen Reagan's *First Father, First Daughter,* in *The New York Times Book Review,* March 26, 1989:

> "Ms. Reagan is the third Reagan child to check in with a book. Patti Davis aired her grievances against her parents in a *roman à clef* about the antiwar daughter of a reactionary governor and his superficial wife; Michael Reagan revealed a lonely childhood in which, unbeknownst to his parents, he was sexually abused by a camp counselor."

**Rosetta Stone.** (roh-ZET-uh) A stone found near Rosetta in northern Egypt in 1799 by Napoleon's troops that provided scholars with the key to deciphering a lost language, Egyptian hieroglyphics. By extension, the term is used to refer to the key to an incomprehensible problem.

The parallel inscriptions on the stone were in three languages: Greek, hieroglyphics (picture writing representing words or sounds) and demotic (a later, simplified form of hieroglyphics). Dr. Thomas Young translated the demotic text in 1819; French Egyptologist J. F. Champollion was then able to construct a complete hieroglyphic alphabet (1821-1822), enabling modern man to understand the ancient Egyptian writings for the first time. The stone, one of the great archaeological finds in history, is now in the British Museum.

The term in use, by Richard Harwood in *The Washington Post*, February 12, 1989:

> "But he had demonstrated to the du Pont heirs a truth known to all the 'insiders' of this city: that in the great commercial bazaar that Washington has become, information is a central and most precious commodity. In the du Pont case, it was the Rosetta Stone that led them to their goal."

**Round Up the Usual Suspects.** Address a problem with an unimaginative approach: blame the customary people or circumstances for what's gone wrong.

The phrase was popularized by the beloved 1942 movie classic *Casablanca*. After two references early in the film, the phrase comes up memorably at the conclusion. The cynical French policeman, Captain Reynaud, deflects the police from arresting the obviously guilty Rick for murder by telling his men, "Major Strasser has been shot. Round up the usual suspects." And off they go, allowing Rick and Reynaud to escape to join the Resistance.

The term in use by Charles Krauthammer in a December 5, 1988, *Time* essay:

> "The first thing a party does after it loses an election is to round up the usual suspects. The Democrats' post mortem

of the Dukakis debacle has produced a fairly standard list of fall guys."

**Rube Goldberg.** Reuben Lucius Goldberg (1883-1970), an American cartoonist whose name has become attached to the complicated, ramshackle contraptions he drew which performed simple tasks in the most complicated ways.

His cartoons—he published nearly 50,000 of them in 72 years, during which time he smoked a total of 118,700 cigars at a cost of $47,480—satirized the technology of modern times. Biographer Peter C. Marzio (who calculated the cigar consumption) in *Rube Goldberg: His Life and Work*, sums up Goldberg's comic contribution: "For Americans, complex machinery has been ever present and ever growing, but few Americans until the arrival of Rube Goldberg saw it as a subject for comedy."

Here's Rube's explanation from a typical cartoon, showing a process in which the whiskers of a bearded man, seated in a chair atop a balloon, brush off the suit of a man standing before him. It starts with a lit candle under a jug:

> "Heat from flame (A) expands home brew in bottle (B) and cork (C) flies out with attached safety razor blade (D), which cuts string (E)—weight (F) drops on strength-testing machine (G) ringing bell (H)—boxing dog (I) thinks round is starting and jumps off chair (J) falling on head of spike (K)—point (L) punctures balloon (M), dropping chair (N), which bobs up and down on spring (O), causing whiskers (P) to brush off clothes with neatness and care." (The cartoon is captioned, "Try our new patent clothes brush.")

The term in use, by Charles Krauthammer in *The Washington Post*, January 6, 1989, commenting on congressional efforts to avoid difficult decisions:

> "Take three elementary functions of the government: 1) balancing the budget, 2) closing obsolete military installations and 3) regulating congressional salaries. Hopelessly afraid of acting on any of these, Congress has constructed an elaborate set of Rube Goldberg devices, to do what

has to be done while taking no responsibility for having done it."

Another example, also from *The Washington Post*, by Tony Korn-heiser, June 3, 1989:

"On Wednesday, Jimmy Connors was given the bum's rush out of the French Open by a 22-year-old punk with a Rube Goldberg serve, a jammed knee and an earring, who buys his racquets at K Mart."

**Rubicon, To Cross the.** Taking a decisive and irrevocable action.

In 49 B.C., Julius Caesar led his army to the banks of the Rubicon, a small river that marked the boundary between Italy and Gaul, and which the Roman Senate had forbidden him to cross. **"The die is cast,"** said Caesar, wading in, knowing full well that this step would mean civil war.

The term in use, in *The Washington Post*, February 14, 1989, in a report on an imminent strike at Eastern Airlines:

" 'We're approaching the Rubicon,' said Robert J. Joedicke, a longtime observer of the industry who is an analyst with Shearson Lehman Hutton, Inc. 'This is the crunch. Somebody backs down or doesn't, but I don't think any of the implications are favorable for the longer-term. . . .' "

Another example, from the *The Christian Science Monitor*, April 3, 1989, in a story on negotiations between the Polish government and the union Solidarity. Writer William Echikson quotes one of the parties:

" 'Both the communists and we crossed the Rubicon,' reflects Tadeusz Mazowiecki, a leading Solidarity negotia-tor. 'It's really surprising how far things went.' "

**Runyon, Damon;** also **Runyonesque** and **Runyonese.** Alfred Damon Runyon (1884-1946) was an American journalist and short story writer who gained fame for his colorful fictional tales of street-wise New Yorkers—bookies, gamblers, fight promoters and other lovable rogues. Among the memorable characters he created were Apple Annie, Joe the Joker and Regret the Horseplayer. Runyon so distinctively used exaggerated, colorful slang and the underworld jargon of the period in his stories that the language became known as "Runyonese." Today colorful underworld or police personalities are called "Runyonesque" even though both the writer and that more innocent time have passed.

Runyon's 1932 collection of stories, *Guys and Dolls*, inspired the 1952 Broadway musical of the same name. Runyon also wrote screenplays, including *Lady for a Day* (1933), *Little Miss Marker* (1934) and *A Slight Case of Murder* (1938).

The term in use, by Shirley Povich, sports editor emeritus of *The Washington Post*, reminiscing on his career in an article for *The Washington Post Magazine*, October 29, 1989:

> "And how many can truthfully say they actually heard a to-be-famous phrase actually enter the language? I did. This was during the 1934 World Series on a cold, blustery day in Detroit. Standing behind me in the upstairs press box was Joe Jacobs, a Damon Runyon character and manager of boxer Max Schmeling. He didn't like baseball much, but the World Series was a place to be seen. Now he was stomping his feet in the chill and drawing his topcoat tighter about him, shivering and unhappy. That's when he muttered to me and my press-box neighbor Paul Gallico, 'I shoulda stood in bed.'"

Another example, from *Village Voice* movie critic Georgia Brown, reviewing *Bloodhounds of Broadway*, December 19, 1989:

> "Anorexic society matron (Julie Hagerty) has a yen for babyfaced gunmen. The door to her mansion is tended by an ancient butler (William Burroughs), whose line, 'Your coat, Sir,' receives the Runyonesque comeback, 'What about it?'"

And from Richard Harrington in *The Washington Post*, November 19, 1989, writing about Don Bluth, creator of animated films:

"Dinosaurs have been good to Don Bluth, as have immigrant mice (*An American Tail*) and, he hopes, rascally dogs, the subject of his new $13 million feature, *All Dogs Go to Heaven*, a lively meld of *Heaven Can Wait*, *Carousel* and Damon Runyon."

# S

**Salad Days.** The days of one's youth, inexperience and innocence; when one is green, exuberant and full of oneself.

The expression goes back a ways. This is from Shakespeare's *Antony and Cleopatra*:

> My salad days,
> When I was green in judgment.

The term in use in more recent times, from *The American Spectator*, February 1988, in a discussion of the Washington summit meeting in December of 1987 between Gorbachev and Reagan:

> "I raised the question with an old Reagan hand who worked closely with the President during the first term, the salad days of that splendidly destabilizing 'Evil Empire' rhetoric."

**Samizdat.** (suh-MEEZ-daht) A Russian word, meaning the underground, clandestine printing and distribution of banned literature in the Soviet Union. The word refers to either the literature or the process of producing it—often simply by producing carbon copies and passing them around.

The term in use, by George F. Will in *The Washington Post*, November 24, 1988, discussing the process of finding people to fill appointive positions in the incoming Bush administration:

> "The hurdle that nominees must clear gets higher and higher as we become more fastidious about sin. This time senators must ask: Did you ever smoke anything nasty in the dorm? Have you circulated *samizdat* copies of the writings of Robert Bork?
>
> "Can't be too careful, so the world will have to wait."

Another example, from Jack Shafer, writing in Washington, D.C.'s *City Paper*, August 18-24, 1989, on the fate of an unpublished article on Washington business mogul Herbert Haft by Washington writer Robert Pack:

> "Driven underground, the story was seized by the journalistic samizdat. Photocopied and rephotocopied, the Pack piece has been passed from one admiring reader to another ever since."

And from *Time*, October 30, 1989:

> "Sony co-founder Akio Morita co-authored *The Japan That Can Say No* for a Japanese audience, but now samizdat English versions are circulating. . . ."

**Sammy Glick.** The term describes someone like the hero of Budd Schulberg's 1941 novel, *What Makes Sammy Run?*. Tough, hard-driving Sammy Glick, crass son of a Jewish immigrant, clawed his way from his humble New York origins to Hollywood success in the movie business.

The term in use, by Karen DeYoung in *The Washington Post*, April 23, 1987, on British author-politician Jeffrey Archer:

> "Well-dressed, clean-shaven and tanned, Archer, 47, appeared during several days on the witness stand to be precisely what he is—a clever, tightly controlled, relentless achiever with a bit of the Sammy Glick about him."

And by Bob Mack, *Spy*, July 1989, describing right-wing journalist Dinesh D'Souza:

> "D'Souza is most famous for his Sammy Glickishness, and for his felicitous nickname, Distort D'Newza."

And David Margolick, commenting on Robert Burt's *Two Jewish Justices: Outcasts in the Promised Land*, *The New York Times*, December 22, 1989:

> "Brandeis, according to Mr. Burt, remained in, and even relished the role of outsider, or, to use the political philosopher Hannah Arendt's term, 'pariah.' . . . Frankfurter, on the other hand, was the '**parvenu**,' in Miss Arendt's terms, a

judicial Sammy Glick, so desperate for acceptance that he became, Mr. Burt wrote, 'an over-eager apologist for the existing order.' "

**Sang-froid.** (song-FRWAH) Coolness, calmness, composure, poise in difficult or dangerous circumstances. French; it literally means coldblooded.

The term in use, by the gossip columnist of *The Chatham Courier*, Chatham, New York, September 15, 1988:

> "Time was, not long ago, when I seemed to be the perfect picture of equanimity. People commented on my sang-froid attitude. . . . But then I stopped smoking. . . ."

And by James M. Markham, writing in *The New York Times*, April 29, 1989, on discontent in NATO:

> "In 1983, France kept its sang-froid and was little moved by the demonstrations that roiled its neighbors, who were said to be afflicted by 'Protestant **angst**.' But today even Francois Mitterrand is sensitive to rising anti-nuclear sentiment among French youth."

And by Judith Miller, *The New York Times*, September 16, 1986:

> "Almost overnight, Paris seems to have become a city under siege. The French, who pride themselves on their sang-froid, have been terrified by the wave of bombings—four in eight days."

**Sans-culottes.** (song COO-lot) Literally, in French, it means "without knee breeches." This generally is thought to come from the days of the French Revolution, and originated as a description of the poor. They did not wear knee breeches as was the fashion for men of the middle and upper classes; instead they wore trousers, or pantaloons.

This difference in clothing emerged as one of the symbols of the revolution, and the most radical elements of the Paris mob came to be called the sans-culottes. Their power in the Revolution grew and reached its peak during the Reign of Terror (1793-1794) in which thousands of people were executed in Paris and in provincial cities. As a sign of the mob's power, politicians proclaimed themselves to be sans-culottes, even though they were middle class lawyers and intellectuals. Certainly their leader, the ruthless **Robespierre**, did not forego his dandified dress. The power of the sans-culottes ended with the overthrow and execution of Robespierre in July 1794.

The term has since come to be applied to extreme radicals, usually with a tinge of proletarian mob violence.

The term in use, by Roger Beard in *The Financial Times*, March 4, 1989, writing on carnival (Mardi Gras) in the French coastal city of Dunkerque (**Dunkirk** to us):

> "Nice, Venice and those other elegant manifestations of carnival are not for the Dunkerqois. Here the masks are of Rocard and Mitterrand rather than Harlequin and Columbine, and there is a cutting edge to the humour which would make the politicians wince. They might dress as aristos, but underneath the paint and the powder they are tough sans culottes."

And another, from *The Financial Times*, December 17, 1986, describing, in an extended French revolutionary metaphor, a debate in the British House of Commons:

> "The Sans Culottes on the Labour benches were in a blood-thirsty mood yesterday as they noisily rolled out the **tumbril** to dispatch Nicholas Ridley, the Environment Secretary, to the scaffold."

And from Gerri Hirshey, *The Washington Post Magazine*, April 12, 1987:

> "Styles may change, but FVs [fashion victims] will be with us as long as the rich flaunt their income with fashion. There is a caution here, even for us sans-culottes sniggering on the sidelines. The FVs' folly is a stubborn thing, but so is our insistent glee in pointing it out."

**Sarajevo.** (SAH-rah-yeh-voh) The town where World War I began.

Sarajevo is a town in Serbia, which was a principality on the Balkan Peninsula (in today's Yugoslavia) when it became the flashpoint for the Great War. The area had been the scene of fighting and political intrigue for decades. [See **Balkanize, Balkanization.**]

Archduke Francis Ferdinand, heir apparent to the Austro-Hungarian throne, and his wife were assassinated in Sarajevo on June 28, 1914 by a Serbian nationalist. The Austrian government was convinced of the complicity of the Serbian government in the plot and on July 28 Austria declared war on Serbia.

Due to the conflicting interests in the region and the network of treaties among the European powers, other declarations followed and soon every major power in Europe was in the war. The assassination in Sarajevo had provided the spark; historians agree that conflict had become inevitable due to the tensions among the European powers. An incident that might have been isolated and controlled in calmer times led instead to a calamitous war. The town's name is used today as a shorthand term for an obscure place which can become the trigger for disastrous events.

The term in use, by columnist George Will, meditating on the history of the income tax in *The Washington Post*, April 13, 1989:

> "But as quickly as Americans could say 'Sarajevo,' war caused government expenditures to soar and international trade (and tariff revenues) to shrink."

**Savile Row.** (SAV-il) A London street known for its tailors of elegant men's clothing. A Savile Row suit is world-famous for the excellence of its tailoring and material, and of course its English style and pricey snob appeal.

The term in use, by Rowland Evans and Robert Novak, in a February 2, 1989, column in *The Washington Post* on the controversial nomination of John Tower to be Secretary of Defense in the Bush administration:

> "They [members of the Senate Armed Services Committee] did not have to like the feisty little Texan who wears

Savile Row suits and a chip on his shoulder. Their clean bill of health showed they shared Bush's respect for Tower's knowledge about defense and intellectual acuity."

And from *The Economist*, December 9, 1989:

"For the wealthy visitor in search of the city's old-world charm, London still offers a long list of things to do. Buying a suit from Savile Row is near the top of the list. The bespoke tailors of the West End are some of the best in the world. The Japanese even acknowledge as much in their language: their word for a three-piece suit is *seiburo*."

**Savonarola.** (sav-uh-nuh-ROH-luh) A name that has become synonymous with militant, zealous reformers.

Giolamo Savonarola (1452-1498) was a monk who came to Florence to preach repentance, denouncing the corruption of the city and of the Papacy. His powerful sermons aroused tremendous emotion and religious fervor, leading to the burning of books and attacks on other influences deemed to be corrupting. He held tremendous power in the city for a brief period, but was ultimately charged with disobedience and then heresy and burned at the stake. He is regarded as one of the forerunners of the Protestant Reformation.

The term in use, by Philip Weiss in *Spy* magazine, November 1988, describing former U.S. Attorney and New York City mayoral candidate Rudolph Giuliani:

"He does not employ musty legalisms. Once, speaking to a group of students, he derided the central principle of his profession: 'The process of training a lawyer is in essence to train someone to see every side of every issue and to argue every side of every issue. That . . . can be very, very destructive of a notion of absolute right and wrong, good and evil, that there are some things that maybe shouldn't be argued by anyone.'

"This Savonarola spiel is not all dramatics, not just Giuliani playing to his public. . . ."

Another example, from Donald Kaul, in the *Des Moines Sunday Register*, July 16, 1989:

> "Mr. Fillmore objected to my calling Newt Gingrich 'the Republican Savonarola,' on the grounds that the priest was better than that. He wrote: 'Savonarola was a sort of 15th century Ralph Nader who preached against the vanities and excesses of his age. . . .' and was a good guy. Sure, and all Gengis Khan wanted to do was rearrange the furniture."

And from Kenneth Turan, *The Washington Post*, November 27, 1989, reviewing a book on David Puttnam, former head of Columbia Pictures:

> "When he left that post barely a year later, he [Puttnam] was reviled as a Savonarola, a dangerous advocate of reform of the most seditious kind."

**Scarlet Pimpernel.** A dashing, mysterious rescuer of those in hopeless circumstances.

The Scarlet Pimpernel, in Baroness Orczy's 1905 novel by that name, pretended to be a hare-brained society fop to disguise his true identity as the daring rescuer of doomed French aristocrats during the French Revolution. The pimpernel, a tiny flower of the primrose family, was the hero's emblem.

The novel was made into a memorable movie in 1934 starring Merle Oberon and a most un-Ashley Wilkes-like Leslie Howard. Howard reprised the role in 1941 in "Pimpernel Smith," playing a mild-mannered professor smuggling fugitives out of Nazi Germany on the eve of World War II.

The character was also brought to the screen by Daffy Duck as "The Scarlet Pumpernickel" (1950).

The term in use, by H.D.S. Greenway, *The Des Moines Register*, October 23, 1989:

> "As the sea sometimes throws up bits of long-lost ship-wrecks on the shore, so did the Soviet prison system last week cough up a few pathetic personal belongings of one of the true heroes of our time. The passport, notebooks and

some loose change belonged to Swedish diplomat Raoul Wallenberg, who disappeared into the Soviets' **Gulag** Archipelago 45 years ago.

"A modern Scarlet Pimpernel, Wallenberg used his diplomatic immunity and the neutrality of Sweden in the last months of World War II to save tens of thousands of Hungarian Jews from death at the hands of the Nazis."

A play on the name, from *Higher Than Hope*, a biography of Nelson Mandela by Fatima Meer, describing Mandela's efforts as an underground organizer against apartheid in South Africa:

"Nelson planned a strategy whereby he would keep the government constantly engaged but himself disguised, secret and inaccessible. The black public thrilled at the adventure that Mandela created. . . .

"The Black Pimpernel was everywhere."


## Schadenfreude. (SHAH-den-FROY-duh) A German word meaning malicious joy, glee at another's misfortune.

The term in use, by economist Paul Samuelson writing in *Newsweek*, August 13, 1973:

"Why have the Watergate hearings brought so little joy? One should have thought the discomfort of the president's admirers might at least have been offset by the Schadenfreude of his critics."


## Sclerosis, Sclerotic. That which is clogged, blocked-up or rigid and inflexible.

It's a medical word, describing body tissues that show abnormal hardening. Perhaps most widely known through the diseases of the arteries—arteriosclerosis and atherosclerosis—it derives from a Greek word, skleros, meaning hard.

The word has expanded from its medical meaning per this example from *The Economist*, January 7, 1989:

"Last year London's galloping sclerosis—road traffic now moves at the same pace as 100 years ago, the tubes and railways are packed—showed that this act may have been necessary but was wholly insufficient."

**Scorched Earth Policy.** Destroying (usually by fire) all crops and supplies that might be of use to an invading army. It is a total war, bitterly fought, that imposes a cruel burden on innocent civilians but intends to starve the foe as he moves away from his source of supply.

The term apparently comes from a translation of a Chinese phrase. *The Oxford English Dictionary* reports a use in the December 6, 1937, *Times* of London, describing the Japanese advance into China and the fears of a particular city's inhabitants as to the reaction of Chinese troops:

> "The populace are still disturbed, in spite of official denials, by wild rumours of a 'scorched earth policy' of burning the city before the Japanese enter."

Edgar Snow's 1941 book *Scorched Earth* attributes the policy to a general on the staff of Chiang-kai-shek.

The term in use, by Marvin Harris, *The Washington Post*, October 22, 1989, reviewing *Lucy's Child: The Discovery of a Human Ancestor*, by Donald Johanson and James Shreeve:

> ". . . Mary Leakey did her best to keep Johanson away from the scene of her life-work. She told the authorities that nothing of significance remained to be discovered at the Gorge. And when that didn't succeed, she resorted to a kind of scorched-earth policy, hastily removing furniture, equipment and supplies from the field station that Johanson intended to use."

**Scylla and Charybdis.** (SIL-uh and kuh-RIB-dis) The nautical equivalent of a rock and a hard place—a choice that leaves no good choice.

Scylla is a huge rock that projects into the Strait of Messina, off the coast of Sicily; Charybdis is a whirlpool in the strait.

The Greeks turned these natural hazards into mythical sea monsters. Scylla had six heads, each with three rows of pointed teeth, and seized and devoured unwary sailors. Charybdis gulped seawater and threw it up again three times a day.

Vessels which managed to evade Scylla would fall prey to Charybdis and vice versa. (Odysseus, hero of the *Odyssey*, managed to pass through the strait in his wanderings after the Trojan war; mythological heroes can sometimes escape mythological monsters with the intervention of a friendly god or goddess.)

The term in use, by Victor Gold in *The American Spectator*, March 1988, describing the hazards of the Iowa caucuses and the New Hampshire primary:

> "Find the candidate who can slip his presidential aspirations past the Scylla of Ames [Iowa]—then, two weeks later, the Charybdis of Concord [New Hampshire]—and you may have a winner."

**Sea Change.** A profound change wrought by the sea, or the action of sea water over time. Today it is a metaphor for a dramatic alteration, metamorphosis or radical change. The phrase appears first in Shakespeare's *The Tempest* (1610), Act I, Scene ii:

> Full fathom five thy father lies,
> Of his bones are coral made:
> Those are pearls that were his eyes:
> Nothing of him that doth fade,
> But doth suffer a Sea-change
> Into something rich, & strange.

This phrase, barks H.W. Fowler, *A Dictionary of Modern English Usage*, "is one of the most importunate & intrusive of irrelevant allusions & hackneyed phrases." Duly chastened, we include it anyway.

The term in use, by Lee Hockstader and Mary Jordan, writing in *The Washington Post*, October 18, 1987, on politics on the Board of Supervisors of Fairfax County, Virginia:

> "In 1975, the county board underwent a political sea change: Herrity was elected chairman and Moore inherited

his role as naysayer. Suddenly Herrity had the chance to practice what he preached."

And a play on the term, from Tom Shales, writing in the *Post* on the new Soviet openness during Ronald Reagan's visit to the Soviet Union, June 1, 1988:

"Demonstrations of the power of television are certainly redundant at this point, but the new receptiveness of the Soviets to TV's prying eye has to be seen as a major departure. A see change."

**Second Coming.** Refers to the triumphant return of Jesus Christ as foretold in the Book of Revelation in the New Testament of the Bible. After **Armageddon** comes the Day of Judgment, when Christ is to return to earth to judge humanity. The righteous are to be rewarded in heaven and sinners sent to eternal damnation.

The term is now used figuratively to refer to a victorious return from obscurity or defeat.

The term in use, in *Maclean's*, January 25, 1988, on the new enterprise being created by computer genius Steven Jobs, cofounder of Apple Computers, Inc.:

"Despite his ability to perpetuate the belief that he is the lone prophet of the next computer revolution, Jobs could find his success at Apple difficult to repeat. Already he has missed some self-imposed deadlines, prompting the joke that 'NeXT' should be named 'Eventually.' Still, some industry experts who have seen NeXT's prototypes say that they are astonishingly powerful. Clearly, it is too soon to rule out a second coming for Steven Jobs."

**Secular Humanism.** A doctrine which, in the eyes of its critics, stresses the achievements of man and ignores the teachings of religion or the role of the deity. The term arises particularly in the context of controversy over the teaching or practice of religion in public schools. It is emotionally and politically loaded, an "attack" phrase that carries powerful and dramatically conflicting meanings for the people using it.

The term is used almost exclusively by its enemies; few people call themselves secular humanists.

Fundamentalist Christians equate secular humanism with an anti-religion they claim is taught in the public schools by virtue of the schools' excluding Christian beliefs from the curriculum.

The term has become a shorthand epithet for much in modern life that conservative religionists don't like: atheism, liberalism, feminism, homosexuality, the theory of evolution, big government, rock music, sexually explicit books and movies, anthropology, the National Council of Churches, Voltaire and the **Enlightenment**.

Humanism, remember, is something else—a philosophical and literary movement that began in the Renaissance and which valued human capabilities, emphasized secular studies such as the humanities, elevated classical ideals and classical forms and rejected medieval religious authority. Renaissance humanists believed that the proper study of man was man, although they did not deny God.

"Secular" humanism is a modern coinage. One early reference was made by noted sociologist C. Wright Mills in an essay written in 1952. Mills said, "Liberals have repeatedly articulated a secular humanism stressing the priceless value of the individual personality and the right of each individual to be dealt with in accordance with rational and understandable laws, to which all power is also subject." The earliest reference found so far goes back to 1933. But fundamentalists claim secular humanism has been designated as a religion by none other than the Supreme Court of the United States. This "authority" came about in an almost whimsical manner—in a footnote to a Supreme Court opinion. In 1961, an atheist filed suit against the state of Maryland because it required that applicants for notary public swear that they believed in God. Justice Hugo Black wrote the court's opinion (*Torcaso v. Watkins*), overruling the Maryland law. He said the protections of the Constitution applied to non-believers as well as believers.

In the now-famous footnote 11, Justice Black added: "Among religions in this country which do not teach what would generally be considered a belief in the existence of God are Buddhism, Taoism, Ethical Culture, Secular Humanism, and others." This of course was irrelevant to the case, since the atheist Torcaso was not a member of any such group.

Justice Black had taken the term from amicus curiae briefs filed in the case, including one from the American Humanist Association—a group that formally embraces secular humanism—which had capitalized the words. The upper-case version found its way into Justice Black's footnote, and a **bête noire** leaped into being.

As Sean Wilentz noted in *The New Republic*, April 25, 1988, "Until 1970 only a few thousand Americans had even heard of the secular humanists, that hearty little band of atheists and world government types. . . . Had Justice Black's pen slipped, the religious right might today be railing against the diabolical effects of Ethical Culturalism."

The term in use, by Senator Jesse Helms, Republican of North Carolina, quoted in *The New York Times*, June 28, 1981:

> "Basically, we're talking about faith in God versus secular humanism."

**Segue.** (SEG-way) A verb, meaning to continue or blend from one part to another without interruption. In music, to move from one composition to another without a break. It is frequently used in show biz, newscasting and politics to mean to move seamlessly from topic A to topic B.

The term in use, by William A. Henry III in *Time*, November 21, 1988, in a review of a production of Samuel Beckett's *Waiting for Godot*:

> "The chief sinner is [Robin] Williams. . . . He scampers. He pounds the ground. He thrusts a big bone into the slave's hands as though it were an Oscar and tells him to 'thank the Academy.' As [Steve] Martin feigns death, Williams hovers over him, murmuring the pet name 'Didi, Didi,' then segues into the theme from 'The Twilight Zone.'"

Another example, from Casey McCabe, *Premiere*, January 1990:

> "Five years ago, Dale Dye pulled into Hollywood with the kind of resume that doesn't exactly open show-business

doors. He was a recently retired Marine Corps captain with zero film experience."

"But Dye engineered a dramatic and unlikely mid-life segue."

**Shanghai.** (shang-high) As a verb, it means to kidnap someone, in particular to press an individual into service as a seaman. In the 19th century days of the China trade, ship captains sometimes obtained the additional hands needed by drugging sailors ashore, carrying them aboard ship and sailing before the men regained consciousness.

Contrary to the belief of many (including the authors), the origin of the term may have had little to do with unsavory doings in the great Chinese seaport of Shanghai. Instead, suggests *Brewer's Dictionary of Phrase and Fable*, it stems from the phrase "ship him to Shanghai," meaning to send someone on a long voyage.

The term in use, by R. Emmett Tyrell, *The American Spectator*, August, 1989:

> "The Hon. Thomas Stephen Foley was shanghaied by fellow Democrats to become Forty-ninth Speaker of the House of Representatives."

**Shangri-La.** A mythical land of peace and eternal youth, supposedly located in Tibet, in James Hilton's 1933 novel *Lost Horizons*. The novel was made into a popular movie starring Ronald Colman in 1937, and the word moved into the language as a term for a tranquil refuge from the pains and difficulties of life.

Franklin D. Roosevelt had some fun with the name. In April 1942, he dodged questions about the launching site (actually the carrier *Hornet*) of the bombers used in the Doolittle Raid over Tokyo, by saying they came "from Shangri-La." Similarly he once announced that two battleships had gone to Shangri-La, a place, Berlin Radio said in a subsequent broadcast, that German authorities had not been able to locate on a map.

Shangri-La was the name Roosevelt gave to the rustic presidential hideaway established at an old CCC camp in the Catoctin Mountains of Maryland. The Navy had fretted that FDR could no longer cruise on the presidential yacht safe from prowling enemy submarines, so this mountaintop conveniently close to Washington was selected as a restful retreat. The place was manned by the yacht's crew and furnished with items from the White House attic. The name is said to have been suggested by the yacht's captain. FDR referred to the place as "USS Shangri-La," and liked to call his visits there "cruises." The presidential retreat is still under Navy jurisdiction.

And ultimately, the name of this fictitious land of peace was given to an American warship. In tribute to Roosevelt and his joke about the launching-point of the Doolittle Raid, the aircraft carrier *Shangri-La* was commissioned in 1944. The ship was decommissioned in 1971.

The presidential retreat was renamed Camp David by Dwight Eisenhower for his grandson in 1953, and has maintained the name ever since.

The term in use, by R.H. Melton, in *The Washington Post*, April 9, 1949, under a Roanoke, Virginia dateline:

> "This used to be the Shangri-La of the state Republican Party, the near-mythic cradle of a fiercely independent and successful brand of GOP politics."

Another example, from Don Terry, *The New York Times*, July 24, 1989, in a story of New York City's Greenwich Village:

> " 'People think the Village is some kind of Shangri-La,' said John Pettinato, the executive director of the Greenwich Village Youth Council, who was born and reared in the area. 'It isn't. The critical problems that face New York City as a whole—crack, crime, homelessness—face the Village, too.' "

**Shermanesque.** An absolute, unequivocal, all-doors-barred refusal to run for office. In 1884, some 20 years after his destruction of Atlanta and march to the sea, the former Union general and Northern hero squelched a movement to draft him as the Republican presidential nominee. In a classic statement of forthright refusal, he informed the GOP national convention: "I will not accept if nominated, and will not serve if elected." He wasn't and didn't.

The term in use, by Virginia's governor-elect Douglas Wilder, referring to a future gubernatorial race between Attorney General Mary Sue Terry and Lieutenant Governor-elect Don Beyer, quoted in *The Washington Post,* November 9, 1989:

> "At least one person, though, seemed intrigued by the prospect of a little elbowing between Beyer and Terry. Wilder, asked about the subject today, noted that Beyer had declined to issue a 'Shermanesque statement' about not challenging Terry, then doubled over in laughter. 'You guys are always looking for grist,' he told reporters. 'You'll get it for four years.' "

Sherman's political injunction was recalled in *The Washington Post* on February 22, 1987:

> "Perhaps it was his keen sense of regional sensibilities that kept Senator Sam Nunn (D-Ga.) from invoking Sherman's words when he told 3,000 supporters Friday night he would not become a candidate for president in 1988. 'Sherman-like statements may be okay in New York,' Nunn said, 'but not in Atlanta.' "

**Sherpa.** A member of a hardy mountaineering tribe of the Himalayas. The tribesmen have gained fame as guides of expeditions to climb the region's mountains. The most famous Sherpa is Tenseng Norgay, who accompanied Sir Edmund Hillary when he became the first man to ascend Mt. Everest in 1953.

The term has come to be part of the diplomatic lexicon, too. Diplomats who do the necessary preparations for East-West summit meetings are sometimes called sherpas by their colleagues and the media, as those who act as guides in scaling the "summit." This use appeared after Hillary's achievement and as the era of meetings of U.S. presidents and U.S.S.R. leaders began in the mid-1950's. The word is also used, more generally, to describe a native or local guide.

The term in use, by Frank Gibney, *The New York Times,* December 3, 1989, reviewing *The Four Little Dragons* (referring to the thriving economies of South Korea, Taiwan, Singapore and Hong Kong) by Brian Kelly and Mark London:

"Then, obviously too shrewd to be taken in by mere propaganda, they found some knowing friends or acquaintances who would tell them what was really going on. These volunteer Sherpas ranged from successful local businessmen with American college educations to fellow drinkers the authors ran into in the evidently innumerable local bars, nightclubs and hostess spas on their tour."

And from William Safire, *The New York Times*, November 27, 1989:

"One practical question is burning in the minds of the President and his pre-summit sherpas: What will it take to get the Red Army completely out of Eastern Europe?"

**The Shot Heard Round the World.** A dramatic, heralding act that achieves broad attention and influences events elsewhere.

The expression appeared in Ralph Waldo Emerson's "Concord Hymn," which was sung at the dedication of a monument in Concord, Massachusetts commemorating the battles of Lexington and Concord on April 19, 1775, in which the first military action was taken against the British—the start of armed insurrection. The line takes note of the significance of the episode for the American Revolution, and the significance of the revolution for the world.

British troops had marched to Concord to seize weapons thought to be stored there. Thanks to the midnight ride of Paul Revere, the countryside was aroused and colonial militia met the British on the green at Lexington. A second confrontation took place at Concord Bridge, of which Emerson wrote:

By the rude bridge that arched the flood,
Their flag to April's breeze unfurled,
Here once the embattled farmers stood,
And fired the shot heard round the world.

In current use, the phrase is used to describe a dramatic or attention-getting action. A play on the term, utilizing Winston Churchill's description of Russia as "a riddle wrapped in a mystery inside an enigma" (radio broadcast, October 1, 1939), by Paul Gigot in a *Wall Street Journal* column, March 31, 1989, discussing Secretary of Defense Richard Cheney's rebuke of the Air Force chief of staff for taking a line that varied from administration policy:

> "Aided by an intrusive Congress, the military bureaucracy can fight elected executive control with the ferocity of British Ghurkas. So Mr. Cheney's rebuke was a shot heard 'round the maze-wrapped-in-a-labyrinth that is the Pentagon."

Another example, from *The New York Times*, in a book review by Christopher Lehman-Haupt, April 3, 1989:

> "To summarize Bobby Thompson's 1951 pennant-winning 'Shot Heard Round the World,' they simply quote Red Smith's report in *The New York Herald Tribune:* 'The art of fiction is dead. Reality has strangled invention. Only the utter impossible, the inexpressibly fantastic, can ever be plausible again.'"

And from *Computerworld*, March 13, 1989, by John Kirkley:

> "Whether storming the barricades or firing the shot heard round the world, when the going gets tough, you're busy just surviving. The personal computer revolution is no exception."

**Shtik** or **Shtick.** Someone's special trait or interest, as in "What's his shtik? What's he selling? What's his routine?"

It is a Yiddish word that is widely used in show business, where it means the "business" employed by actors—grimaces, gestures, whatever, for calling attention to themselves.

Leo Rosten, in his *The Joys of Yiddish*, lists a few other meanings: a piece, as in "a shtik of cake"; a prank; a piece of misconduct, a devious trick or bit of cheating, as in "How did you ever fall for a shtik like that?" A little *shtik*, he says, is a *shtikl*.

The term in use, in *The American Spectator*, July 1988, describing morning proceedings in the U.S. Senate:

> "Senator William Proxmire, a notorious early-riser, wandered about, talking in a loud voice and casting an occasional glance to the gallery to see if he was being noticed. Proxmire's shtik as the crotchety-but-lovable eccentric, which at one time made him the object of an adoring press, has been wearing thin over the last several years; it is now mostly considered a petty annoyance."

**Sick Man of Europe.** Originally the term described the decaying Ottoman Empire, which had once extended from Hungary and the Balkan Peninsula to the south Russian steppes and from Algeria to the Persian Gulf. Its decline lingered over 200 years. The maneuvering of European governments to sustain a balance of power helped to maintain this huge, varied and ancient entity, but its deterioration was inevitable despite efforts at reform led by "**Young Turks**."

Today the phrase is applied to a nation suffering profound political, social or economic difficulty.

The term in use, by Karen DeYoung in *The Washington Post*, November 14, 1988, discussing Britain under the leadership of Prime Minister Margaret Thatcher:

> "That Thatcher has changed this country's image is undeniable. No longer the indebted 'sick man' of the industrialized West, Britain is once again a force to be reckoned with in the world."

Another example, from George Will, in a column in *The Washington Post*, September 14, 1989:

> "Italy, until recently the sick man of Western Europe, is so robust that social scientists should be dizzy."

**Silent Spring.** Shorthand for ecological disaster.

It refers to a spring without songbirds, caused by use of toxic chemicals that poison the food chain and destroy the balance of nature. The allusion is to the title of the influential 1962 book by

Rachel Carson (1907-1964), which raised an early alarm about the effects of herbicides and pesticides on the environment; the book became one of the bases of the environmental movement.

The term in use, by C.L. Sulzberger in *The New York Times*, June 12, 1970:

> "The Caspian Sea is probably the most dramatic battle-ground of Soviet Russia's looming silent spring and to date this battle is being lost to oil, petroleum products, indus-trial and city sewage, ballast and waste from ships."

**Sine Qua Non.** (sih-neh kwah-NOHN) Literally, in Latin, "without which not," meaning a necessary precondition, without which something cannot be.

The term in use, by Thomas Boswell in *The Washington Post*, September 26, 1988:

> "If the last-minute scoring drive for victory is the sine qua non of playing quarterback, then the blindside fumble for a touchdown to kill all hope is the sport's worst knife in the back."

And from Patrick Buchanan, quoted in *The Washington Post*, January 15, 1987, on testing the waters for a presidential candidacy:

> "You've got to have some shot at winning; that's the *sine qua non*."

**Sinister Force.** An expression spawned by the Watergate affair, it has come to be applied (often jeeringly) to thinly disguised wrongdo-ing or to feeble theories offered by obvious malefactors trying to explain away their misdeeds. It springs from the testimony of Alex-ander M. Haig, Richard Nixon's chief of staff, attempting to explain an 18½ minute gap—an erasure—in a key White House audio tape. The taping equipment, installed on Nixon's command in several places in the White House, was voice-activated and picked up conver-sations unbeknownst to virtually everyone.

Haig offered his theory—really a non-theory—in the Watergate trial presided over by federal judge John J. Sirica, who describes the moment in his memoir, *To Set the Record Straight*:

> "In court, Haig went on to offer what he called a 'devil theory.' '. . . perhaps some sinister force had come in and applied the other energy source and taken care of the information on that tape,' he testified.
> ". . . his unhappy choice of words made headlines around the world. Quite by accident, Nixon's closest aide had supplied a description that many people all over the country thought probably fitted the president of the United States as well as anyone."

The term in use, by Lynn Darling, *Newsday*, November 10, 1989, on the abortion debate:

> "Both sides talk of exploitation, and sinister forces fighting for the **hearts and minds** of the American people. Both sides think the system is in thrall to the enemy."

**Sisyphean.** An adjective taken from the name of Sisyphus, a character from Greek mythology. He was punished by Zeus for his misdeeds by having to roll a huge stone up a hill, only to have it roll back again each time. Thus, a Sisyphean task is a burden or labor that never ends.

The term in use, by Lisa W. Foderaro in *The New York Times*, April 12, 1989, writing on efforts to encourage New Yorkers to eat healthfully:

> "While undoing well-worn habits is something of a Sisyphean task, the state is determined to try. From urban neighborhoods to farming villages, the statewide project calls for public service announcements on television and radio, free screenings for blood pressure and cholesterol levels, health fairs and fitness programs."

Another example, from Justin Kaplan's review of David Halberstam's *Summer of '49*, *The New York Times Book Review*, March 28, 1989:

"After the summer of 1949, the Red Sox and the Yankees, afflicted by complacency, the arrogance of power and a racist policy that made them among the last of the major league teams to hire black players, lost some of their stature. The Yankees surrendered their collective personality to what Mr. Halberstam calls 'cold-blooded organizational skill.' And the Red Sox continued to labor unavailingly to escape Sisyphean punishment for having sold Babe Ruth to the Yankees in 1920."

**Situation Ethics.** An ethical system in which acts are judged in their context rather than by absolute principles.

Richard Halloran of *The New York Times* offered one definition in an August 6, 1987 article headlined, "Officers and Gentlemen and Situational Lying":

"In recent years the practice of what military officers refer to as 'situational ethics' has become pervasive. That view of ethics says that a higher end, such as national security, justifies such means as lying and deception."

The term in use, by Doug Wead, a Bush presidential campaign liaison to Republican conservatives, quoted by Fred Barnes in *The New Republic*, December 5, 1988:

"Earlier this year, Wead added, some conservatives were saying it would be fine to lose the presidency in 1988 'so we can come back in 1992 with a real conservative. If we're going to indulge in situational ethics, we're no better than our opponents.' Thank God, he said, that conservatives 'woke up and got behind George Bush.'"

And from David Underhill, *The Christian Century*, May 6, 1987, writing about an Alabama lawsuit over the alleged teaching of **secular humanism** in the public schools:

"Employing the longstanding judicial dictum that freedom of speech does not include the right to set off a trampling panic by shouting 'Fire!' in a crowded theater, the plaintiffs argued that when a text or teacher says 'Situation ethics!' in

323

a crowded classroom, the students are motivated to rush off to sample the ware of the neighborhood dope pusher and burn out."

**Skunkworks** (sometimes **Skunk Works**). A team set up within an organization to expedite a new product or service. Such ad hoc outfits bring together the expertise for rapid, single-minded action, and are able to cut through red tape because they are outside normal channels.

The nickname was applied to the Advance Development Project group established within the Lockheed Corporation during World War II under Clarence L. "Kelly" Johnson. Its mission was to build a jet airplane within 180 days. He set up the group in temporary quarters made from airplane engine packing crates.

Johnson is not sure how the group got its name, but in his autobiography (*Kelly: More Than My Share of It All*) offers this story: since everything the group did was secret, there was much curiosity in the rest of the plant about its activities. An engineer responded to questions with "Oh, he's stirring up some kind of brew." Johnson says, "This brought to mind Al Capp's popular comic strip of the day, 'Lil Abner,' and the hairy Indian who regularly stirred up a big brew, throwing in skunks, old shoes, and other likely material to make his 'kickapoo joy juice.' Thus the Skunk Works was born and named."

Lockheed's Skunkworks not only produced the jet fighter on schedule, but also created the U-2 and SR-71 spy planes.

The term in use, by Melissa Healy in the *Los Angeles Times*, April 29, 1989, in a story on reported sightings of the supersecret Stealth fighter:

"Lockheed Corp. is to build a total of 59 F-117s at its experimental 'skunk works' facility in Palmdale."

Another example, from *The New York Times*, July 16, 1989; writer John Holusha describes the building of equipment with innovative methods at Kodak:

"Mr. Cole was authorized to set up a small design group outside the company's normal structure, known in manufacturing as a 'skunk works.' "

**Slam Dunk.** In basketball, a crowd-pleasing shot in which a player soars into the air and jams the ball into the basket from above the rim, with enough force to shake the rim and sometimes even break it or the backboard. Used in a broader sense, the phrase refers to a spectacular success.

The term in use, by national Democratic Party chairman Ron Brown, as quoted by Robert Kuttner, *The New York Times Magazine*, December 3, 1989:

"For Democrats, for blacks and for liberals, the 1989 election was in Brown's own election-night words, 'a slam dunk.' "

Another example, from Jean M. White, *The Washington Post Book World*, May 21, 1989, headlining an enthusiastic review of Robert B. Parker's latest novel: "Parker's Slam Dunk."

**Slouching Toward Bethlehem.** This phrase from William Butler Yeats' poem, "The Second Coming," describes a vision of an ominous Sphinx-like monster with "a gaze blank and pitiless as the sun":

And what rough beast, its hour come round at last, slouches toward Bethlehem to be born?

The imagery suggests an unknown, frightening future seen from a present in which order is breaking down. Joan Didion chose the phrase as the title of an essay describing the hippie scene in San Francisco's Haight-Ashbury district in the summer of 1967. She explained: "It was the first time I had dealt directly and flatly with the evidence of atomization, the proof that things fall apart. . . . "

The phrase attracts parody. Peter De Vries entitled a comic novel *Slouching Towards Kalamazoo*. And the *City Paper* of Washington, D.C., in a February 19, 1988, movie review, commented:

"Unlike Yeats, 'The Manchurian Candidate' goes grinning toward Bethlehem instead of slouching."

**Slough of Despond.** (slow [as in cow] of des-POND) A fit of deep depression.

The term comes from John Bunyan's *Pilgrim's Progress.* A slough is a bog, a place with deep mud into which the unwary may wander and become stuck. Despond is despondency. The Slough of Despond was one of the many hazards facing **Everyman** on his way to the Celestial City. He wandered in and, weighed down by his sins, was unable to get out until finally rescued by Help.

The term in use by historian Edmund Morris, official biographer of President Reagan, in a letter to the court supporting clemency for Michael Deaver, who was convicted of perjury and admitted that he had suffered from alcoholism (as quoted in *Spy,* February 1989):

"He has passed through the Slough of Despond, and come through curiously purified."

**Sobriquet.** (soh-bree-KAY) A French word meaning nickname or false name.

The term in use by J. J. Hunsecker (speaking of sobriquets!) in his December 1988 *Spy* magazine column of inside gossip on life within *The New York Times:*

"A man long known for his appreciation of form over content, [*Times* executive editor Max] Frankel earned himself the sobriquet 'Max the Ax' for his desire to pare down stories—a move that, in the Sunday *Times* at least, was much welcomed by readers."

Another example, from David Kirby, reviewing Carole Klein's *Gramercy Park: An American **Bloomsbury,*** in *The Village Voice,* January 19, 1988:

"Throughout the book Gramercy Park appears and disappears, like the Maltese Falcon—yes, Dashiell Hammett passed through the neighborhood, staying in the Kenmore Hall Hotel thanks to the generosity of a desk clerk named Nathanael West, who let fellow scribes register under phony names and skip when their bills came due (Hammett is said to have enjoyed the Kenmore Hall's hospitality under the sobriquet 'T. Victrola Blueberry.')"

**Social Darwinism.** Charles Darwin's theory of evolution—"the survival of the fittest"—applied to the economic arena.

English social scientist Herbert Spencer applied Darwin's theory of natural selection to society and concluded that the struggle for existence, unimpeded by government or anyone else, actually contributed most to human progress. The best would make it.

The concept was particularly admired in the post-Civil War United States, especially by those who already enjoyed a leg up. Government interference in the economy was resisted, vast fortunes were made and the privileges and prerogatives of wealth were defended on the grounds that interference would impede human progress. Steel millionaire Andrew Carnegie said that while this "may sometimes be hard for the individual, it is best for the race."

The term in use, by Edmund Morris in *The New York Times Book Review,* reviewing *The Life of Oliver Wendell Holmes* by Sheldon M. Novick, August 20, 1989:

> "Mr. Novick, who is by no means worshipful, feels that 'a kind of fascist ideology' underlay much of Holmes' Social Darwinism. Deep war wounds received during his service in the Union Army, followed by decades of public indifference to his writings, persuaded Holmes that all human affairs, whether vulgar or sublime, were subject to the rule of tooth and claw."

Another example, from an October 20, 1988, *Washington Post* profile of Marilyn Quayle, wife of then vice-presidential candidate Dan Quayle:

> " 'They're right-wing for Indiana, even,' says one fellow student. Another remembers Marilyn Quayle as 'a social Darwinist.' "

**Sodom and Gomorrah.** Bywords for places of moral corruption and rampant sin.

327

In Genesis in the Old Testament, these were cities destroyed by God with **fire and brimstone** because of their wickedness. As the story goes, Abraham persuaded the Lord to spare Sodom if ten righteous men could be found there. They couldn't. The lone righteous man in Sodom, Lot, was warned to flee with his family to escape the city's destruction. God told them not to look back, but Lot's wife couldn't resist and she was turned into a pillar of salt.

The word sodomy—unnatural copulation with a human or an animal—derives from Sodom.

The term in use, by the Moral Majority describing an anti-discrimination bill as "Sodom and Gomorrah legislation," as reported by *The Washington Post*, March 19, 1988.

Another example, from *Newsweek*, March 13, 1989, on the aftermath of the fight over confirmation of John Tower:

> "Meanwhile, the public is left with an image of the Senate as a cockpit of partisan squabbling, the White House as a center of questionable decision making, and the city of Washington as Sodom-and-Gomorrah-by-the-Potomac."

**Solon.** (SOH-lahn) He was an Athenian statesman whose name has become a shorthand term for wise lawmakers. It is a much-loved newspaper headline word, presumably because of its brevity, as in: "Solons Return from Hawaiian Fact-Finding Trip."

Solon of Athens lived from 638 to 558 B.C., had no first name and never took a fact-finding trip to Hawaii. In his nation-state, however, he was granted absolute authority to remedy an economic and political crisis. He repealed the stern code of Draco [see **Draconian**], except for the laws on homicide. He canceled debts on land, forbade debt-slavery (the practice of selling into slavery people who couldn't pay their debts) and opened political office to more citizens by creating citizenship rights based on wealth rather than birth. (At the time, this was progress.) His reforms are considered to be the basis of Athenian democracy.

The term in use, by Curt Suplee in *The Washington Post*, "Outlook," March 5, 1989, on changing public attitude toward alcoholism:

"The signs are ubiquitous, notably in the news media themselves. For generations, drinking was a taboo subject, and the press routinely overlooked solons' most grotesque and conspicuous drunkenness. Now editors are closing the ethanol gap: The current *Newsweek*, for example, devotes a full page to famous Congressional sots."


**Sop to Cerberus.** Giving a sop to Cerberus is a means of bribing one's way out of a bad situation.

In Greek mythology, Cerberus was a watchdog, bearing many heads and a tail of snakes, at the gates of hell. Vergil's *Aeneid* tells how this dog was put to sleep (just a nap) by a honey and poppy cake tossed to him by a sibyl (a prophetess) who was leading the hero Aeneas through the underworld. The Greeks buried honey cakes with their dead to quiet Cerberus.

Incidentally, one of the 12 labors of Hercules was capturing Cerberus. [For another Herculean task, see **Augean Stables**.]

The term in use, by the old wordmeister himself, William Safire, in his essay "Telemarketing Dukakis" in *The New York Times* of August 29, 1988, and speaking, of course, of the Democratic candidate for president:

> "His far-left supporters know this moderate pose is only a sop to Cerberus, and smile at the campaign-time conversion."


**Sotto Voce.** (SAH-toh VOH-chi) In a low voice, an undertone, spoken not to be overheard. In Italian, literally, under the voice. It should not be confused with a stage whisper, which is meant to be heard by an audience (in Italian, "sussoro udibile").

(Of course, if you're heard speaking sotto voce, you haven't been sotto enough.)

The term in use, by Lloyd Grove in *The Washington Post*, March 2, 1989, writing about John G. Tower, whose nomination to become secretary of defense was in trouble because of his alleged heavy drinking. The reader must judge whether Senator Tower, overheard in a Washington cocktail lounge, was speaking *sotto voce* or *sussoro audible*:

> "Then a man who preferred to be identified only as Tower's spokesman approached. 'I'm told, senator,' the man said with a grin, 'that the bars around Capitol Hill are pretty sparsely populated this evening.'
>
> "Tower cupped his hand over his mouth and said sotto voce into his trusted aide's ear: 'They're all back in their hideaways.'
>
> "The two shared a mirthless laugh."

By GOP political consultant Jay Severin on the 1989 New York mayoral race, quoted in *The Washington Post*, September 14, 1989:

> "It's going to boil down to, sotto voce, who do you trust more to crack down on drugs and crime: a white Italian guy from Brooklyn, or a liberal black politician from Manhattan?"

And from *Words That Make A Difference*, by Robert Greenman, quoting a *New York Times* use of the term:

> "On another occasion, in a group of people, I said that my daughter's name was Cambria—'Latin for Wales,' I added, and I heard a woman say to another, sotto voce, 'Imagine naming your daughter after a fish.'"

## South Sea Bubble. One of the earliest bull markets.

In the early 18th century, Europeans and their governments were beginning to learn about large-scale banking and credit in order to pay off huge war debts and to raise money for new commercial ventures. In England, much of the government debt was held through government-chartered companies granted monopolies on particular activities; when stockholders bought shares in the companies, the government would then receive a large cash loan.

The famous East India Company was one such enterprise; the South Sea Company was another. It was given a monopoly on British trade with South America. Rampant speculation developed in South

Sea shares, fed by the apparent success of a similar scheme in France (the Mississippi enterprise) and overblown promises of profits.

A rash of similar enterprises, called "bubbles" at the time, appeared. But in 1720 South Sea stockholders began to sell and financial collapse and scandal ensued. Robert Walpole, a long-time critic of the South Sea scheme, became principal minister to the king. Parliament passed "the Bubble Act" to limit such activities and Walpole's efforts preserved the credit of the British government.

In France the results were more dire. The monarchy's inability to solve the country's financial problems helped bring on the French Revolution.

*An Encyclopedia of World History* calls the bubble "an introduction to modern speculative finance."

"Bubble" continues to describe, aptly, the frenzy of stock speculation which drives prices beyond their rational value —and ends in collapse when the bubble bursts.

Not surprisingly, the term comes up in connection with contemporary financial wheeling and dealing. The term in use, by Martin Lipton, as quoted in *Spy*, February 1989, on the leveraged buyout craze on Wall Street:

> " 'Our nation is blindly rushing to the precipice. As with tulip bulbs [and] South Sea bubbles . . . the denouement will be a crash.' That's Marty Lipton talking—Marty Lipton, the best-known LBO [see **leveraged buyout**] lawyer in the world and the man who, at the very moment he was writing his jeremiad, billed Kraft $20 million or so for his two weeks of legal work on the junk-bond-financed Philip Morris takeover."

**-Speak.** A suffix attached to many words to denote a specialized or particular way of speaking. It is drawn from George Orwell's *1984*. [See **Orwellian**.] In the totalitarian society of Orwell's novel, there are two languages, Oldspeak and Newspeak. Oldspeak is English as we know it; Newspeak is the horrifying new language of dictatorship, which erases history and meaning in words and recreates an ugly, clumsy language that serves the interest of the state.

The term in use, by Gerald F. Seib, *The Wall Street Journal*, June 21, 1989:

> "Thus are the inquiring minds of foreign correspondents taxed these days as they try to interpret Bushspeak for their readers. Far more than other world leaders, American politicians sprinkle their language with slang. And the slangiest is Mr. Bush, who speaks in free-form Americanese, filled with pop-culture colloquialisms and Texas vernacularisms."

And from *The Economist*, July 29, 1989, on competing American and Canadian gold coins:

> "Although the Eagle and the Maple Leaf contain the same amount of gold, the Eagle is padded with more alloys. It is 22-carat—22 parts gold out of a possible 24—while the Maple Leaf is 99.99% pure gold or 'four-nines' in goldspeak."

**Spear Carrier.** Someone with a small, non-distinct role to play, in life or on stage.

In the theater the name is applied to those who, if they don't literally carry spears as part of an army, are the servants, onlookers, anonymous crowds, mobs, pall-bearers, etc. who become part of the background. The term has carried over from the theater to describe loyal foot soldiers in a cause, the humble workers who can be counted on to do the job.

The term in use by Vice President Dan Quayle, as quoted in *The New Republic*, February 6, 1989:

> "Quayle insists he won't be the right's 'spear carrier' in the White House, but he's spent much of his time since the election conferring with nearly every conservative figure in Washington."

Another example, from A.J. Langruth, reviewing the book *Orders from France: The Americans and the French in a Revolutionary World, 1780-1820*, by Roger G. Kennedy, *The Washington Post Book World*, June 4, 1989:

". . . [H]is passion for buildings and their creators is so contagious that men like Benjamin Henry Latrobe and Joseph-Jacques Ramee come to seem like the real heroes of the epoch and **Robespierre** and Napoleon mere spear carriers."

And from the inimitable John Ehrlichman, in his testimony before the Senate Watergate committee, quoted in *The Washington Post*, July 29, 1973:

"There were quite a few spear carriers at the meeting from the White House staff and I was simply there to get information."

**Spin Control.** The efforts by aides to political candidates to influence the interpretation of events—to put their own "spin" on reporters' analyses.

It is news management, plus one. First the event takes place—or is staged—and then the political minions subtly try to influence the press to make certain that the story as reported will have a tone favorable to their employers.

The term may come from tennis, in which a ball may be hit with topspin or backspin to make the shot more difficult to return. Or maybe from throwing a Frisbee. The idea is to put the object in play in the most advantageous manner.

The term in use, by Gilbert Fuchsberg in *The Wall Street Journal*, November 29, 1989, writing on the politics of surveys that rank business schools:

"Desperate to move up a notch in future surveys, like one *U.S. News and World Report* currently is conducting among deans and corporate executives, nearly everyone is playing spin-control. Because deans are often survey participants, they lobby each other for support with letters and brochures touting the latest from their campuses."

The term has developed a variety of forms especially to describe practitioners of the art, such as spinmeister, spin doctor, and this example from *The New York Times*, October 4, 1988:

"All those Highly Informed television reporters are torn with grief. All those eager campaign analysts, all those expert columnists covering the political campaigns, all those political consultants who appear with Bryant and Ted and Peter and Tom—all are deeply distressed.

"The reason? The news that the vice-presidential debate on the major networks . . . will be followed immediately by regular programs, with no political discussion. So there will not be the normal half-hour 'spin' by all the experts who tell all of us unenlightened viewers who won and who lost. . . .

" 'This is clearly an outrage, the end of Western civilization,' wailed John Buckley, a Republican political consultant and master spinner."

**Star Chamber.** A proceeding notable for its arbitrary, cruel and secret nature; the place you'd expect a kangaroo court to sit in.

In English law, the Star Chamber was a notorious court that took its name from the gilt stars decorating the ceiling of its meeting room in the Palace of Westminster in London.

The court was less bound by formal procedure than other courts. It required no juries for indictment or verdict and could act on individual complaints by hauling the accused in to testify under oath.

Opposition arose to such arbitrary use of power in the 17th century during the long struggle between Charles I and Puritan forces in Parliament. For example, an attack by radical Puritan pamphleteer William Prynne on women actors as "notorious whores" was interpreted as aimed at the king's theatrically-inclined queen. (Prynne also objected to mixed dancing and face makeup and long hair on men.) The Court of Star Chamber sentenced Prynne to imprisonment for life, expulsion from the legal profession, an enormous fine, the pillory, and the "cropping" of his ears. For all that, Prynne continued agitating from his cell and three years later the court had his face branded and the rest of his ears sliced off.

Such actions aroused Parliament and the Star Chamber was abolished in 1641. Prynne and other political prisoners were freed. King

Charles lost his war with Parliament and was tried in 1649 by a high court of 67 members of the House of Commons—a tribunal as arbitrary as the Star Chamber. The king was sentenced to death and beheaded within three days.

To finish with prickly-natured William Prynne: he grew his hair long to cover the scars from his lost ears, quarreled with moderate and radical Puritans and was imprisoned for three years for refusing to pay taxes. He came to support restoration of the monarchy and was rewarded by King Charles II with a position as keeper of the records in the Tower of London. He lived, comfortably, for nine years into the reign of Charles II, a period known for its bawdy theatricals, sexual license and face makeup and long hair on men.

The term in use, by *The Wall Street Journal*, March 22, 1989, in an editorial attacking the aggressive investigatory style of Rep. John Dingell (D-Mich.), the chairman of the House Energy and Commerce Committee:

> ". . . he also asserted that the power of congressional investigations makes the House of Representatives the 'grand jury to the nation.' Mr. Dingell's idea of what constitutes the legitimate use of state power suggests the Star Chamber may be closer to reality."

**Stockholm Syndrome.** The phenomenon in which a hostage becomes sympathetic to his captor.

Psychologists say it is an automatic and unconscious defense mechanism for hostages to develop a sympathetic relationship with those who hold them, resulting from their total dependence on their captors and from extreme fear. The reverse sometimes occurs, too: hostage-takers become emotionally attached to their prisoners.

The term takes its name from an incident in Stockholm, Sweden. On August 23, 1973, four employees of the Sveriges Kreditbank were taken hostage in the bank's vault by a gunman, Jan-Erik Olsson, a 32-year-old thief, burglar and prison escapee who was later joined by his former cellmate. The hostages were held for 131 hours. After their release, it was found that the victims had come to fear the police more than their captors. The hostages had feelings of gratitude that their captors had "given their lives back," and after the incident visited the former captors in prison. One female hostage even married one of the hostage-takers.

The term is used figuratively when someone changes sympathies or moves to a friendlier position as a result of contact with those who would normally be considered to be adversaries.

The term in use, by Charles Krauthammer in *The Washington Post*, January 20, 1989, on the efforts of Rita Hauser and other American Jews to make contact with the Palestine Liberation Organization:

> "Embarrassed PLO apologists are saying that Arafat's threat [to kill Palestinian moderates] was never made. Rita Hauser, who gives new meaning to the term 'Stockholm syndrome,' made that denial in the comfort of a Washington TV studio."

**Sturm und Drang.** (SHTURM oond DRAHNG) in German: literally, storm and struggle. It's the name of a German literary movement in the late 18th century, a forerunner to Romanticism, characterized by extravagant drama, passionate emotion, extreme nationalism and opposition to established forms of society and thought. Thus it represented a rebellion against the rationalism of the **Enlightenment.** S&D writers include Goethe and Schiller.

Today, it suggests scenes heavy with emotion.

The term in use, in Nan Robertson's "On Stage" column in *The New York Times*, July 29, 1988, discussing a musical comedy about ex-spouses jailed for nonpayment of alimony, entitled "Welcome to the Club", by Cy Coleman and A.E. Hotchner:

> ". . . the comic Sturm und Drang between her and her husband is a lot of the motor that drives the play,' Mr. Coleman said."

Another example, from Jonathan Alter, writing in *Newsweek*, October 16, 1989:

> "Most of the current *Sturm und Drang* [at NBC] concerns the 'Today' show, which can trace its family problems back

to the leak last March of Bryant Gumbel's famous memo on how to improve the show."

Finally, from an ad for the Audi V-8 Quattro, quoting *Road and Track*, appearing in *The Wall Street Journal*, December 14, 1989:

"Sure, a Jaguar is lovely, and a Lexus or Infiniti is trendy. But when it comes to your cut-and-thrust, Sturm-und-Drang family sedan, only a sturdy Bavarian or sinewy Schwabian will do."

**Sui Generis.** (SOO-ee JEN-er-ihs) Latin, meaning in its own class, the only one of its kind.

The term in use, from a Richard Cohen column in *The Washington Post* of July 21, 1988:

"Dukakis even shuns the label 'liberal' and once rebuked an aide for calling him a reformer. He considers himself sui generis, a politician with no antecedents except the home-town boy who first interested him in politics: John F. Kennedy."

**Sulk Like Achilles in His Tent.** To nurse a grievance and refuse to take part in something important because of a personal annoyance.

This comes from the *Iliad*, the story of the Trojan War. It wasn't his vulnerable heel that caused the Greek superhero to retreat to his tent, but a quarrel over a girl. He and Agamemnon, king of Mycenae and one of the leaders of the Greek expedition against Troy, fought over a slave girl and **Achilles**, in a fit of pique, withdrew from the fighting. The Greeks suffered serious reverses as a result.

The term in use, by Barbara Tuchman in *The Proud Tower*, describing the predominance of belligerent nationalism in imperial Germany at the beginning of the 20th century:

"The other Germany, the Germany of intellect and sentiment, the liberal Germany which lost in 1848 and never tried again, had withdrawn from the arena, content to despise militarism and materialism and sulk in a tent of superior spiritual values."

337

Another example, from David Falkner, writing in *The New York Times*, May 22, 1989 on difficulties experienced by Latin American baseball players in the United States:

> "For more than a year after that, Valenzuela, an enormously proud man from Mexico, was reluctant to speak English. He declined all interviews with the English-speaking news media; he turned an impassive face to a public already swept up in 'Fernando-mania,' and he cast a wary eye around the clubhouse.
>
> "But what might have turned into an Achillean sulk turned out to be a relatively minor incident on an ascending slope of acculturation that some, but not all, Latin American ballplayers in the United States successfully negotiate."

**Svengali.** Someone who exerts tremendous power over another through force of personality or will.

The term comes from a character in George DuMaurier's 1894 novel *Trilby*. Trilby was a beautiful woman who fell under the power of the musician Svengali, a sinister fellow who used hypnosis to turn her into a great singer.

The term in use by *The New York Times*, October 27, 1988:

> "Mrs. Nussbaum, a former editor of children's books, was described as afraid of confronting Mr. Steinberg, whom she said exercised a Svengali-like power over her."

Another example, from Alyn Brodsky's review of *If This Was Happiness: A Biography of Rita Hayworth*, by Barbara Leaming, *The Miami Herald*, February 4, 1990:

> "Rita's fourth marriage, and by far her most self-destructive relationship, was to crooner Dick Haymes—'Mr. Evil,' as he was known. . . . This incredibly loathsome **lounge lizard** almost destroyed her career, as well as her reputation, before she managed to break his Svengali-like hold."

**Sword of Damocles.** (DAM-uh-kleez) A looming threat to one's existence, especially when the danger is forestalled only by fragile protection.

In a Greek legend, Damocles was a hanger-on of Dionysius, real-life ruler of the city-state of Syracuse. According to the story, the ruler grew tired of the constant flattery, and invited Damocles to a great banquet where he was seated under a sword hanging by a single thread or hair. Damocles was too terrified to move as Dionysius demonstrated to him that rulers and others holding power faced danger while enjoying glory.

The term in use, by President John F. Kennedy in a speech to the United Nations General Assembly, September 25, 1963:

> "Today, every inhabitant of this planet must contemplate the day when this planet may no longer be habitable. Every man, woman and child lives under a nuclear sword of Damocles, hanging by the slenderest of threads, capable of being cut at any moment by accident or miscalculation or by madness. The weapons of war must be abolished before they abolish us."

And by economist Alan Sinai, quoted in *The Washington Post*, October 30, 1988:

> "But, Sinai said, 'the legacies of deficits and debt hang like a sword of Damocles over the financial markets and the economy.'"

339

# T

**Take to the Woodshed.** See Woodshed, Take to the.

**Talmudic, Talmudistic.** Labored, overdone, perhaps excessively solemn analysis; hair-splitting.

It comes from the Hebrew *Talmud*, which means "teaching" or "instruction" but is a vast compilation of Jewish oral law, a compendium of debate and commentary (and commentary on commentary on commentary) by scholars who have exhaustively studied and interpreted the Torah (the first five books of the Bible).

The *Talmud* fills 63 books and goes back more than a thousand years. Leo Rosten says in *The Joys of Yiddish*, "The *Talmud* embraces everything from theology to contracts, cosmology to cosmetics, jurisprudence to etiquette, criminal law to diet, delusions and drinking. . . . It illustrates the ways in which Biblical passages can be interpreted, argued over, and reinterpreted. For over the sprawling terrain of the *Talmud* disagreements rage, views clash, arguments are marshaled, advanced, withdrawn. (The effect on the young Jews who studied *Talmud* was to encourage questioning, arguing, refinements of distinction and analysis.)"

To be precise, *The Oxford English Dictionary* says "Talmudic" means "pertaining to the *Talmud*." A "Talmudist" is a Talmudic scholar and one who spends "a good deal of time and intellect in dialectical taffy-pulls," as Rosten puts it. Thus "Talmudistic" is the proper form to suggest something is intricate, solemn or pedantic. However, Talmudic seems to be in more general circulation.

The term in use, in a *Washington Post* article of December 22, 1986, discussing the jokes arising out of disclosures about the Iran-contra affair:

> "Washington wag Christopher J. Mathews, former top aide
> to Tip O'Neill and now president of the Government Re-
> search Corp., said yesterday that in Washington itself, peo-

ple are trying to keep straight faces about the scandal, but that occasionally a glimmer of ribaldry breaks through.

" 'I call it Deep Gloat,' Mathews said. 'That's what the Democrats are feeling about this. Everyone is being very Talmudic and depressed on the surface. I say, "Come on, it's dynamite!" We're seeing the same Reagan m.o. [see **Modus Operandi**] for five years, but this time he finally got caught.' "

**Tammany, Tammany Hall.** (TAM-uh-nee) The name for the headquarters (and for the organization itself) of the Democratic Party in New York City; history has made its name synonymous with corrupt machine politics.

But things started out more hopefully than that. The organization was founded in 1789, one of many such groups established to champion democracy and oppose what was seen as a resurgence of aristocratic tendencies. Tammany (probably a corruption of "Tamenend") was a 17th century chief of the Delaware Indians noted for his wisdom, and "St. Tammany" was adopted as the name of anti-British groups before the revolution to ridicule loyalist societies named for saints. Most of these groups died out, but "Tammany Society, No. 1" was converted into a political machine by Aaron Burr and played a role in Jefferson's election as president in 1800.

Tammany Hall became identified with graft and corruption later in the 19th century, with the activities of the Tweed Ring and subsequent political crooks. Today Tammany Hall remains the most famous of urban political machines, and its name is a byword for corrupt politics.

The term in use, by James Ring Adams in *The American Spectator*, March 1989:

> "The 'D-triple-C' [Democratic Congressional Campaign Committee] was the personal creation and nationwide Tammany of California Congressman Tony Coelho, who has parlayed his fund-raising prowess into the third-ranking position in the House of Representative's [sic] Democratic hierarchy."

In use again, by Robert Kagan, in *The New Republic*, June 12, 1989:

> "The Nicaraguan government's monopoly on power is an even more serious problem today than it was ten years ago. Somoza's Liberal party, corrupt and domineering though it may have been, could never compete with the modern Sandinista party, which is more skilled in politics, mobilization, and the exercise of power than Somoza and his Tammany Hall-style cronies."

**Tar Baby.** A problem you can't get rid of; no matter what you do to escape, it sticks.

From Joel Chandler Harris' famous *Uncle Remus* children's stories, the tar baby is a doll covered with tar. Brer Rabbit comes by and speaks to it, but the tar baby doesn't answer; Brer Rabbit gets angry and hits the tar baby, which sticks to him. The more Brer Rabbit struggles to get free, the tighter the tar baby sticks.

The term in use, from *The Washington Post*, June 21, 1988, summarizing an article in the *Ripon Forum*, a publication of the moderate Republican Ripon Society:

> "And the Ripon Society chairman, Rep. Jim Leach of Iowa, suggests how [George] Bush can rid himself of the Iran-contra tar baby."

And by Robert Hunter of the Center for Strategic and International Studies, quoted in *The New York Times*, May 11, 1989:

> "Reagan didn't have an answer to the drug issue—who does?—so he found it useful to point a finger at Noriega. . . . So Bush inherited this problem, and I salute him for his calm approach so far. He's smart to try not to get himself stuck to this tar baby."

**Teapot Dome.** One of the most celebrated government scandals in American history, whose name became a shorthand term for flagrant cases of government corruption. It also served as something of a measuring stick; newspaper writers used to like to say things like "the worst scandal since Teapot Dome." Watergate came along, but Teapot Dome still has a resonance to it.

Teapot Dome, Wyoming and Elk Hill, California are oil fields designated as reserves for the U.S. Navy. During the administration of President Warren G. Harding (1921-1923), Interior Secretary Albert B. Fall had jurisdiction over these reserves transferred to his department. He then secretly leased them to private oil companies, allowing them to take oil out of U.S. reserves. The executives of the oil companies showed their appreciation by paying Fall hundreds of thousands of dollars in gratuities.

The leases weren't secret for long, and a Senate committee and special commission investigated. Fall ultimately was convicted of bribery. He was the first, but not last, Cabinet officer to be sent to prison.

The term in use, by Congressman James Leach, discussing the contemporary savings and loan scandal, quoted in *Time*, June 12, 1989:

> "House Banking Committee member Jim Leach, an Iowa Republican who refuses to take PAC money, believes this may be the disgrace that brings down the current congressional establishment. 'We're looking at an eleven-figure fraud story that's bigger than Teapot Dome,' he says."

**Tectonic Plates.** A geological term for the huge slabs that make up the earth's crust. There are thought to be twelve or more huge plates that actually drift on the partially molten rock far below the surface of the earth. The shifting, parting or scraping together of these plates causes the formation of mountains and volcanoes and such events as earthquakes. The expression has come into metaphorical use to describe profound changes.

The term in use, by columnist David R. Gergen, *The Los Angeles Times*, June 18, 1989:

> "With the tectonic plates shifting in geopolitics, Bush might be tempted to spend his time in the diplomatic arena."

Another example, from William Safire, *The New York Times*, September 25, 1989:

"The tectonic plates that underlie the American way of living are making loud, grinding noises. Something big is going on in the real America that most of us who live inside urban beltways are missing: proximity is losing its power."

**Tet, Tet Offensive.** A Vietnamese word, it marks the start of the lunar new year, a major holiday in Asia. Tet entered the American lexicon in 1968, and it since has been employed to describe a sudden and demoralizing assault that destroys resolve—a psychological defeat.

The event that gave birth to the American usage began at 3 a.m. on January 31, 1968, when Vietcong guerrillas and North Vietnamese attacked more than 100 military bases and civilian centers in South Vietnam, including the imperial capital of Hue. One assault team even managed to penetrate the U.S. embassy compound in Saigon.

Although the Tet offensive was repelled and ended in a military defeat for the communists, the attack had a devastating psychological effect in the United States. Anti-war feelings had been growing, and the offensive seemed to belie assurances Americans had received from their government that the war was being won. Politically, the scope of the war effort could no longer be maintained. In March, President Lyndon Johnson announced that he would not seek reelection, and took steps to open negotiations with the North Vietnamese.

An example, by Reagan Administration national security advisor Robert McFarlane, as quoted in *The Washington Post*, May 14, 1984:

"Cuba has decided to roughly double the guerrilla force in El Salvador in hopes of mounting a 'Tet-like' offensive there during the U.S. presidential race this fall, national security advisor Robert C. McFarlane charged yesterday."

**Theater of the Absurd.** A scene or set of circumstances that are crazy, illogical—or absurd.

It is from an avante-garde theatrical movement that developed after

World War II. While its playwrights employed timeless themes such as human reaction to death, loneliness and freedom, it presented them in shocking, outrageous and nonsensical ways. The absurdity of the human condition and the futility of trying to cope with it is revealed. Chief dramatists of the movement are Samuel Beckett (*Waiting for Godot*), Jean Genet (*The Maids, The Balcony, The Blacks*) and Eugene Ionesco (*The Bald Soprano*) and Edward Albee (*The Zoo Story*).

The term in use, by Paul Johnson in his 1977 book, *Enemies of Society*:

> "In a world where real distinctions are being deliberately eroded or inverted by pseudo-science, where reason is derided, knowledge assassinated and the most fundamental principles of civilization assaulted, we must not be surprised to find that the United Nations, the fount of international authority—such as it is—should have become the World Theatre of the Absurd, a global madhouse where lunatic falsehood reigns and the voices of the sane can scarcely be heard above the revolutionary and racist din."

Another example, from Elizabeth Bumiller, *The Washington Post*, October 24, 1989:

> "Former president Ronald Reagan is here in the world's richest city [Tokyo] this week, raising money from the Japanese for his presidential library as he earns a $2 million fee, and just in case anyone is nostalgic for Reagan-era extravagance and the theater of the absurd between the former president and the press—it's all back."

The term has spawned a number of similar expressions, some related to theater, some moving beyond to describe theatrical scenes in the real world. Some examples include "Theater of Cruelty," "Theater of Fact" and "Theater of the Streets." An example of the broader usage, from *Newsweek*, May 1, 1989, by Tom Mathews in a breathless profile of *Vanity Fair* editor Tina Brown:

> "She has turned her magazine and apartment into Manhattan's liveliest Theater-of-What's-Happening-Now."

345

**Thermopylae.** The site of one of history's most famous battles, marked by the courageous stand of the Spartans, vastly outnumbered by the Persians.

Thermopylae is a pass between the cliffs of Mount Oeta and the Malic Gulf and was, in ancient times, an entrance into Greece from the north.

In 480 B.C., a small army under the leadership of King Leonidas of Sparta held the pass against the huge invading force (estimated at 180,000) of Xerxes, the Persian king. The Persians ultimately were able to turn the Spartans' flank, guided to a path by a traitor. Leonidas had sent most of his army to safety, but remained to hold the pass as long as possible with his celebrated band of 300 Spartans. These heroes were joined by 700 Thespians. (This conjures up an image of Leonidas recruiting 700 unemployed actors to support his stand. Not quite. They were from the city of Thespiae.)

The defenders' valiant stand has been celebrated ever since, and is commemorated in the epitaph composed by the poet Simonides:

> Go tell the Spartans, thou who passest by
> That here obedient to their laws we lie.

Heroism aside, there was some grumbling among the Greeks at the time about the celebration of Xerxes' ultimate defeat. It seems that Leonidas had sent urgent messages back to Sparta for reinforcements, which never came. Other Greek cities, particularly Athens, were not happy with Sparta's tendency toward isolationism—its unwillingness to do more than protect its own territory in the Peloponnese. Thucydides reports an Athenian comment to Spartan ambassadors: "The Mede [the Persians] had time to come from the ends of the earth to Peloponnese ere any force of yours worthy of the name went out to meet him."

The term in use, by Robert Reno in *Newsday*, February 22, 1989, in a column on the federal budget deficit:

> "But you'd think Bush was defending the pass at Thermopylae. You'd think he was saving us from some hideous fate, from an invasion of carnivorous green slugs, from the toad that ate Nebraska. And all because he figured that a

plea not to increase taxes to adequate levels was a pretty neat way to get elected."

**Thin Red Line.** A thin and valiant line of defense.

The term was probably coined by William Howard Russell of the *Times* of London, one of the world's first war correspondents. He applied it to the brave—and successful—stand made by the 93rd Highlanders against a charge by Russian cavalry in the battle of Balaclava during the Crimean War. (Twenty seconds of history: the war, from 1853-56, was between Russia and the allied powers of Turkey, England, France and Sardinia. At issue was Russian influence in the Middle East. The allies won after a long bloody siege of Sevastopol, the heavily fortified base of the Russian fleet. Balaclava was a key battle. The war is remembered for the disastrous Charge of the Light Brigade, also at Balaclava, and the nursing reforms of Florence Nightingale.)

The 93rd, an infantry regiment, was guarding a point that, if lost, would have enabled the Russians to break through to the town of Balaclava, a key British position. Col. Colin Campbell formed his lines and told his men, "There is no retreat from here! You must die where you stand!" And the reply came, "Ay, ay, Sir Colin; and needs be we'll do that."

Reporter Russell watched from a distant hill and later wrote: "The Russians charged in toward Balaclava. The ground flew beneath the horses' feet; gathering speed at every stride they dashed on towards that thin red streak tipped with steel." (Russell later changed the reference to "line," as did others who wrote about the battle.)

As the Russians approached, the Highlanders themselves showed some inclination to charge, but Campbell ordered them back: "Ninety-third! damn all that eagerness!" So they waited until the thundering ranks of horses were in range and then fired; the charge was broken and the Russians retreated in confusion. After this celebrated incident, the regiment was nicknamed "the thin red line."

Rudyard Kipling immortalized the phrase in his poem *Tommy*, a tribute to the unappreciated ordinary British soldier "Tommy Atkins":

> Then it's Tommy this, an' Tommy that,
> an' "Tommy, 'ow's yer soul?"

> But it's "Thin red line of 'eroes"
> when the drums begin to roll . . . .

A play on the phrase is in the title of a 1988 documentary-detective film, *The Thin Blue Line*, as used by a Dallas prosecuting attorney in his closing speech in the trial of a man accused of murdering a police officer: "the thin blue line of men and women who daily risk their lives by walking into the jaws of death. . . ."

America's West Point has created a phrase that's a cousin: "the long gray line." It refers to the generations of graduates of the United States Military Academy.

A play on the latter, from B. Drummond Ayres Jr., *The New York Times*, July 27, 1989, describing a bizarre incident in which Washington, D.C. police forced a group of prostitutes to walk from downtown to the city line:

> "The police snared about two dozen women, and they were ordered to fall in, single file. Then the march began, down 14th Street, through the darkened business district, past City Hall, across the Mall, on and on until, after more than a mile and a half of grumbling and stumbling, a bridge over the Potomac loomed and beyond the shores of a new jurisdiction, the Commonwealth of Virginia.
>
> "In truth, the long spangled line never made it to Virginia."

**Through a Glass, Darkly.** Having an unclear, obscured vision of reality.

It comes from the New Testament. St. Paul, writing in 1 Corinthians 13:12, explains that man's knowledge is as imperfect as the image in a mirror (in those days, not well polished and thus giving a poor reflection) compared with the knowledge men will enjoy when God's purpose is ultimately revealed. He says: "Now we see through a glass, darkly; but then face to face: now I know in part; but then I shall know even as also I am known."

The term in use, by Tom Shales in a television review in *The Washington Post*, October 25, 1988:

"That's a lot of gloom and doom for one night on one network. A look at prime-time tubal 1988 could almost be called 'Through a Glass Darkly.' "

The term played upon, by economist Paul Samuelson writing on the Watergate scandal in *Newsweek*, August 13, 1973:

"The reason why the never-ending disclosures have been so disquieting is that we begin to see, on the TV tube darkly, the face of Fascism."

**Tilting at Windmills.** Battling imaginary foes, or fighting for an ideal with little hope of victory.

From the classic 1605 novel **Don Quixote** by Miguel de Cervantes, in which a kindly man crazed from reading stories of chivalric adventures decides he should go forth and right the world's wrongs. Among Don Quixote's misadventures is an encounter with windmills, which he sees as threatening giants. Spurring his skinny nag Rocinante, he charges them with his lance, which becomes caught on the sail of one of the mills. Horse and rider are lifted off the ground and fall painfully to earth. ("Tilting," incidentally, is a medieval fight between men mounted on horses and armed with lances.)

The term in use, from a Jonathan Yardley review of the latest Judith Krantz novel in *The Washington Post*, August 3, 1988:

". . . Krantz has achieved the status of brand name, and her books sell automatically; there is nothing that we reviewers, tilting at windmills with our silly little lances, can do either to help her along to greater riches or to arrest her progress in that direction."

**Titanic.** An ocean liner whose famous disaster at sea made her name a metaphor for catastrophe.

On her maiden voyage, with 2,200 people aboard, the British ship struck an iceberg and sank in the North Atlantic on the night of April 14-15, 1912 with the loss of more than 1,500 lives. The *Titanic* was the most opulent and elegant liner in history, and was thought to be unsinkable due to its design of watertight bulkheads and a double-bottomed hull. Confidence in her seaworthiness was such that she only carried enough lifeboats to accommodate half the people on board. The disaster is one of the most haunting and riveting stories of tragedy at sea.

The calamity gave rise to the contemporary expression "rearranging the deckchairs on the *Titanic,*" that is, spending time on inconsequential details when disaster looms.

The term in use, in an article assessing local Republican chances for success in New York City, *The New York Times,* March 20, 1989:

> " 'They say that power corrupts, but the lack of power corrupts, too,' [see **Lord Acton**] said Norman Adler, a political consultant. . . . 'Young people don't want to ship out on the Titanic. You can fit all the people who worked more than 10 hours last year for the Republican Party in a small meeting room at the Plaza.' "

**Torquemada, Tomas de.** (tor-key-MAH-dah, TOH-mahs day) The first inquisitor general of the Spanish Inquisition, his name has become synonymous with cruelty and fanaticism.

The Spanish Inquisition was instituted in about 1480 in Spain and later in its European and Latin American domains, to detect and punish heretics and anyone guilty of offenses against Roman Catholic orthodoxy. (There was also a Roman or papal Inquisition established at Rome in 1542.)

The Inquisition's procedures were secret and arbitrary: the accused was surprised by a sudden summons and could be imprisoned on suspicion. The names of witnesses against the accused were withheld. Torture was allowed, including the torture of witnesses. Punishments ranged from fines to penances to imprisonment, with the most obstinate heretics handed over to the secular authorities for execution, usually by fire. [See **Auto-da-fé.**]

In Spain, the Inquisition was closely linked to the crown and used by the government to centralize its authority during the reign of Ferdinand and Isabella. In addition to eliminating potential opposition, the state seized the property of heretics, thus giving church and state a significant community of interest.

The term in use, by Alan Abelson, in *Barron's*, June 5, 1989:

"Perhaps we should have suspected long before that there was something different about the SEC [Securities and Exchange Commission]. Oh, sure, we were aware, of course, it had changed some since the days when Stanley Sporkin, a.k.a. Torquemada, was in charge of the rack and ate a broker for breakfast every morning."

Another example, from Bob Mack, *Spy*, July 1989, on William F. Buckley:

"Reagan's muddled, middle-of-the-road second term left Buckley to fill *his* syndicated column with pointless crankery—suggesting that the U.S. declare war on Cuba, complaining about a blind man trying to sail across the Atlantic, and offering the Torquemadic suggestion that AIDS carriers be tattooed on the buttocks."

**Troglodyte.** A prehistoric cave-dweller; nowadays, a recluse. Also someone with primitive or degraded ways of thinking.

The term in use, by James J. Kilpatrick, in *The Daily Oklahoman*, January 14, 1976, as quoted in *The Quintessential Dictionary* by I. Moyer Hunsberger:

"If the President [Ford] should win his party's nomination at Kansas City in August, only a handful of super-troglodytes will want to sit on their hands and sulk."

And by Doug Ireland, *The Village Voice*, January 23, 1990:

"Many in the gay community and among the HIV-infected, as well as their families and friends, gave their votes to Dinkins in the primary above all because they thought he was the only candidate who'd give New York City a compassionate health commissioner to replace that moral troglodyte, Stephen Joseph."

**Trojan Horse.** A device used to conceal a conquering force behind an innocent facade, which allows it to be insinuated behind an enemy's defenses.

It was the strategem devised by the Greeks to conquer the city of Troy, as recounted in Homer's *Odyssey* and Vergil's *Aeneid*.

After an unsuccessful 10-year fight, the Greeks came up with the ploy. They constructed a huge wooden horse, filled it with Greek warriors and left it outside the city's gates. The rest of the Greeks pretended to sail away, leaving behind Sinon, who posed as a Greek traitor and convinced the Trojans that the horse was an offering to the goddess Athena, who would reward Troy with her protection if the Trojans would only bring the horse into the city.

The Trojans were warned of possible trickery by **Cassandra** (ignored, as always) and the priest Laocoön ("I fear the Greeks even when bearing gifts"), who was inopportunely strangled by sea serpents. So the warnings did no good, the horse was brought in, and the Greeks emerged and opened the gates to admit their returning army.

The term in use, by Peruvian novelist and presidential candidate Mario Vargas Llosa, as quoted in a *Wall Street Journal* editorial, September 9, 1987:

> "Mr. Vargas Llosa has asked the government 'not to be the Trojan horse that allows communism into Peru.' "

**Trompe l'Oeil.** (TROHMP loy) A visual deception that creates an optical illusion. Literally, in French, to fool the eye.

In architecture, painting or sculpture, the technique makes the viewer see something that is not there, such as paintings on the sides of buildings giving the illusion that one can see through to scenes on the other side, or that make a room appear larger.

In a play on the term by G. B. Trudeau in his "Doonesbury" comic strip, March 16, 1989, millionaire Donald Trump gives directions for the decoration of his yacht's bathroom to artist J.J.:

> "And up on this wall, I want you to paint me a bunch of books. I really respect books, so make 'em look real—to fool people—what do you call that?"
> J.J. responds: "Trump l'oeil."
> "Right. And make 'em all best sellers."

The term in use, by Anton Furst, designer of the movie *Batman*, interviewed on National Public Radio, June 30, 1989: If the ubiquitous Batman logo looked to you like a goofy cartoon mouth with teeth rather than a bat, take comfort. It was deliberate. "It's the trompe l'oeil effect," explained Furst.

Another example, from Robert Hughes, *Time*, January 8, 1990, on an exhibit of the works of 19th-century American painter Frederic E. Church:

> "Church was an inventive showman. *Heart of the Andes*, more than 5 ft. by 9 ft., went on view in a trompe l'oeil architectural frame built, literally, like a picture window, so that one sat down on a bench and had the illusion of gazing from a Victorian living room into sublimity, complete with palms, parrots and Andean campesinos adoring a cross."

**Trouble in River City.** A light-hearted suggestion that difficulties are brewing beneath a seemingly placid surface.

The term comes from the 1957 musical comedy "The Music Man" by Meridith Willson. Con man Professor Harold Hill persuades the people of River City, Iowa that their children can be saved from delinquency only through the formation of a boys' band.

River City, a placid turn-of-the-century town, is the last place where youth is likely to go astray, but Hill warns: "Either you're closing your eyes to a situation you don't wish to acknowledge or you are not aware of the calibre of disaster—indicated by the presence of a pool table in your community." He describes the horrors to follow, as foreshadowed by certain sure warning signs: "The moment your son leaves the house, does he rebuckle his knickerbockers *below the knee?* Is there a nicotine stain on his index finger? A dime novel hidden in the corn crib? That's trouble with a capital T, and that rhymes with P, and that stands for Pool!"

The term in use by Alfred Balk, reviewing *The National Debt* by Lawrence Malkin in *The New York Times Book World*, May 3, 1987, under the headline "Trouble in River City":

> "Ronald Reagan, Mr. Malkin seems to be saying in *The National Debt*, is a modern Music Man. For the pool hall, President Reagan substitutes Communism and Big Gov-

ernment; for the brass band, a military buildup and tax reductions; for the Think System, Reaganomics. What he lacks is a Marian the librarian to provide a happy ending."

**Tumbrel** or **Tumbril.** (TUM-bril) A rough-hewn cart, one that can be tilted for dumping. Tumbrels were used during the French Revolution to carry those sentenced to death from prison to the guillotine. Ever since, the word has been used to evoke the image of those either literally or figuratively being carried to execution.

The term in use, by *The Economist*, May 6, 1989, in reporting international statistics on employment of the death penalty by different nations:

"In the three years to mid-1988 the countries in which the tumbrels rolled most tirelessly were Iran (743 executions or more), South Africa (537+), China (500+), Nigeria (439+), Somalia (150+), Saudi Arabia (140), Pakistan (115+), the United States (66) and the Soviet Union (63+)."

Another example, also from *The Economist*, July 8, 1989:

"Today's revolutionaries all want to overthrow the **ancien regime** of communism bloodlessly. Hardly any want to set the tumbrels rolling—which is just one reason that communists and noncommunists alike should be glad if they succeed."

**Tweedledum and Tweedledee.** Two characters who are so alike that a choice between them is no choice at all.

They are particularly likely to show up at election time. Inevitably two opposing candidates of similar view are going to be compared to Tweedledum and Tweedledee to underscore the assertion that scant difference exists between them.

The Tweedle boys appear as fat little identical twins in Lewis Carroll's *Through the Looking Glass*. Carroll used but did not coin the names himself; they come from a satiric verse by John Byrom

(1692-1763) mocking a quarrel between two groups of musicians whose real differences were very small. But Carroll created the memorable twins.

A play on the names and idea, by Michael Hirschorn in *Spy*, February 1989:

> "[Virginia Senator Paul] Trible didn't run for reelection, claiming that he wanted to spend more time with his family. Many suspect that he was afraid of losing. Maybe, maybe not. As it turned out, his opponent would have been former Democratic governor Chuck Robb, who took over Trible's seat a few weeks ago and is no slouch himself when it comes to thickheadedness. The campaign would have been a race between Tweedledum and Tweedledummer."

**Twist Slowly in the Wind.** The political abandonment of an aide or a subordinate who is left exposed to suffer prolonged public agonies—alone.

This is another phrase that originated in that great hatchery of colorful expressions, the Nixon-Watergate era. It was coined by John Ehrlichman, assistant to President Richard Nixon, discussing L. Patrick Gray, whose nomination to be director of the FBI was under bruising attack in the Senate during March 1973.

Ehrlichman had taped his (March 7 or 8, 1973) conversation with White House counsel John Dean. On July 26, 1973, Sen. Lowell Weicker (D.-Conn.) referred to it during Ehrlichman's appearance before the Watergate committee hearings, a transcript having been provided by Ehrlichman. The exact quote was, as published in *The Washington Post* of July 27, 1973: "Let him hang there. Well, I think we ought to let him hang there. Let him twist slowly, slowly in the wind."

The term in use, from *Time*, July 20, 1987, in "The Fall Guy Fights Back" by Ed Magnuson:

> "On the 'smoking gun' memos in which [Lt. Col. Oliver] North had outlined the diversion plans, [Senate Commit-

tee Counsel Arthur] Liman presented many documents in similar form but on far less significant topics that North had sent to Poindexter for presidential approval. . . . The implication was clear: it would be extraordinary if a proposal for the diversion, with the consequences serious enough to endanger the Reagan presidency, did not reach Ronald Reagan's desk. Unless, of course, North's foxy superiors had really intended to let the eager, can-do Marine twist slowly in the wind."

Another example, from Robert L. Beisner's review of the memoirs of national security expert Paul Nitze, *The Washington Post*, October 22, 1989:

"Nitze should have risked more candor about his most recent history—the daring story of a mid-level bureaucrat trying to outmaneuver Reagan himself in a design to exchange the vision of an Astrodome strategic defense system for sharp cuts in Soviet offensive missiles. Robert McFarlane and, later, [Secretary of State] Shultz quietly cheered Nitze's bid, but both had to disguise their support and both were ready to leave him twisting in the wind at a moment's notice."

**Type A.** From medicine, a behavior pattern characterized by tenseness, impatience and competitive drive, with elements of anger, hostility and aggression. The term was coined in 1972 by American cardiologists Meyer Friedman and Roy Rosenman, who found, in some people, a link between those traits and a tendency to develop coronary heart disease. The term is used to describe both the type of behavior and an individual with these characteristics, and is sometimes contrasted with the more easygoing and placid "type B."

Studies continue to appear on the subject, with revisionist views coming to the fore, e.g., a certain amount of stress is good for you; a competitive drive is o.k., it's the anger that gets you, etc.

The term in use, by Rep. Thomas A. Foley, as the about-to-be

Speaker of the House was quoted in *The Washington Post*, June 1, 1989:

> "While many congressmen are aggressive Type A personalities, Foley says, and focus on a particular issue with great intensity, he sees himself as the Type B mediator who tries 'to reconcile the clash of ideas.'"

# U

**Über.** (OO-ber) A German prefix meaning the ultimate, super, as in Übermensch, or superman.

The term in use, by Alessandra Stanley in *The New Republic*, December 12, 1988, commenting on George Bush's image:

> ". . . in 1988 Bush's early ads borrowed heavily from Reagan and played on the same themes. That's because Bush aides thought they had to sell a product nobody but his mother would buy, George Bush, Uber-prep."

And William Safire, *The New York Times*, November 13, 1989, on a reunited Germany:

> "Mr. Gorbachev doesn't seem to be worried about the coming Uberpower. He probably figures that's for the next Soviet dictator; his role in Russian history is to insure the survival of the state today."

**Ugly American.** The boorish Yankee abroad.

The term comes from *The Ugly American*, a novel by William J. Lederer and Eugene Burdick, and is used to describe any overbearing American being offensive in a foreign country. In the book, however, the particular ugly American was so called because of his appearance but, in fact, was a compassionate American who went into rural areas and wooed Asian peasants away from communism. Since the theme of the novel was the alienation caused by the ignorance, greed and arrogance of Americans in foreign places, the term has come to describe people who exhibit such qualities. And not only Americans have earned the title. The ability to be an obnoxious visitor in a foreign land may be universal.

The term in use, by Costa Rican President Oscar Arias in an interview with Tad Szulc in *Parade* magazine, August 28, 1988:

"If I had to advise Washington on its policy in Latin America, I'd say, 'Please be nice—please stop being the ugly American.' "

And in use by sportswriter Tony Kornheiser, describing Korean anger over the behavior of American fans and athletes at the 1988 Olympic games in Seoul in *The Washington Post*, October 1, 1988:

"It hasn't deterred some Americans from practicing what is construed—particularly by the contentious European press—as Ugly Americanism. Many Americans treat the Olympics like their own private tour group. . . . This behavior is beyond patriotism. It's about rudeness and the automatic right of way that Americans consider their birthright as they travel the world in a clumsy exuberance that other cultures take for bullying."

And even in the comics—in "Mary Worth" on September 30, 1988. In that day's episode, the professor's wife employs the adjectival form to tell him to dress for dinner on their vacation cruise (on which they are accompanied by perpetual freeloader Mary):

"Mary and I refuse to waste our best gowns on a typical ugly-American tourist!"

Finally, from *Spy*, July 1989, by George Kalogerakis:

". . . [A] survey of New Yorkers who work at jobs with a high risk of tourist contact suggests that Europeans have co-opted our notorious traveling comportment along with our jeans and television shows. The Ugly European is at large."

**Ur-.** (oor) A prefix, from German, added to nouns, to mean first, original, very old or primitive.

The term in use, by Martin Amis, *The Moronic Inferno*, in an essay on the revival of *Vanity Fair* magazine:

> "Its name is *Vanity Fair,* and, yes, it is a resuscitation of the spangled original, the ur-glossy that served cafe society from 1914 to 1936."

# V

**Valhalla.** (val-HAL-uh) In Nordic mythology, it's the banqueting-hall of heroes in Asgard, the Scandinavian equivalent of Mount Olympus for the Greek gods. A place in Valhalla is the reward for warriors slain in battle. These heroes go out every day and fight each other for fun, then return to Valhalla in the evenings, their wounds magically healed, to feast mightily on boar and quaff mead by the gallon. The term is used today, often ironically, to describe the reward or place of honor for heroic (or very anti-heroic) warriors or combatants.

The term in use, by Rupert Christiansen in *Vanity Fair*, May 1989, describing the battle over the directorship of the Opera Bastille of Paris, playing full blast on the Nordic mythology themes of Wagnerian opera:

> "Five months later the **Wagnerian** context for this meeting had come to seem all too appropriate. Valhalla, in the shape of a $350 million opera house, stood awaiting its finishing touches, but Daniel Barenboim was barred from crossing the rainbow bridge that led to its portals. From the wings, in apocalyptic unison, a chorus of front pages in Paris, London and New York rallied to his cause."

**Vast Wasteland.** A desolate, unproductive environment.

Newton Minow, chairman of the Federal Communications Commission in the Kennedy Administration, coined the term in a speech to the National Association of Broadcasters in 1961 to describe what he considered the lowest-common-denominator offerings of television programming. The striking phrase moved into the language and is still used to describe television's shortcomings as well as other failures of human effort.

The term in use by Lester Bernstein in *The New York Times*

*Magazine,* February 26, 1989, writing on the business empire of Time, Inc.:

> "Whether or not it can intimidate an acquirer, the attempt to clothe Time Inc.'s huge television franchises in public-service virtue recalls the noble blather with which the networks once defended the vast wasteland of TV. Even for the magazine group, invoking journalistic sanctity as a takeover refuge has a self-serving ring."

**Vet.** A verb meaning to check out, examine closely for deficiencies. A favorite term of the bureaucracy, as in "the document was thoroughly vetted," or to refer to security checks on people who are to be in posts requiring loyalty, discretion and freedom from questionable habits. Newspaper, magazine and book publishers will sometimes have lawyers vet sensitive writings to detect potentially libelous material.

The term comes from the shortening and transforming of "veterinarian" into a verb. Veterinarian became vet and the physical examination of an animal by a vet ultimately became known as vetting.

The term in early use, by Rudyard Kipling in *Traffic and Discoveries* (1904):

> "These are our crowd. . . . They've been vetted, an' we're putting 'em through their paces."

In use again, by *The Economist,* March 4, 1989, describing a benign trend in the behavior of British soccer fans—waving huge inflatable toys:

> "Bananas. Giant ones—six feet tall. Inflatable. Also giant haddocks, sharks, dolphins, women, pink panthers, skeletons, black puddings—Mr. Patrick Barclay, the *Independent's* chief football writer, has seen even an inflatable swimming pool waved aloft.
>
> "This fun, which has made the season one of the most enjoyable for years, is brought to you by the same football fans whose behaviour is so awful that the government is passing a law to vet them. A bill now in the House of Lords

is meant to ensure that all fans have identity cards before they are allowed to enter a football ground."

**Volte-face.** (volt fahs) A reversal of opinion, a complete turnaround, the rejection of a previously held point of view. In French, it means to turn face.

The term in use, by Geoffrey Wheatcroft in *The New Republic*, September 12-19, 1988, reviewing two books by Irish lecturer/writer/parliamentarian/diplomat/historian Conor Cruise O'Brien:

"As he has worked out his view of life in books and articles he has certainly changed his mind, come to see that some things are not as they once seemed. But I do not think that he has performed (unlike many others you could name) a grotesque volte face."

Another example, from John Kenyon's review of Paula Backsheider's biography of 18th-century English writer Daniel Defoe, *The Washington Post Book World*, December 10, 1989:

". . . Defoe's pen was really at the service of anyone who would pay him. He was quite capable of denouncing in print pamphlets he had written himself, and between Sept. 13 and Oct. 9, 1711, he performed one of the most remarkable volte-faces in the history of journalism on the need for peace with France (once he found his paymaster Harley was behind it)."

# W

**Wagnerian.** (vahg-NIHR-ee-uhn) Of, pertaining to or in the style of the works of German composer Richard Wagner (1813-1883). Wagner was notable for his megalomania and extreme German nationalism; his operas (or music dramas, as he called them) were generally based on Norse and Teutonic mythology. His most famous works include *The Flying Dutchman, Tannhäuser, Lohengrin, Tristan and Isolde* and the four-part *Der Ring des Nibelungen.*

He introduced innovations to opera, including the **Leitmotiv**, a significant recurring theme in a work; he also wrote operas composed of continuous music, rather than the older style of aria and recitation.

The adjective, sometimes used in a jocular fashion, suggests something similar to the grandiose Teutonic themes of the composer, and sometimes a comic image of the stout opera diva, complete with spear and horned helmet, as in the example below.

The term in use, by Alan Jay Lerner, in his lyrics for *My Fair Lady* (1956), in which Professor Henry Higgins sings of the dangers of letting a woman in your life: "She'll have a large Wagnerian mother, with a voice that shatters glass!"

Another example, from Stephen Holden in *The New York Times,* July 16, 1989, on developments in music for film soundtracks:

> "Jack Nicholson's fiendish Joker and Michael Keaton's Caped Crusader aren't the only forces that collide in the smash-hit movie 'Batman.' The film's noisy soundtrack presents a pitched battle between the two strains of music that have accompanied movies since the dawn of the sound era: one derived from high culture, the other from pop. The majority of the film's score is loud, post-Wagnerian action music composed by Danny Elfman. Sly, subterranean funk songs by Prince make up the rest."

**Walter Mitty.** A quiet, milquetoasty, retiring fellow who daydreams of performing brave and heroic feats. The fantasies are Mittyesque; the adjective describing Mittylike behavior is Mittyish.

The term comes from the name of a character created by James Thurber in his famous 1939 short story, "The Secret Life of Walter Mitty." The story was made into a movie in 1947, with Danny Kaye playing Walter.

The term in use, by A. M. Rosenthal, *The New York Times*, October 27, 1989:

> "Walter Mitty and I have this dream. Someday Jesse Jackson will call up and say, 'Abe, you are absolutely right: Arafat is no good, the Middle East problem is caused by Arab rejectionism of Israel, left-wing economics is musty, I renounce Farrakhan, and I want to be President of the United States, not the third world.' "

**Waterloo.** The scene of Napoleon's downfall. Thus, "to meet one's Waterloo" is to suffer a staggering setback, a disastrous defeat.

Napoleon had slipped out of exile in March 1815, marched in triumph to Paris and reestablished his rule. The European allies who had defeated and exiled him the year before dropped their own quarrels and rushed their armies into position. The Duke of Wellington concentrated his army of British, Prussian, Dutch and Belgian forces at Brussels.

Not only the army arrived in Brussels: the troops were followed by wives, dependents and thrill-seeking socialites. As Thackeray describes it in his novel, *Vanity Fair,* "There never was, since the days of Darius, such a brilliant train of camp-followers as hung round the Duke of Wellington's army in the Low Countries, in 1815; and led it dancing and feasting, as it were, up to the very brink of battle." Indeed, the night before the battle, Wellington and his officers attended a glittering ball given by the Duchess of Richmond; some of them marched to the battle in their dancing-shoes.

Seeking to defeat his enemies before they could join forces, Napoleon had crossed swiftly into Belgium on June 14. He forced the

Prussian troops to fall back, and on June 17 reached Wellington's lines at Waterloo, a village nine miles from Brussels. The following day, Napoleon made a critical error when he waited through the morning for the ground to dry out after a night of torrential rain before launching his attack. The delay enabled the Prussian army of Marshal Blücher to arrive just in time to reinforce Wellington and tip the balance in favor of the allies.

The French defeat was total. Napoleon fled but was forced to surrender and was sent into exile again—this time to a more stern and isolated venue, the island of St. Helena in the south Atlantic. He died there in 1821.

The term in use, by *The Washington Post* in a November 27, 1988 headline:

> "The Sad, Strange Mind of Col. North: An NSC Colleague Explains Why Ollie Met His Waterloo"

Another example, from Megan Rosenfeld, *The Washington Post*, June 18, 1989, in an article about spas:

> "What I had was a bad case of the My Second Child is 14 Months Old and I Still Can't Fit Into My Old Clothes Blues. . . .
>
> "That, plus the desire for a short break from the adorable children who had brought me to this plump Waterloo—not to mention the husband who, when losing weight is mentioned, says 'What's the big deal? Just stop eating'—led me to think of going to a spa."

**Waving the Bloody Shirt.** Inflammatory rhetoric, usually political in nature, that exploits public prejudice and resentment. The phrase was born in the 19th century when it was applied to Republicans who kept alive Civil War bitterness by blaming the Democratic party for the tragic struggle. The tactic caused such moderate Republicans as Horace Greeley to break with the GOP.

The term in use, by political analyst Kevin Phillips, writing in the *Los Angeles Times*, November 13, 1988:

> "In a sense, the harsh Bush attack ads that hit Dukakis on 'flags and furloughs' were the 1988 equivalent of the 'wav-

ing the bloody shirt' rhetoric used by late 19th century Republicans to keep old Civil War GOP loyalties throbbing."

And a whimsical application from Sam Howe Verhoek, *The New York Times*, May 19, 1988:

"Nobody is waving a bloody shirt in this year's campaign for the board of directors at Co-op City, but mysterious stains in the laundry are a key rallying point."

**Weltanschauung.** (VELT-ahn-show-uhng) A German word meaning a world view, a philosophical conception of the world.

The term in use, by Tom Wolfe, in *Radical Chic and Mau-Mauing the Flak-Catchers*, on publicity about a fundraising party for the Black Panthers given by famed composer and conductor Leonard Bernstein and his wife:

"What the Bernsteins probably did not realize at first was that the story was going out on *The New York Times* News Service wires. In other cities throughout the United States and Europe it was played on page one, typically, to an international chorus of horse laughs or nausea, depending on one's *Weltanschauung*. The English, particularly, milked the story for all it was worth and seemed to derive one of the great cackles of the year from it."

**Whip the Offending Adam, To.** To knock the sin out of someone; to administer a drubbing.

Adam, as the first man, was the first sinner—thus the "offending Adam."

Shakespeare coined the phrase in *Henry V* in describing the transformation of rascally Prince Hal into virtuous monarch:

The breath no sooner left his father's body
But that his wildness, mortified in him,
Seemed to die too; like an angel, came
and whipped the offending Adam out of him,

Leaving his body as a paradise
T' envelop and contain celestial spirits.

The term in use, by Leonore Fleischer in her "Talk of the Trade" column in *Publishers Weekly*, June 9, 1989:

"Birch Lane Press will be publishing Stephen Hanks's *The Game That Changed Pro Football* in September. The game of the title is the 1969 Superbowl III, in which, sparked by star quarterback Joe Namath, the New York Jets of the upstart American Football League whipped the offending Adam (16–7) out of the Baltimore Colts, leaders of the super-heavy National Football League."

**White-bread.** Slang adjective meaning conventional, square, bland, Middle American.

The term in use, by Chuck Conconi in "Personalities," *The Washington Post*, March 23, 1989:

"Drape the juke box in black, and bronze the old saddle shoes. Dick Clark, America's oldest teen-ager, is giving up 'American Bandstand' after 33 years. The white-bread emcee of television's longest-running variety program, the man even your parents loved, has decided it's time to quit next year."

Another example, from Timothy Noah, *The New Republic*, December 25, 1989:

"We live in a country where two boys named Michael Eisner and Jeffrey Katzenberg can grow up to run one of America's great white-bread institutions, the Walt Disney studios. Maybe someday a Spike Lee can attain that dream too."

**White Man's Burden.** As used by Rudyard Kipling in an 1899 poem by that title, the term meant the moral duty and high service of bringing civilization to backward peoples in the colonies. Today the phrase packs a wallop because of its baggage of discredited and defunct imperialism and the condescending and racist elitism of the imperial era. It is used sneeringly to suggest the persistence of such attitudes.

Kipling addressed his poem to the American people as the United States became a colonial power by acquiring the Philippines in the Spanish-American War:

> Take up the white man's burden—
> Send forth the best ye breed—
> Go bind your sons to exile
> To serve your captive's need;
>
> To wait in heavy harness
> On fluttered folk and wild—
> Your new-caught sullen peoples,
> Half devil and half child.

A jocular example of the term in use, from Alfred Hitchcock's 1935 classic, *The 39 Steps:* Blond heroine Pamela, handcuffed to fugitive hero Richard Hannay, demands, "What chance have you got tied to me?" Hannay responds:

> "Keep that question for your husband. Meanwhile, I'll admit you're the White Man's Burden."

A play on the term, by Paul Johnson, in his 1988 book *Intellectuals,* referring to British writer Cyril Connolly:

> "Connolly's accounts of these visits [to the Spanish Civil War], mainly in the *New Statesman,* are acute and a refreshing contrast to the field-grey committed prose most other intellectuals were producing at the time. But they indicate the strain he found in carrying the Left Man's Burden."

**White Noise.** A continuous, unobtrusive background noise which has the effect of masking other sounds.

The term in use, by Frances Fitzgerald in an essay, "The American Millennium," in *Estrangement, America and the World,* edited by Sanford Ungar:

> "Finally, and most important, the life had gone out of Soviet Marxism-Leninism. The Soviet leaders still trum-

369

peted the old phrases, and there were still a lot of excited young men around the world willing to repeat them for the price of a Kalishnikov [a Soviet machine gun], but the words had become little more than white noise."

**Whitehall.** The site of British government offices in London, and thus a shorthand expression for the British government, particularly the permanent establishment, the civil service, the bureaucracy. [See **Foggy Bottom**.] For the French government, especially the foreign office, "Quai D'Orsay" is used in a similar sense. This site along the bank of the River Seine in Paris is the location of government offices.

Whitehall actually is a thoroughfare in the heart of London, near the Houses of Parliament. The street takes its name from a royal palace that was located there from the reign of Henry VIII until William III. All of it burned in 1698 except the famous Banqueting Hall.

An example of use, in *The Economist*, January 14, 1989: an article on the British government's appropriate role in regulating mergers of European electronics companies is entitled "Stand Back, Whitehall."

**Will Rogers.** A beloved American humorist (1879-1935) whose salty observations have become part of the American national folklore.

He was born in Oklahoma (then Indian Territory) with Cherokee ancestry on both parents' sides. His act, as he developed it over the years, consisted of doing tricks with a lariat and making comments about society and politics, seeming to be just a simple cowboy who came up with shrewd observations about the issues of the day. He appeared in films, wrote books and a daily newspaper column and broadcast a Sunday morning radio talk.

His fame and popularity were enormous. His humor was so infectious that he was able to make people laugh at themselves while he offered penetrating commentary on their foibles. He got away with addressing a convention of bankers as "loan sharks and interest hounds."

In 1927, the National Press Club named him "congressman at

large" and he responded: "I certainly regret the disgrace that's been thrust on me here tonight. . . . I certainly have lived, or tried to live, my life so that I would never be a congressman, and I am just as ashamed of the fact I have failed as you are."

Before the stock market crash of 1929, he warned, "You will try to show us that we are prosperous, because we have more. I will show you where we are not prosperous, because we haven't paid for it yet." During the Depression he performed at benefits and donated large sums to relief. He kidded his countrymen: "You hold the distinction of being the only nation ever to go to the poorhouse in an automobile."

His sayings have become cliches. No political season can pass without a pundit quoting him, "I belong to no organized political party; I'm a Democrat."

Will Rogers died in a plane crash in Alaska with aviator Wiley Post in 1935.

Another famous Will Rogers statement invoked, by Richard Cohen, *The Washington Post*, October 31, 1989:

> "The president is a parody of Will Rogers. The late humorist said he never met a man he didn't like. Bush feels the same way about constitutional amendments."

**Willy Loman.** (LOH-man) The central character in Arthur Miller's 1949 play "Death of a Salesman," which won the New York Drama Critics Circle Award and the Pulitzer Prize and is a scathing indictment of America's material success-over-all-else values.

Willy Loman is an aging salesman, whose professional and family lives are crumbling. Neither he nor his two sons have achieved the financial gain and status he yearns for. As playwright Miller sardonically has noted, Willy had broken an unwritten law that says a failure in society and business has no right to live. Says Miller: "The law of success is not administered by statute or church, but it is nearly as powerful in its grip upon men."

As the play ends, Willy loses his job and sees the emptiness of his life. His son Biff tells him, "Pop! I'm a dime a dozen and so are you!" Willy kills himself in the illusory belief that his life insurance money will enable Biff to finally become a success.

The term in use, by Richard Cohen in *The Washington Post*, April 19, 1989, commenting on disclosure of honoraria received by newspaper columnists:

> "Ridicule greeted my disclosures, and I feared reprimand from the Benevolent Protective Order of Newspaper Columnists (BPONC). William Safire reported $18,000 for a single speech. David Broder got $6,000. David Gergen of *U.S. News and World Report* turns out to be the Willie Loman of journalism—on the road constantly. For his smile and shoeshine, a group must generally pay at least $5,000."

Another example, from Bill Keller, *The New York Times*, January 14, 1990:

> "Politically, the breakaway of a republic could be perilous for Mr. Gorbachev, in a way the upheavals in Eastern Europe could not. It would probably embolden hard-liners in the Communist Party Central Committee. (Watching Mr. Gorbachev begging Lithuania to remain Soviet, they must have thought him the most pathetic of figures, the Willy Loman of Soviet leaders.)"

**Witches' Sabbath.** From the folklore of witchcraft, referring to the nocturnal meetings of witches to engage in devil-worship. The application of the Hebrew word "sabbath" (meaning "seventh day," which is also used for the day of Christian worship) to such gatherings may come from the alleged practice of blasphemous parodies of Christian rites—the idea of the "black mass."

*The Encyclopedia of Demonology and Witchcraft* offers another theory—that use of the Hebrew word might have helped to fan hostility towards Jews, Moslems and other groups seen as threats by the medieval Church. After all, references to devil-worshipping rites began to be reported in the 14th and 15th centuries, coinciding with the beginning of the Inquisition. Sects persecuted by the Inquisition were accused of outlandishly cruel and perverse activities in order to arouse public fear and hostility against them.

The term in use, by P.J. O'Rourke, in *Holidays in Hell*:

"My friend Dorothy and I spent a weekend at Heritage USA, the born-again Christian resort and amusement park created by television evangelists Jim and Tammy Bakker, who have been so much in the news. Dorothy and I came to scoff—but went away converted.

"Unfortunately, we were converted to Satanism. Now we're up half the night going to witch's sabbaths and have to spend our free time reciting the Lord's Prayer backward and scouring the neighborhood for black dogs to sacrifice. Frankly, it's a nuisance, but if it keeps us from going to the Heritage USA part of heaven, it will be worth it."

And from *The Sunday Telegraph*, April 2, 1989, a picture of life in the Soviet Union:

"The traffic too has a military appearance: Soviet lorries are Army vehicles, on loan like Soviet ships and aeroplanes for civilian purposes for which they are poorly adapted. Careering lawlessly through this traffic, bringing cars and pedestrians to a frightened standstill, are the convoys of party limousines, with their flashing lights and curtained windows, hurrying like frantic hearses to a witches' sabbath. These are unforgettable images of empire: but an empire founded on force and lies alone. Wherever its rule extends both law and commerce are sacrificed, and society becomes a by-product of the military machine. Is it really possible, after 70 years of subjugation, that such a society can now turn off the machine which created it, and pull out the plug?"

**Witching Hour.** A time "appropriate for witchcraft," according to *The Oxford English Dictionary*; a time for significant, weird or scary happenings. As William Shakespeare puts it in *Hamlet*: " 'Tis now the verie witching time of night, When Churchyards yawne and Hell itself breathes out Contagion to this world."

In contemporary financial lingo, however, the term refers to the time at which stock option contracts and other stock-index futures expire. At that moment, traders who deal in such contracts change their positions, creating an environment in which dramatic price swings can occur with great speed. It is a time of uncertainty, with the possibility of things running out of control.

The term in use, by *The Economist*, March 4, 1989:

> "Officials at Japan's finance ministry and the Tokyo Stock Exchange are unofficially worried. They fear that what went up during Japan's first 'witching hour' on December 7, 1988—when the Nikkei index jumped through 30,000 for the first time—could come down with a thud during the second index-arbitragers' big event on March 7th."

**Woodshed, Take to the.** To be dressed down, scolded. In American rural mythology, behind the woodshed was where father meted out punishment (usually with his belt) on an erring son.

The phrase entered the contemporary political lexicon in 1981 with Reagan budget director David Stockman, who had spoken indiscreetly and frankly with reporter William Greider in a series of interviews. Stockman had confessed that when it came to assessing the budget deficit, "none of us really understands what's going on with all these numbers."

An uproar followed and the White House engaged in some damage control [see **Spin Control**] to get off the hook. Stockman met with the president, then told the White House press corps that he had been "taken to the woodshed."

Writes Christopher Matthews, recounting the episode in his book *Hardball*, "In one small but elegant bit of stagecraft, the West Wing PR folks, running with Stockman's naughty-boy metaphor, shifted the entire media focus from an earth-shaking revelation of unsound public finance to a small soap opera: the betrayal by one young bright young man of his trusting mentor."

The term in use, by the *Chicago Sun-Times*, July 16, 1983:

> "Assuming the Fed is traditionally pliant, why does not Reagan simply take [Federal Reserve Chairman Paul] Volcker into the woodshed and tell him to ease up?"

**Wooster, Bertie.** See Bertie Wooster.

**Wunderkind.** (VOON-der-kint) Wonder child, in German. A child prodigy, one who achieves fame or success at a young age. Frequently the term is applied to adults who attain remarkable success or prominence while still young.

The term was often applied to David Stockman, who was appointed director of the Office of Management and Budget in the Reagan Administration at the age of 34.

(Of course, Stockman's career at OMB led him to be characterized also as an **enfant terrible** and, after his candid statements about the making of Reagan economic policies in an interview [see **Woodshed**] and his book, *The Triumph of Politics*, some probably viewed him as a **quisling,** too.)

The term in use by critic Andrew Sarris in *American Film*, November 1988:

> "If Orson Welles (1915-1985) was famous even before he made *Citizen Kane*, the one-time (and allegedly one-shot) wunderkind was notorious ever after." (Welles produced, directed, partly wrote and starred in *Citizen Kane*, all at the age of 25.)

Another example—another filmmaker—described by movie critic Rita Kempley, *The Washington Post*, August 11, 1989:

> " 'Sex, lies, and videotape' is inspired chitchat, a barefaced Louisiana gabfest written and directed by Steven Soderbergh, a 26-year-old *Wunderkind* preoccupied with *l'amour.*"

# X

**Xanadu.** (ZAN-uh-doo) A poetization of the name of the city of Xandu, or Shang-tu in Mongolia, which is celebrated in Samuel Taylor Coleridge's 1797 poem, *Kubla Khan.* The city was founded by Kublai Khan (1215-1294), a Mongol general and statesman who became emperor of China. Stories of the wealth and power of Kublai Khan were brought to the West in the writings of Marco Polo.

"Xanadu" today means a luxurious or fantastically elaborate home, building or scene; a pleasure palace. We quote you the famous opening lines, which themselves are often alluded to or imitated:

> In Xanadu did Kubla Khan
> A stately pleasure-dome decree:
> Where Alph, the sacred river, ran
> Through caverns measureless to man
> Down to a sunless sea.

Coleridge, poet, essayist, critic, free spirit and dope fiend, claimed to have dreamed the poem in an opium-induced sleep. He began to write it down when he awoke, but was interrupted; when he returned to the work he could no longer remember it. The unfinished poem is nevertheless considered one of his best.

The term in use, by Mark Lilla in *The New Republic*, April 10, 1989:

> "No kidding. Parisians are all excited about a new library. Not just any library, but the biggest in the world—The Really Big Library (*La Trés Grande Bibliothéque*). Anything to replace today's frightening Bastilles of the mind, but why so big? And why in Paris? This will be Mitterrand's Xanadu."

Coleridge is also remembered for *The Rime of the Ancient Mariner* (1798) in which an old man recounts the punishment meted out by supernatural forces to him and his shipmates for his sin in shooting an albatross. The description of a becalmed ship, seared by heat— you remember it, of course, from high school literature class:

Day after day, day after day,
We stuck, without a breath or motion,
As idle as a painted ship
Upon a painted ocean.

Water, water, everywhere
Nor any drop to drink.

# Y

**Yalta.** An old Russian resort on the Black Sea that gains its fame and status as an allusion by virtue of being the site of the February 1945 meeting between Josef Stalin, Winston Churchill and Franklin Roosevelt.

The World War II Allied leaders met as their armies were flooding into Germany, to determine the shape of the postwar world. Much has been said about the agreements reached at Yalta, with many analysts contending that an ailing Roosevelt gave too much away to Stalin and trusted him too much in allowing Soviet influence to prevail in post-war eastern and central Europe. Roosevelt biographer Nathan Miller, on the other hand, notes that Soviet armies already were in the region, and that Churchill and FDR could have done little to change that overwhelming fact.

Stalin also agreed to enter the war against Japan (much desired by Allied military authorities) in exchange for territories lost in the Russo-Japanese War of 1904-1905, the Kurile Islands and concessions in Manchuria. As it turned out, Russian entry into the Pacific war had little significance, coming two days after the dropping of the atomic bomb.

In any event, as **Munich** has come to stand for appeasement of rapacious dictators, so Yalta has become a metaphor for naively trusting those capable of treachery.

The term in use, by Ronald Steel, *The New York Times*, December 1, 1989 (in one of the many analyses inspired by the Malta summit meeting between President Bush and Mikhail Gorbachev):

> " 'Never another Yalta,' says the common wisdom. The common wisdom is wrong. Another Yalta is needed, but this time it should be made to work."

Another example, from Polish prime minister Mazowiecki, quoted by Barry Schweid in a column moved on the Associated Press wire February 23, 1990:

"It is unthinkable in today's democratic world to have this form of Yalta, where one group of countries could decide about another."

**Yellow Journalism.** Sensationalism in the press.

The term is an epithet born in the newspaper circulation wars in the United States during the 1890s. To bolster street sales, big city newspapers, especially those owned by press lords William Randolph Hearst and Joseph Pulitzer, engaged in flashy, exaggerated reporting, lavish illustrations and screaming scare headlines. In the weeks before the Spanish-American War, Hearst's papers promoted war fever with stories calculated to incite hatred of Spain. According to legend, Hearst dispatched artist Frederick Remington to Cuba to provide drawings that would accompany his papers' sensational stories. Remington cabled Hearst he could find no war to illustrate and Hearst is said to have replied: "You furnish the pictures. I'll furnish the war."

The term derives from other features added to newspapers to pique interest—color and comics. In 1896, Pulitzer's *New York World* experimented with printing the color yellow for the first time. According to A *History of the Comic Strip*, by Pierre Couperie et al., a rascally character in the paper's comic strip "Down Hogan's Alley" always wore a long white shirt. (The strip was drawn by Richard Outcault, who later created Buster Brown.) On February 16, the printers colored the shirt yellow. The gambit was a great success and the character was immediately nicknamed the "Yellow Kid." Colored comic sections were soon developed in both competing newspapers.

As Coulton Waugh describes it in *The Comics*, the success of the Yellow Kid began a series of raids, counter-raids and lawsuits between Pulitzer and Hearst to obtain the services of the most successful comic artists. Hearst hired Oucault and his comic; Pulitzer bought him back. Hearst bought Oucault back again, and this time Pulitzer hired another artist to draw a competing Yellow Kid. This contest gave rise to the terms "yellow journalism" and "the yellow press" which were applied to sensation-seeking journalism as a whole.

The term in use, by Stephen Hess of the Brookings Institution, discussing a Washington sex scandal in *The Washington Post*, August 1, 1989:

"In some way, that's a classic story. It's just that the press has become so professional that we have a class structure built in now and we look down our noses at yellow journalism—the kind that Hearst and Pulitzer made their reputations with."

**Yin and Yang.** Terms from Chinese philosophy; they are two opposing cosmic forces. Yin is the feminine, dark, earthly, cold, passive side; yang is the masculine, light, bright, positive principle. These forces, however, are not opposites as we understand them in the West; think more along the lines of a continuous cycle, of balance and harmony. This is summed up, appropriately, by the symbol of the two forces, a circle divided into light and dark fields by an S-shaped curve. Television viewers saw this symbol often during the telecast of the 1988 Olympics from South Korea, for the Korean flag displays the symbol for yin and yang.

The terms in use, by Richard Harrington, writing in *The Washington Post*, September 25, 1989, on Rolling Stones Mick Jagger and Keith Richards:

"They have inspired much definition—Siamese twins with two strong heads pulling in opposite directions, a ship with two mastheads plowing into the sea, the rock-and-roller and the superstar, the warrior and the dilettante, one taking the high road, one the low—but in the mid-Eighties, Yin/Yang became Yin vs. Yang, the Glimmer Twins slid to Grimmer, riffs turned to rifts."

**Young Turks.** Brash young reformers who impetuously rebel against the established order and its champions, frequently referred to as the **Old Guard.**

The original Young Turks were young Turks who, at the beginning of the 20th century, sought to reform and modernize the decaying Ottoman Empire [see **Sick Man of Europe**]. The movement was largely supported by students and in 1908 they deposed the sultan, replaced him with his brother and introduced a number of reforms, hoping to prevent the breakup of the empire. That hope proved futile as territories were lost in the Balkan wars and World War I. Massive changes came with the proclamation of the Turkish Republic in 1923 under the leadership of Mustafa Kemal (who took the name Ataturk, or "father of the Turks").

The term in use, in its most classic and (hackneyed) form, describing the fight among Republicans in the House of Representatives over the position of minority whip. The battle was between old-line Republican Edward Madigan and New Right leader Newt Gingrich. From Jeffrey Birnbaum in *The Wall Street Journal*, March 21, 1989:

> "The 45-year-old Mr. Gingrich, though gray-haired and a 10-year veteran of the House, considers himself the guru of the insurgent 'young turks.'"

# Z

**Zaftig.** "Juicy" or "succulent" in Yiddish, and often applied to a buxom or well-rounded woman.

According to Leo Rosten in *The Joys of Yiddish*, it also means provocative, seminal or germinal, as in, "The book is full of zaftig ideas."

The term in use, from *USA Today*, December 28, 1987:

> "Call her zaftig or fleshy, or pleasingly plump—the heavier woman is 'in' for '88."

**Zeitgeist.** (TSIGHT-gighst) A German word, meaning the spirit of the time, particularly as reflected in the literature or philosophy of a period.

The term in use, by David Finkle in his review of *Memoirs of an Invisible Man* by H. F. Saint in *The New York Times*, May 10, 1987:

> "Updating H. G. Wells' 'Invisible Man' to the 1980s, so that the protagonist is the victim of an accident at a particle physics experimental laboratory, is a clever idea. Making the invisible hero a security analyst pursued by a relentless Government agent in a book published during the year of Dennis Levine, Ivan Boesky and the musical blockbuster 'Les Miserables' is positively prescient.
>
> "Who, a reader wonders, is this H. F. Saint, and how does he come . . . to tap so directly into the Zeitgeist?"

In use again, by Mark Stevens in *The New Republic*, May 18, 1987:

> "Warhol was a floating, almost immaterial presence, seemingly there and not there, a kind of angel of the zeitgeist. When damning an angel, one should remember to admire the wings."

Finally, from Danielle Crittenden, writing in *The Wall Street Journal*, December 6, 1989:

> "If women's magazines are in any way a barometer of a female zeitgeist, then women today are as neurotically insecure and preoccupied with getting married as feminist writers say they were three decades ago."

**Zen.** A sect of Buddhism based on the practice of meditation rather than on adherence to any particular scriptural doctrine.

Zen Buddhism developed in China in the 6th century and spread to Japan in the 12th and 13th centuries. Zen strives for truth or enlightenment through a sudden breakthrough or stroke of insight, called satori, rather than through ritual or good works. The breakthrough can come through meditation, including concentration on problems, called kōan. These are usually paradoxes, such as, "What is the sound of one hand clapping?" Thinking about such problems is seen as a way to enable the mind to break away from the constraints of conventional logic.

Zen's values—strength of character, discipline, tranquility, fearlessness—were much valued in medieval Japan, especially among the warrior class.

Recent western interest in eastern cultures and religion has attracted adherents to Zen in the United States and brought the word into the English language to express the concept of a conceptual breakthrough, a spiritual elevation or a state of euphoria.

The term in use by Steven S. King in *The Washington Post*, September 2, 1988:

> "When conditions approach ideal, though, biking can transcend the realm of mere physical endeavor and affect mental or even spiritual planes. For lack of formal terminology, I call this experience the Zen bike ride."

In use again, by Benjamin J. Stein in *The American Spectator*, December 1988, writing on the success of the Disney studio:

> "If the Disney managers are in Zen synch with their audiences and attendees, they are in even greater synch with

their stockholders, who have gotten rich, despite a stock market crash, off Michael [Eisner] and Mickey [Mouse]'s efforts. The Zen bond between stockholder wishes and management wishes is truly profound."

**Zero-sum Game.** A term from game theory, a branch of mathematics that analyzes competitive situations. Game theory looks at the elements that go into the decision-making of each player, including how each will anticipate the actions of competitors. The theory assumes the players act rationally but also considers such factors as conflicting interests, incomplete information and chance. The theory has come to be applied in many fields, from economics, business and law to strategic planning for national security.

In a zero-sum game, the winner takes all, at the expense of the losers. In world politics in the nuclear age, the danger of such a situation is clear, and policy makers try to avoid it; it is much safer for face-saving factors to be introduced so that both sides can back away from confrontation and claim gains.

The term in use by Fareed Zakaria in *The New Republic*, October 19, 1987, discussing proposals to include ethics in the curriculum of business schools:

"Although capitalism is not a zero-sum game, competition does lie at the heart of the free enterprise system. A firm does not, and should not, consider the potential loss to every competitor as a restraint on its actions. The market as encounter group may be nice, but it wouldn't be very efficient."

**Zut Alors!** (zoot uh-lor) An exclamation of disgust, scorn, refusal or disappointment. It is French, comparable to drat! rats! fie! or pooh!

The term in use, by *The Washington Post*, April 29, 1989, as the headline over a letter to the editor from one Maria P. Terrell, protesting the satiric tone of an article mocking one of the events celebrating the bicentennial of the French Revolution:

"Zut Alors! . . . Too bad there's not a 'mouton national' [national battering ram] to use on Henry Allen for his satiric words about the friendly impulse of the French to share their history with the American people."

Another example, from Peter Gambaccini, *The Village Voice,* April 3, 1990:

"Hertzberg, perhaps trying to match his subject by embarrassing himself as well, wrote of Quayle, 'If he were a woman he would be described as beautiful . . . his mouth is what pulp fiction writers call sensual.' *Zut alors!*"

# BIBLIOGRAPHY

In our research, we relied constantly on the updated editions of these classic reference works: *Benét's Reader's Encyclopedia, Brewer's Dictionary of Phrase and Fable* and *The Oxford English Dictionary, Second Edition* as well as the *Encyclopaedia Britannica*.

Other invaluable sources included *The Facts on File Dictionary of Classical, Biblical and Literary Allusions*, by Lass, Kiremidjian and Goldstein, *An Incomplete Education* by Jones and Wilson, William Safire's *Political Dictionary, The Dictionary of Cultural Literacy* by Hirsch, Kett and Trefil; *Le Mot Juste: A Dictionary of Classical & Foreign Words & Phrases*, Buchanan-Brown et. al.; *The Joys of Yiddish*, by Leo Rosten; *The Morris Dictionary of Word and Phrase Origins*, by William and Mary Morris; Merriam Webster's *12,000 Words; The Barnhart Dictionary Companion* and the *Barnhart Dictionary of New English Since 1963; Black's Law Dictionary*; I. Moyer Hunsberger, *The Quintessential Dictionary; Bartlett's Familiar Quotations*; George Seldes, *The Great Thoughts*.

# ABOUT THE AUTHORS

Elizabeth Webber is a native of Ottumwa, Iowa transplanted to Washington, D.C. A lawyer by training but not inclination, she worked several years in Congress, but managed to make a clean getaway. She is now senior editor with a small but sincere Washington publishing firm and devotes her time to the basics: reading, writing and rowing on the Potomac River.

She attributes her knowledge to a lifelong reading addiction and a career as a professional generalist.

Mike Feinsilber, a Pennsylvanian, has been putting words in print ever since the 5th grade when he established *The Daily Stink*, which partially lived up to its name although it did not come out every day.

He reported for United Press International in Pittsburgh, Columbus, Harrisburg, Newark, New York, Saigon and, after 1968, Washington. He is now reporter-at-large with The Associated Press, where he writes what strikes his fancy and uses allusions when he knows what they mean.

He is married, jogs, gardens and bakes bread.

For additional copies of *Grand Allusions*, write:

Farragut Publishing Company
2033 M Street N.W.
Washington, D.C. 20036

Paperback: $12.95
Hardcover: $21.95

Please include $1.50 for shipping and handling for each copy. Make check or money order payable to Farragut Publishing Company.